THE LEGACY OF PARMENIDES

THE LEGACY OF PARMENIDES

Eleatic Monism and Later Presocratic Thought

Patricia Curd

PARMENIDES
PUBLISHING

PARMENIDES PUBLISHING
Las Vegas 89109

Originally published 1998 by Princeton University Press

This paperback edition, with a new introduction,
published in 2004 by
Parmenides Publishing
in the United States of America

ISBN: 1-930972-15-6

Printed in the United States of America

Publisher's Cataloging-in-Publication Data

Curd, Patricia. 1949 -
The legacy of Parmenides : Eleatic monism and later presocratic thought / Patricia Curd.

p. ; cm.
Includes bibliographical references and indexes.
ISBN: 1-930972-15-6

1. Eleatics. 2. Parmenides–Influence. 3. Pre-Socratic philosophers. I. Title.

B196 .C87 2004
182/.3

10 9 8 7 6 5 4 3 2 1

1-888-PARMENIDES
www.parmenides.com

For M. V. C.

Contents

Preface

This book began as a series of papers on Presocratic issues written in 1990–91 while I was a Junior Fellow at the Center for Hellenic Studies. After returning from the center, I continued to think and to write about the Presocratics, and it became clear to me that I was actually writing a book. In completing it, I have received support and encouragement from a number of people and institutions.

The Center for Hellenic Studies provided a wonderful place to work that first year, and it has welcomed me back on a number of research visits. I am very grateful to the director during my time there, Zeph Stewart, and to the present directors, Kurt Raaflaub and Deborah Boedeker, and to the center's librarian, Ellen Roth.

My work has been supported by a Fellowship for University Teachers from the National Endowment for the Humanities, and by the Center for Humanistic Studies of the School of Liberal Arts at Purdue University; I am thankful for the support of these institutions. In addition, several Faculty Development Grants from the Purdue University School of Liberal Arts subsidized research trips and computer equipment, and I am pleased to acknowledge this valuable assistance. The deans of the School of Liberal Arts, David Caputo and Thomas Adler, were active in their support, as were philosophy department heads William Rowe and Rod Bertolet. The inter-library loan department of the Purdue libraries was indispensable.

An early version of Chapter IV was read at the Princeton Colloquium in Ancient Philosophy in 1992, and I am grateful to the commentator, Christopher Kirwan, for his remarks. Some of the material in Chapters I, II, IV, and V was presented at meetings of the American Philosophical Association and the Society for Ancient Greek Philosophy. My thanks to participants at all these meetings for their comments and suggestions.

I am indebted to Ann Wald, Editor in Chief of Princeton University Press, to her assistant Helen Hsu, and to Marta Steele, who copyedited the book; it has been a joy to work with them. I am grateful for the comments and suggestions of two anonymous readers for the Press.

A number of people deserve special mention. For allowing me to use and to refer to unpublished material, thanks are due to David Furley, Daniel Graham, André Laks, and Kirk Sanders. Carl Huffman, John Kirby, and Alexander Nehamas read and commented on parts of the manuscript and answered many questions. Alexander P. D. Mourelatos was generous with help and advice. James Lesher read and commented on the entire book and answered numerous emails; he deserves particular thanks for his help and his willingness to pursue an argument to its end. My work has been much improved by the comments and suggestions of all these people, and if I have been stubborn enough to ignore some of what they have suggested to me, the fault (and responsibility) is entirely mine. John Cooper, James Lesher, and Alexander Nehamas encouraged me even before this project began, and I am immensely grateful to them for years of support since then. My greatest debt is to Martin Curd, who read and reread, commented and commented again; he has been my best editor and strongest critic, and this book owes much to his patience and philosophical acumen.

Acknowledgments

SOME OF THE MATERIAL in this book is drawn from papers I have published in the past. In all cases I have rethought my positions, in some instances changing my mind. I am grateful to the editors and publishers who have allowed me to draw from this previously printed material. Full citations of these articles will be found in the bibliography.

Some discussions of Heraclitus are adapted from "Knowledge and Unity in Heraclitus," *The Monist* vol. 74 (1991) Copyright © 1991, *The Monist*, La Salle, IL 61301. Reprinted by permission.

Some of the material in Chapters I and II is based on "Parmenidean Monism," *Phronesis* vol. 36 (1991). Used by permission of E. J. Brill.

Part of Chapter III first appeared in "Deception and Belief in Parmenides' *Doxa*," reprinted from *APEIRON: A Journal for Ancient Philosophy and Science* vol. 25 (1992), by permission of Academic Printing and Publishing.

Some of the discussions of Zeno and Melissus are drawn from "Eleatic Monism in Zeno and Melissus," *Ancient Philosophy* vol. 13 (1993) used by permission of *ANCIENT PHILOSOPHY*.

In Chapter VI, fragments of Philolaus, translated by Patricia Curd, originally appeared in *Readings in Ancient Greek Philosophy*, edited by Cohen, Curd, and Reeve, Copyright 1995, Hackett Publishing Co., Inc. Reprinted with permission.

A Note on Texts and Translations

THE USUAL method of referring to the Presocratics has been followed. Each philosopher is assigned a number by DK; where the reference may be unclear, I have included that number. "A" refers to the section of testimonia assigned to each philosopher by DK; "B" refers to the section of fragments accepted as authentic by DK.

Statistical observations are based on and word searches have used the data bank of the *Thesaurus Linguae Graecae* (*TLG*).

Unless otherwise indicated, translations are my own.

For the texts of the fragments and testimonia on the Presocratics, I have, except where noted, followed DK. For Plato, I have used the J. Burnet editions in the Oxford Classical Texts series. Texts for the Commentators on Aristotle follow the editions of the Berlin Academy *Commentaria in Aristotelem Graeca*. Other texts are listed below.

Aeschylus, *Aeschyli Tragoediae*. 2d ed., ed. G. Murray (1955; reprinted Oxford: Clarendon Press, 1960).

Bacchylides, *Bacchylidis Carmina cum Fragmentis,* ed. H. Maehler (post B. Snell), 10th ed. (Leipzig: Teubner, 1970).

Euripides, *Euripidis Fabulae,* ed. G. Murray, vol. 1 (1902; reprinted Oxford: Clarendon Press, 1966).

Herodotus, *Historiae*, ed. C. Hude (Oxford: Clarendon Press, 1908).

Hesiod, *Theogony*, ed. M. L. West (Oxford: Clarendon Press, 1966).

Homer, *Homeri Odyssea,* ed. P. von der Muehll (Basel: Helbing and Lichtenhahn, 1962).

Pindar, *Pindari Carmina cum Fragmentis,* ed. H. Maehler (post B. Snell) (Leipzig: Teubner, pt. 1, 5th ed., 1971; pt. 2, 4th ed., 1975).

Sophocles, *Sophocle,* ed. A. Dain and P. Mazon (vol. 1, 1955; reprinted Paris: Les Belles Lettres, 1958; vol. 2, 1958; reprinted Paris: Les Belles Lettres, 1968).

Thucydides, *Thucydidis Historiae,* ed. H. S. Jones and J. E. Powell, 2 vols. (1942; vol. 1, reprinted Oxford: Clarendon Press, 1970; vol. 2, 2d ed., reprinted Oxford: Clarendon Press, 1967).

Abbreviations

THE FOLLOWING abbreviations have been used throughout.

DG Diels, H. *Doxographi Graeci* (Berlin: Walter de Gruyter, 1965)

DK Diels, H., and W. Kranz, eds. *Die Fragmente der Vorsokratiker.* 3 vols. Reprint of sixth edition (Berlin: Weidmann, 1974)

HGP Guthrie, W K. C. *A History of Greek Philosophy* Vols. I and II (Cambridge: Cambridge University Press, vol. I, 1962; vol. II, 1965)

KR Kirk, G. S., and J. E. Raven. *The Presocratic Philosophers* (Cambridge: Cambridge University Press, 1957)

KRS Kirk, G. S., J. E. Raven, and M. Schofield. *The Presocratic Philosophers.* 2d ed. (Cambridge: Cambridge University Press, 1983)

LSJ Liddell, H. G., R. Scott, and H. S. Jones, eds. *A Greek-English Lexicon.* Rev. ed. (Oxford: Clarendon Press, 1968)

PP Barnes, J. *The Presocratic Philosophers.* 2 vols. (London: Routledge and Kegan Paul, 1979)

Abbreviations for ancient works follow LSJ supplemented by the second edition of the *Oxford Classical Dictionary*, although there are occasional expansions for ease of recognition.

Introduction to the Paperback Version

SINCE *THE LEGACY OF PARMENIDES* was first published in late 1997, I have received many comments, criticisms, and suggestions.[1] Reviews and articles, especially those by Daniel Graham, Alexander Mourelatos, and Alexander Nehamas, offered constructive criticisms that have helped to clarify my thoughts about Parmenides and other early Greek thinkers.[2] With the benefit of time and experience (and with the help of critics), I can see how the original could have been better, and were I writing the book now, I would no doubt put things differently. It is not my intention, in this new introduction, to respond directly and systematically to criticisms, but rather to clarify some parts of my view.

Unlike some commentators, I do not take Parmenides to have forbidden or denied the possibility of genuine cosmology. Rather, his aim is to criticize previous accounts of the nature of things while formulating metatheoretical requirements for an acceptable cosmological account. Such an account must be grounded in metaphysically genuine entities and use mechanisms that do not undermine the reality of those basic things. In the *Alētheia* section of the poem, Parmenides argues that what-is is in such a way that it does not come to be, pass away, or alter, and that anything that is must be a whole of a single kind. Only what genuinely is in this way can be an object of genuine thought and so of knowledge or understanding (see B2, B3, B8.1–6, with the full arguments in B8). Any reliable account of the cosmos that will count as knowledge must be suitably grounded in what-is. Anything that is in the way sanctioned by the arguments of B8 counts as metaphysically basic and could

[1] Chapter or page numbers with no other identification refer to this book. I have made some small changes to the original text and corrected some typographical errors, but this is not a revised or second edition. Since completing *Legacy*, I have been primarily concerned with the pluralists, and as I have spent more time with these thinkers, my views on a number of problems in both Empedocles and Anaxagoras have changed. I give a much fuller (and, I hope, more correct) account of Anaxagoras in *Anaxagoras of Clazomenae*, forthcoming.

[2] Interest in early Greek philosophy is flourishing: Conferences and new publications on the Presocratics have enabled me to learn from colleagues and to rethink a number of questions. The 21st Annual Philosophy Workshop (in honor of Alexander Mourelatos) in March of 1998 and the October 2000 Lille Conference (on the question "Qu'est-ce que la Philosophie Présocratique?") organized by André Laks stand out. Both conferences resulted in volumes that contain exciting new work on the Presocratics, as does *The Cambridge Companion to Early Greek Philosophy* (ed. A.A. Long). For other sources, see the bibliography that follows the acknowledgments section, p. xxvii.

serve as the foundation for a theoretically acceptable account of the world that we perceive.[3]

1. Monisms

I argue that Parmenides advocates predicational monism (a monism about natures or kinds) rather than numerical monism (a monism about things). Numerical, or strict, monism is the claim that there exists only one thing, and this is the monism that has traditionally been attributed to Parmenides. In challenging the traditional account, I contrast numerical monism with both material monism and what I have called predicational monism. Material monism, the view that everything is or comes from a single material stuff, was attributed to the earliest Greek thinkers by Aristotle.[4] The monism that I attribute to Parmenides is neither of these, but a monism about the nature or essence of a thing. Whatever genuinely is must be a strict unity, a whole of a single kind. In discussing this monism, I claim that "each thing that is can be only one thing; it can hold only the one predicate which indicates what it is, and must hold it in a particularly strong way. To be a genuine entity, a thing must be a predicational unity, with a single account of what it is; but it need not be the case that there exists only one such thing" (p. 66). Although I am not entirely happy with the term "predicational monism," I am not sure what name would be better. Here, I would like to clarify the sort of monism that I attribute to Parmenides, especially my claim that what-is can hold only a single predicate. For this, I first need to say more about the inquiry into nature and the force of the *esti* in Parmenides.

Chapter I argues that Parmenides wishes to reform the theory and method of inquiry into nature. Can we attain genuine knowledge of the world reported by the senses? Traditional accounts of the feebleness of human experience as a source of knowledge and Xenophanes' arguments about the fallibility of human understanding had suggested the impossibility of such knowledge.[5]

[3] Thus I take Parmenides to belong squarely to the tradition of natural philosophers. I discuss this tradition more fully in "Presocratics as Philosophers," "New Empedocles," and "Question of Religion." A rejection of this sort of interpretation of Parmenides (and of Empedocles) can be found in the work of Kingsley.

[4] A clear statement of alternative versions of material monism can be found in Algra; Barnes defends Aristotle's view in *PP*. Graham has argued against attributing material monism to the Milesians ("Heraclitus' Criticism," a paper published after *Legacy* had gone to press), opting instead for what he calls a generating substance theory. On this account, Milesian theories begin with a single substance (water, the boundless, air) which then generates but does not underlie all other things. Graham works out this theory persuasively; for a strong argument in favor of material monism, see Mourelatos, forthcoming. In this introduction, I refer to "Milesian Monism," leaving it open which account of their view is correct.

[5] Thanks to the work of Lesher and Mourelatos, I now have a greater appreciation of the importance of Xenophanes. His claims about the lack of divine warrant for human understanding,

Heraclitus had seen that a solution to the problem could be found in a link between the nature of human understanding and what is understood, the *logos* in accordance with which all things happen. The *logos* can only be understood by a soul in the proper state; a hot dry human soul can grasp it (recall that the symbol of the *logos* is fire). But Heraclitus had not given a complete account of the *logos*, nor had he shown how one could be certain that one had indeed understood it. In addition, Heraclitus had (from Parmenides' point of view) conflated what-is and what-is-not.[6] Like Heraclitus, Parmenides sees a natural connection between thought and its object (see B3 and B8.34–37).[7] Crucially, he goes farther in establishing criteria that any object of genuine thought or understanding must meet, and (at the same time, with the same arguments) provides tests for whether those criteria have been met. The argument in the *Alētheia* section of the poem is formal. Parmenides claims that the proper route or way of inquiry will arrive at *what-is* (and argues that any other way of inquiry is impossible since it can lead nowhere). So, any thing that is in the way that the proofs of B8 demand will be something that genuinely is. "What-is" (*to eon*) serves as a formal name for the proper object of knowledge, a placeholder for any entity that is genuinely basic and is thus the right beginning for an account of the nature of things.[8] I argue that the "is" in Parmenides is primarily predicative, and that the predications required by Parmenides' arguments are informative identity statements (pp. 41–42). The only acceptable way to use "is" or *einai* is in the predication of a nature or an essence.[9] Any thing that can be said to be is something that is a basic reality and is what it is essentially. Only what is in this sense of being a nature (what something really or genuinely is) can be an object of genuine knowledge. This means that what-is is both genuinely real and what

---

and the subsequent problems of knowledge and belief are crucial for an understanding of the epistemological problems that Parmenides explores. Recent work by Lesher, Mourelatos, Mogyoródi, and Hermann demonstrates the philosophical importance of Xenophanes.

6 For discussion of Heraclitus and Parmenides, see Graham ("Heraclitus and Parmenides," now published in Caston and Graham), with response by Nehamas (ibid., 45–65).

7 See Long ("Thinking Being" and "Finding Oneself") on the connection between thinking and what-is in Parmenides and other early Greek thinkers. I agree with much of what Long says about the object of thought and the connection between thinking and what-is, although I ams not sure that his commitment to numerical monism in Parmenides will let him maintain the sort of identity between thought and its object that he suggests. According to Long, thinking and being are not the same in essence, but are "co-extensive types, such that their tokens are identical" ("Thinking Being," p. 132n.13; cf. pp. 145–46). Numerical monism might not allow for the plurality of types that he needs. On this point, see also Crystal. For a different account of the relation of thought and what-is in Parmenides' project, see Cherubin.

8 In chapter I, I argue that Parmenides' interest is in metaphysically basic entities, or natures, and that in this he is taking on the attempts of earlier thinkers to explain the fundamental natures of things. Mourelatos rejects this restriction; "Pluralists," pp. 120–21.

9 Thus the force of Aristotle's claim that "being is said in many ways." This is a rejection of the Eleatic (and Platonic—at least pre-*Sophist*) claim that there is but a single acceptable use of "*einai*."

is revealed in true statement and thought.[10] The claim that X is Y, or that Y is what it is to be X, asserts that X is a basic reality, and that its nature is to be Y.

Genuine thought grasps its object in a single act of apprehension, and its object must be a necessary unity that can be understood in that single act. The arguments of B8 point out how what-is is, and one of the signs at the beginning of B8 (at line 4) is that what-is is "a whole of a single kind."[11] This is expanded in the claims that what-is is "all together one, continuous" (B8.5–6) and that it is not divisible (B8.22–24). The indivisibility requirement rules out the possibility that what-is can be identified with a homogeneous mixture or with an entity that can actually be separated into independent parts.[12] The milk and the cream in homogenized milk constitute a unity of sorts, but it does not satisfy Parmenides' criteria precisely because it is an additive unity of milk plus cream, held together by the mixing. Heraclitus's *kykeōn*, the sacred barley drink that falls apart if it is not stirred (22B125) is an analogous case. It is what it is only through the mixture of its parts, and so it is not a unity in the appropriate sense. It is for this reason that I have said that an entity that can satisfy the unity criterion must be *mono*genous rather than *homo*genous. What is homogenous and thoroughly mixed may be the same all the way through, but if it is a mixed sameness, it is actually a plurality rather than a unity. If we think of *to eon* as what is fundamental or basic in an account of what there is, then we can see that what we begin with must be a unity—each thing that is is a unified whole, all of the same sort or kind. In the predication "X is really F" (or "F is what it is to be X"), F (even if it is a statement or proposition expressed in a plurality of words) is the necessarily unified nature of X. Thus, I claim that Parmenides' monism is a monism of

[10] Thus the *esti* is both predicational and veridical. To this extent, both Mourelatos and Kahn are right about the force of the *esti*. I think that disagreements between them are less important than their agreement on these issues (though they perhaps would not agree with this). For discussion of their views, see Kahn, "Parmenides and Plato," (esp. pp. 83–89 and p. 84n.9); for Mourelatos on his view, see "Pluralists," pp. 121–22. Moreover, whatever is in this sense will also exist, but as I noted (p. 39n.42) this is perhaps the least interesting aspect of Parmenides' claim and certainly not the focus of his analysis. The fused sense is becoming more widely accepted, although many scholars still speak of the object of Parmenides' analysis as "what exists." See, for instance, Sedley (pp. 114–15) and Hankinson (p. 68), both of whom note that for the early Greek philosophical use of *esti*, to be is to be something or other, but then speak of "what exists." Hankinson says that "in the most important part of [Parmenides'] deduction it is indeed existence as such which is primarily (although not exclusively) at issue."

[11] I discuss the text and translation of the key term *mounogenes* on pp. 71–73.

[12] Thus my worry (p.72 n.23) whether an Aristotelian essence—like "being a rational animal"—can actually qualify as a Parmenidean one. Insofar as being rational and being an animal are separable, if we think of being a rational animal as being rational *plus* being an animal, it is not a real unity. Aristotle clearly denies that the essence of human beings is an additive unity of this kind, and he is at pains to show that all genuine essences are unities of exactly the sort that concerns Parmenides. I now think that because its definition expresses a genuine unity, the Aristotelian essence "rational animal" would satisfy Parmenides' criteria.

kinds, and that this kind of monism is consistent with numerical pluralism.[13] Anything that is must be one, but there may be more than one such thing.

2. Internal and External Negations

One might agree that what-is must be a whole of a single kind and still argue that this entails that there can exist only one such thing. That is, it might well seem that predicational monism (as I initially described it and as I have amplified it here) entails numerical monism, and that the traditional view that Parmenides is a strict or numerical monist must be correct.[14] There can be no divisions in what-is, and no part of what-is can not be; yet, if there were two or more things, each could be said to be different from, and so not, the others, and so we would be led to the absurd conclusion that what-is is not.

There are, it seems to me, two ways to interpret this objection. First, one might regard *being* or *what-is* as the collective name of anything that is in the way that Parmenides argues for, and view the collection so named as something apart from the things named. Let us, for the sake of example, adopt a tripartite cosmology: suppose that there are three basic entities—water, air, and fire—each of which (*ex hypothesi*) meets Parmenidean requirements.[15] One might think that there are these three *and* that there is also being, which is the collection of the three. This collection is an apparent unity, yet it is divisible into three constituents (water, air, and fire), and so being or what-is is divisible in exactly the way that Parmenides rejects. This seems to me to be a category mistake. Just as (in the Rylean case) there is no university apart from the buildings, the people, and so on, so there is no thing, being, apart from the things that are, and being is therefore not divisible in the way envisioned by this version of the objection.

Here is a more serious version of the objection. If we suppose that there can be a plurality of real things, each with its own specifiable and knowable unified nature, we must say of each that it is different from and so is not each of the others. If we return to our previous sample cosmology: water is different from and so is not fire, fire is different from and so is not air, and air is different from and so is not water. If the only allowable predications are claims about natures or essences, then what it is to be water is to be not-fire, and so on. Thus, plurality demands a negative specification of each

[13] See Nehamas, who contrasts "strict" (numerical) and "kind" monism (or what I call predicational monism). While accepting that what Parmenides says is consistent with kind monism, Nehamas says that "Parmenides' theory was vague: it was not clearly committed to either sort of monism" ("Being/Fire," p. 51). I agree that Parmenides leaves open the question of what actually satisfies his criteria, thus allowing the possibility that, as a matter of fact, only one such entity does so, but I think that his primary concern is with predicational or kind monism.

[14] See Crystal, p. 216 n. 34.

[15] As far as I know, no Presocratic adopted such a cosmology.

thing that is, and this is exactly the sort of negative predication ruled out by the arguments of B8.[16] This is the sort of problem that I consider briefly in section 3 of chapter II. I still think that the suggestion made there is correct: if we distinguish between internal and external negations, we can allow for numerically diverse entities without compromising their internal unity. An internal negation (ruled out by the prohibition against what-is-not) is a negation that would be an integral part of the definition specifying the nature of something that is.[17] An external negation, by contrast, is a negative claim about an entity that is not included in the definition specifying its nature. Definitions specifying the nature of a thing neither entail nor are entailed by statements about the relation between that thing and other basic things. Thus, water can be a basic entity, and earth can be a basic entity, and they are different. The internal-external negations distinction allows one to say that earth differs from water without being committed to the claim that earth then is-not what it is to be water (or is what it is to be not-water), and thus avoids the forbidden assertion that earth is something that both is and is not. Each basic entity is defined independently and added to the list of what is, without its definition including its relations to the other genuinely real things. Thus, on this view, external negations do not entail internal negations.

I think that, given the unitary nature of *einai* at work in Parmenides, he cannot successfully maintain this distinction. I also think that he did not recognize the difficulty in his theory.[18] The problem in such an account becomes clear only later in the history of Greek philosophy.[19] That this seems incredible to us is not an objection to the view: Plato apparently constructs his account of the Forms in the same way. It is only in the late dialogues (*Parmenides*, *Sophist*) that Plato begins to explain the relations among Forms, and in doing so, sees that he must be able to find an acceptable way to distinguish claims about what a Form is in virtue of being the particular Form

16 See Nehamas, "Being/Fire," p. 61. Nehamas makes the point in the course of objecting to my account of the *Doxa*. His claim is that "Parmenides must consider any two distinct entities, not just the traditional opposites, as enantiomorphs in Curd's sense." That is, what it is to be F *is* (in the strong sense) not what it is to be G.

17 Although my discussion is in terms of definitions, this should not be taken to mean that the problems are merely verbal, not metaphysical. The sorts of definitions I mean are "real definitions," and so the negations that I discuss here would turn out to be part of the nature of a thing.

18 Nor, apparently do the Pluralists and the Atomists. It may seem unwarranted to attribute such a confusion or misunderstanding to Parmenides and others. As I point out below, it requires a number of logical distinctions that only become clear in the work of Plato and Aristotle to see and understand this point.

19 Thus, in the First Hypothesis of Plato's *Parmenides* (139b4–139e6), we find the character Parmenides arguing that the One cannot be the same or different because it is not so in virtue of itself (through being one). That is, the One can be only what it is in and of itself (and that is, being one). In the second Hypothesis (142b5–c2), Plato introduces a distinction between being F and having f at the level of the Forms, such that we can say that the One is (what it is to be) one, while having or partaking of being; it will also partake of sameness and difference.

that it is and claims about a Form's relations to other Forms. Making such distinctions requires the notions of substances, essences, and accidents.[20] I contend that it is only through wrestling with the problems posed by Parmenides' restrictions on the proper use of *esti* that later thinkers came to see the necessity of drawing such distinctions.[21]

3. Locomotion and the Specification of How What-is Is

The internal-external negations distinction permits a plurality of unities, each of which is indivisibly what it is. Thus, the pluralists are not ignoring or rejecting Parmenides' requirements on what-is when they postulate a numerical plurality of basic entities. Nevertheless, it might well seem that any pluralist account that attempts to give a rational explanation of the sensible world will contradict the claim in lines B8.26–31 that what-is is *akinēton*. This is often taken as a denial of locomotion: Change of place is impossible and so the motion necessary for mixture and separation cannot take place.[22] That B8.41 includes change of place in the list of names that mortals unsuccessfully attempt to give to what-is lends further support to the claim that what-is must be motionless.[23] This is a strong objection (and indeed I worried about this while I was writing the book). Here is an outline of a response.

There is good reason for thinking that in lines B8.26–31 Parmenides argues against alteration in the nature of what-is rather than against the locomotion of anything that is, just as Mourelatos had suggested.[24] Although this is not the standard view, I think that the Homeric notion of *kinēsis* as *disruption* is what Parmenides intends here; in chapter II.2 I suggest other parallels to support that view. I take *kinēsis* as a general term covering various sorts of change. I would now suggest more strongly than I did earlier that Xenophanes B26 uses the same sense (see p. 87n.57). The first line of B26 claims that the divine remains always in the same state (*tautōi*), not moving/changing (*kinoumenos ouden*);[25] the second line adds "nor is it fitting that he travel

[20] See Nehamas, "Being/Fire" p. 61 n.57; and Mann on "the discovery of things." See also Kahn on Parmenides and Plato.

[21] Palmer gives an extended account of Parmenides' philosophical importance for Plato.

[22] See the review by Graham. Sedley says that according to the goddess's positive account "what-is will prove to be an everlasting, undifferentiated, motionless sphere" ("Parmenides," p. 117). Sedley and I disagree on a number of crucial points in interpreting Parmenides; his lucid interpretation of the structure of the argument in Melissus B1–B4 makes better sense of those fragments than my account in Ch. V.

[23] Mourelatos, "Pluralists," p. 126; Laks, "Vide."

[24] As I note in Chapter II, in adopting this view of change, I follow the arguments of Mourelatos in *Route*.

[25] Most translators and commentators take *en* + *tautōi* as expressing a dative of place ("in the same place"); but I think it should be understood as a dative of state or condition.

to different places at different times." It seems to me that we first have a general statement that god does not change; to this is added, as a separate claim, the assertion that god does not travel, i.e., does not move. Moreover, if, as I think we should, we read the signs at the beginning of B8 adverbially, as claims about how what-is is what it is, the sign that what-is is *atremes*, unshaking, says that what-is is unchangingly what it is. It would be odd to say that what-is must be motionlessly whatever its nature says that it is. The logical point is about alteration, not about locomotion. The later lines B8.26–31 spell out the implication of that sign, and show that Necessity holds what-is in a bond that maintains its steadfast nature. If what-is is what it is unalterably, that is, maintains its nature throughout, then the motion of such a thing would not affect or destroy that nature. If, for instance, Empedocles' earth has a stable nature (as 31B17.27–28 suggests), then it maintains that nature regardless of whether it is here or there (or is moved from here to there).

What then of the rejection of "change of place" in B8.41? I still think that the list of names in B8.40–41 gives us failed mortal characterizations of what-is. That is, mortals have tried to make these attributes fundamental to the nature of what-is. These are then names that mortals have used, thinking that they are referring to what is real, when in fact the names fail to characterize what-is. Such mortal thought has no real object, and the thought of such mortals wanders, unfocused, unable to engage with what-is. A Milesian monist would have to say that it is part of the nature of what-is that it changes into other things; on a generating substance view, the basic substance ceases to be what it is and becomes something else. In Xenophanes' meteorological accounts, cloud that is one set of colors is a rainbow (B32); as glowing and glimmering because of motion, cloud is St. Elmo's fire (A39); and as certain groupings or movements, cloud constitutes comets, shooting stars, meteors, and lightning (A44 and A45).[26] Motion and exchange of color constitute the reality of these things, and Parmenides might well complain that although such mortal thinkers as the Milesians and Xenophanes suppose that they are naming and explaining what-is, neither the phenomena nor the underlying things can pass the tests for what is real.

4. Doxa

Interpreting the *Doxa* remains controversial, especially given the warnings about the beliefs of mortals that occur at the end of B1 and in B8 at the moment when the goddess turns from her account of truth to her story about those mortal beliefs. My proposal in chapter III was to see the *Doxa* as

[26] Mourelatos provides an account of Xenophanes' cloud theory "Terre" and "Astro-Meteorology."

an outline of a rational cosmology, albeit one with a sting. The plan of the cosmology is correct: begin with a plurality of basic entities that can combine through mixture and separation without loss of essence or nature. This would allow for explanations of the various phenomena of the cosmos, including its development. Nevertheless, the story that the goddess tells is not trustworthy because the supposedly basic entities, Light and Night, do not actually qualify as such. Each is said to be what the other is not; this implies that they are opposites of a particular sort (which I call "enantiomorphic"). Enantiomorphic opposites are by nature each precisely what the other is not, and this exhausts the specification of what each is (pp. 107–9). The negations in such opposites are thus internal: to be F just is to be not-G, and to be G just is to be not-F. Such opposites do not each have a single, self-contained nature as required by the arguments of B8. There is no other specification possible in the statement of the nature of such a thing. It is thus a pseudo-entity, which cannot meet the requirements for what-is and thus is not real. Were Light and Night genuinely real entities, they could serve as the grounding for a rational cosmology. In chapter III, I argue that coming to understand what is deceptive about the account of mortal belief reveals a genuine understanding of the goddess's speech. The *Doxa* is a final examination for the *kouros*, who learns how to test such mortal accounts by using the criteria established in B8. Being thus armed against error, the *kouros* is assured that no false beliefs will drive past him (B8.60–61).

I adopted this account primarily because I could see no other way of making sense of all the goddess's claims about her deceptive story.[27] In a recent paper, Alexander Nehamas has offered a persuasive alternative interpretation, suggesting that what is deceptive is not the goddess's account of the sensible world, but that world itself. The world of appearance presents itself to unthinking mortals as all that there is, "masquerading as real when it is only apparent." As long as we keep in mind that what the *Doxa* describes is only apparent and not real, we will not be mistaken in accepting it as a correct cosmological explanation. According to Nehamas, it is "an accurate description . . . of a false world."[28] The naming of the two forms (Light and Night) is right: unlike Milesian monism, which requires the transformation of its basic entity, Parmenides' dualism in the *Doxa* avoids this problem. The basic entities of the cosmology are metaphysically acceptable. The problem is the status of the mixtures that produce the changing objects in the sensible

[27] Nehamas might well be right that there is a "psychological" difficulty with my account: "If," as he puts it, "Parmenides is aware of the problem of opposites and has the right sort of entities up his sleeve, why does he not produce the right cosmology after all?" ("Being/Fire" p. 61). I have felt the force of this sort of objection since before the book was published (the editors of the journal that published an earlier version of the chapter said that they liked the paper but hoped that it was wrong); but, for the reasons I give in Chapter III.1, it seemed to me that no other interpretation would do.

[28] Nehamas, "Being/Fire," pp. 56–63. The passages quoted are on pp. 60 and 63.

world, for those things are both light and night and so are not insofar as they fail to meet the criteria of the *Alētheia*.[29] As I say, I find this account attractive; it avoids the problem that afflicts many other interpretations of treating the *Doxa* as the best false theory, and it offers a persuasive explanation for the wealth of detail that apparently made up the *Doxa*. Nevertheless, there are three difficulties with Nehamas's interpretation. First, why does the goddess say that the story she tells involves deception at some level? The world of experience is deceptive to mortals, who think that it is all that there is (and especially to Milesian monists who think that there is a single basic entity that is transformed into other things). Yet, once we (along with the *kouros*) have learned the truths of the *Alētheia*, we cease to think like mortals and cannot be deceived either by the story or by the pervasiveness of sensory experience. On this account, for us, who know, the sensible world is not deceptive. Second, on Nehamas's account, the world of appearance and the world of being are entirely separate; the one is apprehended by reason, the other by the senses, and they float free of one another.[30] Yet, given his account, we ought to be able to apprehend Light and Night by thought. If they meet the criteria for what-is in B8, we could have knowledge of them through knowing their natures, and then could have derivative true belief about the mixtures they produce, insofar as we understand how those mixtures are constituted by combinations of Light and Night. So, to someone who understands the goddess's story, the world of experience should not be in any way deceptive; indeed it should be the object of true belief justified by an appeal to the genuine entities Light and Night. Finally, Nehamas's account relies on following Coxon's translation and interpretation of B8.53–54: "For they have resolved to name two Forms (of which it is wrong to name only one, wherein men have gone astray)."[31] The "only" is not in the text, and I do not see how to justify its addition. Rather, on the standard translation ("they laid down in their minds two forms for naming, of which it is not right to name one - in which they have gone astray"), the text seems to say that the mistake lies in one of the forms that is named (not that naming only one of the forms is the problem).[32] If this is so, then Light and Night cannot both be named as acceptable entities. Naming both Light and Night is necessary for Nehamas's claim that the *Doxa* gives a correct account of the deceptive sensible world, for the *Doxa* must be a dualism. If we cannot make that move, then it looks as though we have to think that the deception belongs to the details of the mortal account rather than attaching to the world

29 Ibid., pp. 62–3.

30 "Parmenides does not explain the relationship between these two worlds" ("Being/Fire," p. 63).

31 "Being/Fire," p. 62; See Coxon, *Fragments*, p. 76 for the translation, and p. 220 for Coxon's commentary on the line. As Nehamas notes, Coxon takes the comment as a direct criticism of Milesian monism.

32 I discuss the text and translation issues on pp. 109–110.

that is described. We are then left with the problem of determining what is deceptive in the story the goddess tells; it was in order to account for this that I developed my view. These difficulties are not fatal to Nehamas's view but, for the moment, they prevent me from accepting his attractive interpretation of the *Doxa*; so I continue to maintain the account I gave in chapter III.

Acknowledgments

I am very grateful to Parmenides Publishing for the paper version of *The Legacy of Parmenides*; Sara Hermann and Gale Carr have been unfailingly gracious and supportive. Thanks are also due to Ian Malcolm at Princeton University Press, who aided in the necessary transfer of rights. In addition to his careful criticism of *Legacy* in his review in *Apeiron*, Alexander P. D. Mourelatos supplied me with a list of typographical and other errors. Alex's work remains a model of meticulous scholarship and an inspiration; I hope I have corrected the typos—philosophical disagreement will no doubt remain. Many thanks, too, to all the other friends and colleagues who kept track of errors and encouraged me to pursue a paperback version of the volume. My debt to Martin Curd remains and increases.

Supplementary Bibliography

This is a list of sources cited in this introduction; it is far from a complete bibliography of work on Parmenides since *Legacy* went into production in 1996. I have also included several papers that I originally cited as "unpublished," but which have now appeared in print. More comprehensive bibliographical data may be found in *The Pre-Socratics: A Collection of Critical Essays*, edited by A. P. D. Mourelatos; *The Cambridge Companion to Early Greek Philosophy*, edited by A. A. Long; *Bibliographia Praesocratica*, edited by B. Šijaković; and in *The Oxford Handbook to Presocratic Philosophy*, edited by P. Curd and D. H. Graham (forthcoming).

Algra, K. "The Beginnings of Cosmology." In A. A. Long, ed., *Cambridge Companion*, 45–65.

Caston, V., and D. Graham, eds., *Presocratic Philosophy: Essays in Honor of A. P. D. Mourelatos*. Aldershot: Ashgate Publishing Co., 2002.

Cherubin, R. "Λέγειν, Νοεῖν, and Τὸ Ἐόν in Parmenides." *Ancient Philosophy* 21 (2001) 277–303.

Crystal, I. "The Scope of Thought in Parmenides." *Classical Quarterly* 52 (2002) 207–19.

Curd, P. "A New Empedocles? The Implications of the Strasburg Fragments for Presocratic Philosophy." In J. J. Cleary and G. M. Gurtler, eds., *Pro-*

ceedings of the Boston Area Colloquium in Ancient Philosophy 17 (2001) 27–49.

———. "The Metaphysics of Physics: Mixture and Separation in Anaxagoras and Empedocles." In Caston and Graham, eds., *Presocratic Philosophy*, 139–58.

———. "The Presocratics as Philosophers," in Laks and Louguet, eds., *Philosophie*, 115–138.

———. *Anaxagoras of Clazomenae: Fragments. A Text and Translation with Introduction and Commentary*. Forthcoming.

———. "On the Question of Religion and Natural Philosophy in Empedocles." In Apostolos Pierris, ed., *Proceedings of Symposium Philosophiae Antiquae Tertium Myconense: The Empedoclean Cosmos: Structure, Process and the Question of Cyclicity*. Forthcoming.

Curd, P., and D. W. Graham, eds. *The Oxford Handbook of Presocratic Philosophy*. New York and Oxford: Oxford University Press, forthcoming.

Furley, D. "Anaxagoras, Plato, and the Naming of Parts." In Caston and Graham, eds., *Presocratic Philosophy*, 119–26.

Graham, D. W. "Empedocles and Anaxagoras: Responses to Parmenides." In A. A. Long, ed., *Cambridge Companion*, 159–80.

———. "Heraclitus' Criticism of Ionian Philosophy," *Oxford Studies In Ancient Philosophy* 15 (1997) 1–50.

———. Review of P. Curd, *The Legacy of Parmenides*; *Ancient Philosophy* 18 (1998) 435–39.

———. "Heraclitus and Parmenides." In Caston and Graham, eds., *Presocratic Philosophy*, 27–44.

Hankinson, R. J. "Parmenides and the Metaphysics of Changelessness." In Caston and Graham, eds., *Presocratic Philosophy*, 65–80.

Hermann, A. *To Think Like God. Pythagoras and Parmenides: The Origins of Philosophy*. Las Vegas: Parmenides Publishing, 2004.

Kahn, C. H. "Parmenides and Plato." In Caston and Graham, eds., *Presocratic Philosophy*, 81–93.

Kingsley, P. *In the Dark Places of Wisdom*. Inverness, CA: Golden Sufi Publishing, 1999; Reprinted, London: Duckworth, 2001.

———. "Empedocles for the New Millennium." *Ancient Philosophy* 22 (2002) 333–413.

———. *Reality*. Inverness CA: Golden Sufi Publishing, 2004.

Laks, A. *Le Vide et La Haine: Eléments pour Une Histoire Archaïque de la Négativité*. Paris: Presses Universitaires de France, 2004.

Laks, A., and C. Louguet, eds. *Qu'est-ce que la Philosophie Présocratique?* Lille: Presses Universitaires du Septentrion, 2002.

Lesher, J. "Early Interest in Knowledge." In A. A. Long, ed., *Cambridge Companion*, 225–49.

———. "The Humanizing of Knowledge." In P. Curd and D. Graham, eds., *Oxford Handbook*. Forthcoming.

Long, A. A., ed. *The Cambridge Companion to Early Greek Philosophy*. Cambridge: Cambridge University Press, 1999.

———. "Finding Oneself in Greek Philosophy." *Tijdschrift voor Filosofie* 54 (1992) 255–79.

———. "Parmenides on Thinking Being." In J. J. Cleary and W. C. Wians, eds., *Proceedings of the Boston Area Colloquium in Ancient Philosophy* 12 (Lanham: University Press of America: 1996) 125–51 (bibliography on pp. 161–62).

Mann, W.-R. *The Discovery of Things: Aristotle's* Categories *and Their Context*. Princeton: Princeton University Press, 2000.

Mogyoródi, E. "Xenophanes as a Philosopher: Theology and Theodicy." In Laks and Louguet, eds., *Philosophie*, 253–86.

Mourelatos, A. P. D. ed. *The Pre-Socratics: A Collection of Critical Essays*. Princeton: Princeton University Press, 1993.

———. "Parmenides and the Pluralists" Review of P. Curd, *The Legacy of Parmenides. Apeiron* 32 (1999) 117–29.

———. "La Terre et les Étoiles dans la Cosmologie de Xénophane." In Laks and Louguet, eds., *Philosophie*, 331–50.

———. "The Astro-Meteorology of Xenophanes: An Archaic Project in Unified Science." In Curd and Graham, eds., *Oxford Handbook*. Forthcoming.

Nehamas, A. "Parmenidean Being/Heraclitean Fire." In Caston and Graham, eds., *Presocratic Philosophy*, 45–65.

Palmer, J. A. *Plato's Reception of Parmenides*. Oxford: Clarendon Press, 1999.

Sanders, K. "Much Ado About 'Nothing': μηδέν and τὸ μὴ ὄν in Parmenides." *Apeiron* 35 (2002) 87–104.

Sedley, D. "Parmenides and Melissus." In A. A. Long, ed. *Cambridge Companion*, 113–33.

Šijaković, B. *Bibliographia Praesocratica: A Bibliographical Guide to the Studies of Early Greek Philosophy in Its Religious and Scientific Contexts with an Introductory Bibliography on the Historiography of Philosophy*. Paris: Les Belles Lettres 2001.

THE LEGACY OF PARMENIDES

Introduction

PARMENIDES OF ELEA is generally regarded as the most important and influential of the Presocratic philosophers.[1] Through his rejection of what-is-not and his commitment to monism, Parmenides provided a challenge that altered the nature of Presocratic thought. Even Plato, through the character of the Eleatic Stranger in the *Sophist*, refers to him as "Father Parmenides" and suggests that a re-evaluation of his views might be considered a sort of parricide (241d3). The interpretation of Parmenides now dominant (at least among English-speaking philosophers) sees Presocratic philosophy prior to Parmenides as a set of attempts to do what Parmenides claimed could not be done, and later Presocratic thought as a series of efforts to rescue physical inquiry from Parmenides' rejection of change and his monism. It is often argued that if Parmenides is correct, then philosophy and science (as the early philosopher-scientists of Greece understood it) are impossible. But despite Parmenides' arguments, later Presocratics continued to propose cosmological systems to explain the world reported by sense experience. How could they do so if they really understood Parmenides and if Parmenides' influence was as the standard interpretation claims?

The predominant present-day explanations of later Presocratic thought fail adequately to explain an important aspect of these views. For, despite their many differences, the major responses to Parmenides—Atomism, Pluralism, and Plato's Theory of Forms—share a common characteristic: in their explanations of the world reported by the senses, all three posit without justifying argument a numerical plurality of fundamental entities. But if numerical monism is entailed by Parmenides' arguments about what-is, and if monism and the arguments about change entail that science is impossible, then pluralistic theorists cannot defeat or avoid Parmenides' conclusions simply by positing without argument a plurality of basic entities, as they seem to do. The widespread silence about numerical monism among later Presocratics is suggestive. The early Greek philosophers were not shy about voicing disagreements (see, for instance, Heraclitus B40, B42, B129, and Parmenides himself in B6 and B7). While both Anaxagoras and Empedocles

[1] I follow the convention of referring to early Greek philosophers as Presocratics although many of the figures I discuss were active during Socrates' lifetime and are, in that sense, not pre-Socrates at all. The convention allows us to pick out a particular group of thinkers fairly easily, and as long as the chronological discrepancy is kept in mind, it provides a useful name for this group.

note their dissatisfaction with those who claim that coming-to-be is real, and both insist on the genuine reality of their basic entities, neither argues against monism or in favor of numerical pluralism. Rather, they assume that a plurality of basic entities is metaphysically permissible.[2] Thus, on the standard reading of the history of Presocratic philosophy, the Pluralists and the Atomists beg the question against Parmenides, although most interpretations of Presocratic thought dismiss this silence about Parmenides' monism as a minor aspect of the theories of Pluralism and Atomism.[3] But if Parmenides' arguments entail monism, they cannot simply be ignored; nor can the rest of his system legitimately be adopted while pluralism is embraced. The view that Parmenides was a monist is usually based on an existential interpretation of the "is" in Parmenides. On this account, when Parmenides claims that only the route "that it is" is an acceptable path of inquiry, his subject is to be taken as whatever can be thought or studied, and his claim is that whatever can legitimately be inquired into exists; moreover, these arguments are supposed to demonstrate that only one such thing exists.[4]

This book offers an alternative account of the views of Parmenides and his influence on later Presocratic thought, especially Pluralism and Atomism, in the period immediately preceding Plato's Theory of Forms. It challenges what has become the standard account of the development of Pluralism (in the theories of Empedocles and Anaxagoras) and Atomism (adopted by Leucippus and Democritus). This alternative interpretation places Parmenides firmly in the tradition of physical inquiry in Presocratic thought, arguing that Parmenides was concerned with the same problems that had occupied his predecessors (although his concern took a different form). Further, this account explains how Parmenides' metaphysical and cosmological doctrines had a positive influence on his successors, and how they were used and modified by the later Eleatics Zeno and Melissus.

In the course of this book, I shall argue against both the prevailing interpretation of Parmenides' monism and the usual explanation of the "is" in Parmenides. Instead, I shall claim that Parmenides' subject is what it is to be the genuine nature of something, thus linking Parmenides with the inquiries into nature of his philosophical predecessors. On the view for which I shall argue, the "is" that concerns Parmenides is a predicational "is" of a particularly strong sort rather than an existential "is." I accept that Parmenides is a monist, but I deny that he is a numerical monist. Rather, I

[2] Plurality is taken for granted until Diogenes of Apollonia, who was, I think, influenced by Melissus's arguments for numerical monism. I discuss Melissus's arguments in Chap. V, Section 4.

[3] See, for instance, the discussions in such standard histories as KRS or Guthrie, *HGP*, vol. II. The dismissals usually claim that Parmenides' arguments for numerical monism are weak (although it is sometimes unclear wherein commentators think their weakness lies) and thus may safely be ignored by the later Presocratics.

[4] See, for example, Owen's influential "Eleatic Questions."

claim that Parmenides is committed to what I call predicational monism.[5] Numerical monism asserts that there exists only one thing: a complete list of entities in the universe would have only one entry. This is the kind of monism that has traditionally been attributed to Parmenides and (rightly) to Melissus. Predicational monism is the claim that each thing that is can be only one thing; and must be that in a particularly strong way. To be a genuine entity, something that is metaphysically basic, a thing must be a predicational unity, a being of a single kind (*mounogenes*, as Parmenides says in B8.4), with a single account of what it is; but it need not be the case that there exists only one such thing. What must be the case is that the thing itself must be a unified whole. If it is, say *F* (whatever *F* turns out to be), it must be all, only, and completely *F*. On predicational monism, a numerical plurality of such one-beings (as we might call them) is possible.[6] The interpretation of Parmenides' "is" becomes relevant here, for I argue that to be for Parmenides is to be the nature of a thing, what a thing genuinely is, and thus metaphysically basic. The arguments of Parmenides' fragment B8 concern the criteria for what-is, that is, for being the nature of something, where such a nature is what a thing really is. Those arguments purport to show that what-is must be whole, complete, unchanging, and of a single kind. Each thing that is can have only one nature, but there may be many such things that satisfy Parmenides' criteria.[7] These issues are the subjects of Chapters I and II.

The proper interpretation of the second major part of Parmenides' poem, the *Doxa*, is a vexed issue in Parmenides scholarship. On the standard interpretation, Parmenides first argues that scientific inquiry is impossible but then goes on to present his own cosmology. What is his purpose in doing this, particularly since he has announced that the discussion of the cosmology is deceptive (at B8.50–52)? One view of the *Doxa* is that it is entirely false and deceptive and that its purpose is purely dialectical.[8] Another is that while the *Doxa* (and, by extension, all cosmology) is false, it is nevertheless the best (albeit mistaken) account of experience possible. Parmenides' point is that no cosmology as such can ever be rational in the sense of meeting the criteria

[5] Mourelatos (in *Route*) and Barnes ("Eleatic One") have also questioned the predominant view that Parmenides is a numerical monist; Barnes denies any sort of monism to Parmenides, and Mourelatos emphasizes Parmenides' anti-dualism.

[6] Thus, the failure of later Presocratic thinkers to argue for their pluralistic theories, while working within a Parmenidean framework and stressing the reality and predicational unity of their basic entities, is evidence for my view that it is possible for there to be a numerical plurality of entities each of which is predicationally one.

[7] In later terminology we might say that Parmenides is searching for an account of what it is to be the essence of something, although I have avoided the word *essence* because it is an anachronistic term in Presocratic thought. There is, however, a connection between Parmenides' search for what-is and Aristotle's accounts of *ousia* and *to ti ēn einai*; the connection runs through Plato's Theory of Forms, which itself has Parmenidean roots.

[8] This is Owen's view in "Eleatic Questions." He is followed by Mourelatos and Barnes.

for genuine entities that he formulates in B8.[9] In Chapter III, I argue for a different interpretation of the *Doxa*, placing its deception in the unacceptable character of the fundamental entities of the cosmological theory posited in that section of the poem. Parmenides rejects dualistic candidates for the basic entities of a cosmology but does not thereby repudiate all attempts to give a rational explanation of the world as experienced by the senses. On this view Parmenides is rejecting as candidates for theoretically basic entities opposites of a particular sort, since these fail to meet the criteria for what-is that are spelled out in the arguments of B8, and especially the requirement of predicational monism. Thus, the opposites of the *Doxa* are unacceptable as genuine entities. Nevertheless, in the deceptive account told by the goddess, they mix and separate to form the heavens and to account for the various phenomena reported to us by our senses. The lesson of the *Doxa* is neither that cosmology is unacceptable, nor that, as an account of sense-experience, it has lesser value. Rather, I argue that Parmenides supposes that his model in the *Doxa* would yield a rationally grounded cosmology if the basic entities of such a theory met the criteria of B8 for what-is. Further, I maintain that Parmenides' model cosmology, based on a set of basic realities that mix and separate, was just as influential on those Presocratics who came after him as were his arguments about what-is.

Given the interpretation of Parmenides that I argue for, the standard account of Parmenides' influence on later Presocratic philosophy must be revised. Parmenides' predicational monism is consistent with numerical pluralism. For, as long as each thing that is is a unity in the appropriate, predicational, sense, there is no theoretical bar to the reality of more than one such thing. The history of later Presocratic philosophy is, in large part, the history of explorations of the nature of theoretically basic entities, their relation to the world of experience reported by our senses, and their role in explaining that world. The Pluralists (Empedocles and Anaxagoras) and the Atomists (Leucippus and Democritus) accept Parmenides' conclusions that what-is has an unchanging nature and must be one in the appropriate sense. But they do not suppose that Parmenides' conclusions entail that cosmological or other scientific knowledge is impossible. While taking care to point out the unchanging unity and homogeneity of the fundamental elements—the *chrēmata* for Anaxagoras; earth, water, air, and fire (along with Love and Strife) for Empedocles—Anaxagoras and Empedocles see no need to argue for an original plurality. Instead, they fix their attention on the issue of whether the separation and mixture of these elements will account for the apparent changes of the sensible world. Their silence on the issue of monism, their concern with establishing the nature and character of their basic entities, and their interest in explaining the world reported by the senses are, I think, confirmation of the account of

[9] See, for instance, Long in "Principles."

Parmenides for which I argue. Chapter IV is an exploration of the Parmenidean influence on the metaphysical foundations of Pluralism, paying particular attention to the problem of the nature of the "things" (*chrēmata*) in Anaxagoras and the four roots in Empedocles, and to the problem of justifying apparent change through mixture and separation of entities that themselves remain unchanged. Chapter IV also examines Zeno's arguments concerning division and portrays Zeno as arguing that the basic entities adopted by the Pluralists cannot actually succeed in meeting Parmenides' criteria for what-is.

Leucippus and Democritus, too, follow the Parmenidean model in attempting to provide a rational account of how things are. They assert the monogeneous unity of each atom (thus meeting the Parmenidean criteria for what is while avoiding the Zenonian division arguments) and then rely on the mixing and separation of atoms to account for sensible phenomena: "By convention sweet, by convention bitter, by convention hot, by convention cold, by convention color; but in reality atoms and the void" (Democritus B9; B125). A fundamental issue for my interpretation (taken up in Chapter V) is the problem of the reality of void. How can something that the Atomists explicitly called "nothing" and "what-is-not" qualify as real on a Parmenidean model? I argue that the Atomists conceive both atoms and void as entities that have unchanging and knowable characters or natures of their own, thus satisfying the Parmenidean criteria for what-is. Like Parmenides, the later Presocratic cosmologists argue that change is merely apparent and not real, but that nevertheless the phenomenal world can be the subject of rational explanation. But Melissus, the last of the three Eleatics, objects to all pluralistic theories, on the grounds that, first, pluralism itself is incompatible with the correct account of what-is, and second, that in any case, pluralistic theories cannot successfully account for the world reported to us by our senses. In these arguments Melissus goes beyond Parmenides.[10]

The book concludes (in Chapter VI) with short discussions of Philolaus and Diogenes of Apollonia, closing with an account of the influence of Parmenides' monism on the development of Plato's metaphysical and epistemological views in the Theory of Forms. Plato's Theory of Forms is frequently seen as an original theory, strikingly different from the philosophical theories of those philosophers (other than Socrates) who preceded Plato. I suggest that there is a strong Eleatic influence on Plato's views from the beginnings in the early dialogues, and that Parmenides' arguments about what-is lie

[10] The three Eleatics, while sharing certain basic assumptions, differ importantly from each other. Eleaticism was not, I shall argue, a monolithic set of views, and Zeno and Melissus were not merely parroting Parmenides' arguments. Rather, they had distinct theories of their own which sometimes conflict with those of Parmenides or go beyond anything to which Parmenides himself was committed.

behind certain of the most remarkable and important parts of Plato's theory, especially self-predication and participation. Thus the Platonic system itself is part of the legacy of Parmenides.

My subject is the philosophical basis of Parmenides' theories and the significance of his views for later Presocratic thought. Although I discuss cosmology, my inquiry is not concerned with Presocratic cosmology as such. Thus, I do not examine the various accounts of the cosmic whirls, or the composition of the stars and planets, nor do I discuss the several Presocratic theories about the formation of the earth, or about the beings that inhabit the earth. Moreover, other facets of the theories of these Presocratic thinkers are also passed over lightly. Empedocles and Democritus, for instance, had interesting claims to make about how human beings ought to live. These issues are important and interesting in their own right, but they are not the subject of this book. Here I am exploring how the metaphysical arguments of Parmenides affected the course of Presocratic thought, how he criticizes earlier theories of what there is, and how those criticisms helped to shape the metaphysical framework accepted by those who followed him. Because of the fundamental character of Parmenides' arguments and claims, other aspects of Presocratic theories are, indirectly, affected by them, and in not discussing them, I do not mean to suggest that they are irrelevant to an understanding of the nature of Presocratic philosophy, or that they are unimportant details that are unworthy of examination. But because my subject is the direct effect of Parmenides' meta-theoretical arguments on the principles that shape the foundations of Presocratic thought about what there is, I will have little to say about the details of cosmological or other aspects of the theories that I discuss. The story I tell may, in some aspects, be similar to traditional accounts of the influence of Parmenides; but there is an important difference in emphasis, because I see later Presocratic philosophers as accepting Parmenides' arguments rather than attempting to avoid them, and as positively influenced by both the *Alētheia* and the *Doxa* of Parmenides' poem. I do not interpret those later thinkers as battling with or trying to maneuver around Parmenidean numerical monism. They are not attempting to avoid certain of Parmenides' arguments but are rather seeking to engage in rational cosmology, an inquiry into the nature of things that takes account of Parmenides' metaphysical insights and arguments.

Before turning to these issues in the following chapters, I consider some questions that are preliminary to the arguments that form the main part of the book. I begin by examining an account of Parmenides that has been widely accepted, exploring some of the deficiencies I see in this view of Parmenides and his importance for later Presocratic thought. I then turn to the vexed problem of the chronology of fifth-century thinkers. Finally, I close with some brief comments on Parmenides B1—the first, introductory, section of his philosophical poem.

1. The Standard Interpretation of Parmenides

Most recent English-language discussions of Parmenides have been influenced by G.E.L. Owen's account of Parmenides' theory and its place in Presocratic thought. Owen's view (or various versions and adaptations of it) has become the standard interpretation of Parmenides.[11] I argue against Owen's views in Chapters I and II; here I explore the explanation of the development of Presocratic thought to which Owen's account (or one like it) is committed. I believe that my interpretation of Parmenides and the development of Presocratic philosophy makes better sense of the history of Presocratic thought, at least as we have it in the surviving fragments.[12]

Any explanation of the thought of Parmenides must give an account of the nature of the *esti* (it is) in B2 and throughout the poem, and also explain the subject of that *esti*. Owen's view is that the subject of the *esti* is "what can be thought or spoken of" and that the *esti* is existential.[13] Thus, according to Owen, Parmenides' doctrine is that only what can be thought or spoken of can exist and indeed must exist. And, given the arguments of B8, only one such thing can and must exist; a solitary thing, neither coming to be nor passing away, nor subject to any changes, constitutes what there is.[14] Barnes suggests a modification of Owen's view. According to Barnes, rather

[11] In most English-language accounts of Parmenides, the assumption is that the Owen view (or a version of it) is correct. However, Tarán's interpretation is an alternative to the Owen view, taking Parmenides' subject to be Being. I discuss Tarán's account below, in n. 27.

[12] I do not suggest that I prove that what I call the standard accounts, and those views based on them, are false. Rather, I think that the story that I tell makes better sense of the history of Presocratic philosophy. The fragmentary nature of the evidence, and the difficulties in interpreting that evidence (particularly the testimonia) make it unlikely that any interpretation can be counted as final or definitive. What I have tried to do in this book is to interpret the fragments and testimonia as carefully as I can, imposing as few preconceptions on the material as possible. It is impossible to read Presocratic philosophy as the Presocratics themselves did; any interpretation is filtered through contemporary philosophical attitudes and colored by knowledge of "what happened next" (as evidenced by the very name "Presocratics"). But this does not, I think, mean that we cannot have grounds for preferring one interpretation of the evidence to another. On the issue of different interpretations of Presocratic thought, see Mourelatos, "Alternatives." I discuss several current interpretations of Parmenides in this section, but I do not pretend that this is a comprehensive survey of views on Parmenides, nor do I intend it as such. Such comprehensive surveys may be found in Tarán, Guthrie, and Bormann. Here my object is to discuss two views of Parmenides: one that makes Parmenides' subject "what can be thought or investigated" and another claiming that Parmenides' subject is Being. Mourelatos, in *Route* and in a number of papers, offers an important and attractive alternative to the interpretations of Parmenides that I have discussed here. I see my own view as a development of Mourelatos's account of the *Alētheia* section of Parmenides' poem, and say more about the details of his account, and about the similarities and differences between his view and mine, in Chapters I and II.

[13] Owen, "Eleatic," pp. 14–16.

[14] Owen's view is accepted by (among others) Stokes (*One and Many*), Furley (in his *Encyclopedia of Philosophy* article on Parmenides, although he opts for a "fused" interpretation

than investigating "in a Kantian fashion, the implications of rationality," Parmenides explores "the possibility, not exactly of rational thought, but of scientific research."[15] Like Owen, Barnes adopts an existential reading of Parmenides' *esti*, and so, according to Barnes, Parmenides is claiming that whatever is the object of study exists.[16] Unlike Owen, Barnes does not think that Parmenides was committed to numerical monism, so he does not find in Parmenides a claim that only one such object of study can, indeed must, exist.[17]

This interpretation of Parmenides' argument faces a number of difficulties. The question of who it is that Parmenides is attacking has long exercised commentators. No predecessor of Parmenides, at least as far as we know, had held that one can or ought to inquire into what does not exist. Rather, the Presocratic thinkers who preceded Parmenides sought to explain the physical phenomena of the world reported by the senses, offering accounts both of the development of the *kosmos* and of the physical, astronomical, and meteorological characteristics of that *kosmos*. There was, as far as the surviving evidence shows, no worry about or interest in the sorts of questions about "meaning, reference, and existence"[18] that the Owen-Barnes

of the *esti* in "Notes"), Gallop (*Parmenides*), and McKirahan. See also Chap. I, n. 9. In his later work Owen gave up the existential reading of the *esti* (see Chap. I, n. 7), but his existential interpretation in "Eleatic" remains influential. O'Brien rejects much of Owen's interpretation, but he, too, opts for an existential reading of the *esti* (see his claims throughout "Le Poème de Parménide").

15 Both quotations occur on p. 163 of vol. I of Barnes's *PP*.

16 My formulation is intentionally loose here, in order to capture some unclarities that Barnes finds in Parmenides' views. Barnes takes it that Parmenides' claim does not decide between claims about the inquiry into and so the existence of (1a) "things of a certain sort (stars, winds, horses)" and (1b) particular things ("the sun, Boreas, Pegasus") (*PP*, vol. I, p. 163). Furthermore, according to Barnes, Parmenides does not "see that two distinct propositions are on view" in the modal operators of the second halves of lines B2.3 and B2.5. According to Barnes, Parmenides' claim is neutral between (2a) "If a thing is studied, it has the property of necessary existence" and (2b) "It is necessarily true that anything studied exists" (*PP*, vol. I, p. 164).

17 A version of Barnes's view seems to be adopted by Schofield in KRS (see pp. 245–46). Like Barnes, Schofield claims that the subject of the *esti* is "any subject of inquiry whatever" (p. 245), but he allows that both predicative and existential interpretations of the *esti* are possible: "Parmenides' use of *estin* is simultaneously existential and predicative ... but not therefore ... confused" (p. 246). Nonetheless, it should be noted that, while adopting the fused *esti*, Schofield stresses the existential component: he interprets the negative way as primarily an attempt to make negative existential claims (see p. 246). According to Schofield, Parmenides' claim that a non-existence assertion expresses "no clear thought" is paradoxical, "but like all good paradoxes it forces us to examine more deeply our grasp of the concepts it employs—notably in this case the relations between meaning, reference, and existence" (p. 246). Unlike Barnes, Schofield thinks that Parmenides is committed to numerical monism, although he finds the argument for monism unclear (p. 251). A re-examination of some of these issues is to be found in Mason, who suggests that in exploring connections between thought and reality Parmenides is concerned to give an account of how properly to characterize what is.

18 See Schofield in KRS, p. 246.

view attributes to Parmenides. Owen specifically denies that Parmenides' target was any of the cosmological views (or assumptions required by the cosmological views) of his predecessors, and Barnes takes a similar position. Both take Parmenides' target to be the assumption that things can be talked about or studied when they do not exist; Owen claims that ordinary persons who think that some things are non-existent or that some things exist here but not there are those who take "the path of mortals" and are thus the object of Parmenides' scorn in B6.[19] What evidence is there for this explanation of Parmenides' target? Owen and Barnes offer none that connects Parmenides with the views or arguments of earlier philosophers.[20] On this account Parmenides is outside the developmental line of Presocratic thought and is apparently unconcerned to criticize the details of the philosophical views of his predecessors. Moreover, on the standard view, given that those who came after him apparently feel free to ignore parts of his arguments, Parmenides would seem to be irrelevant to the further development of Presocratic philosophy. Owen does not explain how later Presocratic theories could respond to Parmenides while still doing cosmology and engaging in inquiry. According to Barnes, a philosopher who truly understood Parmenides would not engage in physical inquiry at all: "*a priori* ratiocination reveals that the phenomena which science attempts to understand and explain are figments of our deceptive senses; the scientist has little or nothing to investigate—let him turn to poetry or to gardening."[21] But later Presocratic thinkers were clearly influenced by Parmenides' arguments (the evidence for this claim will be examined in Chapters IV and V). The question is the nature of that influence. On the standard account, the later Presocratics, such as the Pluralists and the Atomists, failing to see the futility of engaging in cosmological inquiry, try to answer Parmenides by agreeing that coming-to-be and passing-away are not real. Nevertheless, they still attempt to give rational accounts of the changing sensible world, insisting that a plurality of unchanging things underlie and

[19] Owen, "Eleatic," pp. 14–15; Barnes, *PP*, vol. I, pp. 165–70.

[20] Barnes offers a passage from the *Dissoi Logoi*. But it is much later than Parmenides and is no doubt influenced by later philosophical debates, including the work of the Sophists. (On the *Dissoi Logoi*, see Robinson, *Contrasting Arguments*. Robinson argues [pp. 34–41] for a date of around 403–395 for the *Dissoi Logoi*.) Owen says, "I am not of course denying that some of the ideas employed in the course of [Parmenides'] argument may have been inherited from earlier theorists. This must be true of some of the cosmogony, and probably at least the idea of πεῖρας in the Ἀλήθεια" ("Eleatic," p. 16, n. 51). But Owen does not admit that the earlier Presocratics had any other importance for Parmenides, although he also claims in the last sentence of his article that Parmenides "wished to demolish" the tradition of earlier Presocratic cosmologies. As ordinary persons as well as practitioners of inquiry, earlier Presocratic thinkers would be the target of Parmenides' arguments. But Owen does not see in Parmenides any special concern with earlier cosmological thought and inquiry.

[21] Barnes, *PP*, vol. II, p. 3.

explain that world.[22] Moreover, these later Presocratics give no attention to problems of reference and meaning, offering no evidence that they recognized these issues as Parmenides' concerns. So either they must have badly misunderstood Parmenides, or else their answers were quite feeble.[23] On this account the first genuine response to Parmenides comes in Plato's *Sophist*, and this is the view of the relation between Plato and Eleaticism taken by a majority of commentators. Furthermore, on interpretations like those of Owen and Barnes, the role of the *Doxa* section of Parmenides' poem is unexplained. Owen says that the point of the *Doxa* is entirely dialectic; Barnes claims that the *Doxa* is entirely false.[24] Yet (as far as we can tell from the evidence) the *Doxa* occupied a large part of Parmenides' poem, and it, too, seems to have influenced later Presocratic thinkers. How is this to be explained? On the view of Owen and Barnes, that the *Doxa* is entirely false and dialectical in purpose, no answer to this question is forthcoming. Nor is there an adequate explanation of this influence on the widely accepted alternative view, that the *Doxa* (as a dualism of opposed principles) represents the best false account that mortals give.[25] On these interpretations of the *Doxa*, the philosophers who come after Parmenides

22 Plurality is not a problem for Barnes, who doubts that Parmenides was a numerical monist. But later Presocratic pluralism is an embarrassment for other commentators. The usual response is to claim, as Schofield does in KRS, or as Inwood does in *Empedocles*, that Parmenides' arguments for monism are weak.

23 This seems to be Barnes's view. See *PP*, vol. I, p. 155, where he suggests that "their defence was often frail and unconvincing," and vol. II, p. 3, where Barnes acknowledges that there is "much of interest and much of permanent influence" in later Presocratic systems but implies that rather than being "genuine answers to the Eleatic metaphysics" they are "obstinate attempts to follow an out-moded profession." (Barnes raises the point for later discussion, but its appearance on the first page of a chapter called "The Ionian Revival" suggests that it is his view.) Kirk and Raven (in KR, p. 319) gave a different view of the lessons that later Presocratic thinkers had to learn from Parmenides. According to them, each of the systems that followed Parmenides "is, in its own way, a deliberate reply to Parmenides." According to KR, Parmenides "seemed ... to have established once and for all" four principles which all cosmologists must adopt (at least until Plato revealed "the fallacies on which they were based"). These four principles are that "Being ... must not be allowed to spring from Not-Being," that void is impossible, that "plurality cannot come from an original unity," and that motion must be explained rather than assumed. This account has been influential—I once had these principles quoted to me verbatim by someone objecting to my account of later Presocratic thought—but it is rightly challenged in the second edition of *The Presocratic Philosophers* (KRS), where, in a more nuanced introduction to those philosophers who constitute "The Ionian Response," it is claimed that only the principle that what-is cannot come from what-is-not is accepted by all of Anaxagoras, Empedocles, the Atomists, and Diogenes of Apollonia. KRS accept that "Parmenides' metaphysics dominated fifth-century Ionian philosophy" but seem to limit his influence to "the findings of the *Truth* [section of Parmenides' poem] (mediated, in the atomists' case, by Melissus)" (KRS, p. 351).

24 Owen, "Eleatic," p. 9; Barnes, *PP*, vol. I, pp. 156–57.

25 This is the interpretation advanced by Long in "Principles." I discuss various accounts of the *Doxa* in more detail in Chap. III.

misunderstand him, by engaging in cosmology and endorsing a plurality of basic entities and by accepting aspects of the *Doxa* as a model for an acceptable cosmology.[26]

On the standard interpretation we must either attribute serious misunderstandings of Parmenides to later Presocratic thinkers or claim that they felt free to ignore his arguments while accepting certain of his assumptions about what-is.[27] While it is possible that this account is an accurate representation of the history of later Presocratic philosophy, I would prefer to adopt a more charitable view of Parmenides' successors; I believe that the interpretation of Parmenides offered here allows

[26] The errors are slightly different on Barnes's account, for Barnes does not accept that Parmenides was a monist. But, as the passage quoted above demonstrates, Barnes clearly understands the later Presocratics as mistaken in thinking that Parmenides' unrefuted arguments are compatible with the practice of inquiry into nature.

[27] Tarán's interpretation of Parmenides offers an alternative to the Owen-Barnes view but shares a number of difficulties with it. According to Tarán, Parmenides' subject is Being, and Parmenides' doctrine is that "whatever exists (whatever this is) can have only the characteristic of existence plus certain determinations established by reasoning" (*Parmenides*, p. 38). Parmenides is a numerical monist whose arguments demonstrate that the changing, phenomenal world of the senses is an illusion. Consequently, any attempt to explain the appearance of change and difference in the phenomenal world is doomed to failure. Tarán interprets later Presocratic thinkers as attempting to reconcile Parmenides' account of Being with phenomenal change, by appealing to basic real things that can be rearranged. This proposed reconciliation must fail because (1) it assumes, falsely, that more than one thing can exist, and (2) it ignores Parmenides' argument that the world of phenomenal change is unreal. On Tarán's view, then, all of Parmenides' predecessors are refuted, as are all of his successors who attempt to explain the sensible world. This account shares with the Owen-Barnes interpretation the problems of explaining the purpose of the *Doxa* and making sense of later responses to Parmenides. Like Barnes, Tarán must hold that later Presocratics misunderstood Parmenides, for they attempt exactly what (on Tarán's interpretation) his arguments forbid. Moreover, Tarán's account also has difficulty with the partial acceptance of Parmenides' arguments that he thinks can be found in later theories. For on Tarán's interpretation, the pluralism of later theories is a double problem. First, Tarán claims that Parmenides had argued that Being is unique (he finds the assertion of uniqueness at B8.34–41), so the sheer assumption of plurality by pluralistic theories is inconsistent with Parmenides' arguments. Second, for Tarán, the uniqueness of Being is part of the proof that the sensible world is an illusion. So on his view, while accepting the arguments against coming-to-be and passing-away (which are part of the proof that Being alone can be), the Pluralists (and Atomists) then demonstrate their misunderstanding of Parmenides by trying to explain an illusion by appeal to an impossible plurality. Their acceptance of certain of Parmenides' arguments demonstrates that later Presocratics understood him to some extent and took his views seriously, but their insistence on continuing to try to engage in physical inquiry (without arguing against Parmenides' claims that such inquiry is impossible) illustrates that their understanding was only partial. Not only did Parmenides' Presocratic successors misunderstand the force of Parmenides' arguments for monism; they failed to appreciate the falsity of the *Doxa* and instead, mistakenly, took Parmenides' inclusion of it in his poem as a suggestion that cosmological inquiry was both possible and acceptable. For criticisms of Tarán's view that the subject of Parmenides' account is Being, see Robinson, "Ascertainment of the Real," p. 628, who argues that Tarán's understanding of *einai* as "Being" (and his translation to *to eon* as "Being") "is without linguistic parallel."

this.[28] The difficulties I raise do not prove that the interpretations that I have discussed are false. Parmenides may have been a historically independent innovator and a thinker far ahead of his time. Later Presocratic thinkers may have misunderstood the force of his arguments or felt free to ignore them. However, I think that an interpretation that settles Parmenides' views more securely in the history of Presocratic philosophy, and that does not attribute to later Presocratic thinkers fundamental misunderstanding of Parmenides' arguments or only incomplete acceptance of his doctrines is both desirable and possible.[29] In this book I argue for an alternative account of Parmenides

[28] Coxon's account of Parmenides' place in the history of Presocratic thought is broader than those of the Owen-Barnes view and of Tarán. Coxon interprets Parmenides as criticizing philosophical theories that suppose that the physical world is real and that change, particularly change of a "primary substance," is possible (Coxon, *Fragments*, p. 18). Coxon denies that the polemics of B6 are directed at ordinary persons. As evidence, he cites Parmenides' assertion that the forbidden route is a way of inquiry, and the claims of B8.54. He picks out Anaximenes and Heraclitus as special targets. For Coxon there is also a special connection with Pythagoreanism in Parmenides' work. He sees Parmenides as a critic of Pythagorean ideas who was nevertheless deeply influenced by them. Indeed, according to Coxon, "Parmenides represents himself in the prologue as a Pythagorean philosopher at the crisis of his career" (p. 170). This claim is difficult to support in the face of our overwhelming ignorance of the details of pre-Parmenidean Pythagoreanism. Unlike Tarán, Coxon adopts a predicative reading of Parmenides' *esti*, but like him says that Parmenides' subject is Being (Coxon's discussion of these issues in *Fragments* is on pp. 19–21). This he equates with reality, for he takes Parmenides' poem to be an attempt to answer the question, "What must reality be, if it is knowable by the human mind, and what is the nature of human experience?" (*Fragments*, p. 19). On Coxon's view, Parmenides' answer is that Being must be changeless (and timeless), unique, and indivisible. It is not clear what Coxon intends by the claim that "Being" is Parmenides' subject. According to Coxon, Parmenides regards "Being itself as the only legitimate subject of enquiry" and considers "the predicates asserted of this subject as the names, not of attributes of Being, but of Being itself." (*Fragments*, p. 194; see also pp. 20–21). Parmenides' successors, according to Coxon, sought to "evade" his conclusions, and to "re-establish the reality of the sensible world in the face of Parmenides' arguments" (p. 22). All adopted some of Parmenides' views but rejected numerical monism. Coxon sees this rejection as correct, for on his view of the *Doxa*, Parmenides argues that any account of the appearances of the physical world must not be monistic but dualistic. (It is for this reason that Coxon calls Diogenes of Apollonia reactionary and says that he "betrays a remarkable insensitivity to Parmenides' criticism"; *Fragments*, pp. 185–86.) But, according to Coxon, these thinkers erred in applying Parmenides' claims not to Being, but to elements of the physical world. I reject Coxon's account of the subject (see Renehan's review of Coxon; Renehan quotes Burnet to good effect against this account on p. 398), as well as his account of the *Doxa* (see Chap. III). Moreover, for Coxon, too, later Presocratic thinkers must be seen as not fully appreciating the force of Parmenides' arguments, for they do not argue against his conclusions but simply assert, in the face of them, that rational accounts of the sensible world can be given.

[29] It might be suggested that the assertion of numerical pluralism in the face of an argument for what-is that entails numerical monism is less a misunderstanding than a defiant rejection of this part of Parmenides' arguments. Pluralistic accounts may thus demonstrate the flaws of Parmenides' argument simply by giving pluralist-based accounts of the sensible world. But, as I shall argue, numerical monism (if it is to be found in Parmenides) is a consequence of the rejection of what-is-not. Parmenides' successors cannot consistently refuse to accept just

and of the history of later Presocratic thought. Rejecting the view that Parmenides' *esti* is existential, I maintain that Parmenides' concern is to explore the natures of metaphysically basic entities in an explanation of the world reported by the senses, a concern in which the *Doxa* plays an important role. On my view Parmenides is engaged in a metaphysical analysis of the possibility of the sort of physical inquiry that had engaged his predecessors, and his conclusions are of great interest and importance to those philosophers who came after him. His work is thus firmly in the tradition of Presocratic philosophical thought and inquiry. Because, as I argue, Parmenides was not a numerical monist (although he was indeed a monist of another sort, adopting what I call predicational monism), the pluralism of later theories is not a difficulty to be overcome or explained away. Indeed, I count such pluralism, together with the concern that later Presocratics have to show that their basic substances are genuine entities that meet Parmenidean criteria, as evidence for my account of Parmenides. Moreover, I shall argue that there is a positive lesson to be learned from the *Doxa*; although it is deceptive, it serves as a model for a successful account of the world reported by the senses. All these aspects of interpretation go together and allow for an explanation of Parmenides' views and of his role in the history of Presocratic thought that both recognizes his overwhelming importance for Presocratic (and Platonic) philosophy and also sees him as part of the Presocratic tradition, aware of and criticizing his predecessors and posing important philosophical problems for his successors.

2. Chronology

No area of Presocratics studies is without controversy. One of the more contentious issues is the chronological ordering of the philosophers who came after Parmenides. The evidence we have (from such sources as Apollodorus or Diogenes Laertius) is usually of little help, and there are few fixed dates to use as benchmarks, so we must rely primarily on internal evidence, which is notoriously difficult to decipher and which is particularly subject to conflicting interpretations. In this book I have settled on an order for the Presocratic thinkers I discuss, but I do not pretend that this arrangement is the only one possible. Here I discuss the chronology that I adopt.

In the *Parmenides*, Plato describes a meeting between Socrates and Parmenides, who, along with Zeno, had come to Athens for the Great Pan-

---

this part of Parmenides' argument while at the same time accepting his basic premises about what-is. So, I claim, on the views that see Parmenides as a numerical monist, his successors either seriously misunderstood Parmenides' arguments or were bad logicians. I prefer to avoid both conclusions if possible.

athenaic Festival. In the dialogue Plato says that Parmenides was about sixty-five, Zeno about forty, and Socrates very young (*Prm.* 127b3–4; c4–5).[30] Given a birthdate of about 470 B.C. for Socrates, the meeting must have taken place around the time of the Great Panathenaea of 450;[31] that would place Parmenides' birth at sometime around 515. Unfortunately, knowing the likely date of Parmenides' birth does not help to establish the time of his philosophical work or when that work became available to others (unless we adopt a convention like Apollodorus's, and place a man's *acmē* in his fortieth year). Nevertheless, it seems reasonable to think that Parmenides' poem had been written by the end of the first twenty-five or thirty years of the fifth century. This would place Parmenides after Xenophanes, Pythagoras, and Heraclitus.[32]

Some have found responses to Xenophanes or Pythagoreanism in Parmenides' work; Heraclitus, with his theory of the unity of the opposites and his interest in distinguishing things in accordance with nature, is I think, more important as an influence.[33] Michael Stokes claims that Heraclitus was of no importance to Parmenides, and that considerations of Heraclitean views were irrelevant to an understanding of Parmenides. His view is based on rejecting the claim that one of two repudiated ways in Parmenides' B6 is to be identified with theories that can be traced to Heraclitus.[34] Stokes's case rests on his own reading of B6, and on the claim that Parmenides can be understood independently of any considerations of the views of Heraclitus. Daniel Graham has recently challenged Stokes's claims and has shown that there are a large number of literary parallels between Parmenides and Heraclitus, and that these parallels suggest that Parmenides knew Heraclitus's

[30] Although there are reasons for doubting that the views attributed to Parmenides in the *Parmenides* accurately reflect those of the historical Parmenides (see Chap. VI, Section 2), there is, I think, little reason to distrust Plato's claims about the probable ages of Parmenides and Zeno.

[31] See Allen, *Parmenides*, p. 64. The festival was held in August.

[32] On Xenophanes' dates, see Lesher, *Xenophanes*, p. 3; on Heraclitus, see Kahn, *Art and Thought*, p. 1.

[33] KRS claim that there are "echoes, not merely verbal, of Xenophanes' theology and epistemology in Parmenides" and suggest that Parmenides may have been imitating Xenophanes when he chose to write in hexameter verse (p. 241). Coxon sees Parmenides as offering a "radical revision" of Xenophanes' theology (*Fragments*, p. 18). It is generally agreed that Plato's claim that Parmenides was a follower of Xenophanes (*Sph.* 242d4–6) is an overstatement. Coxon places far more emphasis on a Pythagorean connection (*Fragments*, p. 18), but given our ignorance of the details of pre-Parmenidean Pythagorean theory, such claims are difficult to evaluate.

[34] Stokes, *One and Many*, pp. 109–27. Stokes claims that treating Parmenides and Heraclitus as independent of one another is justified "even if Parmenides did know of Heraclitus, at least until it is shown (as it has never been) that Parmenides would have written even so much as a single syllable differently if Heraclitus had never opened his mouth or set pen to papyrus" (ibid., p. 127).

work.[35] Graham further argues that there are good philosophical reasons (aside from considerations of B6) for reading Parmenides in the light of Heraclitean claims. I shall maintain that the reading of B6 suggested by Owen, which Stokes accepts and uses as evidence for his claims against Heraclitean influence, is not the best way to understand that passage.[36] Thus, I shall argue that there is no good reason to accept Stokes's claim that Parmenides must be considered independently of Heraclitus (and, incidentally, of every other Presocratic philosopher). I shall suggest that Heraclitus and other early Presocratic thinkers were of great importance to Parmenides, and that it is illuminating to think of him as working within a tradition of views about what there is and how we come to understand the world reported by the senses.

It is with the post-Parmenidean Presocratics that the real difficulties of chronology appear. First, there is the problem of the relations among Anaxagoras, Empedocles, and Zeno; then Leucippus, Democritus, Melissus, and Diogenes of Apollonia must be incorporated into the scheme. Many of these thinkers were contemporaries, and any order of discussion (implying a chronological order) is apt to give rise to questions and objections. Despite the difficulty in fixing the chronology, I shall assume that Anaxagoras wrote earlier than Empedocles.[37] Moreover, I shall consider Zeno as reacting to claims that can be found in both Anaxagoras and Empedocles.[38] The usual view is that the Atomists were responding to Zeno in making their basic entities indivisible, and also to Melissus, whose B8 is sometimes (mistakenly, I shall argue) taken as sanctioning a view like the atomic theory, which makes each basic thing (each atom, in this case) like Melissus's One. But Melissus

[35] Graham, "Heraclitus and Parmenides," presented at the October 1994 meeting of the Society for Ancient Greek Philosophy, Binghamton, NY. I am grateful to Prof. Graham for sending me a copy of his as yet unpublished paper and allowing me to refer to it. I have also argued elsewhere (in "Monism" and in "Deception") that Heraclitus was an important influence on Parmenides.

[36] In his influential "Eleatic Questions," Owen argues that Parmenides is best understood independently of the Presocratic tradition. I argue against Owen's' view in Chap. I. On B6, see Chap. I, Section 3.

[37] In placing Anaxagoras before Empedocles, I follow O'Brien, who argues that "Empedocles wrote later than Anaxagoras, and was influenced by him." For O'Brien's defense of this view, see "Relation"; the passage quoted is on p. 113. O'Brien is joined in this view by Schofield, *Essay,* p. 35 with n. 86 (Schofield also places Anaxagoras earlier than Zeno, pp. 80–82); by Sider, *Anaxagoras*, pp. 5–6, who agrees on the relative dates of Anaxagoras and Empedocles; by Kahn in "Historical Position"; by Inwood in his *Empedocles*; and by Furth, in "Anaxagoras." Wright reverses the chronology, placing Empedocles first; she sees Anaxagoras replying to Empedocles and to Zeno. Mansfeld argues vigorously for the priority of Empedocles' work in "Chronology." Woodbury, in "Anaxagoras and Athens," responds to Mansfeld, showing that the evidence for Anaxagoras in Athens places him earlier than Empedocles.

[38] Furley examines the possibility that Zeno was attacking Anaxagoras ("Anaxagoras in Response," esp. pp. 58–62), while Longrigg argues that Zeno responded to Empedocles ("Zeno's Cosmology?").

seems also to be arguing against atomism when he denies the reality of void. One solution of the difficulty is to see Melissus as perhaps coming between Leucippus and Democritus, with Melissus attacking certain aspects of Leucippus's version of atomism and Democritus defending atomism against Melissus's arguments.[39] I have placed my discussion of Melissus at the end of the chapter in which I deal with Atomism, to allow for this possibility, but I do not mean to imply by this that I am certain that this is the correct order. I discuss Philolaus and Diogenes of Apollonia (both of whom may have been, roughly, contemporaries of Melissus) in the final chapter of the book.[40] The ordering of the post-Parmenidean philosophers that I have chosen is not certain; but it is not therefore arbitrary. While internal evidence, such as near quotations, or philosophical commitments can be quite slippery, I have reasons for the positions I have taken, and throughout the book argue for the claims of influence and chronology that I make.

3. The Proem

Parmenides' poem is written in hexameter verse, opening with an introduction that describes a journey by a young man, a *kouros*, to meet a goddess.[41] This goddess speaks to him, telling him that it is right that he "learn all things" (B1.28: χρεὼ δέ σε πάντα πυθέσθαι); her teachings constitute the remainder of the poem.[42] This opening fragment, with its story of mares, a speeding chariot (with glowing and sounding axle), maidens (daughters

[39] On the possibility that Leucippus antedates Melissus, see Klowski. Barnes (*PP*, vol. II, pp. 40–75) and Solmsen ("Abdera's Arguments") have both argued that the Atomist commitment to void is a response to Zeno's divisibility arguments, and that Melissus's argument against motion and void is aimed at the Atomist position. On the other hand, Tannery claimed that Melissus was not acquainted with the work of Anaxagoras, Empedocles, or the Atomists (*l'Histoire*; Tannery's discussion of Melissus is on pp. 271–83.) We have reports that Melissus commanded the Samian navy that defeated Pericles in 441, but we do not know Melissus's age at the time or whether he had completed, was engaged in, or was just beginning his philosophical work.

[40] Huffman puts Philolaus later than Anaxagoras and Empedocles (*Philolaus*, p. 9). Philolaus was born about 470, and Huffman thinks his work was circulated no earlier than 440; thus the writings of Anaxagoras and Empedocles could have preceded his. Diller's arguments that Melissus was attacking both Leucippus and Diogenes of Apollonia have been roundly rejected. But KRS agree (p. 437n.1) that "the chronology of these three thinkers is admittedly loose enough to allow that they were all active, as Diller suggests, in the decade 440–430 B.C."

[41] Diogenes Laertius lists Parmenides among those who left but a single work (*Lives*, I.16). On the term *kouros* as having a special religious meaning, see Burkert, "Proömium."

[42] Approximately 150 lines of Greek remain. There are a number of fragments that are parts of lines or (in the case of B15a) a single word. B18 survives in a Latin translation, and there is a passage in Plato's *Theaetetus* (180e1) that, according to Cornford, constitutes a separate fragment. I discuss the Cornford fragment in Chap. II, n. 72. See Coxon, *Fragments*, pp. 1–7, on the manuscript tradition.

of the sun), the House of Night, the Gates of the paths of Night and Day (complete with a thorough discussion of the posts, doors, and the keys that open them), guarded by "much-avenging Justice" (*Dikē polupoinos*), has been alternatively exhaustively analyzed and ignored by commentators.[43] The apparent influences of Homer and Hesiod on the proem have been catalogued, but there is little general agreement about how fragment 1 is to be interpreted.[44] It seems clear that the proem has an allegorical aspect, but it is not clear what the allegory is about.[45] Some commentators have seen the journey as one to light and enlightenment, others as a progress along the road to the House of Night, but despite claims to the contrary, the topography of the poem is confusing, and I do not think that it is clear where the *kouros* has gone.[46] Further, there are difficulties in deciphering any allegorical elements: are they meant to allude to the *Doxa* or to the *Alētheia* sections of the poem? If they are to be interpreted in light of the *Doxa*, there is the question of why Parmenides should have included, at the very opening of his poem, allegorical references to a part of the work that most commentators take to be altogether false. Although connections with other early Greek poetry can be found, I suspect that no interpretation of certain elements of the proem can ever be confidently accepted. The evidence for the sources of this aspect of Parmenides' thought and for other early use of allegory is just too meager for certainty.[47]

[43] For discussion of various interpretations of B1, see Fränkel, "Studies," pp. 1–14, and *Early Greek,* pp. 351–53; Bowra, "Proem"; Verdenius, "Parmenides' Conception"; Mansfeld, *Offenbarung*, chap. IV, pp. 222–73; Tarán, *Parmenides,* pp. 22–31; Guthrie, *HGP*, vol. II, pp. 6–13; and Bormann, pp. 56–69. For more recent interpretations, see (among others) Burkert, "Proömium"; Furley, "Notes"; Coxon, *Fragments*, pp. 153–71; Bollack, "Cosmologies"; Laks, "Proem." On the other hand, Barnes comments on the journey part of the proem (lines 1–27): "The poem began with a long allegorical prologue, the interpretation of which is for the most part of little philosophical importance" (*PP,* vol I, p. 156). Floyd ("Verse") links the proem with Parmenides' purposes in writing in verse: according to Floyd, verse allows Parmenides to include both truth and opinion in the same work.

[44] On influences from Homer and Hesiod, see Havelock, "Parmenides"; Schwabl, "Hesiod und Parmenides"; Mourelatos, *Route*, chap. 1; Pellikaan-Engel; Pfeiffer; and Coxon, *Fragments*. Kingsley finds Babylonian influence (*Ancient Philosophy*, pp. 54–55 and pp. 392–93); others, including Burkert, have seen influence from the Orphic tradition.

[45] Sextus Empiricus provides an account of an ancient allegorical interpretation at *M.* VII.112–14. Laks ("Proem") provides a comprehensive treatment of allegorical interpretations. (I am grateful to Professor Laks for allowing me to use and to refer to his as yet unpublished paper.)

[46] On the first view, see Fränkel, "Studies," pp. 5–6. On the latter, see Morrison, "Er"; Burkert, "Proömium"; and Furley, "Notes." See also Coxon, *Fragments*, pp. 13–17, who says that "the journey to the goddess is an anticipation of death" (p. 16). Mourelatos argues (*Route*, pp. 15–16) that "the honest conclusion from all this is that the topography of the journey is blurred beyond recognition." See also Fränkel, "Studies," p. 5: "there is no route that can be located."

[47] A major obstacle to understanding is our lack of evidence about pre-Parmenidean Pythagorean thought. Coxon argues for heavy Pythagorean influence on Parmenides, and he

But this pessimism concerning the allegorical significance of the *kouros*'s journey need not prevent confidence concerning other claims about the proem. The opening lines of the poem share with other poetry of Parmenides' time a representation of a process of inspiration, together with an appeal to divine authorization for the truths that the poem as a whole will impart to its hearers and readers.[48] Parmenides, like other poets of his time, attributed to the divine the inspiration that allowed him to have the insights that are given in the body of the poem. But unlike other surviving pre-Parmenidean appeals to the Muses or representations of divine inspiration, Parmenides' inspired poem is a work of philosophy.[49] This may seem to undercut the point of Parmenides' arguments, but the goddess herself gives no evidence that there is any conflict between her divinely inspired address to Parmenides and the use of rational thinking or judging. It is, after all, the goddess herself who tells the *kouros* (at B7.5–6) to "judge by reasoning the much contested testing" (κρῖναι δὲ λόγῳ πολύδηριν ἔλεγχον) that she has spoken.[50] There is a difference between appealing to a goddess as the source of one's inspiration and using divine authority as the justification for one's claims; and Parmenides' appeal falls under the former rather than the latter classification. Despite representing the *kouros* as the recipient of the goddess's story, Parmenides does not show him as a passive hearer of what the goddess has to say. She exhorts him to take charge of his *noos* and to judge for himself the claims that she makes.[51] Divine inspiration might have been necessary for Parmenides to achieve his insights, but only hard philosophical thought and judgment will show whether those insights are true.[52]

---

may well be correct. But there is so little evidence that it is quite difficult to be confident about picking out any details in Parmenides as particularly influenced by the Pythagoreans.

48 For a discussion of these issues, particularly of the similarities with other poetical accounts of inspiration, see Lesher, "Significance." Lesher argues that, despite the fact that there is no manuscript authority for *astē* in line B1.3 (as Coxon had pointed out in 1968), there are good reasons for thinking that the line indeed originally read κατὰ πάντ' ἄστη. Lesher also clearly formulates and discusses the apparent problem of an appeal to the authority of a goddess to guarantee philosophical arguments (see esp. pp. 16–19).

49 There is reason to think that we lack the opening lines of any of Xenophanes' poems; thus we do not know if he also had such introductions to his philosophical poems (or even if we can distinguish strictly philosophical works among Xenophanes' oeuvre). Nor do we know if such an appeal to divine authority was standard practice among Pythagoreans. Empedocles invokes the Muses (in B3, B4, B131), but he may be following Parmenides rather than an earlier philosophical tradition.

50 On this translation of B7.5–6, see Chap. I, nn. 107 and 109. I further discuss the role of argument in Parmenides' work in "Eleatic Arguments."

51 On the contrast between the passivity of the *kouros* during the chariot ride and the goddess's commands to him once her account has begun, see Lesher, "Parmenides' Critique," p. 29. I discuss these issues further in Chap. I, Section 2; see also n. 72 in that chapter.

52 Any reader of Hesiod will know that the Muses can be misleading if they wish. See the Muses' claim at *Th.* 27–28: ἴδμεν ψεύδεα πολλὰ λέγειν ἐτύμοισιν ὁμοῖα, ἴδμεν δ' εὖτ'

Whatever the setting of the proem, one of the things that is clear is its distance from the world of everyday human life. The goddess emphasizes this in her welcome to the *kouros*, describing (at B1.27) the route he has traveled to her as "far from the beaten path of human beings" (ἦ γὰρ ἀπ' ἀνθρώπων ἐκτὸς πάτου ἐστίν). To reach the goddess, the chariot has traveled as far as the gates of the paths of Day and Night and has then gone through those gates and traveled onward on the road to meet the goddess who narrates the story (B1.20–21). The distant setting (wherever it is) of the meeting of *kouros* and goddess, the details of the daughters of the sun and the great gates, and the presence of goddess herself combine to indicate that this is no ordinary journey, and that the story Parmenides has to tell is no ordinary story. The goddess's narrative will be about philosophical inquiry, knowledge, and its object, but the setting suggests that the usual methods of investigation, adopted by those the goddess calls mortals, will not be appropriate in evaluating or using the information that the goddess will impart.

After greeting and reassuring the *kouros*, the goddess tells him what he will learn from her:

> ... χρεὼ δέ σε πάντα πυθέσθαι
> ἠμὲν ἀληθείης εὐπειθέος[53] ἀτρεμὲς ἦτορ
> ἠδὲ βροτῶν δόξας, ταῖς οὐκ ἔνι πίστις ἀληθής.
> ἀλλ' ἔμπης καὶ ταῦτα μαθήσεαι, ὡς τὰ δοκοῦντα
> χρῆν δοκίμως εἶναι, διὰ παντὸς πάντα περ ὄντα.[54] (B1.28–32)

> ... it is right that you learn all things,
> both the unshaking heart of well-persuasive truth
> and the beliefs of mortals, in which there is no true trust.
> But nevertheless you shall learn these things, too, how it were right that
> the things that seem be reliably, being indeed, the whole of things.

In promising that the kouros will learn "all things," the goddess in effect guarantees a full account of both what is true and what is (mistakenly)

ἐθέλωμεν ἀληθέα γηρύσασθαι (We know how to say many false things resembling the truth, but when we wish we know how to speak the truth). In his commentary on the *Theogony*, West notes the similarity between the Muses' description of themselves and the portrayal of Odysseus at *Od.* XIX.203. The muses' assertion is often invoked in explanations of why the goddess includes both the *Alētheia* and the *Doxa* in her account. But if (as Hesiod suggests) divine deception is possible, the goddess's claims should be subject to independent check by reasoning.

53 For εὐπειθέος rather than εὐκυκλέος, I here follow the arguments of Mourelatos; see *Route*, pp. 154–56, with n. 50 (which lists modern agreements and disagreements with the reading). See also Coxon, *Fragments,* p. 168, and Finkelberg, "Parmenides' Foundation," p. 65. Tarán, Guthrie, and Bormann follow DK in reading εὐκυκλέος.

54 Following Owen, I read περ ὄντα rather than περῶντα here. See Chap. III, nn. 48 and 52.

deemed by mortals to be the case. Later, in B8 (at lines 60–61), she tells the *kouros* that he will learn the beliefs of mortals so that he will never be overtaken or misleadingly persuaded by these beliefs. In B1 there is no clear statement of the nature of the persuasive truth that the goddess will impart, but lines 31–32 (which recount the error of mortals) provide a clue, especially when those lines are considered in the light of B1.29, which promises an account of persuasive truth.[55]

According to the goddess, the error of mortals is in thinking that the things that seem (*ta dokounta*), whatever they are, are reliably or genuinely. *Dokimōs* here must mean something like "genuinely" or "really."[56] The implication is that something is *dokimōs* just in case it has been certifiably attested, or passed specific tests, for a *dokimasia* is an examination or trial. That which is reliably is something that has passed (or could pass) some test for what is, and so, being reliably, would therefore qualify as "well-persuasive truth" (*alētheia eupeithēs*).[57] Mortals are wrong in taking the things that seem (*ta dokounta*) to be genuinely real; what they believe to be true is, as a matter of fact, false. Their error may result from failing to understand the tests for reliable being so that they mistake things that merely seem for things that are genuinely or they may even be uncritical enough to think that there are no such tests.[58] B7, with its references to the organs of sense experience, indicates that mortals are misled by sensory perception into taking to be real what they perceive, while B1.32 suggests that this error comes about because mortals mistake *ta dokounta* for the whole of things. *Ta dokounta* are the only things that can be perceived through the senses; mortals, thinking that sense experience is a reliable guide to what is real, thus take them to constitute the genuine nature of things, without realizing that what is genuinely real may not be available through sense perception alone.

In promising to teach the *kouros* "all things," the goddess undertakes to impart to him what he must know to avoid the errors of mortals. Thus he must learn what it is for something to be reliably, and he must learn both the criteria for reliability and the tests that will allow him to investigate and to evaluate various claims for trustworthy and reliable being, or what-is. In

[55] For the argument that these lines contain the goddess's account of mortal error, see Owen, "Eleatic," pp. 3–9. Although I disagree with Owen's claim that the *Doxa* is unrelentingly false (see Chap. III below), I accept his account of these lines of the proem.

[56] Owen, "Eleatic," p. 6: "where *dokimōs* is attested elsewhere (Aeschylus, *Persae* 547; Xenophon, *Cyr*. 1.6.7) the lexica and the editors rightly translate it 'really, genuinely' . . . . The *dokimos* is the reliable man."

[57] On the connection between being reliably and qualifying as well-persuasive truth, see Lesher, "Parmenides' Critique" and "Philosophical Interest."

[58] Lines B1.31–32 thus contain an early contrast between seeming and being; see also Xenophanes B34 and B35.

order to teach the *kouros* these things, then, the goddess must undertake a full investigation into what-is, showing the *kouros* how he is to inquire into what-is and what he must look for while he is doing so. Her teachings, as they appear in Parmenides' arguments, are recounted in the rest of the poem, and they and their influence on later Presocratic thought are the subject of the remainder of this book.

I

Parmenides and the Inquiry into Nature

εἰ δ' ἄγ' ἐγὼν ἐρέω, κόμισαι δὲ σὺ μῦθον ἀκούσας,
αἵπερ ὁδοὶ μοῦναι διζήσιός εἰσι νοῆσαι·
ἡ μὲν ὅπως ἔστιν τε καὶ ὡς οὐκ ἔστι μὴ εἶναι,
Πειθοῦς ἐστι κέλευθος (ἀληθείῃ γὰρ ὀπηδεῖ),
ἡ δ' ὡς οὐκ ἔστιν τε καὶ ὡς χρεών ἐστι μὴ εἶναι,
τὴν δή τοι φράζω παναπευθέα ἔμμεν ἀταρπόν·
οὔτε γὰρ ἂν γνοίης τό γε μὴ ἐόν (οὐ γὰρ ἀνυστόν)
οὔτε φράσαις. (28B2)

Come now, and I will tell you, and you, hearing, preserve the story,
the only routes of inquiry there are for thinking;
the one that it is and that it cannot not be
is the path of Persuasion (for it attends on truth)
the other, that it is not and that it is right that it not be,
this I point out to you is a path wholly inscrutable
for you could not know what is not (for it is not to be accomplished)
nor could you point it out.

In the *Alētheia* section of his poem, Parmenides argues that the proper route of inquiry will lead to genuine thought about and understanding of what-is. But is what Parmenides proposes connected to the scientific inquiries undertaken by the Ionian philosophers who came before him? This chapter examines that issue, focusing on Parmenides' response to the philosophical search for the nature, or *physis* of a thing.

The goddess who welcomes the *kouros* describes what she will teach him, and, mentioning Right and Justice, she links her claims with the force of necessity and stresses that he will learn "all things":

. . . ἐπεὶ οὔτι σε μοῖρα κακὴ προὔπεμπε νέεσθαι
τήνδ' ὁδόν (ἦ γὰρ ἀπ' ἀνθρώπων ἐκτὸς πάτου ἐστίν),
ἀλλὰ Θέμις τε Δίκη τε. χρεὼ δέ σε πάντα πυθέσθαι
ἠμὲν ἀληθείης εὐπειθέος[1] ἀτρεμὲς ἦτορ
ἠδὲ βροτῶν δόξας, ταῖς οὐκ ἔνι πίστις ἀληθής. (28B1.26–30)

. . . since no ill fate sent you out to travel
this route (for it is indeed far from the beaten track of human beings)

[1] For εὐπειθέος rather than εὐκυκλέος, see Introduction, n. 53.

but Right and Justice. It is right that you should learn all things
both the unshaken heart of well-persuasive truth
and the beliefs of mortals, in which there is no true trust.

Not only will the youth learn "well-persuasive truth," he will also learn about the untrustworthy beliefs of mortals. B10 offers further information about these beliefs:[2]

εἴσῃ δ' αἰθερίαν τε φύσιν τά τ' ἐν αἰθέρι πάντα
σήματα καὶ καθαρᾶς εὐαγέος ἠελίοιο
λαμπάδος ἔργ' ἀΐδηλα καὶ ὁππόθεν ἐξεγένοντο,
ἔργα τε κύκλωπος πεύσῃ περίφοιτα σελήνης
καὶ φύσιν, εἰδήσεις δὲ καὶ οὐρανὸν ἀμφὶς ἔχοντα
ἔνθεν ἔφυ τε καὶ ὥς μιν ἄγουσ(α) ἐπέδησεν Ἀνάγκη
πείρατ' ἔχειν ἄστρων.

And you will know the nature[3] of the aether and all the signs
in the aether and the destructive works of the bright sun's
pure torch, and from whence they came to be,
and you will learn the wandering works of the round-eyed moon
and its nature, and you will know also the surrounding heaven,
whence it grew and how Necessity led and bound it
to hold the limits of the stars.

Despite declaring that there is no "true trust" in the beliefs of mortals, the goddess is prepared to say that, from her teaching, the youth will learn the nature (*physis*) of the aether and of the moon; and that he will know how the "surrounding heaven" arose and the forces that shaped its development. Twice in B10 (at 10.1 and 10.5), forms of *oida* (to know) are used, suggesting that the youth will have knowledge of these things. Further, at B8.60–61 the goddess tells the youth that she will "relate the whole likely-seeming ordering in order that no opinion of mortals shall ever overtake you" (τόν σοι ἐγὼ διάκοσμον ἐοικότα πάντα φατίζω, ὡς οὐ μή ποτέ τίς σε βροτῶν γνώμη παρελάσσῃ). The strength of the goddess's claim here shows that her teaching, in both the *Alētheia* and the *Doxa*, will arm the youth against errors

[2] Bicknell ("Parmenides, fragment 10") has suggested that B10 actually belongs to the proem, rather than to the *Doxa* proper. It might also fit at the end of B8, listing the things to be learned in the *Doxa*. In either case B10 contains claims that belong to the *Doxa* section of the poem and that are to be connected with the mortal beliefs mentioned at B1.30.

[3] Coxon (in *Fragments*) translates *physis* as "origin" rather than as "nature." On p. 227 he notes the connection between the two notions, quoting Aristotle *Ph.* II.1.193b12ff. In the natural things that Aristotle studies and that are the concern of the earlier Presocratic philosophers, there is a connection between a thing's *physis* and its origin, growth, and development. What a thing is, for this sort of thing, includes its development and change.

in cosmological thinking.[4] The beliefs of mortals, which are contrasted with "the unshaking heart of well-persuasive truth," are all about the nature of things and appear, from our fragmentary evidence, to have been modeled on Ionian inquiry into the *kosmos*.

In "Eleatic Questions" G.E.L. Owen rejected the claim that Parmenides "wrote his poem in the broad tradition of Ionian and Italian cosmology."[5] Indeed, according to Owen, the intent of Parmenides' arguments is to put an end to Ionian speculation; comparing Parmenides with Descartes, he claims that both are radical pioneers whose arguments "cut free of inherited premisses."[6] To support his claim about Parmenides' innovation, Owen argued that the subject of the *esti* and of the arguments of B2 and B8 is "simply what can be talked or thought about" and that Parmenides' point is to prove that what can be said or thought must exist and must have the attributes proved in B8. Thus, the *esti* that is the basis of the arguments is existential.[7] According to Owen, the result of Parmenides' argument is that there exists only a single, unchanging thing; thus the Ionian search for an explanation of a plurality of changing entities is pointless.[8] Owen's view of the subject and the *esti* has proved influential; it is followed in most histories

[4] The goddess can so arm the youth only if she teaches him the principles that underlie any acceptable cosmology. The goddess cannot hope to prevent any and all mortal opinion from "racing past" the youth except by teaching him principles by which to judge any belief that he is faced with (compare with Descartes's strategy in the *First Meditation*). The principles follow from the rejection of what-is-not in B2, and in the judgments based on the *krisis* "is or is not." Thus the goddess both gives the truth to the *kouros* (in telling him, in the *Alētheia*, about the nature of what-is) and (through the *krisis* and the arguments of B8) gives him the means by which to judge other theories of what there is. Further, through the accounts of both the *Alētheia* and the *Doxa* the *kouros* learns how to evaluate other explanations of what the senses report.

[5] Owen, "Eleatic," p. 3.

[6] Owen, "Eleatic," p. 16. According to Owen (p. 3), interpreting Parmenides as part of the tradition of Ionian cosmology depends on three points, all of which he rejects. First, the cosmogony presented in the *Doxa* must have some "measure of truth or reliability"; second, Parmenides' arguments in the *Alētheia* begin from "assumptions derived from earlier cosmologists and are concerned merely to work out the implications" of these assumptions; third, these views take the arguments of B8 to prove the existence of a spherical universe. I hold none of these views, as they are stated by Owen; but I shall argue that Owen is wrong to claim that Parmenides is working independently of Ionian speculation about the *kosmos*. Further, I argue that the issue of the reliability of the *Doxa* is more complicated than Owen suggests.

[7] Owen gave up this view of the *esti* by the time of the publication of his work on Plato's *Prm.* and *Sph.*, adopting instead a version of the fused account of the verb. See his "Notes on Ryle's Plato" and "Plato on Not-Being" (especially pp. 104-8 with nn. 3 and 6); see also Kahn, "Retrospect," p. 25nn.37 and 38.

[8] Perhaps we should also include the early Pythagoreans here as well. Heraclitus claims (in B129) that Pythagoras "pursued *historiē* further than anyone else." Any claim about early Pythagoreanism must remain conjectural, because of the difficulties in determining the content of Pre-Parmenidean Pythagorean theories. The earliest Pythagorean for whom we have good evidence is Philolaus, but I suspect that the split between the *akusmatikoi* and the *mathematikoi* may predate Parmenides; if so, Parmenides may have the latter in mind as well. Parmenides'

of Presocratic thought, and in much recent work on Parmenides.[9] There have been dissenters from this account of both the subject and the nature of the *esti*, but it seems fair to say that the account, presented by Owen in "Eleatic Questions," has become the standard interpretation of Parmenides.[10]

Owen's account is, I think, mistaken, both in its interpretation of the *esti* and in its insistence on Parmenides' independence from earlier cosmological thought and speculation. I shall suggest that, rather than rejecting the study of nature, and of what there genuinely is, Parmenides seeks to make it legitimate, by proposing criteria that a successful theory of what there is must meet, and showing that such a theory must be grounded in principles that are metaphysically and epistemologically justified. In the *Alētheia* Parmenides argues that there are certain basic requirements that anything that is must fulfill, while in the *Doxa* he presents a model for a successful cosmology, provided that the fundamental entities of such a cosmological theory meet the standards of the *Alētheia*.[11] In this chapter I explore the issue of the Presocratic inquiry into nature and what there is, arguing that

---

relation to the Pythagoreans is unclear, although Coxon suggests that Parmenides was trained in the Pythagorean tradition and that the poem constitutes his rejection of Pythagorean doctrine (*Fragments*, pp. 18–19; 170). Whatever the relation, it is probable that Parmenides knew well the Pythagorean views.

[9] See for instance, Guthrie's account in *HGP*, vol. II (pp. 13–20), although Guthrie sees Parmenides' poem as criticizing earlier cosmologists who had tried to say and think that what does not exist exists; see also the accounts in KRS, Barnes (*PP*, vol. I), and McKirahan. D. J. Furley adopts Owen's account of both the *esti* and its subject in his entry on Parmenides in the *Encyclopedia of Philosophy* (although he later opts for a fused *esti*), as does Stokes in *One and Many*. The existential reading is also to be found in Gallop's text, translation and notes on Parmenides, and he explicitly defends the existential view in " 'Is' or 'Is Not'?" The existential reading is the basis of Finkelberg's account in "Parmenides' Foundation," although he rejects other aspects of Owen's view. O'Brien, too, accepts the existential reading ("Le Poème de Parménide"). Furth, although he adopts a "fused" *esti*, accepts Owen's account of the subject of the *esti* (in "Elements"). Owen's view of the deception of the *Doxa* has had less universal acceptance.

[10] Kahn has argued against the existential *esti* in many papers; see especially "Being in Parmenides and Plato," "The Thesis of Parmenides," "The Greek Verb 'To Be' and the Concept of Being," "Why Existence Does Not Emerge as a Distinct Concept in Greek Philosophy," and "Retrospect." Furth, "Elements," followed by Furley, in "Notes," and by Goldin, opts for a fused *esti*. Mason suggests that a characterizing sense of *esti* is at work. A.P.D. Mourelatos (in *Route* and elsewhere) rejects both the existential reading and Owen's account of the subject, opting for a predicational reading of the *esti*. On Mourelatos' view, the *esti* "directly captures or calls forth the characteristic nature, true identity, intrinsic reality, or essence" of a thing ("Determinacy," p. 53). I discuss Mourelatos's interpretation further, below; as shall be seen, my view owes a great debt to Mourelatos's.

[11] I shall argue that the error of mortals is to try to begin with entities that are defined as opposites, so that neither is a genuine entity. In this way, the *Doxa* embodies the thought of mortals who think "that to be and not to be are the same and not the same" (B6.8–9). On this view, mortals do not err in doing physics or cosmology; rather their mistake is in the natures of the entities on which they ground their scientific theories. I turn to the *Doxa* in Chap. III.

an interpretation of Parmenides' *esti* that links it with that inquiry allows us to read the text from B2 through B7 in a unified manner, gives a good reason why the negative route of inquiry must be avoided, and makes sense of Parmenides' abuse of mortals as two-headed wanderers who fail to make the correct decision about what-is and what-is-not.

1. The Problem of the Argument in *Alētheia*

At B8.1–2 the goddess tells the youth that a "single account of the route that it is still remains" (. . . μόνος δ' ἔτι μῦθος ὁδοῖο λείπεται ὡς ἔστιν). That this "single account" is said to "still remain" (*eti* . . . *leipetai*) suggests that this was the correct account all along, and that the discussion (in B6 and B7) of the route of mortals, the route of is-not, was only a temporary side trip into an examination of a route of inquiry that could not be genuine. In examining fragments B2–B7, it is difficult to determine just where the repudiation of the route of what-is-not has taken place; it is even more difficult, perhaps, to determine the form the repudiation takes. Parmenides' claim that only the route of what-is is possible is often analyzed as a disjunctive syllogism that occurs primarily in B2 (B3 is sometimes included as part of the argument of B2).[12] The problem is that the premise that rejects the route of what-is-not is, on the face of it, woefully unsupported. B2.7–8 asserts that what-is-not can be neither known nor pointed out (οὔτε γὰρ ἂν γνοίης τό γε μὴ ἐόν [οὐ γὰρ ἀνυστόν] οὔτε φράσαις). But there is no support offered for this assertion. B3 seems to complete the line B2.8; if we read it that way, we get the added claim "for the same thing is for thinking and for being" (. . . τὸ γὰρ αὐτὸ νοεῖν ἐστίν τε καὶ εἶναι). But again, this is declared, not argued for. B2 does not present two equally viable alternatives and argue against one of them.[13] Rather, the

[12] This analysis is implicit in Owen's claims, and it is stated explicitly by Gallop and by Furley. In "Eleatic," Owen says, "the goddess maintains that to the question 'Does it exist?' only a positive answer can be given; the negative is ruled out by the plea that what does not exist cannot be distinguished in thought or speech (B2.7–8); and this plea is basic to the following arguments and recalled more than once in them (B8.8–9, 17–18, probably 34–6). . . . The goddess' premiss in this opening game is that what does not exist cannot be thought or spoken of or, what comes to the same, that what can be thought or spoken of exists. . . . It is the prior point that Parmenides seems anxious to establish in the opening couplet of B6 . . ." (pp. 14–15). Owen links this move in the argument with Parmenides' independence from earlier cosmological tradition, likening Parmenides to Descartes: "both arguments cut free of inherited premisses, both start from an assumption whose denial is peculiarly self-refuting" (p. 16). Gallop's view is that "the argument . . . takes the following logical form: i/ either 'is' or 'is not' (and not both); ii/ not 'is not'; therefore iii/ 'is.' It is expressly summarized in these terms at 8.15–16" (*Parmenides*, p. 7). Furley makes this interpretation the basis of his discussion in "Truth." For criticism of this analysis of the argument, see Lesher, "Parmenides' Critique" and "Cognition," and Finkelberg, "Parmenides' Foundation."

[13] See Mourelatos, "Determinacy and Indeterminacy," pp. 49–50; see also Lesher, "Parmenides' Critique of Thinking," pp. 12–16.

route of what-is is presented as a "path of Persuasion" because it "attends upon Truth" (Πειθοῦς ἐστι κέλευθος [ἀληθείῃ γὰρ ὀπηδεῖ] B2.4), while the path of what-is-not is denigrated even as it is presented. "That, I point out to you is a path wholly inscrutable"[14] (τὴν δή τοι φράζω παναπευθέα ἔμμεν ἀταρπόν B2.6). The *esti* route is introduced in B2 as the right route and that of *ouk esti* is introduced as impossible. So, while the argument presented in B2 indeed has the form of a disjunctive syllogism, it cannot constitute a proof that only the route of what-is is possible, for we do not know that the second premise (that what-is-not is impossible) is true, and B2 offers no support for that claim.

B6.1 reinforces the availability of what-is, stressing its connection with thought and speech. B6.2ff. and B7 strengthen the claim against *ouk esti*; but as before, in neither case is there an argument to show the necessity or impossibility of the route. Indeed, the passages show how rather than that the negative route fails. That is, B6 and B7 show us unfortunate mortals who try to say and think that what-is-not is. So the closest we come to an account of the unacceptability of *ouk esti* and the acceptability of the *esti* route are the claims of B2.6–7 and B3 about the connection between thought and what-is. Lesher has argued that these claims could not be the crucial premise (or even a premise at all) in an argument against the route of what-is-not, on the grounds that such an interpretation of B2.6–7 and B3 (as well as Parmenides' other comments about thought and being in the *Alētheia*) would make mortal thought impossible rather than incorrect; moreover, the claims about the impossibility of saying and thinking what-is-not are themselves, on the face of it, improbable.[15] On the existential reading of the *esti*, the premise would be that it is not possible to say, think, or know what does not exist. Since this is a controversial claim, one would expect Parmenides to argue for it rather than merely assert it. One solution to this difficulty is offered by Lesher; he argues that the statements of B2.6–7, B3, B6.1–2 are all proleptic: they look forward to what will be proved in the arguments of B8.[16]

The proleptic reading rests on two assumptions: (1) that the claim in B2.7–8 is controversial and counterintuitive and (2) that the arguments of B8 show that what-is-not (read as what does not exist) can be neither said nor thought. Let us examine these assumptions, beginning with (2). For the proleptic analysis of the structure of the argument to be correct, we should have to find (a) that *ouk esti* has been rejected by the end of the positive

[14] Or "without report" (Coxon), "from which no tidings ever come" (Mourelatos).

[15] Lesher, "Parmenides' Critique" and "Cognition," p. 25n.50. Lesher's claim depends on an existential reading of the *esti*.

[16] Lesher, "Cognition," p. 25n.50: ". . . by the end of the argument it will be shown that one cannot think of, speak of, or know 'what is not,' since *by then it will have become clear* that what is there to be thought of, spoken of, and known is only 'what is.' In short, the real work of refuting the 'is not' way of thinking may have been carried out simply through the multiple proofs of fr. 8" (emphasis in original).

arguments in B8 (before, that is, the goddess announces that she is ceasing her trustworthy account at B8.50) and (b) that the impossibility of the *ouk esti* route (and more particularly the fact that what-is-not is neither sayable nor thinkable) is not used as a premise in the proofs of the signs of B8.[17]

I take it that (a) is uncontroversial, for on any interpretation of the argument in B2-B8 the *ouk esti* route has been rejected by B8.50. So I will concentrate on claim (b).

B8.1–2's assertion that only a single story remains (that of the route that it is) implies that the route of not-being has already been discarded.[18] This might be another of the goddess's proleptic remarks, so in order to avoid begging the question, we cannot rely on these lines as part of an argument against the proleptic reading. After the announcement of the signs, the goddess first shows that what-is has no coming to be nor growth (lines B8.6–7). And here, immediately, there is reliance on the principle that what-is-not is unsayable and unthinkable:

> ... τίνα γὰρ γέννναν διζήσεαι αὐτοῦ;
> πῇ πόθεν αὐξηθέν; οὔτ' ἐκ μὴ ἐόντος ἐάσσω
> φάσθαι σ' οὐδὲ νοεῖν· οὐ γὰρ φατὸν οὐδὲ νοητόν
> ἔστιν ὅπως οὐκ ἔστι. (B8.6–9)
>
> ... for what birth of it will you seek out?
> How, and whence grown? Neither from what is not shall I allow
> you to say or think; for it is not to be said or thought
> that it is not.

The goddess rejects a coming-to-be for what-is on the grounds that there is no what-is-not from which what-is could come to be: what-is-not is neither knowable nor sayable and thus, seemingly, it is impossible as a

[17] Lesher seems to allow that the impossibility of what-is-not might be used as a premise in B8: "During the course of her critical examination [in B8], each of the various respects in which one might imagine that what is not might be ... is considered. But in each case, in order to think that *what is* is involved in not being, in some respect, we must also think that in the same manner *what is not* is—which violates the principle stated at the outset of fragment 7 ... 'never shall this prevail: that things that are not are' " ("Cognition," p. 25). But B7 does not offer an argument against the *ouk esti* route: it merely states that it cannot be proved that what-is-not is, and points out the predicament of mortals who attempt the impossible route. The claim that it cannot be proved ("it cannot prevail") that what-is-not is itself depends on the principles enunciated in B2 and B3, for the structure of B2 shows that the rejection of what-is-not (B2.5–6) depends on B2.7–8. (B2.7–8 is a *gar* clause that seems to explain the assertion of lines 5–6.)

[18] B8.1–2 might also be read as the claim that the route that it is remains an account of something that is one or single (although I find this a less natural reading of the line). On either reading of B8.1–2, the suggestion would be that the negative route has been rejected. I am here assuming that there is but one negative route, and that the so-called fully negative route and the route of mortals are, in fact, the same. I discuss this issue in Section 3, below.

source for what-is.[19] In the next lines the coming to be from what-is-not is further rejected: there is no reason why what-is should come to be from what-is-not. Nor can anything else that is come to be alongside what-is. So there is no coming to be in any form for what-is.[20] All these arguments ultimately rest on the same principle, as the goddess announces at B8.15–18:

> . . . ἡ δὲ κρίσις περὶ τούτων ἐν τῷδ' ἔστιν·
> ἔστιν ἢ οὐκ ἔστιν· κέκριται δ' οὖν, ὥσπερ ἀνάγκη,
> τὴν μὲν ἐᾶν ἀνόητον ἀνώνυμον (οὐ γὰρ ἀληθής
> ἔστιν ὁδός), τὴν δ' ὥστε πέλειν καὶ ἐτήτυμον εἶναι.
>
> . . . and the decision about these is in this:
> is or is not; and it has been decided, just as is necessary,
> to leave the one unthinkable and unnamed (for it is not a true
> route), and the other to be and to be genuine.

The use of the perfect *kekritai* (it has been decided) suggests that the decision is not one that is going to be made or is in the process of being made, but one that has already been made in fact and that stands for all time.[21] The use of *anankē* (necessity) in the line further strengthens the notion that the judgment that what-is-not is "unthinkable and unnamed" holds not just in B2, or in Parmenides' poem, but always. This reinforces the claim that the prohibition on what-is-not as a source for what-is in B8.7–9 rests on a rejection of the route of what-is-not as unsayable and unthinkable, which has already taken place by the time the arguments of B8 begin. The rejection of birth, coming-to-be, and perishing is crucial for the arguments that follow, for the claim that what-is is changeless or immobile (*akinēton*) in B8.26–31 is based on the unavailability of coming to be and perishing, and the changelessness of what-is is a reason for its completeness (the completeness proof at B8.32–33 is introduced by *houneken*). The dependence of the later arguments on the earlier ones suggests that the pronouncement against thinking that what-is could have its birth or growth in what-is-not is not here proleptic. It does not look forward to a further proof that will in turn justify the claim that

[19] Exactly how this claim should be interpreted must wait for an analysis of the assertion that what-is-not is neither sayable nor thinkable. At this point, my claim is simply that this assertion serves as a premise in the argument rather than something that is yet to be proved. I shall suggest later that the problem with what-is-not is that there is nothing that it is in itself, so to try to say or think it is to try to say or think nothing at all.

[20] For an analysis of the nested structure of these arguments, see Mourelatos, *Route*, pp. 98–103. He points out the importance of the claim that "is not" is not allowable because unspeakable and unthinkable on p. 99. The argument at B8.9–10 depends on an application of the principle of sufficient reason, but as part of the nested arguments against coming-to-be, it ultimately rests on the impossibility that what-is-not is. I further discuss the arguments of B8 in Chap. II, Section 2.

[21] See Smyth, §§1852 (p. 413), §1945, 1946 (p. 434).

what-is-not is not to be said or thought, but is itself a crucial premise in the arguments against birth and growth.

The strongest evidence that B8 contains the proof that what-is-not is unthinkable and unknowable is in lines B8.34–38; in those lines the connection between thought and what-is receives specific attention:

> ταὐτὸν δ' ἐστὶ νοεῖν τε καὶ οὕνεκέν ἐστι νόημα·
> οὐ γὰρ ἄνευ τοῦ ἐόντος, ἐν ᾧ πεφατισμένον ἐστίν,
> εὑρήσεις τὸ νοεῖν· οὐδὲν γὰρ ⟨ἢ⟩ ἔστιν ἢ ἔσται[22]
> ἄλλο πάρεξ τοῦ ἐόντος, ἐπεὶ τό γε Μοῖρ' ἐπέδησεν
> οὖλον ἀκίνητόν τ' ἔμεναι . . . (B8.34–38)
>
> The same thing is for thinking and wherefore there is thought;
> for not without being, in which it has been expressed,[23]
> will you find thinking; for nothing else either is or will be
> except what-is, since Fate shackled just this
> to be whole and unchanging.

Here Parmenides claims that thinking and what-is are essentially connected and are so in a way that rules out the possibility that what-is-not can be thought. The reason is given in lines 36–38: there is nothing besides what-is to be thought, because it was what-is that Fate (a personification of necessity) shackled to be whole and unchanging (and there are further arguments that only what is whole and unchanging can be). Here is an explicit argument for the connection between what-is and thought, and a justification for the principle that lies behind B2.7–8 and B3. Moreover, these lines are the heart of one of the fundamental arguments of the poem.[24] So we might expect that this is the crucial argument that proves that what-is-not is neither knowable nor sayable. But I do not think that this is an independent argument for the conclusion that there is only what-is and so only what-is can be thought (or said). Note that "nothing else either is or will be except what-is," because it was just what-is that Fate shackles or holds in fetters as whole and unchanging. So the availability of what-is for thought depends on the wholeness and unchanging character of what-is. Those characteristics of completeness and immobility are themselves explicitly said to be based on the fact that coming to be and perishing are impossible: at B8.26–27, what-is is immovable in the hold of great bonds and without start or stop, "since coming to be and perishing have wandered far away and true trust drove

[22] Coxon, *Fragments*, prints οὐδὲ χρόνος ἐστὶν ἢ ἔσται, with the note "scripsi" (p. 71; his discussion of the line is on pp. 210–11). For further discussion and reasons for rejecting Coxon's insertion of *chronos* here, see Renehan, pp. 399–400.

[23] Exploring the implications of this line, Mourelatos helpfully suggests the paraphrase "to which it is committed." See Mourelatos, *Route*, p. 172, with n. 23.

[24] Mourelatos, *Route*, p. 165: the lines occur "in the climactic section of the poem's central argument."

them out" (ἐπεὶ γένεσις καὶ ὄλεθρος τῆλε μάλ' ἐπλάχθησαν, ἀπῶσε δὲ πίστις ἀληθής B8.27–28). But as we have seen, the rejection of coming to be and passing away itself crucially depends on the impossibility of saying or thinking what-is-not.

Given these considerations, I conclude that the claim that what-is-not cannot be thought or said is not itself proved in B8 but rather plays a crucial part in the proofs in that fragment. So, then, I think we should accept the claim of B8.1–2 that only the story of a single route remains, because the route of what-is-not has been rejected by the time the arguments of B8 begin. It is clear that there has not been a proof of the unacceptability of the way of not-being; there is a valid argument in the form of a disjunctive syllogism, but there is no support for the second premise. Rather the route of what-is-not is introduced as impossible because it requires that we say or think what-is-not. Moreover, I suspect that Parmenides did not think that this was a controversial claim. The controversy enters in the further claim that the path of mortals actually is the forbidden path of not-being. What the arguments of B8 show, what we are to judge, is that the mortal accounts of what-is involve change, coming to be, and so on, and so turn out to be on the prohibited negative way. Parmenides' point is that there are indeed only two ways of thought and inquiry (just as B2 claims) and that mortals are deceived into thinking that their way, involving as it does opposites, change, coming to be, and passing away, is not actually the negative route.[25]

But now what of the claim that the principle that what-is-not cannot be said or thought is too controversial to be asserted without proof? Is Parmenides guilty of assuming a crucial and questionable premise? What has seemed to commentators to be both controversial and counter-intuitive about Parmenides' principle is explained by Owen:

> The goddess maintains that to the question, "Does it exist?" only a positive answer can be given; the negative is ruled out by the plea that what does not exist cannot be distinguished in thought or speech (B2.7–8), and this plea is basic to the following arguments and recalled more than once in them. . . . The goddess's premise in this opening game is that what does not exist cannot be thought or spoken of, or, what comes to the same, that what can be thought or spoken of exists. But this, after all, is far from self-evident. The plain men whose daily uses of language make up the second wrong path hold that plenty of things can be talked about which do not exist: they need not wait for Gorgias to tell them that they can think of Scylla and Chimaera.[26]

[25] I argue for all these points below.

[26] Owen, "Eleatic Questions," p. 14. The view that Owen and Lesher take of the import of B2.7–8 and B3 may also be found in (among others) Tarán (*Parmenides*), KRS, Stokes (*One and Many*), Barnes (*PP*), Furth ("Elements"), and Gallop (*Parmenides*).

At the heart of Parmenides' argument, then, is an unproved assertion about the impossibility of thinking or speaking of what does not exist. This is a controversial claim, and if it were the basis of Parmenides' argument, he would be guilty of the errors that have been attributed to him.[27] But why assume that the existential reading is the correct one? This question moves us into the heart of a perennial problem in Parmenides studies. I suggest that the *esti* is not to be read existentially and that when the existential reading is abandoned, Parmenides' claim that the route of what-is-not is unsayable and unthinkable becomes far less controversial. Moreover, with a different understanding of the *esti*, its subject and the structure of the argument of B2-B8 become clearer.

2. Parmenides' *esti* and the Search for Nature

Much recent Parmenides scholarship has focused on two questions. First, what subject, if any, is to be supplied for the subjectless *esti* of the goddess's claims in B2? Second, what is the sense of the verb "to be" at work in Parmenides' assertions about what-is? The two issues are related; if, for instance, one thinks that the subject of B2 is "what can exist," it is natural to take the verb in its existential sense in B2 and in the crucial claims about what-is in B3, B6, and B8. Arguments for and against the existential, veridical, predicative (in many guises), and "fused" senses of the verb "to be" in Parmenides have been advanced.[28] It is worth noting how little ground has been gained or conceded on any side; and although there is little agreement about the actual sense of "to be" at work in B2, there is no disagreement about which fragments are crucial. To substantiate their claims, the supporters of the existential interpretation point to the same passages in Parmenides as those used by the proponents of the veridical sense to defend their account. Thus, a major problem in determining the sense of "to be" at work in the poem is the apparent ambiguity of the evidence to be found in the text.[29]

[27] See, for instance, Owen, "Eleatic," pp. 14–16, with nn. 45 and 47. Barnes (in *PP*) argues that Parmenides is committed to the claim that "if X does not exist, X cannot exist" (his premise 11, p. 166, vol. I) and sees it as an "obvious and offensive" flaw in Parmenides' argument (vol. I, p. 167).

[28] The existential reading is the most widely adopted; see n. 9, above. The veridical "to be" appears in Kahn's work, while a predicative "is" appears in Calogero, Mourelatos, Ketchum, and Austin (*Being*) (the type of predication differs in these authors). The fused sense of "is" is most prominent in Furth's "Elements of Eleatic Ontology," although Furley ("Notes"), Schofield (in KRS), and Goldin, among others, also accept Furth's account. But it should be noted that those who follow Furth in adopting the fused account have a tendency to stress and to focus on the existential component in the *esti*.

[29] It is, I think, worth noting that proponents of the veridical and predicative senses rely on texts other than Parmenides as well as the text of Parmenides as evidence for their interpretation

The difficulty in answering these questions suggests that the wrong issue is being raised at the wrong time. I suspect that beginning by searching for the correct sense of the verb "to be" is a mistake. The motifs of the route together with Parmenides' stress on the notion of inquiry (*dizēsis*) and the proper route of inquiry for thought suggest that Parmenides' concern was as much methodological as metaphysical. What, he asks, is the right way to ask and to answer certain questions? Just what questions Parmenides is concerned with answering correctly might become more obvious by considering what Parmenides sees as an incorrect answer: the *Doxa*. Parmenides does not describe the *Doxa* as false; rather, he says that there is something deceptive in the story that the goddess tells about it (B8.50–53). Thus, in reading and thinking about the *Doxa*, we must be on our guard not to be led astray. But clearly Parmenides thinks that the route that leads to the *Doxa* is not a genuine route of inquiry; the true or genuine route is described at B2.4 as the path of Persuasion and it is said to attend upon truth (compare B1.29, where the youth is told that he will learn the unshaking heart of well-persuasive truth: ἀληθείης εὐπειθέος ἀτρεμὲς ἦτορ).[30] In contrast, there is no true trust (*pistis alēthēs*) in the opinions of mortals (B1.30). B6 and B7 show that those who take the path of inquiry that results in the *Doxa* are straying and wandering far from the secure path of persuasion.

I shall return to the perplexing question of what is wrong with the *Doxa* in a later chapter; for now I attend to the question of what the *Doxa* is about. There, speaking in the voice of mortals, the goddess offers an account of the *kosmos*, beginning with the two forms that are fundamental to it: Light and Night (B8.53–59). These are the basic entities on which depends everything else in the scheme of the *Doxa*, and however we interpret the difficult lines at B8.53–4, it is clear that mortals have made an error in their laying down of these forms. Indeed the goddess says that they have "gone astray" (*peplanēmenoi eisin*); and this links the project of mortals in the *Doxa* with the route of the heedless mortals of B6 and B7 who "wander,

---

of the *esti*. See, for instance, Mourelatos, *Route*, "X is Really Y," and "Determinacy"; see also Kahn's numerous works on the verb "to be." Those who interpret the *esti* as "exists" are less inclined to look for parallels outside of Parmenides (except, perhaps, in Plato's *Sophist*, where they see an existential sense primarily at work as well). This is consistent with the view (which I hold to be mistaken) that Parmenides was not concerned with cosmological issues and can be understood independently of his predecessors.

[30] I here follow the traditional translation and interpretation. There is no definite article attached to *ētor* in the text of B1.29. Coxon has noted that *ētor* "is never used in Greek except of a human or divine person" and argues that it must have such a use here (*Fragments*, p. 168). Lesher proposes to take the line literally, as a promise that the goddess will teach the *kouros* what it is to have a heart full of truth ("Emergence," p. 32nn.65 and 66). Lesher notes parallel treatments in Homer of *ētor* as a psychic faculty. But the contrast between the two sorts of things that the *kouros* will learn in B1.29–30 (introduced by *ēmen* and *ēde*) suggests an exhaustive distinction between the many opinions of mortals (in which there is no true trust) and the core truth that the goddess will reveal.

knowing nothing, two-headed" (B6.4–5: βροτοὶ εἰδότες οὐδὲν πλάττονται, δίκρανοι). But the youth has been told to keep his thought (*noēma*) away from this path (B7.2), and so it seems likely that it embodies the error that the "much-contested elenchus" is designed to prevent in the thought of the youth. In addition to arming the youth with the multiple testing process of B8, the goddess also tells him that what she will impart to him in her "deceptive story" will guarantee that he will never be overtaken by the opinions of mortals, and this is consistent with the introductory comments at the end of B1 about what the youth will learn. All this suggests that the truth of *Alētheia* and the mistake of the *Doxa* are related in a fundamental way.

Now, if we consider the *Doxa*, the error is not one of attempted reference to the non-existent but is rather the attempt to begin an account of what there is with entities in which "is" and "is not" are illegitimately mixed.[31] The problem with such entities is not that their names try but fail to refer to non-existents,[32] but that there is a fundamental problem with the natures of these entities. The problems of mortals on the path of what-is-not, as expressed in B6 and B7 with their images of wanderings, back-turning paths, and confusion, suggest that these entities are too vague to be known, too incomplete to be genuine, too indeterminate to serve as the trustworthy basis of an account of the *kosmos*.[33] This suggests that the goddess's message in *Alētheia* is about how to avoid this very mistake; it is about how to think about what-is so as to avoid the problems of error, vagueness, and wandering *noos* that plague mortals.

The connection between thought or inquiry and what-is is fundamental in Parmenides' poem and is at the heart of the disputes about the nature of the *esti* and the structure of Parmenides' argument. While it seems clear that *noos* and *noein* are primarily connected with thinking, conceiving, and understanding rather than knowing,[34] Parmenides also sees a special connection between *noos* and what-is. Error results when *noos* is led astray or is not properly controlled and is allowed to wander away from its proper goal or object (B6, B7). But just what this thinking or understanding is about is still, at this point, unclear. Some other instances of *noos* and *noein* outside of the

31 I take it that this is uncontroversial. No matter what view we ultimately take of the *Doxa*, it is the case that "is" and "is not" are illegitimately mixed here.

32 If this were the error the youth is warned against, one supposes that the *Doxa* would look more like the discussion between Parmenides and Betathon in Furth's imaginative reconstruction (in "Elements"). But instead, we have in the *Doxa* a fairly commonplace Presocratic cosmology.

33 See Mourelatos, "Determinacy," and chap. 3 of *Route*.

34 Kahn ("Thesis") and Furley ("Notes," p. 35n.34) opt for "knowing" rather than "thinking." But see Barnes, *PP*, vol. I, pp. 158ff.; and also Lesher, "Cognition," esp. section 4 and n. 54, p. 27. The classic discussions of the notions are those of von Fritz on *noos* and *noein* in Homer and in Presocratic thought. But as work by Mourelatos and especially Lesher has shown, the notions are broader than von Fritz thought, not only in Presocratic thought but also in Homer. See Lesher, "Perceiving and Knowing," "Cognition," and *Xenophanes*, pp. 103–4.

Parmenidean context may help here. In a famous fragment (DK 22B40), Heraclitus chastises four famous polymaths:

> πολυμαθίη νόον[35] οὐ διδάσκει· Ἡσίοδον γὰρ ἂν ἐδίδαξε
> καὶ Πυθαγόρην, αὖτίς τε Ξενοφάνεά τε καὶ Ἑκαταῖον.
>
> Much learning does not teach understanding; else it would have taught Hesiod and Pythagoras, and again Xenophanes and Hecataeus.

Heraclitus is willing to assert that Hesiod, Pythagoras, Xenophanes, and Hecataeus have much learning; but he questions whether they have *noos*. Now, in this context, *noos* does not seem to mean simply "thought," but rather "understanding"[36] of the deeper significance of the things they have learned; in other words, the four have gathered much information but do not actually have knowledge. More specifically, of course, Heraclitus is accusing the four of not grasping the *logos* and all that is entailed by that grasping. What they miss, in their various ways (for it is not the case that all four fail to have *noos* in the same way, other than the general failure to grasp the *logos*), is the underlying nature of things as they really are. This is what one who understands the *logos* knows.[37] Now, if this is what the polymaths lack, it is clear that *noos* in this context must mean more than simply "thought" or "thinking." Heraclitus would surely not deny that the polymaths had many thoughts. Rather the mass of thought they have does not add up to understanding, so Heraclitus might say that the polymaths cannot "think straight." This use of *noos* also occurs in two other Heraclitus fragments. In B104 Heraclitus chastises those who put their trust in popular bards (like Homer and Hesiod) and "take the mob for their teacher"; of these unknowing folk (he describes them as *ouk eidotes*) Heraclitus asks, "What *noos* or *phrēn* (wit) do they have?" In asking this he is clearly treating *noos* as more than a faculty of thought; rather it is again understanding that is lacking. Finally, in B114, Heraclitus argues that those who would speak with *noos* must cling to what is common to all: the *logos*, which is identified as common (in B2), if difficult to discern. In all these cases, understanding (*noos*) involves seeing beyond the obvious in order to attain genuine understanding; and given its connection with *logos*, the understanding seems to be of a fundamental sort, of how things really are. Now, while there is difference between Heraclitus

[35] Marcovich, following Schleiermacher, and others (rightly) rejects νόον ἔχειν, which appears in both Athenaeus (XIII 610B) and Clement (*Strom.* I 93.1); both Athenaeus and Clement give partial rather than complete quotations of the fragment. Robinson (*Heraclitus*) and Kahn (*Art and Thought*) agree with Marcovich; KRS do not. Marcovich notes that KR printed νόον ἔχειν in the passage from Diogenes Laertius in which the entire fragment appears; but that νόον ἔχειν does not occur in the Diogenes Laertius MSS (ἔχειν is retained in KRS).

[36] Marcovich and KRS translate "intelligence"; Robinson and Kahn opt for "understanding." Lesher ("Cognition," p. 16) chooses "wisdom."

[37] I have dealt with these issues more fully in "Knowledge and Unity."

and Parmenides on this point—Parmenides grants *noos* to the mortals in B6, although he denies that they properly control their *noos*—there is a shared notion that *noos*, properly used, gains understanding. The mortals in Parmenides B6 are said to have a wandering *noos* (*plaktos noos* B6.6) and thus to be "amazed," thinking that "to be and not to be are the same and not the same" (B6.7–8). This is the fundamental mistake in Parmenides, for one whose *noos* wanders or is not under control suffers from a signal failure of understanding; differing degrees of *noos* (or control of *noos*) mark different degrees of comprehension or understanding.[38]

In the *Odyssey*, Penelope is considered to be supreme in *noos* and *mētis* (for instance at *Od*. XIX.325–26),[39] and she proves this in her test for the identity of Odysseus. Relying on Odysseus's private knowledge of their bed, she provides a trial for the tattered beggar that reveals his true identity. In this she reveals her own *noos*, for she has devised a test that goes straight to the heart of the issue at hand, and that the beggar must pass or fail cleanly, with no opportunity for cheating or a lucky guess. Thus, Penelope's *noos* works to make Odysseus reveal himself. But here too, *noos* must be more than mere thought; after all, many women have many thoughts; yet they do not win the respect Homer has for Penelope.[40] Both Penelope and Odysseus are contrasted with the suitors (whose leader is, after all, Antinoös), but even the suitors have thoughts; what they lack (to a shocking degree) is understanding, or the realization of the genuine meaning of a situation. That is, they fail to have *noos* in that their thought veers away from what-is to what-is-not, with disastrous consequences. Once Penelope has used her *noos* to test Odysseus, what has she learned? I am inclined to say that what she now understands is the identity (that is, the nature) of the man in front of her, that is, she now knows who he is. She might well say, "This is Odysseus." And in saying this she is saying far more than simply, "The man in front of me exists." (She could certainly know that without knowing who he is.) But to know that the man in front of her is indeed Odysseus, she must know certain things about Odysseus (that he is the man with a certain scar, that he knows certain facts about a certain bed, and so on). Her *noos* has led her to a genuine understanding of the nature of the man, and this involves rather more than existence claims.[41]

38 In the *Doxa* (in B16) Parmenides gives a naturalistic theory of *noos* that could account for differences of degree of *noos*.

39 Lattimore translates the occurrence of *epiphrōn mētis* at XIX.326 as "thoughtful good sense"; Fagles as "shrewd good sense." *Mētis* (often translated "cunning") is a notoriously difficult notion. On the concept of *mētis* in Greek literature, see Detienne and Vernant.

40 Consider the P. G. Wodehouse character, Madeline Bassett: she has many thoughts about many things (including that "the stars are God's daisy chain"). But one would hardly, on these grounds, call her "rich in *noos*."

41 Compare Penelope's knowing the identity of Odysseus to Socrates' claim at *Meno* 71b3–8 that one cannot know the qualities of a thing until one knows what that thing is, using the

In the same way, the "is" in Parmenides that seems to be the natural home of *noos*, to which *noos* travels if it takes the proper route of inquiry (*hodos dizēsios*), is more than an existential "is." Rather, it is predicative in a certain fundamental sense: what we know in knowing what-is is the real or genuine character of a thing; thus it is what we know when we know just what something genuinely is, or what it is to be that thing.[42] I take Parmenides' *esti* to be an informative identity claim, an assertion that, when true, reveals the nature of a thing, saying just what something is. This account has deep affinities with Mourelatos's account of what he calls a "speculative 'is.' "[43] According to Mourelatos, the speculative "is" serves as the answer to the question "what is it?" such that it gives "a complete exposure of, and insight into, the identity of a thing to such an extent and in such a manner that no further questions with respect to that thing need or may arise."[44] A speculative "is," according to Mourelatos, "makes a claim of novel

---

example of Meno: "someone who does not know who in the world Meno is can say nothing about him, whether he is handsome (*kalos*), or rich or well-born (or the opposite)." This is not a question about whether or not Meno exists, but about who he is, his nature. In the case of a person, that would include his family and his place in the world, his provenance (on this issue, see Nehamas, "Meno's Paradox"). Plato is often accused of confusing understanding that something is *f* with understanding the nature of *f*. Plato's adoption of just this sort of "is" is the source of that "confusion." See Nehamas, "Self-Predication."

42 This will, of course, include knowing that this thing (whatever it is) exists, but that is a secondary consideration, and the existence of the thing follows along, as it were, from the fact that it is a nature or essence of something. This is the proper response to a query raised by M. Matthen. In his review of Coxon, he asks, "Isn't 'reality' just that which *exists*?" (p. 156). The answer is yes, of course, but just thinking about existence will not get you to a proper account of what-is, whereas Parmenides' full account of what-is (as we shall see) gives us both a real being and an existent thing. See Kahn, "Restrospect," p. 16: "it is highly unlikely that either Parmenides or his readers would understand a bare unadorned *esti* as meaning primarily or predominantly 'it exists.' " Kahn argues for a primarily veridical sense of *esti* in Parmenides, but he claims that "there is no real incompatibility between [his] reading of the Parmenidean *esti* and Mourelatos' proposal to regard the thesis as a predicative sentence frame: '__ is __' (with '__ is not __' for the negation). The basic copula function of *esti* in Greek will assure that, on *any* reading of the thesis, this sentence form is immediately felt to be implied" ("Retrospect," p. 26n.44). Ketchum argues for a predicative sense of *esti* in "Parmenides." But his account differs from the one offered here. First, Ketchum agrees with Owen that the subject is "whatever can be thought or spoken of" (p. 174). I am here suggesting that Parmenides' subject is an entity of a certain kind, one that plays a fundamental role in an explanation of what there is. Second, Ketchum does not take the *esti* to reveal the nature of a thing but seems to read it as an ordinary predication. This makes it difficult for him to provide a coherent analysis of the arguments of B8. According to Ketchum, Parmenides' point is "that what is not anything simply can't be mentioned, discussed, or thought of while mentioning, discussing, or thinking" (p. 189). But Ketchum takes the argument for this to occur at B6.1–2; he provides a short analysis of B8.6–7 but otherwise does not explain the role of B8 in Parmenides' arguments. Nor does Ketchum say anything about monism in Parmenides.

43 Mourelatos, *Route*, pp. 56–61. Professor Mourelatos tells me that in a forthcoming modern Greek translation of *Route,* the "speculative 'is' " is called "a predication of speculative identity."

44 Ibid., p. 57.

description and discovery . . . ; given the predicate, no further predications of that type, either of that particular predicate or on that particular subjects, are necessary or even possible."[45] In later articles, Mourelatos rejected the term "speculative predication," opting for a slightly different explication of the *esti* in Parmenides.[46] Mourelatos now says that this "is," which he connects with what he calls a "naive metaphysics of things," serves "to make direct contact with reality."[47] It is not to be identified simply with the copula nor with the "is" of identity, but "might be called the 'is' of introduction and recognition, since it has its paradigm . . . in acquaintance."[48] A claim that "*X* is *F*" serves, according to Mourelatos, "to evoke or call forth the thing

45 Ibid. It should be noted that there are two claims here (and in the previous quotation), that no further questions or predications about the thing (1) need arise, or (2) may arise ("are even possible"). Presumably, no further questions need arise because a successful speculative predication, in "exposing" the identity of a thing, gives such complete information that no useful information would be elicited by further questions and nothing helpful would be added by further predications. No further questions (and no further predications) can arise, I think, because the information provided in a speculative predication uniquely identifies its subject. Only one such speculative predication per item is allowed (because of the complete identification of a thing that a speculative predication gives).

46 See especially "Naive Metaphysics" and "Determinacy." In "Determinacy" (p. 53n.18) Mourelatos says of speculative predication, "I am now dissatisfied not just with that piece of terminology but with the description I gave . . . of the hybrid copula/identity use. As paradigms of the use, I postulated Milesian contexts of the form 'It is water,' 'It is air'—a maneuver that now strikes me as question begging. Moreover, the translation 'really is' for *esti*, which the account in terms of 'speculative predication' tended to suggest, had the effect of projecting artificial complexities into the analysis of the argument in 'Truth.' " I would agree that "is really" is not the best way to translate *esti*; but I do maintain that the arguments of B8 do explore what criteria a claim about what something really or reliably is must meet; the appropriateness of thinking about what something "really is" is signaled by the use of *dokimōs* in B1.32, even though that use occurs in a discussion of mistaken mortal beliefs. Mortals believe (mistakenly) that what the senses report is something that genuinely is. My view is not, I think, identical with Mourelatos's speculative predication, though it is related to that view. Mourelatos says that speculative predications express an asymmetrical relation: "If *X* is *Y*, it does not follow that *Y* is *X*" (p. 57). I would argue that the lack of symmetry in the relation is not as strong as Mourelatos suggests: what occurs in the *Y* place in the sentence, as uniquely expressing the nature of *X*, is what *X* really is, although *X* does not express *Y*'s nature as *Y* expresses the nature of *X*. But nevertheless, the expressions "*X*" and "*Y*" could be used interchangeably in claims about the world (thus the relation between the two is actually identity, although an informative identity). As I read the "is" in Parmenides, the subject can only be something that would count as a basic entity in an explanation of how things are, and the arguments of B8 indicate how such a thing must be if it is indeed a genuine or basic entity. An assertion like Anaximenes' that air is the real, and thus the fundamental, entity in his cosmology is an example of the kind of claim I have in mind; but it fails to be true, because air will turn out to be subject to change, divisible, more here and less there and not wholly and completely what it is (as applying the arguments of B8 to it will show). Finally, unlike Mourelatos, who does not discuss B3 or B6.1–2, I think that the view of Parmenides' *esti* as an informative identity can account for these passages.

47 Mourelatos, "Naive Metaphysics," p. 20.

48 Ibid.

named by '*F*.' "[49] Because the naive metaphysician conceives of a world that is composed solely of things, to say that "*X* is *F*" is to gesture toward the thing in a special way. The object of knowledge, for Mourelatos, is thus literally a thing that is picked out by a term that must, if it is to name successfully, pick out the whole of the thing in a completely positive way.[50] Thus, when one says "*X* is *F*," gesturing toward a thing, one apparently claims that "*F*" constitutes *X* and reveals exactly what *X* is. Thus, there is a significant core of similarity between the two accounts of the "is" that Mourelatos gives.[51]

This shared core notion seems to me to be a good way to begin to think about Parmenides' *esti* claims, because it clearly connects with the Presocratic notions of inquiry and of the nature of a thing that could be reached through such inquiry.[52] When one says that something is *F*, say, one purports to reveal the nature of the thing to such an extent that we

49 Ibid.

50 This interpretation of Mourelatos's claim about this "is" of introduction and recognition is suggested by what he says, particularly about negations, in "Naive Metaphysics," and about "kennings and formulaic epithets" in "Determinacy." On pp. 52–53 of "Determinacy," Mourelatos says, "Statements of this type imply that the second referring expression somehow directly captures or calls forth the characteristic *nature*, true *identity*, intrinsic *reality*, or *essence* of that which is *merely* referred to by the subject expression" (italics in original); he intends this to replace his account of asymmetry in *Route*.

51 I agree with Mourelatos's second account of the "is" to the extent that he thinks that such an "is" reveals the nature of a thing or what a thing is, but I am less sure about the metaphysical and epistemological claims that go along with the view developed in the later papers. I am not convinced that the naive metaphysics of things, as Mourelatos formulates it, best captures the Presocratic outlook, although I agree that, for instance, the early Presocratics tended to think of the opposites as real things, each with an independent reality. (Mourelatos argues that Heraclitus was the first Presocratic to challenge the naive metaphysics; I think that the notions of opposites and opposition in Heraclitus have more affinities with earlier Presocratic views than Mourelatos allows.) Further, I find the earlier account of speculative predication, with its connection with inquiry, more helpful in placing Parmenides correctly in the context of Presocratic thought. Mourelatos's later accounts of an "is" of introduction and recognition are based on Homeric examples (Mourelatos's examples: "This is Ajax, wall of the Achaeans" [*Iliad* III.229], "There's a certain island, in mid-sea ..." [*Od*. IV.844], "There was among the Trojans one Dares, bountiful, blameless ... " [*Iliad* V.9]) that do not attempt to explain fundamental natures in a cosmological setting. Mourelatos's later accounts seem to me to connect less perspicuously with the Presocratic tradition of inquiry into nature, or what there is, than did the original account of speculative predication. Mourelatos suggests that the examples in the account of speculative predication in *Route* may be question-begging. But I argue in this chapter that the inquiry into the nature of things is an established practice of early Presocratic thought, and that an informative identity claim, or speculative "is," is an appropriate way to explain that thought.

52 See *Route*, pp. 62–68. My notion of an informative identity claim about the nature of a thing was suggested by Mourelatos's original notion of a speculative "is" and is similar to it (and different from it) in the ways I have indicated. Mourelatos also links the Parmenidean *esti* with the concept of *physis*, adopting Kirk's view that *physis* need not always be linked with the concept of growth (Kirk's claims are on p. 228 of his *Heraclitus*); though Mourelatos claims that Parmenides "conceived the cognitive quest as directed toward ἀλήθεια rather than φύσις" (*Route*, p. 63). This is correct; but I see Parmenides' arguments in *Alētheia* as connecting

know just what the thing actually or really is. This claim is about what-is, because in a successful claim, the thing which is *F* is a thing that genuinely or reliably is. It is an identity statement, for it claims an identity between the thing we are examining and its nature; but it can also be informative, for the claim explains the thing and may well tell us something we did not yet know or have just discovered about the thing.[53] It tells us that the thing we are considering is reliably, or genuinely (*esti dokimōs* as B1.32 has it) just what it is. Because such a thing is a genuine or reliable entity, it can be a genuine object of thought or inquiry and could function as a basic entity in a cosmology.[54] Knowing the criteria for such an acceptable informative identity claim would be of great value, for we could then test claims about what there is to see if they indeed succeed in telling us about what-is. Such tests are the *poludēris elenchos* of the arguments of B8; these tests combine the notions of inquiry, thought, and genuine entities. It is this link among inquiry (*dizēsis*), thought (*noein*), and what-is that gives Parmenides' claims their strength. It has been often pointed out that the noun *dizēsis* appears to be Parmenides' own invention, but it is connected with the verb *dizēsthai* (to seek, to inquire) which appears in Homer and Heraclitus (among others).[55]

"You seek honey-sweet homecoming, glorious Odysseus," (Νόστον δίζηαι μελιηδέα, φαίδιμ' Ὀδυσσεῦ), says Tiresias in the underworld (*Od.* XI.100); here the idea of a quest is subsumed in the sense of seeking or searching at the heart of *dizēsthai*, for Odysseus, the most famous wanderer, is in search of home, and this quest is of the utmost importance to him. The same sense of searching and questing occurs in Heraclitus. He uses forms of *dizēsthai* twice, in B22 and in B101. In B22, Heraclitus asserts that "those

---

with the earlier Presocratic search for *physis* because Parmenides seeks to explicate the notion of what a thing really is as that which it is as a whole, unchangingly, etc. See also note 65, below.

53 On the issue of informative identity statements, see Kripke, "Identity and Necessity," esp. pp. 84–88. Kripke argues that questions of (epistemological) a prioricity and (metaphysical) necessity must be scrupulously distinguished; when this is done, it can be seen that " 'Hesperus is Phosphorus' is (or can be) an empirical discovery ... [and] that it is necessary" ("Identity and Necessity," p. 89n.13). Thus, true identity statements are not only necessary, they can also be informative, telling us things we did not know before. I do not, of course, claim that these are notions that would have figured in Parmenides' thought about what-is; rather, I suggest that it is helpful to think of Parmenides' *esti* as making informative identity claims about the nature of a thing.

54 I think that few claims of the form "is *F*" will actually qualify as successful predications. Only things with genuine natures can meet Parmenides' criteria and thus be the appropriate objects of inquiry. On the view I argue for, only the metaphysically basic entity (or entities) in a successful (i.e., rational) cosmology will qualify.

55 See Mourelatos, *Route*, pp. 67–68; Coxon, *Fragments*, p. 173. Mourelatos, rightly, draws parallels with Heraclitus: "for Heraclitus [δίζησις] is directed to that which is hidden and inaccessible to unthinking mortals: It is a 'delving into' and a 'quest for' the φύσις of things. For Parmenides it is a quest for ἀλήθεια" (p. 68). I shall have more to say below about the connection in Heraclitus between *physis* and *alētheia* and its significance for Parmenides.

seeking (*hoi dizēmenoi*) gold dig up a lot of earth and find little," while in B101 he claims, "I inquired into myself (*edizēsamēn emeōuton*)." In both cases, as in the example from the *Odyssey*, the search is actually a quest for something of value. Heraclitus's suggestion is that one can, by diligent searching, grasp the truth and find the hidden prize: the search for gold can be read as a metaphor for the search for knowledge and the *logos*, while the quest for oneself is the pursuit of insight and self-knowledge.[56] Considering these two fragments together, we can see the connection between searching and inquiry: Heraclitus is not merely searching for himself (he is, after all, there all along), but he is inquiring into himself in a special way. Heraclitus comments on the search for self at B45: "One would never discover the limits of soul (*psychēs peirata*), even if one were to travel every road, so deep a *logos* does it have." The need to dig deeply is reinforced by B123: "Nature loves to hide" (φύσις κρύπτεσθαι φιλεῖ); this suggests, not that the search or inquiry is futile, but that it is difficult and that it takes care and time to reach understanding. B123 makes explicit the connection between search or inquiry and the concept of *physis*, or the nature of a thing. At the very beginning of his work, Heraclitus has stressed the importance of *physis* and has provided a hint to what one who succeeds in the quest for *physis* will find: "people are like the inexperienced when they experience such words and deeds as I set forth, distinguishing each thing according to its nature (κατὰ φύσιν διαιρέων ἕκαστον), and pointing out how it is (καὶ φράζων ὅκως ἔχει)." The usual connection of *physis* is with growth, or with the appearance and development of a thing. But here Heraclitus expands the notion by linking it with what a thing really is, and in Parmenides the notion of what a thing is will be further extended by Parmenides' insistence that the genuine character of a thing is not subject to change.[57] According to Heraclitus, one who grasps this nature, or *physis*, of a thing, in accordance with the *Logos*, will have insight into what it really or genuinely is. Thus those who comprehend the *physis* will have true understanding and are to be contrasted with the polymaths castigated in B40. The understanding (*noos*) the polymaths lack is the ability to distinguish each thing and to say how it is; they cannot, in short, give the *physis* of anything. In B1 Heraclitus not only

[56] It is possible to read B22 as a criticism of those practicing traditional inquiry: they are in search of truth about the *kosmos* but find little. But Heraclitus, too, is a searcher; he has the advantage of knowing the *logos*, which serves as the basis of an explanation. While disapproving of the method adopted by those he criticizes in B22, Heraclitus shares in their search for nature (*physis*), or what a thing genuinely is (as he indicates in B1 and in B123).

[57] I think that *physis*, or "nature," can include this notion of the unchanging character of what a thing is in Heraclitus as well. Although there is change in the sensible world, and this change is manifested through the growth and development of a thing (its *physis*), the *logos* itself is unchanging and it is through knowing the *logos* that one comes to be able "to distinguish each thing according to its nature and say how it is." Further, no matter how much a thing may grow and develop, it still remains just what it is, and that, too, is a function of its *physis*.

indicates that to give the *physis* is to distinguish a thing, to set it apart from all others, or to define it, he also says that he will point out or indicate what the thing is, using a form of *phrazō* to make his point. That word, as we know, has a significant role in Parmenides, especially in the goddess's fundamental assertions in B2. There she tells him "what routes of quest/inquiry (*hodoi dizēsios*) alone there are for thinking (or understanding) (*noēsai*)"; as we have seen, she rejects the route of what-is-not: "that, I point out to you is a path altogether inscrutable" (τὴν δή τοι φράζω παναπευθέα ἔμμεν ἀταρπόν) B2.6. It is an "inscrutable path" because it is a path of inquiry that could never lead to the real or genuine character of a thing.

There is a single use of *physis* in Homer, at *Odyssey* X.303. Odysseus tells of having received from Hermes a magic herb, moly, which will help him and his men escape from Circe. Hermes explains that the herb will make Odysseus immune to Circe's poisons and he instructs Odysseus on how to use it to free his men (287ff.).

> Ὣς ἄρα φωνήσας πόρε φάρμακον ἀργειφόντης
> ἐκ γαίης ἐρύσας καί μοι φύσιν αὐτοῦ ἔδειξε·
> ῥίζῃ μὲν μέλαν ἔσκε, γάλακτι δὲ εἴκελον ἄνθος·
> μῶλυ δέ μιν καλέουσι θεοί· χαλεπὸν δέ τ' ὀρύσσειν
> ἀνδράσι γε θνητοῖσι· θεοὶ δέ τε πάντα δύνανται.
>
> (*Od.* X.302–6)

> Speaking thus, Argeïphontes gave me the drug
> having plucked it from the earth, and he showed me its *physis*;
> it was black at the root, but with a blossom like milk;
> The gods call it moly; and it is difficult for mortal
> men to dig up, but the gods have all powers.

Hermes not only gives the fabulous herb to Odysseus, he shows him its *physis*. We are told (by Odysseus) the name of the herb, what it looks like, the sort of place it grows, and that it is difficult for mortals to dig up. In addition, Hermes tells Odysseus of its protective properties, explaining what it will do to him, and why it will protect him from Circe (lines 290ff.). It is likely that here in Homer *physis* means simply a thing's outward form or appearance (as it often seems to in Pindar), related as it is to *phuō* (grow).[58]

But in the passage we can, I think, see a precursor of Heraclitus's notion of setting out the limits or boundaries of a thing by giving its *physis*.

Physis itself does not appear in the extant fragments of Xenophanes, but B32 explains that the rainbow is really a cloud:

[58] See *N.* VI.5 and *I.* IV.49; compare with *O.* II.86–88. There is a similar development in the meaning of *eidos*, which originally means a thing's shape or outward appearance and comes to mean "form" in Plato. Given Parmenides' restriction of the use of *phuō* and *physis* to the *Doxa* section of his poem, he seems to think that this link between the *physis* of a thing and its growth or development is quite strong.

ἥν τ' Ἶριν καλέουσι, νέφος καὶ τοῦτο πέφυκε,
πορφύρεον καὶ φοινίκεον καὶ χλωρὸν ἰδέσθαι.

And she whom they call Iris, this too is by nature cloud,
purple, red, and greenish-yellow to see.

Despite other explanations that have been offered, the nature of the rainbow, or what the rainbow actually is, is revealed to be a certain sort of cloud. In Xenophanes A39 (Aetius II.18.1) we find a similar explanation. The *Dioskouroi* (St. Elmo's fire) are said to be "little clouds glimmering because of their kind of motion." Both here and in the explanation of the rainbow, we have Xenophanes beginning with something that is often taken to be divine or supernatural, and then showing or arguing that its nature is really to be a cloud of a particular kind.[59] In B29 Xenophanes asserts that everything that comes to be or grows is really earth and water. That is, all the myriad forms of life that we perceive are such that they are really (in their true natures) earth and water. Xenophanes thus does just what Heraclitus says he will do in his fragment 1, "distinguishing each thing according to its nature, and showing how it is." Moreover, Xenophanes makes clear how he comes to know the natures of these things, for in fragment 18 he suggests that the proper path to understanding the *physis* or nature of something is inquiry:

οὔτοι ἀπ' ἀρχῆς πάντα θεοὶ θνητοῖσ' ὑπέδειξαν
ἀλλὰ χρόνῳ ζητοῦντες ἐφευρίσκουσιν ἄμεινον

Not from the beginning did the gods reveal all things to mortals,
but, in time, inquiring, they find out better.[60]

The same notion of the nature, or *physis*, of a thing also appears in the mid fifth century in Herodotus. While there are a number of appearances where *physis* most likely means something like "natural order," several other occurrences are of interest because of their similarities to the Xenophanean and Heraclitean uses.[61] In Book II, in his discussions of the animals of Egypt, Herodotus describes the crocodile and the hippopotamus and says that in doing so he is giving the *physis* of each. At II.68 Herodotus undertakes an account of the crocodile, describing its physical appearance, its feeding and nesting habits, its size, its daily activities, its ability to see well on land and not at all under water, and so on. Herodotus begins his account by saying,

[59] See Lesher, *Xenophanes*, pp. 141–44, and Mourelatos, "X is Really Y," pp. 281–85. Mourelatos points out (p. 282) that Xenophanes' claim is not only a rejection of supernatural explanations, but also a criticism of other naturalistic explanations, for he corrects Anaximenes' account of the rainbow (see Anaximenes A18, A7).

[60] On this interpretation of Xenophanes B18, see Lesher, *Xenophanes*, pp. 150–55, and "Xenophanes on Inquiry."

[61] See III.22.16, mentioning the *physis* of wheat; III.116.5–6, where Herodotus remarks that he hesitates to believe in one-eyed men who otherwise have a *physis* like other human beings.

"The nature (*physis*) of the crocodile is the following." *Physis* appears again in II.71 in the account of the appearance, size, voice, and thick hide of the hippopotamus. Though the account of the hippopotamus is less complete than that of the crocodile, Herodotus seems to aim at the same sort of story about it. In explaining the natures of these animals, he tells us what it is to be these sorts of beast, what one would need to know in order to be said to have an understanding of the crocodile or the hippopotamus. So here in Herodotus, as well as in Heraclitus and Xenophanes, *physis* gives an insight into what a thing is.

A connection between the *physis* of a thing and truth (a term that brings us back to Parmenides) appears in another Heraclitus fragment. At B112[62] Heraclitus links the two notions in his account of sound thinking:

> σωφρονεῖν ἀρετὴ μεγίστη καὶ σοφίη, ἀληθέα λέγειν καὶ ποιεῖν κατὰ φύσιν ἐπαΐοντας.
>
> Sound thinking is the greatest virtue and wisdom, to speak the truth and to act according to nature, with understanding.

Heraclitus here suggests that wisdom is to be equated with sound thinking and that it consists in speaking the truth and acting in accordance with the nature of things.[63] The fragment claims that one can do this only if one perceives or understands each thing "according to its nature" (*kata physin*). Unless one grasps just how things are, or what each thing is, one cannot engage in sound thinking. Heraclitus's reference to *physis* echoes his words in B1, and the claim that thinking well is the greatest excellence and wisdom links 112 with 22B2, and its assertion that what is common must be followed (and that a private understanding never counts as wisdom). Moreover, B112 also connects with B41, where we learn that the wise is one (ἓν τὸ σοφόν): knowing the plan that steers all things. But knowing this means knowing the actual nature of things according to the *logos*. Fragment 112 thus brings together a number of important issues in Heraclitus's conception of knowledge or understanding. But it also brings in the notion of truth. Without

62 Kirk and Marcovich reject B112 (following Schleiermacher and Heidel); Marcovich says that it is "no more than a late (probably Stoic) imitation of Heraclitus" (p. 96). Kahn, on the other hand, argues that there is no justification for suspecting the fragment (*Art and Thought*, pp. 119–23); it comes, he says, from a section of Stobaeus where we find other indisputably genuine fragments of Heraclitus and no other disputed ones. Moreover, if B112 is rejected, it leaves Heraclitus "with nothing really original to say on *sōphrosynē*, the paramount virtue of his age" (p. 120). This, by itself, is certainly not decisive. But it adds its weight to other considerations. Kahn therefore concludes that there is no reason to regard B112 as spurious, and good reason to accept it. Robinson (*Heraclitus*, p. 154) follows Kahn.

63 See Kahn, *Art and Thought*, p. 122, on this. Here the connection of *physis* and truth suggests that the *physis* of a thing is not itself subject to change, even though the thing itself may develop and change.

this knowledge of the *physis* of things, Heraclitus insists, one cannot think or act in accordance with the truth; one will be led astray.

But while the notions of *physis* and search play an important role in Heraclitus's theory, and while it is useful to think of the Milesians and even the Pythagoreans as searching for the nature of the *kosmos*, in these philosophers there is little analysis of the proper way to go about the inquiry into what a thing is, little account of a philosophically proper method of search.[64] It is in Parmenides that the method of the search for what a thing is itself becomes a philosophical issue as much as the question of the correct understanding of what there is.[65]

The error of the *Doxa* suggests that Parmenides is arguing for the proper understanding of the character of theoretically fundamental entities in an

64 In both Xenophanes and Heraclitus, there is discussion of how one determines the truth. Xenophanes B18 and B34, for instance, discuss the value and the limitations of inquiry. Heraclitus is eager to reject certain methods of truth seeking (Ionian inquiry, reliance on popular poets and bards). But there is not, at least in the extant fragments of Xenophanes and Heraclitus, a systematic analysis of the right way to go about searching for and testing truth such as we find in Parmenides. I think that Heraclitus was worried by the methodological issue, and that he offered an account of the nature of the knowledge involved in asking and answering questions about *physis*. But Heraclitus does not seem to have given much thought to the problem of error in determining the *physis* of a thing (he sees that error is a problem, but he does not analyze the nature of error). From Parmenides' point of view, Heraclitus's very awareness of these problems makes him a particular target. Heraclitus's solution (in the unity of opposites) is (from the Parmenidean position) quite untenable, for reasons that Heraclitus's own theory should have made clear.

65 There is thus an important connection between the earlier notion of *physis* and Parmenides' account of what it is to be a thing. J. Lesher has suggested to me that the term *physis* probably retains a connection with development and growth, which it gets through its root in *phuō*; and it is likely for this reason that Parmenides restricts his uses of *physis* and *phuō* to the *Doxa* section of his poem. But, as I have argued here, there is evidence that even in the Greek of Parmenides' time the word held intimations of what a thing really is, what its permanent character is. Thus in Pindar (at *O*. II.86–88) the poet claims that "the wise man is one who knows many things by nature" (σοφὸς ὁ πολλὰ εἰδὼς φυᾷ); *O*. IX.100 marks a contrast between that which comes by nature and the merit that comes merely through training. At *Pr*. 489–91 Aeschylus represents Prometheus as claiming through his analysis of the flights of certain birds he knew "which are by nature lucky and auspicious" (οἵτινές τε δεξιοὶ φύσιν εὐωνύμους τε). By the time of Sophocles, we find the use of *physis* to mean "settled character," or what a thing actually is. See, for instance, *Tr*. 1062–63: "a woman, a female being in nature not a man" (γυνὴ δέ, θῆλυς οὖσα κοὐκ ἀνδρὸς φύσιν). Thus, Parmenides' claims about what requirements must be met by a claim about what a thing genuinely or reliably is (what it really is) are a way of reforming earlier views about *physis* and are relevant to issues of what it is to produce a rational cosmology. This view of the relation between Parmenides' account of what something really is and earlier inquiry into *physis* is similar to that taken by Mourelatos in *Route* (pp. 62–63), but I am less persuaded than Mourelatos by Kirk's attempts (in *Heraclitus*, p. 228 with n. 1) to remove the concept of growth and development from *physis* (thus, in the end, Mourelatos is right to claim that Parmenides turns his attention to *alētheia* rather than to *physis*). Lovejoy ("Meaning of Φύσις") argued that *physis* in Presocratic thought should almost always be taken as "genuine nature" (even in Empedocles B8); but I do not think that his account of Empedocles' use of *physis* is correct. Empedocles is committed to denying that mortal things have a nature

account of how things are. The error of mortals is to think that the world is such that its fundamental entities can combine both what-is and what-is-not.[66]

Parmenides criticizes both the result of mortal inquiry and its method. The notions of questing, of routes, and of understanding come together in the goddess's statement at B2.2 of "the only routes of inquiry there are for thinking:" αἵπερ ὁδοὶ μοῦναι διζήσιός εἰσι νοῆσαι. The routes are alternative paths of inquiry, and the connection of *dizēsis* with a quest suggests that the object is understanding of or genuine thought about something of consequence.[67] If the goal of the search is true understanding, then the goddess is pointing out the only routes to it (and, of course, one of them will not be a genuine route at all). The goddess does not reveal the content of the understanding that is to be gained by following the proper route; rather she both criticizes the route that mortals take (in B6 and B7), showing that it leads nowhere, and explains (in fragment 8) the route that will lead to success. The motif of the route suggests that Parmenides is both criticizing the results of mortal inquiries and repudiating the method mortals use to arrive at those results.[68] Led by habit into ignoring the signs on the route, lacking control over their *noos*, and failing to make the right decision (*krisis*), mortals are going about their inquiries in the wrong way, failing to test at each stage of inquiry; thus they never can arrive at complete understanding and their theories will never be trustworthy.[69]

---

or "inner character" of their own, but the force of B8 is to deny that what seem to be cases of coming-to-be and passing away—the growth and destruction of mortal things—are really what they seem. Instead, they are cases of mixture and separation of what is real (the four roots). On various uses of *physis*, especially compared with *einai*, see Holwerda, ΦΥΣΙΣ.

66 This might suggest that I think that the "mortals" that Parmenides denounces are to be identified exclusively with previous philosophers (as, for instance, Coxon, *Fragments*, p. 183). I certainly think that Parmenides' philosophical predecessors are to be included in the ranks of mortals, but ordinary folk are there as well. After all, the Ionian practitioners of *historia* are trying to provide an explanatory account of the *kosmos* as it appears to ordinary people. (This is true even of Heraclitus: what the *logos* explains is the underlying unity that accounts for and makes possible the multiplicitous changes in the world as it is experienced.) So mortals and philosophers have a shared conception of how things are.

67 See Mourelatos, *Route*, chap. 2, esp. pp. 67–70.

68 This is true because the signs in B8 function both as characteristics of the natures that are reached by proper inquiry and regulating principles for that inquiry.

69 The subject of the inquiry is not explicitly stated; but it does not follow that Parmenides intends his analysis to apply to any inquiry whatever. This is to be contrasted with Furth's view that the notion of "inquiry" here is perfectly general: "I shall understand Parmenides to mean any investigation of 'what is' in the sense of what is so, or what is the case; any procedure aimed at ascertaining the facts. . . . Nor need any restriction be placed on the subject matter—whatever Parmenides is saying will apply equally well to ascertaining whether there is animal life on Mars, or a rational root to a certain equation, or an amount of tribute that will satisfy the Persians, or whether Socrates is flying, or any broad-leaved plants are deciduous" (Furth, "Elements," p. 249). Furth's wide understanding of Parmenides' point seems to be echoed in Barnes's claim that Parmenides' subject is whatever is the object of study (*PP,* vol. I, pp. 163–65).

The possibility of error resulting from the malfunction or misuse of *noos* is crucial for understanding its role in Parmenides. While B3 asserts that "the same thing is for thinking and for being" (τὸ γὰρ αὐτὸ νοεῖν ἐστίν τε καὶ εἶναι),[70] Parmenides also suggests at B6.6 and B7.2–6 that *noos* can be led astray into taking the wrong path so that it comes to be connected with *Doxa* rather than with *Alētheia* (this is suggested by the appearance of both *noos* and *noēma* in B16). The misuse of *noos* results in its missing or otherwise failing to connect with its proper object, what-is.[71] This is implicit in the abuse of mortals in B6 and B7. At B6.5–6 the goddess says that "helplessness guides their wandering *noos* (ἀμηχανίη . . . ἰθύνει πλακτὸν νόον)"; the implication is that mortals, having failed to keep their thought from the forbidden route, are guided by a mistaken, deceived, and altogether helpless *noos*. Mortals fail in controlling *noos*; not understanding the nature of its proper object, they fail to steer it properly. So, their *noos* wanders, having no genuine object on which to fix. In such a state and on such a route, they can never hope to reach persuasive truth, which is itself connected with what-is.[72] And although the subject of the routes of inquiry is not explicitly stated, the evidence marshaled above suggests that it is the genuine nature of a thing.

It is, then, hardly surprising that the goddess introduces the way of is-not as impossible. If the routes of inquiry for thinking in B2 are ways of investigating or reaching what a thing genuinely is, then the route of is-not cannot succeed. For what would it be to give a negative account of what something really is? It would be to say "it is not this, or this, or this . . ." and such a route can never be completed; it is not *anuston*. Something that was negative in this sense would be nothing in particular, and it is clear that one cannot think of something that is nothing in particular (we might think of the Cyclopes who misinterpret Polyphemus's cry that he is being harmed by "No-Man."). Mortals would deny that this is the route of inquiry that they take. But Parmenides' argument is that the theories adopted by mortals, committed as they are to coming-to-be and passing away, or to change, actually consign mortals to the negative route. If something changes from being, say, *F* to being *G*, it cannot actually have been either *F* or *G*. What it actually is remains inscrutable and indeterminate. Thus, mortals end

[70] Compare with Coxon's "for the same thing is for conceiving as is for being" (Coxon, *Fragments*, p. 54). On *noein* in this fragment, see Finkelberg, "Parmenides' Foundation," pp. 55–56 and esp. n. 48. See also Heidel, "On Certain Fragments," pp. 720–23.

[71] Barnes notes that even in its traditional uses, there is no guarantee that *noein* will always be veridical (*PP*, vol. I, p. 158).

[72] Lesher argues that in Parmenides human beings are for the first time said to be capable of controlling and directing *noos*. See "Parmenides' Critique of Thinking," p. 29. Lesher contrasts the picture of the *kouros* as controlling his *noos*, and testing the goddess's claims, with the traditional poetic depiction of mortals as helpless and passive, as in Archilochus fr. 70, and Homer, *Od*. XVIII.136–37.

up on the route of what-is-not, whether they intended to take it or not. B6 and B7 show the fate of those who try to take this route: their path is backward turning, and they wander, getting nowhere. The reason for this is shown in the proofs of B8: these mortal views will always end up involving what-is-not, and that is impossible. Thus, Parmenides' rejection of what-is-not in B2 ("for you could not know what-is-not [for that is not to be accomplished] nor could you point it out") depends not so much on a "law of thought" about the impossibility of thinking of what is non-existent, but on the practical impossibility of giving a genuine account of what a thing is that involves commitments to negations.[73] So, rejecting the existential reading of *esti* will allow us both to tell a coherent story about the structure of the argument and to see Parmenides as a crucial figure in the development of Presocratic thought about cosmology and the nature of what-is.

I suggest the following structure for the *Alētheia* (as we have it in the extant fragments). First, in B2, the goddess announces that there are two routes of inquiry possible, and in announcing them she indicates that only one of them is a genuine, i.e., successful route. It is successful because it is persuasive and trustworthy, and it leads to truth. The other is not a genuine route because it leads literally nowhere. One can wander along it, but taking such a route will never lead thought to its desired destination. The reason why the routes have the character they do is given in B2.7–8: "for you could neither know what-is-not (for it is not to be accomplished [*ou ... anuston*[74]]) nor could you point it out" and in B3: "the same thing is for thinking and for being." In B6 the goddess repeats her assertion that what-is is while what is nothing (that which is not) is not. The youth is bidden to consider this, and then the goddess lays out her plan for the rest of the poem: she will lead the youth through the correct route (B8.1–50) and then through the *Doxa*, the route of is-not, pointing out the path that mortals take, thinking they are saying and thinking what-is when in fact they are on the negative route. B6 and B7 finish the preliminary story of those on the forbidden path that is mentioned at B6.4–5, giving an account of the fate of mortals on the negative route. The youth is then (B7.2–6) exhorted to keep his thought (*noēma*) from that route, and told how to manage that task: he must judge for himself the much-contesting trials that the goddess will lay out in B8.1–49. There she shows how to try or test a claim: is it

[73] On this view, the claim at B6.1–2 that what-is "can be, while nothing cannot" points out that what-is-not is that which has no character or nature at all: it is not anything in particular, thus nothing at all, and so not something that can be said or thought. The sense here is still fundamentally predicative rather than primarily existential and is captured well by Mourelatos's "characterizing" sense of nothing or what-is-not. See Mourelatos, "Determinacy" and " 'Nothing' "; see also Kahn, "Retrospect," pp. 26–27n.45.

[74] Mourelatos's suggestion about the ambiguity of *anuston* here is quite suggestive. See "Determinacy," pp. 49–50. Neither can the journey along the route be completed, nor can an account of what-is-not be completed, because what-is-not is itself indeterminate and not fixed.

on the route of what-is or of what-is-not? Any purported claim about what-is that fails the tests enumerated in the signs of B8.2–4 is really a claim about what-is-not.[75] We learn in B8.1–49 the formal characteristics of something that passes the tests for what-is. I now turn to the details of the arguments in B2-B7.

3. Mortal Error and the Routes of Inquiry

In B2 the goddess introduces the routes of inquiry, presenting the positive route as "the path of Persuasion" and characterizing the negative path as not a genuine route at all. In the remaining fragments before B8, she offers further claims about the proper and improper routes of inquiry while, at the same time, withholding the actual details of the content of the positive route, which come in B8.[76] These fragments reinforce the unacceptability of the negative route by showing the difficulties encountered by those who try to follow it in their inquiries, and contrasting those difficulties with the coherent thought of one who takes the positive route. At the end of the sequence, and just before B8, the youth is exhorted to judge for himself the claims made by the goddess. These fragments present some difficulties. Just as the content of the proper route is not provided before B8, in B6 and B7 there are few details given of the error committed by mortals (those details come in the *Doxa*). This lack of specificity about mortal error has led to questions about the mistake mortals make and the number of routes that the goddess actually discusses. In this section I discuss these issues and suggest that it is correct to think that there are only two routes considered in the poem, and that the mortal confusion chronicled in B6 and B7 is caused by the attempt to make the rejected path of B2 a route of inquiry.

B4 exhorts us to consider what-is, and describes the connected, focused nature of what-is:

> λεῦσσε δ' ὅμως ἀπεόντα νόῳ παρεόντα βεβαίως·
> οὐ ̣γὰρ ἀποτμήξει τὸ ἐὸν τοῦ ἐόντος ἔχεσθαι

[75] In this sense the signs (*sēmata*) along the route in B8 also function as metaphorical turnstiles. I do not mean to suggest that the *sēmata* are literally meant as gates, but only that each sign gives a condition that a thing that is must meet. A failure to meet the criterion blocks further passage down the route of what-is. Because the signs delimit necessary characteristics of what-is, an account of what-is that fails to satisfy a *sēma* can be cast aside with no further examination.

[76] This assumes that the arrangement of fragments as we now have them is roughly correct. I am well aware that this assumption may be wrong, and that there may be important parts of Parmenides' arguments missing. I do not find other arrangements of the fragments DK numbers from B2-B7 any more persuasive or compelling than the DK arrangement (see, for instance, Coxon's arrangement in *Fragments*). All an interpreter of Parmenides can do is to try to make the best sense possible out of the surviving fragments.

οὔτε σκιδνάμενον πάντῃ πάντως κατὰ κόσμον
οὔτε συνιστάμενον. (B4)

Look on things which, though far off, are firmly present to the mind;
for you will not cut off what is from holding to what is,
neither dispersing everywhere in every way in order,
nor gathering together.

The claim is that what may seem far off (the goddess's truth that is "far from the beaten track of human beings," perhaps [B1.27]), is nevertheless present to the mind and is to be considered. Given the connection between thought and what-is announced in B3, the natural reading is that we are to consider or think about what-is. This, no matter how remote it may seem, is actually firmly present to the mind, or understanding, as all genuine thought is about what-is, and what-is cannot be cut off from itself. The fragment has both metaphysical and epistemological implications. There is no what-is-not that could cut off or disperse what-is, so what-is all alike is, and is whole and continuous (as will be argued in B8). There are no internal divisions that would allow it to be broken or separated from itself; thus what-is cannot be scattered and gathered but is all together.[77] Moreover, because what-is has this character, it is all present to *noos* and can be grasped by the attentive mind.[78] This is yet another indication of how thought or understanding is committed to what-is (see B8.34–36). One whose *noos* is focused on what-is has a direct, clear, and single-minded grasp of it, unlike the two-headed mortals of B6.5.

B4, the picture of mortals whose wandering *noos* is guided by helplessness (B6.5–9), and the exhortation to keep one's thought (*noēma*) away from the route of inquiry taken by mortals (B7.2), all suggest that there is a choice or decision that can be made concerning thought about what-is; it is up to us to decide which path of inquiry to take. This is, at first glance, denied by the opening of B6:

It is necessary that what is for saying and thinking be; for it can be
but nothing cannot; this I bid you ponder. (B6.1–2)

[77] The similarity of the language suggests a criticism of Heraclitus here (see B10). His "things brought together" contain and so shift between opposites; in contrast, Parmenides claims that what-is is stable. It is also tempting to read this fragment as a criticism of Anaximenes, whose fundamental being, air, is changed into other things by condensation and rarefaction. "Dispersing in every way" and "gathering together," air seems to change in its very nature by becoming other things and not simply underlying them, and thus, according to Parmenides, cannot be a genuine entity.

[78] Xenophanes, in B34, had suggested that one can have sure and certain knowledge only about what one has experienced directly. In this he echoes the Homeric view that knowledge comes either from direct experience or as something provided by a reliable source (see, for instance, the invocation of the Muses to tell the poet all about the Achaian fighters at Troy at *Iliad* II.484–92). Parmenides responds that what-is is always "firmly present to the mind" and so can be known reliably.

The claim that "it is necessary that ..." (*chrē*) suggests one might read the claim as "necessarily, what is for speaking and for thinking is"; and then the exhortation to control our *noos* so as not to say and think what is not becomes otiose. On this reading, it looks as though we have no choice but to say and think what-is, for nothing else is possible. But I think that this is an over-interpretation of *chrē*. The necessity here is that of something's being right or proper, something that ought to be the case, rather than the technical sense of "necessarily."[79] So the opening claim of B6 is better read as "it is right that what is for saying and thinking be; for what-is can be, but nothing cannot." This then gives some force to the goddess's appeal that we ponder her claim, and to the lines that follow. For there she describes her plan for the rest of the poem and the predicament of mortals who have not learned the lesson that she is teaching here. Thinking of all these things, and keeping in mind the claims of B2 and B6.1–2, her hearers will be in a position to avoid the blandishments of much-experienced habit (*ethos polupeiron* B7.3), and to judge the much-contested testing and challenge (*poludēris elenchos* B7.5) of the goddess, and to make the proper choice about a route of inquiry.

In making that choice, we need to be clear about how many routes of inquiry there are. The standard view is that there are three, the route of what-is, the route of what-is-not, and the route that attempts to combine what-is and what-is-not; and that the goddess undertakes to rule out two wrong or improper routes.[80] This account of the goddess's plan is based on the pronouncements at B6.1–5:

> χρὴ τὸ λέγειν τε νοεῖν τ' ἐὸν ἔμμεναι· ἔστι γὰρ εἶναι,
> μηδὲν δ' οὐκ ἔστιν·[81] τά σ' ἐγὼ φράζεσθαι ἄνωγα.

[79] See Mourelatos, *Route*, Appendix III, pp. 277–78. See also Kerferd's concurring remarks in his review of Bormann (p. 130).

[80] For full discussions of this issue, see Cordero, "Les deux chemins," and Nehamas, "Parmenides' Three Ways."

[81] These lines present a number of difficulties, both of text and of interpretation. Cordero notes that Tarán's re-examination of the manuscripts shows that they actually read χρὴ τὸ λέγειν τὸ νοεῖν τ' ἐόν ἔμμεναι in line 1 ("Les deux chemins," pp. 24–25n.1; "Texte de Parménide," pp. 19–20; for Cordero's translation, see n. 91, below). O'Brien adopts this reading, and like Cordero, takes the two occurrences of τό as demonstratives (O'Brien, "Le Poème de Parménide," p. 24; see also pp. 197ff.). Coxon notes the manuscript readings but accepts Karsten's proposal of τὸ λέγειν τε νοεῖν, which was incorporated into Diels' text of Simplicius's commentary and into the text of DK (*Fragments*, p. 55; Cordero examines the history of the DK version in n. 1 of "Les deux chemins" referred to above). I here follow Coxon in retaining the DK text. The interpretation of B6.1–2 is also open to dispute. Owen, who takes the subject to be "what can be thought or spoken of" and the *esti* to be existential, finds these lines to contain a "celebrated fallacy," that of "the so-called *de re* interpretation of modal statements" ("Eleatic," p. 15 and n.4). Robinson defends Parmenides against Owen in "The Real" and "Ascertainment." Ketchum, who accepts Owen's account of the subject, but reads the *esti* as predicative ("what is is something or other"), claims that the argument "seems cogent enough" ("Parmenides,"

πρώτης γὰρ σ' ἀφ' ὁδοῦ ταύτης διζήσιος ⟨εἴργω⟩,
αὐτὰρ ἔπειτ' ἀπὸ τῆς, ἣν δὴ βροτοὶ εἰδότες οὐδέν
πλάττονται, δίκρανοι ... (B6.1–5)

It is right that what is for saying and thinking be; for it can be
but nothing cannot; this I bid you ponder.
For I hold you back from this first way of inquiry
and then again from that, on which mortals, knowing nothing,
wander, two-headed ...

There are two reasons to think that this text commits the goddess to ruling out two ways, leaving the third in command. First, the whole of B6.1–2a is a statement of the positive route (although this has not always been recognized[82]), for the claim that nothing cannot be is part of the genuine path of inquiry. Second, if this is the case, then, when the goddess says that she bars the *kouros* "from this first route" in B6.3, she can hardly mean to bar him from the positive route. So, in saying ἀφ' ὁδοῦ ταύτης διζήσιος, the goddess must refer to some route other than the one she has just adumbrated in B6.1–2a, one that must be a negative path. Thus, when she then adds, "and then again from that (route)" and specifically mentions mortals, she must refer to yet another negative route. The route of mortals (the so-called third route) seems to combine what-is and what-is-not, so the first negative route (apparently referred to at B6.3) must be a completely negative route, which simply asserts that what-is-not is.

As is well known, there are difficulties with this view. There is, in the text as it stands, simply no first negative route mentioned. A number of suggestions have been made to deal with this. Some have taken the short statement μηδὲν δ' οὐκ ἔστιν at B6.2a to be a compressed statement of the purely negative route. But Tarán, Cordero, and Nehamas have argued persuasively that this cannot be correct.[83] One solution to the difficulty

p. 177). For further discussion of the lines, and a defense of Parmenides against Owen's claims, see Goldin, who accepts the Tarán reading of the lines as reported by Cordero.

82 On B6.1–2a as a statement of the positive route, see Tarán (*Parmenides*, pp. 54–58), Cordero ("Les deux chemins"), and Nehamas ("Parmenides' Three Ways").

83 Barnes argues that there is no positive route mentioned in B6; rather, the fragment discusses two negative routes. According to Barnes, lines 4–9 mention the route of mortals (which Barnes glosses as maintaining "both that it is and that it is not"). But the route of mortals is not the "first road" of line 3; that is the purely negative route. According to Barnes, B6.1–2 is not a statement of the positive route, but the *end* of an argument against the purely negative route that began at B2.7–8 (*PP*, vol. I, pp. 159–60). So the "first road of inquiry" mentioned in B6 and from which we are held back is actually the purely negative route and there is no mention of a positive route in B6. This is improbable. Tarán's argument that B6.1–2a contains the positive route is convincing (and Barnes provides no argument against it). Barnes assumes that B3 comes at the end of B2, but then the connection of B6.1–2, as a statement of the purely negative route, with the end of the complex of B2 and B3 is quite unclear. B2 ends with a rejection of the negative route, saying that what-is-not can be neither known nor pointed out (B2.7–8). B3, which claims

of B6.3 (the most drastic) is to posit a lacuna of varying lengths at the end of the line.[84] Tarán, rejecting the view that there are three routes in total, with two negative ways, suggests that the lacuna said something to indicate that the "holding back" from the first way (the positive way) was only temporary, and to suggest that the goddess would return to it presently. This leaves Parmenides with only one negative route, which is discussed in B6.3ff. and B7; having discussed them, the goddess returns to the positive route in B8.1ff. Stokes, rejecting Tarán's account, opts for a lacuna after 6.3 that contained a statement of the completely negative route. Thus, Stokes maintains the traditional view of two negative routes. The necessary gap, according to Stokes, could have been in the manuscripts of Simplicius that have come down to us, or, as Stokes conjectures, there may have been a gap in Simplicius's own source, also coming after line 3.[85] Finkelberg agrees that there must be a lacuna but he says little about its content.[86] He actually sees three rejected routes in B6-B7: one that asserts that Being does not exist (his view of B6.3 plus the projected lacuna); one that asserts that both Being and not-Being exist (B6.4–9), and one that asserts the existence of not-Being (B7.1–2).[87]

All of these interpretations (except Tarán's) share the view that we are free to ignore Parmenides' suggestions in his poem that there are only two routes of inquiry. In several places the goddess indicates that there are only two routes to be considered. First, at the end of B1, she says that the *kouros* will learn "all things"; and she explains this as first, "the unshaking heart of persuasive truth (ἠμὲν ἀληθείης εὐπειθέος ἀτρεμὲς ἦτορ)" (B1.29) and then "the beliefs of mortals in which there is no true trust (ἠδὲ βροτῶν δόξας, ταῖς οὐκ ἔνι πίστις ἀληθής)" (B1.30). No "third route" appears here in the programmatic announcement that governs the whole poem. Second, in B2.1–2 the goddess claims explicitly that she will introduce the only routes of inquiry that there are:

---

that "the same thing is for thinking as for being" supports the positive route against the negative route. On Barnes's view, the opening of B6 continues the argument begun at the end of B2 against the route of what-is-not. So the goddess must, on Barnes's account, be referring to the negative route of B2 when she says that she holds us back from the first route of inquiry. But if we look back to B2, the first route mentioned is the positive route of what-is, not the negative route of what-is-not. So there is, on Barnes's view, still the problem of what the "first route" actually refers to. Barnes's account has affinities with Owen's. Owen sees the opening lines of B6 as establishing "that what can be talked or thought about must exist" ("Eleatic Questions," p. 15). This in turn, according to Owen, supports B2.7–8 (p. 11).

84 Tarán (*Parmenides*), Stokes (*One and Many*), Finkelberg ("Parmenides' Foundation") all adopt this expedient. There is disagreement about whether the gap occurred in the transmission of Simplicius's work, or whether it was already in Simplicius's text of Parmenides.

85 See Stokes, *One and Many*, pp. 112–15. Stokes's rejection of Tarán's account is on p. 113; his positive account is on pp. 113–15.

86 Finkelberg, "Parmenides' Foundation," p. 60n.60; p. 61n.65.

87 Ibid., pp. 61–62n.65.

εἰ δ' ἄγ' ἐγὼν ἐρέω, κόμισαι δὲ σὺ μῦθον ἀκούσας,
αἵπερ ὁδοὶ μοῦναι διζήσιός εἰσι νοῆσαι

Come now, and I will tell you, and you, hearing, preserve the story,
the only routes of inquiry there are for thinking.

When she actually introduces routes in B2, there are only two. The first is clearly the proper route of what-is, introduced in B2.3–4, while the second is the route of what-is-not, introduced at B2.5–7. It is reasonable, at this point in the development of the poem, for a hearer or reader to link the first route with the "unshaking heart of persuasive truth" already mentioned at B1.29, especially as the goddess herself marks the connection through the notion of persuasion, saying that the first route is one that "is the path of Persuasion (for it attends upon truth)" (Πειθοῦς ἐστι κέλευθος [ἀληθείῃ γὰρ ὀπηδεῖ]). Moreover, identifying the second route of B2 with the beliefs of mortals mentioned at B1.30 is also reasonable, for the goddess characterizes the negative route of B2.5–7 as one that is "wholly without report," or a route that is not genuine; this claim is consistent with the view that the beliefs of mortals lack "true trust." The goddess says the *kouros* will learn two sorts of things (the truth and then the beliefs of mortals) and she then goes on to suggest that there are two corresponding routes of inquiry. Further, fragments B6.4 through B7 constitute an admonition against mortal beliefs,[88] and then B8 (clearly the account of the positive route) begins with a claim that only a single story of a route remains. So, leaving out B6.1–3 for the moment, we have a preliminary account that suggests that two sorts of views will be discussed (B1.28–30), a claim that the only possible routes of inquiry are about to be introduced (B2.1–2), followed by a discussion of two routes only (B2.3–8), and a warning against one route, the route of mortals in B6.4–7. Indeed, the only reason for looking for more than two routes is the difficulty of reconciling B6.3 with the rest of the first seven extant fragments.

That difficulty rests on the goddess's claim that she will first bar us from a certain route of inquiry: πρώτης γὰρ σ' ἀφ' ὁδοῦ ταύτης διζήσιος εἴργω (for I bar you from this first path of inquiry). But that claim itself presents a problem. There is no manuscript authority for *eirgō*: in all of the surviving manuscripts in which B6.3 appears, the verse ends at *dizēsios*.[89] The Aldine edition (Venice, 1526) of Simplicius's *Commentary* had dealt with the incomplete line by printing B6.3 as πρώτης γὰρ ἀφ' ὁδοῦ ταύτης

[88] There seems no good reason to think that B7 discusses two routes, or that it is anything other than a discussion of the route of mortals. See Cordero, "Les deux chemins" pp. 11–12; and Nehamas, "Parmenides' Three Ways," pp. 100–101. Cordero grants that there is a resemblance between 6.3 and 7.1, "but it is a matter of an external resemblance and so deceptive" (p. 11; see also n. 89, p. 28).

[89] Cordero, "Les deux chemins," p. 10. In his n. 81 (p. 28), Cordero records the following manuscript variations in line 6.3: "*Cod.* B and *Cod.* C, τ' in place of σ'; Cod. G, nothing between γάρ and ἀφ'."

διζήσιος εἶργε νόημα (For hold back your thought from this route of inquiry). The addition of *eirge noēma* was followed by later editors, although they made other changes to the line.[90] Diels, following the spirit of the Aldine and what he took to be the example of B7.2 (thus retaining σ'), printed the now familiar πρώτης γὰρ σ' ἀφ' ὁδοῦ ταύτης διζήσιος ⟨εἴργω⟩ in the Berlin edition of Simplicius's *Commentary*, and he followed this in his *Parmenides* and in the editions of *Die Fragmente der Vorsokratiker*. But the lack of manuscript authority should make us wary, particularly as the difficulty in making 6.3 fit with the rest of the fragments can be traced to the presence of *eirgō*. Cordero and Nehamas independently argue that the goddess says that there are only two routes, that all the discussions of the *krisis* point to only two possibilities, and that the structure of B6 itself makes *eirgō* an extremely unlikely choice for Parmenides here. Both suggest replacing *eirgō* with a form of *archein* (to begin), Cordero choosing πρώτης γὰρ τ' ἀφ' ὁδοῦ ταύτης διζήσιος ἄρξει (for you will begin from this first route of inquiry[91]), Nehamas completing the line as πρώτης γὰρ σ(οι)[92] ἀφ' ὁδοῦ ταύτης διζήσιος ἄρξω (For first I will begin for you from this way of inquiry).[93] Both of these suggestions make sense of B6: the goddess begins with a statement of the positive route, exhorting the youth to ponder that claim. Then she lays out her plan for the rest of the poem; first will come the discussion of the content of the positive route (B8.1–49) and then a discussion of the details of the route of mortals (the *Doxa*: B8.50 to the end of the fragments as we have them), with a short description of the plight of mortals on that route in B6.5–9 and a warning to avoid it in B7.[94] On this view, the structure of the fragments preceding B8 becomes clearer, and there is no need to posit a third route

90 See Cordero, "Les deux chemins," p. 11 for full discussion of the history of this line between the Aldine and Diels editions.

91 Cordero gives the whole sequence from B6.1 as "Il est nécessaire de dire et de penser qu'il y a de l'être; parce qu'être est possible et le néant n'existe pas. Je t'invite a méditer cela, car tu commenceras par ce premier chemin de la recherche, et ensuite par celui par lequel . . . " ("Les deux chemins," p. 24).

92 On σ' as an elision of σοί, see Nehamas, "On Parmenides' Three Ways," p. 104 with notes. Nehamas cites parallel elisions of σοί at *Iliad* I.170–71, (probably) *Iliad* XXI.122–23, and Sappho, "Ode to Aphrodite," 18–19.

93 Nehamas discusses the use of *archein* with *apo* on p. 105 of "On Parmenides' Three Ways"; see also Cordero, "Les deux chemins," p. 22.

94 Finkelberg objects to Cordero's reading of the passage (he does not mention Nehamas), claiming that Cordero's interpretation "destroys the general line of Parmenides' argumentation and is hardly compatible with B8.1–2" (Parmenides' Foundation," p. 61n.61). Rather than destroying Parmenides' argument, the replacement of *eirgō* gives a coherent structure to the first part of the *Alētheia*; it may not be compatible with Finkelberg's account of the argument, but that is a different matter. Finkelberg's account relies on an existential reading of the *esti* and requires that there be three mistaken routes (not two, as on most interpretations). Both of these assumptions seem to me dubious. I do not see the force of Finkelberg's complaint about B8.1–2. There is no reason why, on either Cordero's or Nehamas's view, we cannot understand the negative route to have been rejected by B8.1 (indeed, it is characterized as impossible as it is

that would disturb the dualistic underpinnings of the whole poem.[95] I think that the Nehamas reconstruction of the line is slightly preferable, for it keeps the action of the poem centered on the goddess who tells the story. Moreover, it makes a nice parallel with B8.50–52, where the goddess announces that she is ending her discussion of the genuine route of inquiry:

> ἐν τῷ σοι παύω πιστὸν λόγον ἠδὲ νόημα
> ἀμφὶς ἀληθείης· δόξας δ' ἀπὸ τοῦδε βροτείας
> μάνθανε κόσμον ἐμῶν ἐπέων ἀπατηλὸν ἀκούων.
>
> Here I bring to an end for you my trustworthy speech and thought
> about truth; from here on learn mortal beliefs
> listening to the deceptive order of my words.

The goddess announces that she is concluding her story of the true route and beginning her account of mortal belief. This line matches up with B6.3 in that at B8.50 the goddess says *soi pauō* (I bring to an end for you), which parallels *soi arxō* at 6.3 (I begin for you). Further, the goddess marks the beginning of her untrustworthy account: *apo toude* (from here); in B6.3 we have *apo ... tautēs* (from this [route]).[96] Besides the linguistic echoes, the passage at B8.50–52 is in agreement with the proposed emendment of B6.3 in two ways. First, it confirms that the plan was to begin with the genuine route that leads to truth and then to go on to the spurious route that mortals take. Second, it shows that the structure of the claim at B6.3 is consistent with the goddess's practice throughout the poem. Like any good teacher, eager that her pupil not get lost, she began by announcing her strategy (B1.28–30), enunciating the basic principles that she will follow (B2); then, as she begins to carry out her plan she repeats the procedure (B6.3–4); and again, halfway through carrying it out, she pauses to remind her hearer where they are in the plan that she had sketched earlier (B8.50–52).[97]

If there is but a single negative route, what is it? B2 claims that there are two routes of inquiry: "the one that it is and that it is not possible not

---

introduced). The goddess says that the negative route is not a genuine route, yet B6 and B7 show that mortals try to follow it. Having first learned the details of the only genuine path, the positive route (in B8.1–49), the *kouros* is then given the content of the negative route (in the *Doxa*), knowing that account to be deceptive, yet needing to learn it (and its principles) so that the goddess's claim at B8.61 will be fulfilled: no opinion of mortals will overtake him.

95 As Nehamas puts it, "Fragment B6 does not therefore reject any way of inquiry. On the contrary, it says that the goddess will follow (demonstrate) two methods of inquiring into nature—and which is just what she does." Nehamas, "On Parmenides' Three Ways," p. 105.

96 I am indebted to Alexander Nehamas for his suggestions about this passage.

97 Compare also the remarks at B8.60–61, also using a first person singular verb (*phatizō*) with *soi*. I suspect that there may have been some sort of similar remark at the end of the *Doxa*. In reporting B19 (*in de Caelo* 558.8–11), Simplicius says that it comes after Parmenides has described the order (*diakosmēsis*) of perception but he does not say that B19 marks the conclusion of the poem.

to be" (B2.3) and "the other that it is not and that it is right that it not be" (B2.5). One impetus for the claim that there are actually two negative routes has come from interpreting the route of B2.5 as one that says that what in no way is at all, is.[98] This leaves room for a so-called mortal route, which takes its character from the description of mortals at B6.8–9. There, mortals are said to think that "to be and not be are the same and not the same" (οἷς τὸ πέλειν τε καὶ οὐκ εἶναι ταὐτὸν νενόμισται κοὐ ταὐτόν). Accordingly, the route mortals take is supposed to be one that combines what-is and what-is-not as opposed to the routes that say purely "it is" or "it is not."

But once one has attempted to say or think "what is not" in any way at all one is immediately on the negative route, not on some third route that is supposed to be intermediate between the routes of being and not being. In B8 Parmenides will prove that to deviate in any way from the route that it is—that route that is the path of persuasion which attends upon truth (B2.4)—is to take the forbidden route of what is not. Any failure to satisfy the criteria that are laid out in B8, any account of a thing that makes that thing something that can come to be or pass away, or something divisible, or changing, or imperfect, is to take the route that is essentially negative and thus ruled out by the *krisis* "is or is not?"

> . . . ἡ δὲ κρίσις περὶ τούτων ἐν τῷδ' ἔστιν·
> ἔστιν ἢ οὐκ ἔστιν· κέκριται δ' οὖν, ὥσπερ ἀνάγκη,
> τὴν μὲν ἐᾶν ἀνόητον ἀνώνυμον (οὐ γὰρ ἀληθής
> ἔστιν ὁδός), τὴν δ' ὥστε πέλειν καὶ ἐτήτυμον εἶναι.
>
> (B8.15–18)

> . . . and the decision about these things is in this:
> is or is not; and it has been decided, just as is necessary,
> to leave the one unthinkable and unnamed (for it is not a true
> route), and the other to be and to be genuine.

Any hint of what-is-not in an account of what a thing really is disqualifies that account, for it is one that was reached via the negative route and so is not a genuine account at all. What Parmenides will show in B8 is that, despite appearances, mortals turn out to be on the negative path, though they think they are on the positive route. It is precisely in this belief that their "two-headedness" (B6.5) lies. For they believe that their account is of what something genuinely is, while they are at the same time (and unknowingly) actually saying something negative. Thus, agreeing that negative accounts are wrong, while at the same time trying to give an account that, according to the criteria of B8, turns out to be negative,

[98] This is often given as saying or thinking that non-existence exists. I have already discussed why I do not think this is the proper reading of the *esti* in Parmenides.

they must genuinely think that to be and not be are the same and not the same. It is this unwitting embrace of the negative route that the goddess refers to in her claim at B6.5–6 that "helplessness in their breasts guides their wandering *noos*" (ἀμηχανίη γὰρ ἐν αὐτῶν στήθεσιν ἰθύνει πλακτὸν νόον). Because they do not control their *noos* and pay attention to the *krisis*, mortals, who begin on the positive route, unwittingly wander off that route and on to the negative one; thus they deserve the epithet the goddess uses of them: they are hordes without judgment (*akrita phula*). Their failure to control *noos* and their lack of judgment is what leads them to be carried along "deaf as well as blind" (κωφοὶ ὁμῶς τυφλοί τε B6.7). Now, *kōphos* means "dull" or "obtuse" as much as "deaf," and *tuphlos* also can be used of errors in thought,[99] and this is surely the meaning intended here.[100] Mortals are obtuse and blind to the truth; they are "amazed" (*tethēpotes* B6.7) and are "carried along," uncritical, rather than systematically making their own way along the genuine route of inquiry.[101] Because of mortals' confusion about their own views, and their conflation of what-is and what-is-not, "the path of all is backward-turning" (πάντων δὲ παλίντροπός ἐστι κέλευθος B6.9).[102]

Having sketched out the state of mortals who conflate the two routes, in B7 the goddess once more exhorts the *kouros*:

> οὐ γὰρ μήποτε τοῦτο δαμῇ εἶναι μὴ ἐόντα·
> ἀλλὰ σύ τῆσδ' ἀφ' ὁδοῦ διζήσιος εἶργε νόημα,
> μηδέ σ' ἔθος πολύπειρον ὁδὸν κατὰ τήνδε βιάσθω,
> νωμᾶν ἄσκοπον ὄμμα καὶ ἠχήεσσαν ἀκουήν
> καὶ γλῶσσαν, κρῖναι δὲ λόγῳ πολύδηριν ἔλεγχον
> ἐξ ἐμέθεν ῥηθέντα.

99 Most commentators seem to take the terms this way, though without specifically discussing the line. Tarán treats *tuphlos* as characterizing intellectual error; see p. 63. He finds a parallel use in Pindar (*Pae.* 7b 13ff.). Coxon, on the other hand, takes the terms literally, as a "failure in the exercise of the senses" (*Fragments*, p. 186).

100 See, for instance, Sophocles, *O.T.* 370–71: σοὶ δὲ τοῦτ' οὐκ ἔστ', ἐπεὶ τυφλὸς τά τ' ὦτα τόν τε νοῦν τά τ' ὄμματ' εἶ (it is not for you because you are blind in your ears and your *nous* as well as in your eyes).

101 Heraclitus had used similar language to make a similar complaint: at 22B34 he says that those who are uncomprehending (of the *logos*) "hear as the deaf do" (ἀξύνετοι ἀκούσαντες κωφοῖσιν ἐοίκασι).

102 Does *pantōn* refer to the beliefs of mortals, to the path mortals take, or to things in the phenomenal world? I think the most natural reading is to take it as part of the goddess's abuse of mortals themselves and so to refer to both their beliefs and the path they follow (which are, after all, related). Because their *noos* wanders, they cannot keep on the straight or genuine path of inquiry, and so both their journey, and also their accounts of what things are, are backward turning. I think that is particularly true of the mortal belief given in the *Doxa*, where the fundamental entities, Light and Night, turn out to be opposites that must each be defined in terms of what the other is not. I discuss this further in Chap. III.

For never shall this be forced through:[103] that things that are not are;
but you hold back your thought from this route of inquiry,
nor let much-experienced habit force you along this path,
to ply an aimless eye and resounding ear
and tongue, but judge by *logos* the much-contested testing
spoken by me.

She begins by recapitulating her claim about the impossibility of what-is-not (first made in the assertion at B2.5–8 that the route of what-is-not is not a genuine route): what-is-not cannot be and can never be proved to be. Nevertheless, habit or custom may overcome us and through inattention we may wander onto the negative route. But if we do so, in attempting to give a negative explanation of the character of a thing, we are plying an aimless eye and echoing ear and tongue as we wander this route, and we will actually learn nothing and say nothing.[104] Lines B7.4–5 are often taken as criticism of attempts to base an account of what-is on sensory experience.[105] This is undeniable; for certainly accounts of what-is that are based on experience will attempt to say that what-is comes into being, changes, is in different ways at different times, and so on. But we can also read these lines as predicting the condition of one who tries to give a negative account of what a thing really is. To say that *X* is really not-*F*, or to attribute to *X* a nature or character that contains negative elements is to make a statement that is steeped in vagueness, which gives one nothing on which to pin one's thought and so *noos* is left wandering. For such a one, there is nothing on which to fix a therefore "aimless eye"; his tongue "echoes," for in saying that what-is both is and is not, he is saying nothing, as he tries to formulate the negative account. On the other hand, a proper explanation, which goes straight to the

[103] The common translation of οὐ γὰρ μήποτε τοῦτο δαμῇ as "never shall this be proved" has been challenged by Coxon (*Fragments*, p. 190). Coxon takes *damnēmi* "in its regular sense of 'be defeated' " and takes *touto* to refer to the *poludēris elenchos* of line 5. This seems a rather long way for the reference to go. Tarán translates "never shall this be forced" (*Parmenides*, p. 73; see his discussion on pp. 73–75). In the context of the goddess's assertion that the *kouros* must judge and think for himself, the claim that what-is-not is can be forced through only by being proved to be the case. See also Mourelatos, *Route*, p. 28n.57. There is a connection with the testing of line 5, for what-is-not can never "win the contest" by surviving the tests the goddess proposes.

[104] The eye is "aimless" because there is nothing definite on which it can be fixed; the tongue "echoes" because it says both what is and what is not; likewise the ear, having nothing definite to hear, gives false readings, Sense perception cannot be a trustworthy source of understanding since it does not direct *noos* to what-is, but rather attempts to represent what-is-not. See Mourelatos, " 'Nothing,' " who carefully distinguishes the existential and characterizing senses of nothing and not-being. Parmenides objects to the attempt to characterize a thing negatively and suggests that reliance on sense perception will always, through misdirecting *noos*, encourage one to make such an attempt.

[105] See, for instance, Lesher, "Philosophical Interest," pp. 24–25; Coxon, *Fragments*, pp. 189–92; Coxon also reads B6.5–9 as an attack on belief in the reality of sensible objects.

genuine nature of a thing, gives us a meaningful story to be told, and a target at which to aim our thought.[106] While this route is not a genuine route of inquiry (because what is not cannot be), it is one easy to attempt, through custom or habit or inattention. Thus, the stern warning of B7 not to become a victim of habit and sloppy thought, but to judge by thought, argument, or reasoning the many-faceted test that the goddess speaks.[107]

The goddess's *poludēris elenchos* is a multiple testing of and challenge to a candidate for what-is.[108] The *elenchos* tests the candidate for genuineness, using the tests that are signaled by the many signs of B8.2–3 (ταύτῃ δ' ἐπὶ σήματ' ἔασι πολλὰ μάλ'). Because B8 will enumerate (and argue for) several criteria for what is, the *elenchos* can be said to be *poludēris*, or "much-contesting" or "much contested." Further, because the tests involve checking a candidate against a criterion, the process will result in a *krisis* that is made on the basis of judgments, first, about the fittingness of the sign, and second, about whether the candidate actually satisfies the criterion announced in the sign. The first judgment comes in listening to and evaluating the goddess's own arguments in B8.1–49, while the second occurs in putting the arguments of B8 to use in assessing claims about what-is. Thus, we must judge, on the evidence, using our capacities to think and understand, rather than letting our thought (*noēma*) be persuaded by habit or past experience, in contrast to the mortals on the mistaken way. Those taking the genuine path of inquiry

[106] See Mourelatos, "Determinacy and Indeterminacy," p. 59: "Just as the structure of wandering is random-like, un-targeted (cf. B7.4 . . .) and centrifugal, the structure of the sort of 'intelligent pointing' (*phrazein*) involved in directing ourselves to the real thing is centripetal and target-oriented." The wandering, unfixed eye and echoing tongue are particularly apt as descriptions of trying to give an explanation in terms of opposites that are each defined as the negation of the other. Such an account can never be completed. This constitutes an answer to objections to Mourelatos's position raised by Furley in "Notes."

[107] Mourelatos has argued against taking *poludēris elenchos* as "much-contested testing" (*Route*, p. 91n.46). Following Verdenius, he notes that the aorist *rhēthenta* "shows that the ἔλεγχος has already been delivered." Thus it cannot, he argues, refer to arguments that are going to be given in B8. He interprets *elenchos* as being closer to the Homeric notion of "blame" or "reproach"—thus the goddess issues a "very contentious challenge" (Mourelatos's translation) in B6 and B7; and it is this challenge that the *kouros* must judge. Lesher has, I think, shown that the notion of testing is included in uses of *elenchos* at the time of Parmenides (see "Parmenides' Critique"), but he has difficulty in finding where a testing of the appropriate sort has taken place before the end of B7. These views can, I think, be reconciled. The goddess denounces mortal thinking in B6 and B7; this is invective (an *elenchos* in the old, Homeric, sense), and it has indeed been spoken by the end of B7. But the *kouros* must not accept the goddess's claims simply because it is she who has uttered them. He must judge, putting her words to the test, an *elenchos* in the sense of "trying" or "testing." And since the tests themselves are arguments that the goddess utters, the *poludēris elenchos* in this sense also comes from the goddess. Her invective is justified only to the extent that the tests of B8 succeed in ruling out all and only unsuccessful candidates for what-is.

[108] Rather than the "refutation" that disqualifies the negative route, as Furley would have it (Furley, "Truth"). See Lesher, "Parmenides' Critique of Thinking," and "Philosophical Interest in Cognition," pp. 24–26, esp. n. 49, on this issue.

can be said to judge by *logos*, here understood as "thought," "reckoning," or "discourse."[109] Thus, they make a judgment, not on the basis of habit or experience, but after having listened to and considered the account that the goddess has given in the *Alētheia* and in the *Doxa*.

One who has judged correctly will succeed in following out an inquiry on the road "that it is," and will complete an account of what something genuinely is. But, even at the end of B7, we do not yet know what such an account will be like. It is in working through the details of the arguments of B8 that we learn the criteria required of any successful story of the nature or character of a thing. And it is in B8 that we meet a crucial and most controversial aspect of Parmenides' theory, his monism. It is to those issues that I turn in the next chapter.

[109] For a survey of uses of *logos* see Guthrie, *HGP*, vol. I, pp. 419–24. It is probable that *logos* here does not mean "reason," if by that we mean the faculty of reason. But it might well mean something like "thought" or "reasoning:" "As early as Parmenides, *logos* in this sense can be opposed, as thought or reasoning, to mere sensation" (Guthrie, *HGP*, vol. I, p. 421). In Aeschylus, *logos* commonly means "story" or "account"; but it occasionally has overtones of "thought" or "argument," with overtones of consideration and reckoning. At *Pers*. 170–71, the Queen asks for advice, urging that her advisors "become counselors of the *logos* for me" (σύμβουλοι λόγου τοῦδέ μοι γένεσθε). Similarly, at *Ch*. 521, Orestes claims "the work is in vain; ὧδ' ἔχει λόγος," literally, "the *logos* is this," which could be taken as "That's how I reckon it." Finally, at *Eu*. 227 the chorus of Eumenides urge Apollo, τιμὰς σὺ μὴ ξύντεμνε τὰς ἐμὰς λόγῳ: "Do not curtail my honors by *logos*." Apollo is trying to persuade the Eumenides to leave Orestes alone; he gives them reasons, so the translation "by argument" is possible. In all three of these occurrences of *logos*, there is a process of taking thought, and of reckoning or argument occurring. In Euripides, *Medea* 872, Guthrie understands "I had a *logos* with myself" as "I have thought it over." It is, I think, this sense that is at work in B7.5. It is worth noting that while Coxon translates *logos* as "discourse," in his commentary on the passage he glosses it as "judge by reason" (p. 192).

II

Parmenides' Monism and the Arguments of B8

AN INTERPRETATION of Parmenides that places his interests firmly in the tradition of Presocratic cosmology, and that argues that Parmenides was more interested in reforming cosmological inquiry than in rejecting it (such as the one that I have offered in the previous chapter) faces one obvious objection: Parmenides is widely supposed to be a monist, who insists that only a single thing (variously called "the One," "the All," or even "Being") exists. One of the earliest records of this view of Parmenides is in Plato's dialogue, the *Parmenides,* in which Zeno describes himself as having defended his master's monism from the attacks of those who find such a view ridiculous (*Prm.* 128b7–e4). Parmenides is shown as adopting his own thesis "that there is a One" as a subject for the "laborious game" that constitutes the second part of the dialogue (*Prm.* 137b3–4).[1] Similar accounts of Parmenides' monism are found in Aristotle and Theophrastus, and in the doxography that descends from them.[2]

It is a commonplace (as common as the assertion that Parmenides was a monist) that the arguments of Parmenides were crucial to those philosophers who came after him; indeed it is inviting to read the history of later Presocratic philosophy as a series of responses to those arguments.[3] But the major post-Parmenidean theories, Pluralism, Atomism, and Plato's Theory of Forms, different though they be in many respects, share a common characteristic: all posit a numerical plurality of fundamental entities. Moreover, those who

[1] Other references to Parmenides' monism in Plato are at *Tht.* 180e and *Sph.* 242d.

[2] Aristotle *Metaph.* 986b18; Simplicius (*in Ph.* 115.11ff.; 28A28) attributes monism to Parmenides, quoting Theophrastus, Eudemus, and Alexander; Plutarch, in *adv. Col* (1114D; 28A34) claims that Parmenides calls "what belongs to the realm of intellect 'one and being.' " Hippolytus (*Haer.* I.11; 28A23) attributes to Parmenides the claims that "the all is one and eternal and ungenerated and spherical." See Barnes, "Eleatic One," p. 3n.8, who notes that much Neoplatonist interpretation of Parmenides is "unhistorical."

[3] Such a view is to be found in many (English) histories of Greek philosophy: for instance in Guthrie (*HGP*), in Kirk and Raven (KR, followed in KRS), and in McKirahan. It is implicit in the section heading of Barnes's *PP*: the sections are called "Eden," "The Serpent," and "Paradise Regained." Although Barnes is careful to avoid over-stressing the "response to Parmenides" aspect of Presocratic thought, he speaks of the "Neo-Ionian counter-reformation" (vol. II, p. 15; see also pp. 11–15 of that volume). For a different view of the relations between the Eleatics and later Presocratic thinkers, see Mourelatos, "Quality."

adopt pluralistic theories give no arguments to justify their pluralism. Such an assumption of pluralism, without argument, would beg the question against Parmenides the monist.[4] While the tradition that Parmenides is a monist is strong, doubts have been raised.[5] Is Parmenides a monist? If so, what sort of monist is he? In this chapter I shall argue for an interpretation of Parmenides' monism that makes his view compatible with a plurality of basic entities. On the view that I shall defend, an explanation of the nature of the things that are and of the *kosmos* can begin with a plurality of metaphysically basic entities yet still meet the requirements for an acceptable theory that Parmenides lays out in B8.

1. Monism

It is possible to distinguish at least three varieties of monism: material, numerical, and what I call predicational monism. The first asserts that there is a single underlying stuff out of which the *kosmos* is made. Such a material monism is consistent with the existence in the world of many things or items, but each is made out of or is a modification of the single material stuff. This is the monism of Thales and Anaximenes.[6] The second, numerical

[4] It might be objected that the Pluralists do not actually beg the question against Parmenides: if he gives an argument whose conclusion is *M*, while they provide an argument that concludes *not-M,* then they have succeeded in showing his argument to be unsound without begging the question. But this is not the Pluralists' procedure. They begin by positing a numerical plurality, rather than arguing for it; this is the unacceptable move. Some commentators have explained the Pluralist reluctance to argue for Pluralism by claiming that such an argument is not necessary. Furth calls the absence of an argument for Pluralism in Anaxagoras a "trifling objection" ("Philosophical Hero," p. 103n.8), while Inwood claims that Parmenides' lack of "a clear argument against plurality" shows that Empedocles "need not argue for plurality" (*Empedocles*, pp. 23–24).

[5] The view that Parmenides was a numerical monist is to be found in all the standard histories of Presocratic thought (except Barnes's), and in most discussions of Parmenides. Barnes's comment is particularly apt: "Monism is such a familiar feature of Eleatic thought that it is rarely discussed: there are plenty of confident ascriptions . . . but few argue for the ascription or attempt to imagine what real monism means" ("Eleatic One", p. 2n.3). For questions about Parmenides' monism, see Jones; Barnes, "Eleatic One," and *PP*, vol. I, pp. 204–7; Mourelatos, *Route* and "Alternatives"; and Solmsen, "The 'Eleatic One' in Melissus" and "The Tradition about Zeno." I raised doubts in "Monism," and here develop further ideas I first proposed there. In response to Solmsen on Zeno, see Vlastos, "Plato's Testimony." Jones's comment ("Way of Truth," p. 296) is appropriate: "The important point [is] that [Parmenides] did hold that reality is one and continuous. This, however, does not as such commit him to any position as regards the question of whether or not being, as a whole, is one monolithic lump. He can maintain quite consistently that all that he has shown is that all the various entities in the world have each the same ontological status."

[6] The case of Anaximander is more complex. He begins with a single thing, the *apeiron*, and from it the *kosmos* as we know it comes to be through a series of stages, beginning when "something productive of hot and cold" [Plutarch], *Strom.* 2; 12A10) separated out of the

monism, claims that there is only one thing or item in the universe. This is the monism that has traditionally been attributed to Parmenides and to Melissus.[7] It is not clear whether or not numerical monism also admits the possibility that the single item can hold more than one predicate. It may or may not be permissible to say any more than "what-is is."[8] The third, predicational monism, is the claim that each thing that is can be only one thing; it can hold only the one predicate that indicates what it is, and must hold it in a particularly strong way. To be a genuine entity, a thing must be a predicational unity, with a single account of what it is; but it need not be the case that there exists only one such thing. Rather, the thing itself must be a unified whole. If it is, say *F*, it must be all, only, and completely *F*. On predicational monism, a numerical plurality of such one-beings (as we might call them) is possible.

There are a number of combinations possible among these three sorts of monism; for example, a theory might adopt both predicational and numerical monism; a numerical monist might also hold material monism; numerical pluralism might be combined with material monism or with predicational monism. For instance, Anaximenes' assertions about air suggest material monism, yet he claims that there are numerically many objects, distinguished by the degree of condensation or rarefaction of the single material constituent that they all have in common.

In this chapter I argue that Parmenides is indeed a monist, though he adopts neither material nor numerical monism. Rather, his arguments in B8 about the only genuine route of inquiry show him to be committed to predicational monism.[9] Whatever genuinely is must be a predicational unity; but this is consistent with there being many things, each of which is one

---

apeiron. The action of these opposites then is responsible for the rest of the becoming that takes place (because the ball of flame that they give rise to is the source of the sun, moon, stars, etc.). If we are willing to countenance the *apeiron* as some kind of matter-stuff, then Anaximander, too, is a material monist.

7 This is what is normally meant when "monism" *simpliciter* is attributed to Parmenides; Barnes calls it "real monism" and contrasts it with material monism. "Eleatic One," p. 2: " 'Exactly one thing exists.' That is the intoxicating thesis of 'real' monism. It is, of course, utterly distinct from its milksop homonym, 'material' monism, which maintains that everything is made of some single matter or stuff."

8 Furth, in "Elements," takes the stronger view; the weaker is to be found in Austin, *Being*.

9 Barnes, then, is correct (in "Eleatic One") to deny that Parmenides adopts numerical monism (although I do not endorse all of his particular arguments against real monism). But Barnes rejects the ascription of any sort of monism to Parmenides. Because Barnes insists on an existential "is" in Parmenides and does not recognize the possibility of predicational monism, he does not consider that Parmenides is committed to a type of monism. Parmenides himself speaks of the unity of what-is and argues that being is both *suneches* (continuous) and *mounogenes* (of a single kind). I will argue that these claims (along with the other signs of B8.1–6) commit Parmenides to predicational monism. I do not, of course, mean that Parmenides formulated a theory to which he gave the name *predicational monism*. Rather, given that these three types of monism can be distinguished, attributing this view to him helps to clarify Parmenides' position.

in the appropriate sense. In the arguments of B2 to B7, as we have seen, Parmenides shows that only the route of what-is is a genuine path of inquiry. But the content of that route has not yet been discussed. That is the task of the arguments of B8.1–49, where the signs along the genuine path are given and explained. It is there that we find a monism that is consistent with numerical plurality and is suitable for a theory that seeks to account for the appropriate way to explain the nature of a thing in a world that may contain many entities. There is a symmetry between natures and accounts or explanations of natures throughout the poem. The *sēmata* of B8 both point out the characteristics of what-is and serve as principles to be followed in reaching an adequate account of what-is.[10] The evidence of the fragments themselves, particularly the emphasis on the proper "route of inquiry for thinking" suggests that Parmenides was interested both in the criteria for a proper account of what-is—that is, the fundamental entity or entities in an account of nature of the *kosmos*—as well as in the metaphysical requirements any such entity must meet.[11] As such, this interest need not constrain him to adopt monism of any sort. But working through the arguments of B8, we shall find that only those entities that are predicationally one can satisfy the requirements for what-is that are elucidated in those arguments, and so only an account that preserves predicational monism can succeed.

B4 provides a preliminary hint about the internal unity of what-is.[12] In the last chapter I argued that B4 has both epistemological and metaphysical implications. It asserts that what-is is firmly present to the mind (νόῳ παρεόντα βεβαίως):

> οὐ γὰρ ἀποτμήξει τὸ ἐὸν τοῦ ἐόντος ἔχεσθαι
> οὔτε σκιδνάμενον πάντῃ πάντως κατὰ κόσμον
> οὔτε συνιστάμενον. (B4.2–4)
>
> for you will not cut off what is from holding to what is,
> neither dispersing in every way everywhere in order,
> nor gathering together.

Aristotle distinguishes between two sorts of monism in his claim in *Metaph.* I.5 that Parmenides concerns himself with what is one in *logos* while Melissus concentrates on what is one in matter (986b18–21).

[10] This is why Parmenides can implicitly criticize the route of mortals in B8 while spelling out what it is to be a fundamental entity. The *krisis* "is or is not" that functions in the arguments of B8 as a means to determining the characteristics of what-is also works as a test for an acceptable route of inquiry, or for an acceptable account of what there is.

[11] Such an entity, after all, is the goal of the route of inquiry.

[12] Because there is no context provided for B4, we cannot be sure just where in the first part of the poem it comes. (Clement, our only source for the complete fragment, quotes it in the midst of a discussion of hope and remarks that Parmenides speaks in a riddling fashion here.) Given the transition to the *Doxa* in B8, it seems likely (as a number of commentators point out) that it was meant to be read before the specific arguments of B8.

The connection between authentic thinking and what-is, expressed in B3, guarantees that genuine thought about what-is will be true; but that guarantee of truth holds only if what-is is itself something that holds together. The last three lines of B4 promise that there are no internal distinctions or gaps in what-is that could allow *noos* to wander away from it on to the path of what-is-not. In contrast to the "things grasped together" (*sullapsies*) of Heraclitus B10, which are both wholes and not wholes, both brought together and separated, and both consonant and dissonant,[13] what-is in Parmenides is at rest and stable, all together and so able to be grasped by inquiring *noos*. But a lack of internal divisions does not entail that there are no external numerical divisions; there is no insistence that there can only be numerically one such being. Rather, there are no predicational divisions within what-is, for all of it is alike—just what it is. Should it be *F*, it is all and only *F* with no possibility that it can also be *G*. For if it were such a plurality, it could be scattered in thought into its *F* and *G* components. Its predicational unity guarantees that it can be understood by thought, with no internal negations that would prevent *noos* from grasping it, or that would allow *noos* to wander away from what-is onto the negative route.

Fragment 8 opens with the claim that a single route remains and with an announcement of the signs that are to be found on the route. The signs are preliminary statements of the character of what-is:

> . . . μόνος δ' ἔτι μῦθος ὁδοῖο
> λείπεται ὡς ἔστιν· ταύτῃ δ' ἐπὶ σήματ' ἔασι
> πολλὰ μάλ', ὡς ἀγένητον ἐὸν καὶ ἀνώλεθρόν ἐστιν,
> οὖλον μουνογενές[14] τε καὶ ἀτρεμὲς ἠδὲ τέλειον·[15]
> οὐδέ ποτ' ἦν οὐδ' ἔσται, ἐπεὶ νῦν ἔστιν ὁμοῦ πᾶν
> ἕν, συνεχές· (B8.1–6)

> . . . a single account still
> remains of the route that it is; and on this route there are
> very many signs, that what is is ungenerable and imperishable,
> a whole of a single kind, and unshaking and complete;
> nor was it nor will it be, since it is now all together
> one, cohesive.

[13] Reading συλλάψιες here with Kirk, Marcovich, Kahn (*Art and Thought*), and Robinson (*Heraclitus*). For discussions of the difficulties of this text, see Kirk and Marcovich. This fragment is probably a discussion of things grasped by the mind or understanding and the unity of opposites: ἐκ πάντων ἓν καὶ ἐξ ἑνὸς πάντα.

[14] On οὖλον μουνογενές (found in Simplicius, Philoponus, Clement, Eusebius, and Theodoretus; though Eusebius and Theodoretus also give μοῦνον μουνογενές) rather than DK's ἐστι γὰρ οὐλομελές (following Plutarch), see Tarán, *Parmenides*, pp. 88–93, Coxon, *Fragments*, p. 195, and Barnes, "Eleatic One," pp. 8–9 with notes.

[15] ἠδὲ τέλειον: following Owen ("Eleatic Questions," Additional Note A, pp. 23–24); see also Coxon, *Fragments*, pp. 195–96. DK: ἠδ' ἀτέλεστον.

Lines B8.1–6 do not contain Parmenides' arguments about the character of what-is; rather these lines are what the goddess says they are: announcements of the signs that will lead thought along the correct route of inquiry into what is. The actual proofs that establish the character of what-is appear in the later lines B8.6–49. This prologue to the arguments announces four signs of what-is. It is (1) ungenerable and indestructible, (2) indivisible, (3) immobile, and (4) complete or perfect. It is difficult to determine exactly the relations among these characteristics. It is true that in B5 the goddess has said that it does not matter where she begins: "for I shall return there again" (τόθι γὰρ πάλιν ἵξομαι αὖθις). But these two lines of B5 have themselves proved puzzling, for the proper route, as it is illustrated in B8, is not circular, and to look for such a circular path is to put the emphasis in the wrong place. What the goddess says in B2, B6, B7, and B8 indicates that the route to what-is leads straight on to what-is, in contrast with the wandering and backward-turning route that mortals take. The goddess's remarks in B5 should be taken, not as a description of the route, but as an account of the various characteristics of what-is. The various attributes of what-is are related as connected aspects of one and the same thing, and they are linked because each attribute follows directly or indirectly from the *krisis* or decision between is and is not. The fundamental character of what-is depends on the impossibility of what-is-not, and once that is granted, one comes to see that the various attributes of what-is interconnect. Whatever aspect of what-is that we begin with, we will eventually reach the others.[16] So, it does not matter to the goddess where she begins in the catalogue of the nature of what-is; she will end up there again by coming full circle in her story of how it is. Her hearers move toward what-is by working through the proofs of B8 and applying the *krisis*. But what-is is simply there: whole and complete, unchanging and cohesive; and it makes no difference where the description of what-is, or the arguments about it, begin, for any one of its attributes ultimately entails all the others.

Lines 4 and 5–6 of the announcement attribute some sort of unity to what is. But should we identify this unity with numerical monism? I shall argue that it is not numerical but predicational monism that is announced here, for only a predicational unity can satisfy both the requirement of B2 that what-is be and have no tinge of what-is-not, and the criteria for what-is explored in B8.6–49.

The programmatic announcement of B8.1–6 says that the genuine route of inquiry leads to something that is ungenerable and imperishable; a perfect, complete, and cohesive whole of a single kind. What could such a thing be?

[16] This is the case even if some of the attributes of what-is depend on others; for instance, it seems that the discussions of the characteristics "unshaking" and "complete" depend on the proofs of ungenerability and cohesiveness. Were we to begin with the completeness of what-is, we would have to pause to consider whether anything else could come to be in order to complete it, or whether it is divisible and so could lack a part of itself.

In the last chapter I argued that Parmenides was concerned with the proper route of inquiry into the nature of a thing. If that is so, then he is discussing the ultimate entities that his predecessors thought to underlie and explain the appearances of the sensible world.[17] If this is the issue that Parmenides is addressing, then simple numerical or even material monism miss the mark as adequate answers to his concerns. Thales apparently said that there is only one genuinely real thing: water.[18] But clearly this material monism could not be a proper response to Parmenides' arguments. For Parmenides asks if the water that Thales postulates as an underlying reality can actually serve in that capacity. If it turns out that water is generable, or perishable, or is not a complete and cohesive whole of a single kind, then despite being a

[17] At this point it is irrelevant whether or not Parmenides thinks one can actually succeed in giving such an account of the sensible world; that depends on the interpretation we give of B1.28–30 and of the *Doxa*. These are issues I take up in Chap. III. A different view of Parmenides' aims is given in a series of articles by T. M. Robinson. (See "Ascertainment of the Real," "Parmenides on the Real," and "Parmenides and Heraclitus.") Robinson rightly argues that Parmenides' concern is what can be known or ascertained, rather than what can simply be thought, as on Owen's view, and he maintains that the correct object of such ascertainment is "the real"—that which is. On Robinson's view, the real is, for Parmenides, eternal and is a partless whole or totality; it is thus "co-extensive with what is normally referred to as the world, in the sense of all that exists and/or all that is the case" ("Parmenides and Heraclitus," p. 157). This reality cannot be divided into smaller parts that can themselves be the objects of discernment (thus Robinson seems committed to a genuine numerical monism for what is real), although mortal thinkers take themselves to be ascertaining the real when they perceive a plurality of changing sensible objects; indeed, the real is the "unappreciated referent" of various mortal assertions ("Ascertainment," pp. 631 and 632). Robinson takes literally the likening of the completeness of what is to the bulk of a well-rounded sphere: "these references . . . seem to me still most naturally taken literally as a reference to a limited, spheroid reality" ("Parmenides on the Real," p. 56). Genuine ascertainment is always formulable; one who knows is able to give an account: "Reality, knowledge and a rational account (λόγος) go hand in hand" ("Parmenides and Heraclitus," p. 157). On Robinson's view, human perception and language is misleading insofar as it presents a real that is fragmented and changing; nevertheless, human utterances and thoughts are valuable because they "point obliquely to the fact that there is a real to be so misdescribed" ("Parmenides and Heraclitus," p. 162). The world of change that is reported by our senses is not "non-existent"; it is simply "the world—our world—as it presents itself to opinion (δόξα)" ("Parmenides and Heraclitus," p. 165). There is much that is attractive in this view. Robinson's emphasis on the essential interconnectedness of what-is and what can be known points out an important aspect of Parmenides' thought, and his account of how mortal thought aims at but misses what-is seems right. I am less convinced that Parmenides' subject is the real in its totality, if by that is meant a single thing, rather than all the things that genuinely are, and as will be seen in my analyses of the relevant passages in B8, I am not convinced that the comparison with the bulk of a sphere should be read literally. My reading of the *Doxa* section of the poem also differs from Robinson's.

[18] This, at any rate, is one way to interpret Aristotle's claim that for Thales water is the ultimate principle of what there is (*Metaph.* 986b17–27). At issue is whether or not Thales would say that water itself changes, and whether the various things that come to be out of water have being in their own right. Should he claim that only watery stuff (or matter) is real, then he would be both a numerical and a material monist.

single thing that is supposedly named or called "what-is," it cannot be a genuine entity and thus cannot constitute the nature of anything. If Thales were to accept Parmenides' claims that what-is is complete, whole, ungenerable, and imperishable, he would be, so far, correct, for Parmenides would concede that Thales had given the right requirements for what there is. If, in agreeing with Parmenides, Thales were to add that water satisfies these criteria, then he and Parmenides would have something further to discuss: it must be shown that in underlying the phenomenal world, water itself does not undergo any of the processes of change, or admit any sort of not-being, in the ways that are forbidden by the arguments of B8. Parmenides gives the criteria for the genuine reality of what there is, and it remains to be seen whether or not any of the candidates for the position are successful.

At B8.4 what-is (*to eon*) is said to be *mounogenes*, "of a single kind." LSJ refer to B8.4 as evidence for the translation of *mounogenes* as "unique," and this is the translation adopted by Coxon and Tarán. Thus the appearance of *mounogenes* in the list of signs would seem to support numerical monism in Parmenides. But both Mourelatos and Barnes argue that in Parmenides *mounogenes* should be understood as deriving from *genos* ("kind" or "genus") rather than from *gignesthai* (to come to be).[19] Thus, what-is is *mounogenes* in the sense of "belonging to only one kind" rather than "only-begotten" or "unique."[20] It is precisely its being *mounogenes* that guarantees the claims of B4 that what-is cannot be scattered and gathered. That it is of a single kind ensures the internal monogeneity of what-is: and this is precisely predicational monism.[21] Lines B8.22–25, which argue that *to eon*

[19] Mourelatos, *Route*, pp. 113–14; Barnes, "Eleatic One," pp. 8–9 (with n. 23), 17.

[20] As Barnes has pointed out ("Eleatic One," p. 22), given that Parmenides is about to argue that there is no coming-to-be for what-is and has announced that it is *agenēton* (ungenerable) in B8.3, it would be odd for him to assert that this *agenēton* (unbegotten) thing is *mounogenes*—an "only-begotten" thing. Mourelatos notes the parallel with Hesiod, *Op.* 11–12. Hesiod asserts that there is not a single kind of strife, but two: οὐκ ἄρα μοῦνον ἔην Ἐρίδων γένος . . .; Parmenides claims that what-is is *mounogenes*. See West, *Hesiod: Works and Days*, pp. 142–43.

[21] Makin, criticizing the view for which I argued in "Monism" (*Indifference,* p. 46n.38), asserts that the only monism that Parmenides argues for is numerical monism. Makin claims that homogeneity alone will not guarantee predicational monism, for something can be a homogeneous spherical warm green solid. But Parmenides does not claim that what-is is merely homogeneous; he says that it is monogeneous, of a single kind, which precludes there being two kinds smoothly mixed together. So, on Parmenides' view, Makin's warm, green, spherical solid is ruled out from the beginning; such a thing would both be and not be in the forbidden sense. Further, Makin claims that Parmenides' argument that what-is is indivisible entails numerical monism. There are two problems with this. First, it depends on an existential reading of the *esti* in Parmenides which Makin adopts without argument (although on p. 31 he mentions a possible predicational reading without exploring the implications of such a view for the claim that what-is is indivisible). On predicational monism each thing that is is indivisible, in a manner consistent with Parmenides' argument in B8. Those claims show how what-is is: it is indivisibly, wholly, and so on. Second, because Makin discusses only lines B8.22–25, he does

is not divisible, and which contain the arguments that correspond to the announcement that what-is is *mounogenes*, echo the claims of B4. There is nothing internal to what-is that could prevent it from cohering with itself (B8.23); "it is all full of what is" (πᾶν δ' ἔμπλεόν ἐστιν ἐόντος B8.24), and so "it is all cohesive; what is draws near to what is" (τῷ ξυνεχὲς πᾶν ἐστιν· ἐὸν γὰρ ἐόντι πελάζει B8.25). Its cohesiveness guarantees that what-is cannot be divided from itself, which further ensures that it is all alike.[22] But this entails that whatever characteristic something that is has, that thing can have only that character, for it is *mounogenes*.[23] It is exactly this point that Plato

not consider how the various arguments of B8 depend on one another and work together to present a unified picture of the nature of what-is. This restriction to four lines of B8 means that Makin does not link the claim that what-is is indivisible with the claim that it is *mounogenes*, and that he does not discuss what being *mounogenes* and indivisible might mean in the larger context of Parmenides' whole project. Makin's comments on p. 33 suggest that he thinks that Parmenides' subject is something one might call "Being as a whole," which cannot be divided into the discrete units of a numerical plurality: "What-is is homogeneous in that it is a seamless whole." But I do not think that this is Parmenides' subject or that Makin's arguments rule out the possibility of a plurality of predicational wholes. Makin does not consider the possibility that Parmenides' concern might be something other than "what can be thought about." My arguments here and in "Monism" depend on a view of Parmenides developed by considering the larger issues raised by the poem as a whole. I discuss B8.22–25 more fully below, in Section 2.

22 It might be thought that the assertion that what-is is *mounogenes*, when combined with the claim that "what-is draws near to what is" (ἐὸν γὰρ ἐόντι πελάζει), which appears in the proof of this sign (at B8.25), means that all of what-is belongs to the single kind, being. This would entail that there is indeed but a single thing, being, and Parmenides would be committed to numerical monism. If this is correct, then when Parmenides speaks of *to eon*, we must understand him to mean by it "being" rather than "what is." Burnet argued persuasively that this is not correct; see also Robinson, "Ascertainment of the Real," p. 628, who argues that "το ἐόν . . . unpacks simply and neutrally into 'that which is.' " Moreover, this reading of the line is at odds with the strongly predicative reading of the *esti*. This reading of the *esti* is, as I have argued in Chap. I, the most likely in the overall context of the poem.

23 The linking of *xuneches* with *mounogenes* is important here, for that link excludes certain sorts of apparent unities that might be thought to be *xuneches*. Consider the number 5. It is a whole, and it seems to be continuous; yet it also appears to be both varied and divisible, since it contains within itself both 3 and 2. The same difficulty arises with certain complex Aristotelian forms (for instance, if to be a human being is to be a rational animal, here is a unity that is continuous, but apparently varied, and in some sense, divisible). Were Parmenides to be confronted with such apparent counter-examples, I think that he would deny that these are actual unities. For the number 5, on post-Parmenidean Pythagorean number theory, is actually composed out of odd and even and is thus not a real unity but a combination (see Alexander, *in Metaph.* 39.8–13). As such it is not *mounogenes*. The same response, from Parmenides' point of view, might well be given to the problem of the unity of an Aristotelian (or late Platonic) form (and Aristotle himself worries about the unity of definition in *Metaph.* VII.12). These examples raise problems for the Parmenidean view but are not, I think, genuine counter-examples to this account of Parmenides. While they depend on notions of unity that develop out of Parmenides' concern with internal predicational monism, they are formulated in terms that already involve rejecting fundamental aspects of Parmenides' account, and particularly the notion that what is must be *mounogenes*. In the *Sophist* Plato puts the difficulty in terms of how we can call one thing by many names (251a5–6) and presents this as part of the solution to the problem

sees and exploits in his account of the Form of Beauty in the *Symposium*, saying there that the form is *monoeides* (one in form, 211b1). The parallel between Plato and Parmenides is striking, for Plato takes over predicational monism from Parmenides in the notion that a form is single-in-genus, while accepting that this is consistent with a plurality of forms.[24]

The word *hen* (one) appears in line 6 of the programmatic announcement. It is clear that Parmenides wishes to attribute some sort of unity to what is; but the claim need not commit him to numerical monism. For here *hen* is part of the attribution of cohesiveness to what-is.[25] Tarán, Gallop, and Coxon, along with KRS, all place a comma after *pan* in line 4, just before the *hen* of line 5. But Mourelatos, followed by Austin, argues that the words ἐπεὶ νῦν ἔστιν ὁμοῦ πᾶν ἕν (since it is now all [of it] together one) in lines 5–6 mark a single sequence of thought, directed at the internal unity of what is, which prevents it from differing in the past or future. This unity is then glossed by *suneches* (cohesive), which follows in line 6. As part of the larger claim about the cohesive nature of what is, the assertion that *to eon* is *hen* reads much more naturally as a claim about the internal or predicational unity of what-is (only what is one can be) rather than as an assertion of numerical monism (only one thing can be).

This interpretation provides a means for understanding Parmenides' depiction of the predicament of the mortals in B6 and B7. Mortals are undiscerning hordes (B6.7); knowing nothing they wander two-headed (B6.5); moreover they have wandering minds (B6.6) and their path turns back on itself (B6.9). Parmenides' charge that they are uncritical (*akrita*) connects their fate with the much-contested testing (*poludēris elenchos*) of B7.5, the *krisis* of B8.15–16, and the first statement of the routes of inquiry in B2 (to which lines B8.15–16 also refer). These uncritical mortals neither understand the nature of the decision they are to make, nor, "thinking that to be and not to be are the same and not the same," do they even manage to formulate the *krisis* correctly. B7 asserts that those who take the route of mortals ply "an aimless eye" and an "echoing ear and tongue," suggesting that they fail to speak and think truly about what-is even though they are attempting to do so.

---

of not-being that involves a testing of the arguments of Parmenides (241d3–8). The Eleatic Stranger's comments at 241d3–8 are a reminder of the *poludēris elenchos* of B7.5.

24 The *Symposium* claims about Beauty occur at 210e6–211b5, in the midst of a passage that is remarkable for its Parmenidean echoes. Plato uses *monoeides* several times in accounts of the Forms: at *Smp.* 211e4 as well as 211b1; at *Phd.* 78d5, 80b2, and 83e2; and at *Rep.* 612a4 (in a discussion of the soul). At *Tht.* 205d1 and *Ti.* 59b2, *monoeides* appears in contexts that show that it means "single in nature or kind." See Mourelatos, *Route*, p. 178; Solmsen, "Parmenides and Perfect Beauty"; Nehamas, "Self-Predication." I further discuss Parmenidean influence on Plato in Chap. VI, Section 2.

25 Barnes reaches a similar conclusion about these lines, though by a different route. As noted above, I disagree with Barnes in that he does not consider that the lines might attribute some type of monism other than numerical monism to Parmenides. See Barnes, "Eleatic One," pp. 9–11.

In trying to give an account of what-is and explain phenomenal experience without understanding the true character of such inquiry, they settle for a conception of what-is that is no real account at all, because it divides what-is predicationally or entails its predicational division. Water, for example, changes into *X* and so is both *X* and not-*X*; the indefinite (*to apeiron*) gives rise to something new that is productive of hot and cold; opposites are said to constitute a unity. Mortals attempt to make it the case that what-is both is and is not, but insofar as it is supposed to be genuinely or reliably *F* and *G* at the same time, it turns out to be neither *F* nor *G*. Explicating how *F*-ness and *G*-ness together constitute an entity involves explaining how *G* is essentially *G* and not-*F*, and how *F* is essentially *F* and not-*G* (and all of this must go on together). Such an account cannot be completed, because of the endless loop of explanation, so that path of inquiry is "backward-turning." Here is a classic case of thinking that "to be and not to be are the same and not the same," for the proposed, allegedly simple account of what-is includes within it both what-is and what-is-not. The *noos* of mortals who attempt to think this way must indeed wander, for in such a mixed, negative, and indeterminate account there is no real or stable object (what-is) on which *noos* can fix. In contrast to the wandering *noos* of mortals, Parmenides insists on the calm connection of *noos* and what-is in B3, and B4, and in the companion lines B8.34–38.

The signs along the genuine route of inquiry thus suggest that Parmenides is committed to a type of monism. But that monism is predicational rather than numerical. To be a genuine entity, and thus a proper object of inquiry, a thing must be "ungenerable and imperishable, a whole of a single kind, and unshaking and complete." These characteristics guarantee that this entity is a single, cohesive whole that is not subject to change. As such, it is something that genuinely or reliably is, and its nature can be grasped and understood by *noos* and it can be a fundamental entity in a cosmological explanation. Why must a genuine entity have such characteristics? Parmenides argues that these attributes are entailed by the judgment that only what-is can be, that what-is-not is impossible. The force of the lines B8.15–16 is that the *krisis* in these matters lies in the claim "is or is not," which reminds us of B2 and its assertion that only the route of what-is is a genuine route of inquiry for thinking. The only way to guarantee that something is a genuine or reliable entity is to test it to see if there is in it any possibility of what-is-not. The tests are explained in the "proofs" of B8, which also explore the characteristics of what-is. According to the signs and the arguments that correspond to them, any purported entity that is generable or perishable, of more than one kind, subject to change or incomplete, and which is not a single, continuous whole, is something that is not, and so cannot be a genuine entity.[26] It is these arguments that constitute the much-contested test

[26] See Coxon, *Fragments*, pp. 193–94. Coxon reads B8 "as an account of the monuments on the way.... To follow the real way is to inquire what other assertions the assertion ἔστιν

(the *poludēris elenchos*) mentioned by the goddess at B7.5; and it is to these arguments that I now turn.

2. The Arguments of B8

The heart of Parmenides' argument about what-is occurs in lines 6–49 of B8. The characteristics of what-is are explicated and shown to follow from the assertions about the routes of inquiry made in B2. The positive route (the only genuine route of inquiry) is characterized as "it is and it is not possible that it not be" (ἡ . . . ὅπως ἔστιν τε καὶ ὡς οὐκ ἔστι μὴ εἶναι B2.3). In B8 Parmenides explores the characteristics that are consistent with that route.[27] Each characteristic is shown to belong to what is on the grounds that it is impossible that what-is be otherwise, because its being otherwise would entail the reality of what-is-not. Thus, what-is can be neither generable nor perishable, is not divisible, and is not incomplete.[28]

While it is evident that lines B8.1–6a are an announcement of the characteristics that will be attributed to what-is in the arguments of lines B8.6b-49, it is not entirely clear how the signs tally with the arguments in the later lines. Indeed, lines 5–6 contain a repetition of certain of the signs announced in B8.3–4. For instance, the assertion of B8.5 that what-is "neither was nor will be" (οὐδέ ποτ' ἦν οὐδ' ἔσται) corresponds to and amplifies the claim of 8.3 that it is ungenerable and indestructible. Further, the announcement at B.8.5–6 that what-is is "all of it together one, cohesive" (ὁμοῦ πᾶν ἕν, συνεχές) echoes the remark at 8.4 that it is "a whole of a single kind" (*oulon mounogenes*). The two signs that are not repeated are "unshaking" (*atremes*) and "complete" (*teleion*). Although these last two seem to be independent signs of what-is, the discussions of them in the body of B8 suggest that there are close connections between Parmenides' arguments for them and the proofs of the other two signs. Nevertheless, despite these complications and unclarities, a fairly close correspondence between the announcement and the arguments can be found. In B8.3 Parmenides asserts that what-is is ungenerable and indestructible, while B8.5 claims that it neither was nor will be, and lines B8.6–21 provide a series of arguments against generation

(now reformulated as ἐόν ἐστιν) entails, i.e., what further predicates are to be associated with 'Being' by the copulative 'is.' " This is, I think, true. But it is also the case that the arguments of B8 test any purported thing that is; because these are the predicates that "are to be associated with Being," we can try any entity to see that it has all and only those attributes.

27 Thus, it is important to work through these arguments both for an understanding of Parmenides' own claims and for understanding how later Presocratic thinkers modeled their own accounts of what-is using Parmenides' criteria.

28 These attributions of negative predicates to what-is show that Parmenides is not ruling out the possibility of negative predication per se. On the issue of negative predications in Parmenides, see Austin, *Being*, chap. 1.

and destruction.[29] Lines B8.22–25 argue that what-is is not divisible, and that it is all continuous (*xuneches*); this argument corresponds to the sign "cohesive" announced at B8.5b-6a, and to the claim that what-is is a whole of a single kind (*mounogenes*), marked at B8.4a. At 8.4b what-is is said to be "unshaking" (*atremes*) and this characteristic is explored in the arguments of B8.26–31 under the rubric "unchanging" or "motionless" (*akinēton*). Finally, the completeness of what-is (announced at B8.4) is considered at B8.32–33 and 42–49. These lines surround and connect with an examination, in lines B8.34–41, of the relation of thought and what-is, a discussion that echoes the earlier linking of thinking and *noos* with what-is in B2, B3, and B4.

The arguments concerning coming-to-be and passing-away work through various ways that what-is might come to be, showing that none is allowable. What unites the arguments is the claim that any sort of coming-to-be is grounded in what-is-not, and, as what-is-not is impossible, so is coming-to-be.[30] The first part of the argument is in lines B8.6–11, where it is argued that there can be no beginning (birth) for what-is.[31]

> . . . τίνα γὰρ γένναν διζήσεαι αὐτοῦ;
> πῇ πόθεν αὐξηθέν; οὔτ' ἐκ μὴ ἐόντος ἐάσσω
> φάσθαι σ' οὐδὲ νοεῖν· οὐ γὰρ φατὸν οὐδὲ νοητόν
> ἔστιν ὅπως οὐκ ἔστι. τί δ' ἄν μιν καὶ χρέος ὦρσεν
> ὕστερον ἢ πρόσθεν, τοῦ μηδενὸς ἀρξάμενον, φῦν;
> οὕτως ἢ πάμπαν πελέναι χρεών ἐστιν ἢ οὐχί. (B8.6–11)

> . . . for what birth will you seek out for it?
> in what way, having grown from what? Nor from what is not will I allow you
> to say or think, for it is not to be said or thought
> that it is not. And then what need could have impelled it,
> later or earlier, starting from nothing, to grow?
> Thus it is necessary that it either altogether is or not at all.

Parmenides considers only the possibility that what-is could come from what-is-not; and this is surely the correct method. For, if it came from what-is, then we would have to begin further back (as it were), asking of *that*, where it came from, and so on. But it is impossible that what-is should come from what-is-not. First, if what-is were to have come to be and developed from

29 As almost all commentators have pointed out, there is no separate argument against destruction; rather, there is simply the claim at B8.14 that Justice will not allow what-is to perish. I shall have more to say about this below.

30 Lines B8.9–10 contain an argument from sufficient reason; but even this ultimately depends on the impossibility that what-is could come from what-is-not, for there is nothing in what-is-not that could impel the birth or coming-to-be of what-is.

31 In seeing three separate steps in the arguments about coming-to-be, I follow Mourelatos (see *Route*, pp. 96–103). In their commentaries on B8, neither Tarán nor Coxon show how the various moves made in lines 6–21 are connected to the overall argument.

its birth, it must have come to be from something. The only candidate is what-is-not (because of the danger of regress if we look to what-is); but it is impossible for what-is-not to be the source of what-is because what-is-not cannot be. It is unsayable and unthinkable (just as was said in B2.5–7). Thus, what-is is not subject to birth with its attendant growth and development but is stable. Moreover, even if what-is could have come from what-is-not, there is a further argument against that possibility. If there were only what-is-not, what could have pushed what-is into being at just the time it came to be? Here Parmenides relies on an argument from sufficient reason and finds that there is nothing (no "need") in what-is-not that could serve as the catalyst to begin the process of the birth of what-is. The final line of the section simply reminds us that the claim of B2.3 guarantees that what-is will have no part of what-is-not: it altogether is, for any deviation from what-is pulls us off the genuine path of inquiry onto the path of what-is-not.

Whom is Parmenides attacking here? We cannot be sure. Perhaps Parmenides was simply exploring the logical possibility that what-is can come from what-is-not. But there is a case of coming to be and growth in earlier Presocratic thought that Parmenides might have had in mind. According to pseudo-Plutarch, Anaximander had said that the *apeiron* was the cause of the generation and destruction of the *kosmos* (12A10), and although the details are hazy, they include first, the coming to be of "the heavens and all the worlds" and then, with respect to this world, "he says that at the coming-to-be of this *kosmos* something productive of hot and cold separated off from the eternal and from it a ball of flame grew around the air around the earth, like bark around a tree" (φησὶ δέ τι[32] ἐκ τοῦ ἀιδίου γόνιμον θερμοῦ τε καὶ ψυχροῦ κατὰ τὴν γένεσιν τοῦδε τοῦ κόσμου ἀποκριθῆναι καί τινα ἐκ τούτου φλογὸς σφαῖραν περιφυῆναι τῷ περὶ τὴν γῆν ἀέρι ὡς τῷ δένδρῳ φλοιόν). The first problem with this account is the nature of the *apeiron* itself. If it is truly indefinite or unlimited, as its name implies, then it has no fundamental character or nature. Thus, according to Parmenides, it is not anything at all and so counts as what-is-not. As such it certainly cannot function as a fundamental entity in Anaximander's theory. Moreover, the theory requires this indefinite, unlimited stuff to give rise to all the heavens. But how can this happen, given the nature of the *apeiron*? Why could anything come to be out of the *apeiron*? There is no reason to be found within the *apeiron* itself, and nothing else to which to appeal. So Anaximander's theory, as reported by pseudo-Plutarch, falls afoul of both steps in Parmenides' argument here. Whatever something genuinely is cannot be something that becomes; it must always remain just what it is.

But suppose there is something that has not come to be (i.e., has no birth). Might not that thing grow and change? In the next part of the argument, Parmenides argues that it cannot.

32 For τι here, I follow Hölscher, "Anaximander," p. 290; Kahn, *Anaximander*, p. 57n. b.

οὐδέ ποτ' ἐκ μὴ ἐόντος[33] ἐφήσει πίστιος ἰσχύς
γίγνεσθαί τι παρ' αὐτό· τοῦ εἵνεκεν οὔτε γενέσθαι
οὔτ' ὄλλυσθαι ἀνῆκε Δίκη χαλάσασα πέδῃσιν,
ἀλλ' ἔχει· ἡ δὲ κρίσις περὶ τούτων ἐν τῷδ' ἔστιν·
ἔστιν ἢ οὐκ ἔστιν· κέκριται δ' οὖν, ὥσπερ ἀνάγκη,
τὴν μὲν ἐᾶν ἀνόητον ἀνώνυμον (οὐ γὰρ ἀληθής
ἔστιν ὁδός), τὴν δ' ὥστε πέλειν καὶ ἐτήτυμον εἶναι.

(B8.12–18)

Nor will the force of trust permit anything to come to be from
what is not alongside it. On account of this neither coming to be
nor perishing would Justice allow, loosening the fetters,
but holds fast. And the decision about these is in this:
is or is not; and it has been decided, just as is necessary,
to leave the one unthinkable and unnamed (for it is not a true
route), and the other to be and to be genuine.

Although birth has been ruled out for what-is, it still might be the case that it could grow by having something added to it. But this is rejected on the grounds that what is added must come from what-is-not (for again, it is what-is that we are considering adding something to, and it cannot be added to itself). "What-is-not" should here be interpreted predicationally.[34] What is not-*f* cannot give rise to anything that could be added to what is *f*, for what is not-*f* is not itself a genuine thing in the first place. Thus, to return to the case of Anaximander, the claim that a ball of flame grew around the air surrounding the earth turns out to be nonsense, if all there was in the beginning was the hot and the cold. The cold cannot give rise to the hot, and the hot itself cannot grow or expand. The claim is even more nonsensical once we realize that the hot and cold were somehow generated from the *apeiron*.[35] The real character of a genuine entity is not subject to such changes through

[33] ἐκ μὴ ἐόντος: this follows the text of DK, accepted by Mourelatos (*Route*), Gallop (*Parmenides*), and Coxon (*Fragments*). On the argument for leaving the text unchanged, see Austin, "Genesis and Motion," and Sanders, "Much Ado." Tarán emends to ἐκ τοῦ ἐόντος. See Tarán, pp. 95–104 and Stokes, *One and Many*, p. 131. For an argument against taking this as a dilemma, see Barnes, *PP*, vol. I, pp. 184–85; Gallop, *Parmenides*, n.42, pp. 34–35. See also Stough, "Parmenides' Way Of Truth," and Schofield, "Eternity," p. 116n.18.

[34] For a defense of the predicational reading of "what-is-not" in this line, see Sanders, "Much Ado," a paper read at the Nineteenth Annual Worshop on Ancient Philosophy at Texas A and M University in March 1996. Sanders understands *to auto* in line 13 as a reference to the *mē eon* of line 12. I prefer to read it as a reference to what-is, the subject of the whole discussion of B8. I am grateful to Mr. Sanders for a copy of his paper and for his permission to refer to it.

[35] I do not claim that Parmenides actually had Anaximander in mind here; I merely wish to show that earlier cosmological theories can provide likely targets. Similar arguments could be constructed against other theories. For instance, Anaximenes' reliance on condensation and rarefaction to fuel changes in air such that it becomes other things also falls afoul of Parmenides' arguments.

addition; it is, as Parmenides says, held fast. The image of Justice holding what-is tightly in fetters shows that Parmenides thought that these claims hold of necessity. The reason why it is necessary is given in the next lines: the *krisis* "is or is not" guarantees the claim. For what-is-not cannot be; it is nameless and unthinkable and so cannot be the source for any addition to what-is. In referring to the *krisis*, and recalling the claim of B2.7–8 that what-is-not can be neither said nor thought, Parmenides makes clear that the characteristics of what-is that are demonstrated in B8 follow inexorably from the claim that what-is can be while what-is-not cannot.

Line B8.14 says that not only is coming-to-be ruled out but also perishing; this is the first mention of passing away in the proofs, and it is merely a mention. There is no separate proof that what-is cannot perish. This is, perhaps, not unexpected. For if what-is were to perish, it would become what-is-not. But there is neither any becoming for what-is, nor is there any what-is-not; so for what-is to perish is impossible.[36] The summary of the proofs about generation (at lines 19–21) also mentions perishing; but it is significant that there perishing or destruction is said to be "unheard of" (*apustos*).

Finally, Parmenides argues against coming-to-be in general. There can be no coming-to-be for what-is now, there cannot have been any in the past, and there cannot be any in the future:

πῶς δ' ἂν ἔπειτα πέλοι τὸ ἐόν[37] ; πῶς δ' ἄν κε γένοιτο;
εἰ γὰρ ἔγεντ', οὐκ ἔστ', οὐδ' εἴ ποτε μέλλει ἔσεσθαι.
τὼς γένεσις μὲν ἀπέσβεσται καὶ ἄπυστος ὄλεθρος. (B8.19–21)

And how could what-is be hereafter? And how could it come to be?
For if it came to be, it is not, nor if it is going to be at some time.
So has coming-to-be been extinguished, and unheard-of destruction.

Parmenides here rules out any and all coming-to-be; in whatever form, at whatever time, it is incompatible with what-is, which maintains its own character always.[38] Note that here the argument moves immediately from the consideration of coming-to-be to its impossibility. If something came

[36] Even in the cosmology of Anaximander, the *apeiron* remains while (at least on one interpretation of 12B1) things come to be from it and pass away into it.

[37] Coxon follows the mss and prints πέλοιτο ἐόν. But see Renehan's review of Coxon, which argues that although this reading gives the same sense as that in the version accepted here (Parmenides does occasionally use *eon* without the article; see B8.3 and 25 for instance), Coxon's translation and interpretation (making the subject "what becomes") is most improbable. Kranz accepts the emendation of Karsten and Stein: ἔπειτ' ἀπόλοιτο ἐόν; Tarán (*Parmenides*, p. 104) argues that the emendation is unnecessary because "the fact [that what-is cannot perish] has already been mentioned (cf. line 14) and the demonstration of it was implied [in lines 13–15]."

[38] The issue of whether or not Parmenides intended to invoke a timeless "is" here has, in recent scholarship, been heavily debated since Owen took issue with Fränkel's rejection of

to be, then it is not now. Why? Becoming always involves beginning from what-is-not,[39] and any admixture of what-is-not immediately moves us from the genuine route of what-is to the impossible path of what-is-not. What something genuinely is (its nature) is not something that can come to be (for it is subject to all the arguments against birth already marshaled); moreover, if the nature of a thing is something that is going to be, it is not now and thus cannot be; for what-is-not can never give rise to what-is. By the time we reach B8.21, Parmenides has rejected the notions of birth and of growth (B8.6–11), of addition (B8.11–18), and finally any sort of coming to be (B8.19–21). Thus scientific inquiry is stymied if the nature of a thing is itself subject to change.[40]

Do these lines contain an argument for monism? I do not think that they do; all they say is that whatever is always has been and always will be and is not subject to change. There may be numerically many real things or only one genuinely real thing; but there cannot come to be more or fewer such things. Moreover, there is no explicit argument in these lines for predicational

---

the "timeless" interpretation (Fränkel, "Studies in Parmenides," p. 46n.86; Owen, "Timeless Present"). Guthrie (*HGP*, vol. II, pp. 29–30) follows Owen's view. The view that Parmenides means to distinguish a timeless *esti* or to invoke a timeless eternity has been challenged by Tarán (*Parmenides* and "Perpetual Duration"), Stough ("Way of Truth," pp. 99–100), Stokes (*One and Many*, pp. 128–30), Schofield ("Eternity"), Robinson ("Parmenides on the Real," pp. 58–59), and Gallop (*Parmenides*, pp. 13–14). See also the exchanges between Groarke ("Parmenides' Timeless Universe") and Matthen ("Parmenides' Denial of Past and Future"); and also Sorabji (chapter 8 of *Time, Creation, and the Continuum*). Tarán (*Parmenides*, pp. 175–88) provides a history of the debate and a summary of various positions that have been taken. See also Collobert, *L'Être*, pp. 155–95. Mourelatos (*Route*, pp. 103–11) separates the issues of whether or not the *esti* is tenseless, and whether or not *to eon* is a timeless entity. He seems to take the evidence as inconclusive and argues that we cannot claim that Parmenides "denies the reality of time"; he concludes that what-is is independent of any one part of time, but that this may not commit Parmenides to "a doctrine of timelessness" (p. 120). Barnes (*PP*, vol. I, pp. 190–94) surveys the issue and concludes "that Parmenides did not have a firm grasp of the inordinately slippery fish he held in his hand" (p. 194). I follow Schofield in his conclusion that the text supports only the more cautious conclusion that Parmenides denies to what-is any coming to be at any time (though I do not endorse Schofield's arguments involving "the interpolator"). I take Parmenides to be claiming that the genuine nature of a thing (what it is to be that thing) neither comes to be (at any time) nor changes; but I do not think that the text as it stands can tell us whether Parmenides thought that such natures stood outside of time as, perhaps, Plato meant his Forms to do even before he wrote the *Timaeus*. Melissus argues that what-is is eternal in 30B1 and B3.

39 Note that Aristotle, in his analysis of change, agrees with this, in that coming to be is from something that is not, in the sense of something different; see *Ph.* I.7. Aristotle, of course, rejects the full Parmenidean conclusion, arguing that certain types of becoming can be philosophically respectable.

40 In the concluding line of the whole set of arguments (B8.21), he again mentions destruction or passing away but, as before (in line 14), there is only a mention rather than a special argument against it. It is for this reason that ἔπειτ' ἀπόλοιτο ἐόν has been proposed for B8.19. But I think that Tarán's claims about the structure of Parmenides' argument tell against the suggestion. See note 37, above.

monism. If we were to suppose it possible for a thing to have a multiple nature that is expressed in several predicates, as long as that nature neither comes to be nor passes away, nor has anything added to it, these arguments have nothing to say that would prevent such a case. But predicational pluralism is ruled out by the next proof, that of indivisibility.

There are two announcements that correspond to the proof of indivisibility: at B8.5–6, what-is is said to be "all together one, cohesive" (ὁμοῦ πᾶν ἕν, συνεχές); and at B8.4, the first announcement of the sign says that what-is is a whole of a single kind: *oulon mounogenes*. However we interpret the proof in lines B8.22–25, the interpretation should be consistent with both signs.

> οὐδὲ διαιρετόν ἐστιν, ἐπεὶ πᾶν ἐστιν ὁμοῖον·
> οὐδέ τι τῇ μᾶλλον, τό κεν εἴργοι μιν συνέχεσθαι,
> οὐδέ τι χειρότερον, πᾶν δ' ἔμπλεόν ἐστιν ἐόντος.
> τῷ ξυνεχὲς πᾶν ἐστιν· ἐὸν γὰρ ἐόντι πελάζει. (B8.22–25)

> Nor is it divisible, since it is all alike;
> Nor is there somewhat more here, which would prevent it from cohering,
> nor somewhat less there, but all is completely full of what is.
> Thus it is all continuous, for what is draws near to what is.

Parmenides claims that what-is is not subject to separation or division, because there are no dissimilarities within it that could mark such divisions. What-is is all alike. I have argued in Chapter I that Parmenides' subject is the nature of a thing (that which identifies a thing as what it is and as a basic entity); he is here arguing that such a nature must be all alike and therefore subject to no divisions, unitary. This corresponds to the claim in the list of signs that what-is is monogeneous (*mounogenes*);[41] being all of one kind, it cannot be further subdivided. If it is true that to be *F* is the nature of a thing, then it is all and only *F* (for it cannot be divided into *F* and say, *G*), and is fully *F* (for there is no part of it that is more or less *F* than any other part, which would keep it from being completely or cohesively *F*). We might recall fragment 1 of Heraclitus where he says he is "distinguishing each thing according to its nature, saying how it is" (κατὰ φύσιν διαιρέων ἕκαστον καὶ φράζων ὅκως ἔχει). That is, he will divide up the world, saying what each thing is by nature. Heraclitus's "distinguishing" (*diaireōn*) and Parmenides' "divisible" (*diaireton* B8.22) are forms of the same word. Parmenides argues that once one has reached the genuine character or reality of a thing, one's account of what the thing is has been completed, for there are no more

[41] I prefer the rather awkward "monogeneous" here to the more usual "homogeneous." The former stresses the single-natured character of what-is that Parmenides is discussing here; "homogeneous" suggests (at least in modern English) the notion of "thoroughly mixed," which implies parts or aspects that are separable in principle even if not in actuality. Parmenides is unwilling to countenance that the character of a genuine entity can be even in principle divisible.

distinctions to be made within the account (or the thing). Because the being of the thing in question is uniform, and subject to no more distinctions or divisions, it is cohesive and a unity. As Parmenides says at B8.5–6, it is "all [of it] together one, cohesive" (ὁμοῦ πᾶν ἕν, συνεχές). The argument at B8.22–25 stresses the wholeness and uniformity of the account given: there are no degrees of *F*-ness if a thing is by nature *F*. So it is "all full of what-is." And thus it is all cohesive or continuous (τῷ ξυνεχὲς πᾶν ἐστιν B8.25). The depiction of the cohesiveness of what-is is strengthened by Parmenides' claim that "what-is draws near to (*pelazei*) what-is." What-is is never separated from itself, so the nature of a thing coheres and makes up a unity that constitutes what it is to be that thing.

An apparent peculiarity of this passage is that there is, strictly speaking, no independent argument in these lines. Rather, Parmenides presents a series of assertions about the cohesiveness and uniformity of what-is. The lines are a further conclusion to be drawn from the *krisis* at B8.15–16. Because it is impossible that there should be any of what-is-not in an account of what a thing is, a thing's nature must be *mounogenes*. And that means that it must be cohesive and all alike, with no "more or less." The reliance on the *krisis* as the basis of the claims here in lines 22–25 underlies the assertion that what-is draws near to what-is. Thus, despite the apparent lack of argument, lines B8.22–25 do contain an inference, whose premises are contained in the reminder of the *krisis* at lines B8.15–16.

Many discussions of this passage (lines 22–25) treat it as a commitment to the spatial or temporal indivisibility of what-is;[42] and most see it at the same time as an argument for numerical monism. But I think that this interpretation depends crucially on reading the *esti* in Parmenides as existential, and, as I have already argued, this is not the best interpretation available. On these readings, the continuous character of what-is turns into a plenum, which allows no separation between entities ("it cannot exist here but not there, etc."), so there is no possibility of a number of entities. But, as I have claimed in Chapter I, there is reason not to take Parmenides as concerned with Existence, Being, or "the all," but rather as concerned with what it is to be the genuine nature or character of a thing. Parmenides is thus discussing the internal unity of an entity, and not the relations among entities. How many entities meet these requirements is an open question. There is a hint that this is the proper interpretation in Aristotle. In the *Metaphysics*, at I.5 (986b18–20 = DK 28A24), Aristotle contrasts Parmenides and Melissus, noting that while Melissus was concerned with what is one in matter (κατὰ τὴν ὕλην), Parmenides "seems to fasten on what is one in account (or:

42 Owen interprets in terms of time ("Timeless Present"), followed by Barnes ("Eleatic One" p. 12); Tugwell interprets the passage as concerned with spatial continuity. Coxon (*Fragments*) opts for both time and space or either (pp. 204–5).

definition)" (Παρμενίδης ... ἔοικε τοῦ κατὰ τὸν λόγον ἑνὸς ἅπτεσθαι).[43] This unity of definition or account is just what we meet with in lines B8.22–25, and is just what we might expect in lines corresponding to the preliminary announcement that what-is is *mounogenes*.

Having argued that what-is can have no connection with coming to be, and that it is cohesive and single in nature, Parmenides next shows that it is unchanging.

> αὐτὰρ ἀκίνητον μεγάλων ἐν πείρασι δεσμῶν
> ἔστιν ἄναρχον ἄπαυστον, ἐπεὶ γένεσις καὶ ὄλεθρος
> τῆλε μαλ' ἐπλάχθησαν, ἀπῶσε δὲ πίστις ἀληθής.
> ταὐτόν τ' ἐν ταὐτῷ τε μένον καθ' ἑαυτό τε κεῖται
> χοὔτως ἔμπεδον αὖθι μένει· κρατερὴ γὰρ Ἀνάγκη
> πείρατος ἐν δεσμοῖσιν ἔχει, τό μιν ἀμφὶς ἐέργει.[44]
>
> (B8.26–31)

> Further, changeless in the limits of great bonds
> it is without start or stop, since coming to be and passing away
> have wandered very far away, and true trust drove them out.
> Remaining the same and in the same it lies by itself
> and remains there steadfast: for mighty Necessity
> holds it in the limits of a bond, which holds it in all around.

There are two immediate questions about these lines. First, how is *akinēton*, which I have translated "changeless," to be interpreted? Second, what is the argument in this passage? The two questions are related, for I shall argue that the passage does not contain an independent argument but instead further develops the consequences of the argument against coming-to-be that appeared in lines 6–21.[45] This suggests that the subject of lines 26–31 is change rather than locomotion.

I begin with the second issue, that of whether there is an independent argument in these lines. Line 26 begins "*autar*," a particle that is, in this case,

[43] Parmenides is further contrasted with Xenophanes, who "looking to the whole heaven says that the one is god" (εἰς τὸν ὅλον οὐρανὸν ἀποβλέψας τὸ ἓν εἶναί φησι τὸν θεόν *Metaph.* 986b24–5).

[44] I follow Mourelatos (*Route*) and Gallop (*Parmenides*) in putting a period rather than a comma here as DK, Tarán (*Parmenides*), Bormann, and Coxon (*Fragments*) do.

[45] In the discussion of the preliminary announcement, it was noted that the signs corresponding to "changeless" and to "cohesive" were repeated in lines 5–6, after the initial list of four signs has been given. The repetition marks their fundamental character and their importance in underlying the signs "unshaking" (*atremes*) and "complete" (*teleion*) that conclude the initial listing of characteristics of what-is in lines B8.3–4. The characteristics of what-is that are discussed from this point in the text show the importance of the two "fundamental" characteristics.

progressive.[46] So we are to be told something further about the character of what-is. What we are told is that it is *akinēton* and "without start or stop," held within the limits of mighty fetters, because (*epei*) there is no coming-to-be or passing away. The link with the earlier argument against genesis and destruction is strengthened by the assertion that it was "true trust" (*pistis alēthēs*) that "drove out" coming-to-be and perishing (line 28).[47] That is a reminder of the contention, made in the midst of the arguments against coming-to-be, that "the force of trust" (*pistios ischus* [12]) will not permit anything to come to be in addition to what is.[48] Because there is no coming to be or passing away for it, what-is always remains the same, in the same state. It is "by itself" because nothing can be added to or taken away from it (another way of saying that it does not alter or change). And, as Parmenides insists, by using the images of constraint and bonds, it is necessary that what-is be stable. It could change only if it can become what it is not, and if what-is-not can come to be. But neither becoming nor passing away is possible; so what-is remains always the same. The demonstration of the stable and unchanging nature of what-is thus depends upon the earlier proof that there is no coming-to-be or passing away. So in these lines we have, not an independent proof that what-is is *akinēton*, but a derivation from the earlier denial of genesis and destruction.

No matter whether *akinēton* is translated "changeless" or "motionless," lines 26–31 are often taken as an argument against motion. A problem with this interpretation is that the denial of coming-to-be and passing away does not lead naturally to a rejection of motion—there is no obvious inference from the one to the other.[49] One response to the objection is to argue that at this time no genuine distinction between qualitative alteration and motion was made,

46 See Denniston, p. 55. It is unlikely that *autar* would have a "strongly adversative" sense in these lines, for we have just been told that what-is is cohesive and indivisible, and its character as "unchanging" can be seen as a further implication of its cohesiveness. If *autar* has any adversative role here, it may be to warn us not to take the claim that what-is "draws near" (*pelazei*) to what-is literally, but as a metaphor, illustrating the cohesiveness of what-is.

47 Not only has "true trust" driven out genesis and destruction, they have "wandered very far away," showing their connection with the wandering *noos* of mortals, and the path of what-is-not on which mortals wander (B6).

48 There is also a reminder of the reliability of the goddess's claims in the echo of the characterization (at B1.30) of mortal beliefs as those "in which there is no true trust" (ταῖς οὐκ ἔνι πίστις ἀληθής).

49 Tarán (*Parmenides*), pp. 109–13. Kirk and Stokes ("Parmenides' Refutation") argue that Parmenides is rejecting motion; they read *akinēton* at B8.26 as "unmoving" but acknowledge that at B8.38 *akinēton* "probably refers to change in general" (p. 4n.1). Coxon seems to opt for "unchanging" and says that *akinēton* is "deduced from the premises in lines 30–33, i.e., Being is 'unvarying' not because becoming and perishing have been banished from it but because its perfection exempts it from variation" (*Fragments*, p. 207). But it is difficult to see how Parmenides can rely on premises that have yet to be given and that actually follow from the immobility of what-is. For Parmenides will argue that because what-is is unchanging it is complete. Mourelatos (*Route*, pp. 117–20) suggests that *kinēsis* should be understood

and that *akinēton* therefore covers both sorts of change indiscriminately.[50] I doubt that this can be maintained. Heraclitus is able to mark the distinction, saying in B125 that the barley drink falls apart if it is not moved or stirred (⟨*mē*⟩ *kinoumenos*), while also claiming, in B67, that god alters (*alloioutai*).[51] And even if B125 is classified as a paraphrase rather than a quotation, it is the appearance of a form of *alloioun* in B67 that is relevant to showing that the distinction could have been made at this time. But while the two forms of change can be distinguished, it is possible to read Parmenides' denial of *kinēsis* as a denial of alteration in the nature of a thing.[52] What-is is not subject to being moved out of or away from itself; that is, it does not change or develop in any way. The earlier rejection of coming-to-be and passing away is relevant to showing that this sort of alteration is impossible for what-is, for in this sort of change one state of affairs ceases while another comes to be; but the elimination of genesis and destruction is not relevant to a rejection of locomotion.

This interpretation of Parmenides' use of *akinēton* is, I think, strengthened by considering the Homeric notion of *kinēsis*. The basic conception in Homer is that of pushing or rousing a thing, disrupting or budging it out of the place it occupies.[53] This typically implies a displacement, rather than sustained locomotion. Now, while these are all terms that can be read as implying motion, they also suggest a disruption or change in something as well. Though the primary meaning may be to push or rouse something, this use in Homer can license a use of *kinēsis* and related terms in later writers that is not primarily locomotive. It appears in Bacchylides V. 200, where the prayer is that Zeus will "protect them unmoved in peace";[54] and Coxon notes

---

as a violent egress of what-is from its natural place. But, if this is meant as a form of motion, his view leaves unanswered the question of how this is deduced from the absence of coming-to-be and perishing. I think that Mourelatos's view actually amounts to a rejection of alteration.

50 This is Tarán's solution (*Parmenides*, pp. 109–13). He concludes (p. 113) that "for [Parmenides] motion and change imply each other."

51 On the problem of Heraclitus B125, see Marcovich (pp. 156–57), Kirk (pp. 256–57). Mackenzie discusses the difficulties of the fragment in "The Moving Posset"; *kinoumenos* appears in all three versions of the fragment that she considers.

52 In Plato's *Prm.*, for instance, *kinēsis* functions as a general term encompassing both locomotion and alteration. In showing that the One neither moves nor rests, at 138b8–c1, Parmenides says that "if it were moving it would either change place or alter; for these are the only motions" (κινούμενόν γε ἢ φέροιτο ἢ ἀλλοιοῖτο ἄν· αὗται γὰρ μόναι κινήσεις).

53 See Cunliffe, *s.v. kineō*, p. 227. In epics, forms of *kineō* are used when Zeus rouses himself, another form of displacement or disturbance rather than simple motion. In Heraclitus B125, the movement necessary to keep the *kykēon* whole is something more like a violent agitation than a gentle stirring (although it is perhaps part of Heraclitus's paradoxical view of things that the violent agitation is necessary to maintain the posset's identity as the *kykēon* rather than as simply a layered collection of ingredients). See also Mourelatos, *Route*, pp. 117–19, who stresses the Homeric roots of Parmenides' claim, and Guthrie, *HGP*, vol. I, p. 382.

54 τοὺς ὁ μεγιστοπάτωρ Ζεὺς ἀκινήτους ἐν εἰρήν[ᾳ φυλάσσοι.

Sophocles' use of *akinētos pelei* to mean "is steadfast."[55] It is undeniable that the words used by Parmenides have a meaning that can be locomotive; but they can be used metaphorically as well. Parmenides, after all, uses language in a number of picturesque ways. There are the images of wanderings and chains (not to mention "two-headed mortals"), the metaphor of the sphere, and the crucially important motif of the route. It is, I think, the use of *kinēsis* as displacement or disturbance from a state, understood as the alteration or change in what a thing is, that is at work in lines 26–31. This sort of change, a shift in the very nature of a thing, would be particularly violent and disruptive. This interpretation allows us to make sense of Parmenides' claims even though the passage, as it stands, cannot function as an argument against *kinēsis* when it is interpreted as locomotion.

A further difficulty with treating this passage specifically as an argument against locomotion is the incongruity of there being such an argument embedded in a discussion of the necessary character of the nature of a thing. Why would we expect that what something truly is should be subject to motion at all? But it might be the case that the nature of a thing—what it is to be that thing—might undergo displacement, understood as alteration or development. It is this that Parmenides is ruling out. The nature of a thing is not only permanent (subject to no becoming or passing away), it is also stable, undergoing no alteration; what-is does not become different from, and so alienated from itself. It is self-contained, isolated from and independent of everything else; this is indicated by the declaration that "remaining the same and in the same, it lies by itself and remains there steadfast."[56] The preliminary statement of the characteristics of what-is in lines 3–6 included the assertion that what-is is unshaken or calm (*atremes*), recalling the goddess's promise in B1.29 that the *kouros* will learn "the unshaken heart of well-persuasive truth" (ἀληθείης εὐπειθέος ἀτρεμὲς ἦτορ); this is another indication that what is being argued for is the internal stability of what-is rather than its literal immobility.

[55] Coxon, *Fragments,* p. 206. See also Thucydides (a late example). At II.61.2, Pericles contrasts his own steadfastness with the mutability of the Assembly: "I am the same and I have not altered; it is you who have changed" (καὶ ἐγὼ μὲν ὁ αὐτός εἰμι καὶ οὐκ ἐξίσταμαι· ὑμεῖς δὲ μεταβάλλετε). Both *existanai* and *metaballein* can have implications of motion or locomotion; but Pericles' comment, which describes his character, is certainly not addressed to his staying in one place and the assembly's moving, except metaphorically.

[56] Compare this with Plato's description of Beauty itself in the *Symp.* (211a8–b2): "nor is it anywhere in something else, such as in an animal, or in earth, or in the heaven or in anything else, but itself by itself with itself it is always one in form (ἀλλ' αὐτὸ καθ' αὑτὸ μεθ' αὑτοῦ μονοειδὲς ἀεὶ ὄν)." The phrase "itself by itself" (αὐτὸ καθ' αὑτό) also appears in the *Phd.* (at 100b5–7), where Socrates sets out the hypothesis that there is a Form of Beauty "itself by itself" and also Forms of Good and Large "and all the others." See Chap. VI, Section 2.

In asserting that what-is "remains the same and in the same," Parmenides echoes Xenophanes' description of an unmoving or unchanging god in 21B26.[57] On one interpretation of Xenophanes' view, it is not becoming or suitable for a god to move from place to place, in contrast to the Olympian gods in Homer who are always rushing about intervening in the affairs of mortals. Such behavior is considered unbecoming to a god. But Xenophanes might be less concerned with criticizing the Olympian gods' penchant for travel and interference in the affairs of humans than in exploring what characteristics are consistent with the claim that his one god is "greatest among gods and men" (21B23). A being that moved about would fail to meet the criteria for the greatest being.[58] Rather, god is self-contained and stable; thus not subject to alteration. Similarly, Parmenides claims, it is inappropriate that what accounts for the character of a thing as the thing that it is, would be subject to change; rather, that nature remains always the same. Something that was subject to change or alteration would fail to meet the criteria for what-is. This corrects Heraclitus, who, in B67, asserts that god becomes everything (day night, winter summer, war peace, satiety hunger), by altering (*alloioutai*).[59] Parmenides regards Heraclitus's account as wrongheaded, illicitly mixing what-is with what-is-not. If the purported character or nature of something undergoes alteration, it cannot genuinely be the character of anything, for it fails to meet the criterion of stability and steadfastness that what-is must meet. Moreover, as Parmenides will argue in lines 34–38, being unstable, it could not be grasped by *noos*. Whether or not a thing moves seems irrelevant to its capacity to be known. Odysseus remains just who he is no matter where he is. It is only if he changed his character as well as his appearance and his location that one might be justified in doubting that the returned stranger is truly Odysseus. When Parmenides asserts that what-is is *akinēton*, he is, therefore, insisting that the nature of a thing, what gives it its identity as the sort of thing it is, cannot be subject to the disruption of itself that would come with alteration or change.[60] Thus, natures are both permanent (without coming-to-be or passing away) and stable (not subject to change).

The final proof, that which corresponds to the sign *teleion* (complete), occurs in two parts (lines 32–33, and 42–49), separated by a discussion of the

[57] Xenophanes B26: αἰεὶ δ' ἐν ταὐτῷ μίμνει κινούμενος οὐδέν: "he always remains in the same, altering not at all." This can be read as a reference both to motion and to alteration of character.

[58] See Lesher, *Xenophanes*, pp. 112–13, esp. p. 113: "In particular, [Xenophanes] holds that one god is *megistos* . . . , a view which if understood in terms of power would entail instant and complete accomplishment of divine wishes and intentions across enormous expanses of space and time. . . . Traveling about, localized activity or effect . . . would all be alien to such a conception."

[59] Both the text and the meaning of Heraclitus B67 are disputed. See Kirk (pp. 184–201) and Marcovich (pp. 413–17) for discussions of the alternatives.

[60] I take it that Mourelatos's discussion of *akinēton* (in *Route*) comes to much the same conclusion.

relation of thought to what-is (lines B8.34–41).[61] The intervening discussion is relevant to the completeness of what-is, for what-is, as complete, is the natural home of thought; but the discussion is not a part of the proof of completeness, nor is what Parmenides says there germane only to that proof. Nevertheless, because of the relevance of lines 33–41 to the second part of the proof of completeness, I shall consider the parts of the proof and the discussion of thought and what-is in the order in which they appear in B8.

οὕνεκεν οὐκ ἀτελεύτητον τὸ ἐὸν θέμις εἶναι·
ἔστι γὰρ οὐκ ἐπιδευές· ἐὸν δ' ἂν παντὸς ἐδεῖτο.[62]

(B8.32–33)

Wherefore, it is not right that what-is be incomplete;
for it is not in need; for if it were, it would lack everything.

Because what-is is restrained or held in, and because it is cohesive (the results of the two preceding arguments), it is complete, here understood as being completely or fully what it is. Being complete involves being fully finished, achieved, or accomplished.[63] There is nothing to be added; it is perfected or completed as it is. If there were anything missing from it, it would not be just what it is and so would lack "everything." The argument succeeds because of the character of its subject. What-is, the subject of the discussions, is the basic nature of a thing; it is what it is to be something, say *F*. To be the nature of *F* is to be all and only what *F* is; so, if this purported nature of *F* (which is what it is to be *F*) were to lack something it would lack or fall short in being *F*; but to be in need that way is to be not-*F*. Thus, our purported nature of *F* could not actually be the nature of anything at all.

The completeness of what-is is guaranteed by its unchanging character (whence the "wherefore" [*houneken*] in line 32). As we have seen, that characteristic depends on its being indivisible and not subject to coming to be or passing away. So the proof of completeness brings together into a whole

[61] Coxon (*Fragments*) treats lines 32 and 33 as part of the argument that what-is is *akinēton* (but what has incompleteness to do with proving immobility?), while Schofield ("Eternity") takes 32–33 to be the only argument for perfection; according to Schofield, lines 42–49 argue for the equipoise of what is (he reads ἠδ' ἀτάλαντον at the end of B8.4); see "Eternity," p. 115n.16.

[62] Coxon prints ἔστι γὰρ οὐκ ἐπιδεές· μὴ ἐὸν δ' ἂν παντὸς ἐδεῖτο, with the translation "for it is not defective, whereas Not-being would lack everything." Although, according to Coxon, "the manuscript evidence is slightly in favor of . . . ἐπιδευές, . . . it is clear that ἐπιδεές (scanned as trisyllabic by synizesis) is correct, for the deletion of μή in the succeeding phrase is paleographically and exegetically indefensible" (Coxon, *Fragments*, p. 208). The argument is given in Coxon, "Manuscript Tradition," pp. 72–73. I follow DK, Tarán (*Parmenides*), Mourelatos (*Route*), Bormann, and Gallop (*Parmenides*). For a defense, see Mourelatos, *Route*, p. 122n.22, who points out that the text Coxon defends gives us a "weak, almost platitudinous statement, which, quite apart from considerations of rhetoric, provides only contrast, but no support for the preceding clause."

[63] See LSJ on *teleutē* and related terms.

all of the essential characteristics of what-is: because it has no coming-to-be, is indivisible, and is not subject to alteration, what-is is completed and perfected.

Because it has this character, what-is is the ideal object of thought; and it is the connection between thinking and what-is that Parmenides explores in the next lines.[64]

ταὐτὸν δ' ἐστὶ νοεῖν τε καὶ οὕνεκέν ἐστι νόημα·
οὐ γὰρ ἄνευ τοῦ ἐόντος, ἐν ᾧ πεφατισμένον ἐστίν,
εὑρήσεις τὸ νοεῖν· οὐδὲν γὰρ ⟨ἢ⟩ ἔστιν ἢ ἔσται[65]
ἄλλο πάρεξ τοῦ ἐόντος, ἐπεὶ τό γε Μοῖρ' ἐπέδησεν
οὖλον ἀκίνητόν τ' ἔμεναι· τῷ πάντ(α) ὀνόμασται[66]
ὅσσα βροτοὶ κατέθεντο πεποιθότες εἶναι ἀληθῆ,
γίγνεσθαί τε καὶ ὄλλυσθαι, εἶναί τε καὶ οὐχί,
καὶ τόπον ἀλλάσσειν διά τε χρόα φανὸν ἀμείβειν. (B8.34–41)

And the same thing is for thinking and wherefore there is thought;
for not without what-is, in which it is expressed,
will you find thinking; for nothing either is or will be
except what-is, since Fate shackled just this
to be whole and unchanging; with respect to this have all names been given
as many as mortals laid down, trusting them to be true,
to come to be and to pass away, to be and not to be,
and to change place and to exchange bright color.

The passage opens with a reminder of the statement of the connection between thought and what-is that had been given in B3. But there is an additional point: not only is it the case that "the same thing is for thinking and for being" (B3), but what-is is also that on account of which there is thought (hence the *houneken* of line 34). This is further explicated in the next lines: what-is is the necessary condition of thinking, and thinking is committed

[64] The passage is sometimes taken as a comment on the inadequacy of mortal thought; see for instance, Coxon (*Fragments*, pp. 208–12), Tarán (*Parmenides*, pp. 141–44), Barnes ("Eleatic One," p. 13). It would be odd, however, to find such a claim in the midst of Parmenides' discussion of the character of what-is. The passage reads more naturally as an account of the fit between thinking and what-is, stressing that what-is alone is the true object of thought. We then have a reminder, not of the stupidity or inanity of mortal thinking, but that mortal thought, inadequate though it might be, aims at or tries to reach what-is, which is the natural home of thinking or inquiry. These lines then fit comfortably both with the discussions of the relation of *noos* and what-is in B2, B3, and B4, and with the rejection of mortal attempts at inquiry in B6 and B7.

[65] On Coxon's version of the line, see Chap. I, n. 22.

[66] For ὀνόμασται here, see Woodbury, "Parmenides on Names"; Mourelatos, *Route*, pp. 180–91; and Robinson, "Ascertainment of the Real," pp. 631–32. Although I accept Woodbury's philological arguments for ὀνόμασται rather than the ὄνομ(α) ἔσται of DK, Tarán, and Coxon, for philosophical reasons my interpretation of the line is closer to that of Mourelatos.

to what-is. These lines reaffirm the connection between thinking and what-is that Parmenides had stressed in fragments B2, 3, and 4. Thinking is committed to what-is (*pephatismenon*);[67] that is, the aim or target of thought or mind (*noos*) is what-is and thought finds its completion or fulfillment there. This passage fits neatly just after the preliminary discussion of the completion or perfection of what-is, the object of thought. We should recall that the thinking that Parmenides is concerned with in the earlier fragments is inquiry or *dizēsis* into the nature of a thing; thus thought must be about what something is. The fit between *noos* and what-is is further secured by the claim that "it was just this that Fate shackled to be whole and unchanging." The mention of *Moira*, Fate, not only continues the personifications of necessity that are scattered throughout the poem but also stresses the inevitability of the connection between thinking and what-is. The features of what-is that have been enumerated in B8 (its unchanging character, its wholeness, and its perfection) guarantee that it can be altogether grasped by *noos* and that in aiming at what-is *noos* will not be led astray or forced into wandering by the incursion of what-is-not. Thus, thinking and what-is form an ideally suited pair: thought aims at what-is and what-is has just the nature that makes it the suitable object of thinking.

All inquiry aims at what-is, even when those practicing inquiry have been mistaken about its true character. Lines B8.38–41 point out that when mortals give their mistaken accounts of the *kosmos*, they are attempting to name or describe what-is, even when they do not realize it. Just as the mortals of B6 and B7 do not grasp that theirs is the route of what-is-not, so here they do not understand that their attempts fail when they try to name what-is in affirming things that have characters that come to be and pass away, change place and color. These names fail to connect with anything, because they try to attribute to what-is characteristics that entail that what-is is not. A genuine name reveals the nature of a thing, but that which comes to be

[67] For discussions of *pephatismenon*, see Tarán (*Parmenides*), pp. 123–28, and Mourelatos, *Route*, pp. 170–72. Coxon (*Fragments*) translates "when one thing has been said of another" and claims that "though Parmenides discriminates assertions which express conceiving from those which do not, his monism precludes him from ascribing any reality to conceiving, unless this may be regarded as in the strictest sense identifying the individual's mind with the One Being" (p. 210). Coxon treats the entire section from lines 34 to 41 as a rejection of "human experience" (pp. 208–9); this strikes me as improbable, particularly because the argument depends on the dubious οὐδὲ χρόνος ἐστὶν ἢ ἔσται in line 36. Moreover, the placement of the lines, surrounded by claims about the completeness or perfection of what-is suggests that the passage is a further consideration of what-is rather than a rejection of human experience. The arguments of B8 up to this point have been concerned with the character of what-is, and this is the topic to which we return in lines 42 to 48. It would be odd were this sustained discussion, where the subject is what-is, to be suddenly interrupted for a rejection of human experience. When the subject does turn to human views or experience, that turn is marked by the goddess's specific statement that she is about to "cease her trustworthy account" and begin a discussion of mortal thought in lines 50ff.

and passes away, changes place or exchanges bright color fails to be such a thing, for it fails to meet the criteria that have been set out in B8, and so it is actually what-is-not.[68] But what-is-not cannot be genuinely named. As B8.16–18 say, it follows from the basic *krisis*, or "decision," between what-is and what-is-not that what-is-not is to be let go as un-thought and un-named "because it is not a true route."[69] Inquiry into what-is-not does not constitute "a true route," because it wanders away from what-is, actually goes nowhere, and we learn nothing from it.

Lines 36–37 are often supposed to contain an argument for numerical monism, for here Parmenides claims that "nothing either is or will be except what-is, since Fate shackled just this to be whole and unchanging" (οὐδὲν γὰρ ⟨ἤ⟩ ἐστιν ἢ ἔσται ἄλλο πάρεξ τοῦ ἐόντος, ἐπεὶ τό γε Μοῖρ' ἐπέδησεν οὖλον ἀκίνητόν τ' ἔμεναι).[70] But if we recall that Parmenides' subject is what it is to be the character or nature of thing, the likelihood that Parmenides is committing himself to numerical monism is diminished. The subject in these lines is the connection between thought or inquiry into a thing's nature and what-is; Parmenides insists that thought must connect with what-is because there simply is no way for the account of the nature of something to be either overtly or implicitly negative.[71] Anything negative would present us with something too vague and indeterminate to be thought about and would thus put us on the route of what-is-not. There is nothing outside of what-is, as it is characterized in the arguments here in B8, that could serve as an account of what it is to be something. But this does not entail that there must be only one instance of what-is. All that follows is that every instance of what-is must be one in the appropriate sense. It is only when we read the *esti* existentially and assume that the subject is something like "the all," that a commitment to numerical monism could even begin to look plausible here. But as we saw in Chapter I, there are good reasons not to read the *esti* existentially, and there is no place in B8 where it is reasonable to suppose that "the all"

[68] Thus the correctness of Mourelatos's arguments against the standard text and translation. Parmenides is not saying that what mortals offer are " 'mere' names" (indeed, there is nothing in the Greek that corresponds to 'mere,' which translators add). Rather mortals attempt to name and elevate to the status of real that which must be left nameless. Mourelatos, *Route*, n. 41, pp. 182–83.

[69] B8.15–18: ἡ δὲ κρίσις περὶ τούτων ἐν τῷδ' ἔστιν· ἔστιν ἢ οὐκ ἔστιν· κέκριται δ' οὖν, ὥσπερ ἀνάγκη, τὴν μὲν ἐᾶν ἀνόητον ἀνώνυμον (οὐ γὰρ ἀληθὴς ἔστιν ὁδός), τὴν δ' ὥστε πέλειν καὶ ἐτήτυμον εἶναι (and the decision about these is in this: is or is not; and it has been decided, just as is necessary, to leave the one unthinkable and unnamed [for it is not a true route], and the other to be and to be genuine).

[70] The claim here is that, in Tarán's words, "there is nothing else besides Being, i.e., Being is the only thing there is" (Tarán, *Parmenides*, p. 190); see also pp. 135–36; Stokes, *One and Many*, pp. 141–44.

[71] The connection between thinking and inquiry is established as the fundamental issue in B2.2 where the goddess claims that her subject is the routes of inquiry available for thinking: αἵπερ ὁδοὶ μοῦναι διζήσιός εἰσι νοῆσαι.

is what Parmenides is talking about.[72] Moreover, a commitment to numerical monism would seem to require a sign and a proof all to itself, rather than a comment in a passage in B8 that returns to an issue (the relation of thinking and what-is) that has already been discussed in fragments B3, 4, and 5. If it were the case that numerical monism were Parmenides' chief contribution to the philosophical inquiry of his day, we might well expect to find a fuller discussion of it than he apparently provides (or to which any of the partisans of numerical monism among commentators is able to point).

The final lines of the discussion of the character of what-is return to and expand on its perfection. Here that perfection and the uniform, unified, character of what-is is expressed in the metaphor of the sphere.

> αὐτὰρ ἐπεὶ πεῖρας πύματον, τετελεσμένον ἐστί,[73]
> πάντοθεν εὐκύκλου σφαίρης ἐναλίγκιον ὄγκῳ,
> μέσσοθεν ἰσοπαλὲς πάντῃ· τὸ γὰρ οὔτε τι μεῖζον
> οὔτε τι βαιότερον πελέναι χρεόν ἐστι τῇ ἢ τῇ·
> οὔτε γὰρ οὐκ ἐόν ἐστι, τό κεν παύοι μιν ἱκνεῖσθαι
> εἰς ὁμόν, οὔτ' ἐόν ἐστιν ὅπως εἴη κεν ἐόντος
> τῇ μᾶλλον τῇ δ' ἧσσον, ἐπεὶ πᾶν ἐστιν ἄσυλον·
> οἷ γὰρ πάντοθεν ἶσον, ὁμῶς ἐν πείρασι κύρει. (B8.42–49)

> Further, since there is an outermost limit, it is completed,
> like the bulk of a sphere well-rounded from every side,
> from the center evenly matched everywhere: for it may be neither
> somewhat larger
> nor somewhat smaller here or there;
> for there is neither what is not, which might prevent it from reaching
> the same, nor is there any way in which what is could be
> here more or there less than what is, since it is all inviolate;
> for equal to itself from every direction, it lies equally in the bounds.

These lines pick up and continue the argument about the perfection of what-is that began in lines 32–33. These earlier lines had claimed that what-is is completed or perfected because it is in need of or lacks nothing, while

[72] Indeed, the only place where a such a subject seems even possible is in the so-called Cornford fragment; but even there (despite Cornford's own view) rendering *toi panti* as "the All" seems dubious. Perry, pp. 2–3, points out that "when [Parmenides] uses *pas* to describe being, it has adverbial force, 'in its entirety, completely.' " Mourelatos discusses various possible translations and opts for "Such [or 'alone'], immobile, is that for which as a whole the name is: 'to be' " (Mourelatos, *Route*, pp. 185–86). See Perry for a discussion of the history of the debate about the line. Perry, following Diels and Tarán (*Parmenides*), argues that it is not a separate fragment but a misstatement or adaptation of B8.38. Coxon likewise takes the line to be variation on B8.38 (Coxon, *Fragments*, p. 3n.1). I agree with Perry and Coxon.

[73] I follow Diels, Mourelatos (*Route*), and Gallop (*Parmenides*) in putting a comma here, rather than after *pantothen* in the next line. See Mourelatos, *Route*, p. 124n.24 on both the punctuation and the structure of the next line.

the later passage stresses the link between the limits or boundaries of what-is and its completion. Those boundaries first appear in line 26, and in the lines that follow the images of limits reappear several times, often linked with a personification of Necessity. The images intensify until we finally reach the resemblance of what-is to the bulk or expanse of a sphere, perfectly composed, unchanging, and held firmly within bonds. The lines that separate the two phases of the proof of perfection also stress the bonds or limits of what-is (the "shackles" of Fate), for it is those bonds that make what-is the perfect partner to thinking. The names that mortals try to use to get to what-is, change of place, exchange of bright color, to be and not to be, fail to connect with what-is because the names imply that which is not limited or which can escape the bonds into what-is-not. Those names indicate that what-is can change its aspect or character, or that how it is depends on how one looks at it. But the final argument about its perfection shows that this is not the case: like a sphere, what-is is always the same, no matter from what direction or angle one approaches it. Because of its predicational unity, what-is, like the sphere, does not present a different character to different observers, for there is only the single character that is there to be observed. The sphere analogy is just that, an analogy. If one understands what-is, one understands it in its entirety, and anyone else's understanding of it will be exactly the same.

Elements of previous discussions of signs resurface here. The rejection of what-is-not from B2 is part of the claim that there is no what-is-not that would prevent what-is from being uniform, and part of the proof of the indivisibility and cohesiveness of what-is also reappear. In that proof (in lines 22–25), Parmenides argued that what-is is indivisible because "it is all alike." Further, he claimed that there is not "somewhat more here, which would prevent it from cohering, nor somewhat less there, but all is completely full of what is" (B8.23–24). In these lines the claim that what-is is "neither somewhat more nor somewhat less" argues that to be *F* is to be uniformly *F* with no possibility of gaps or differences in the *F*-ness that something is. In the later lines dealing with perfection, the same point is used to show that genuinely being *F* entails being perfectly *F* throughout, with no possibility of being more or less *F*, which would allow just the sort of perspectival differences that arise in the names mortals have tried to give to what-is. Those perspectival differences depend on a multiplicity of characters or natures and so on the being of what-is-not, which would make room for not-*F*. But there is no what-is-not that would thwart the completeness of what-is. The assertion that "it is all inviolate" emphasizes the predicational unity of what-is, for none of it is such as would allow it to be more or less, which would permit the intrusion of what-is-not. The image of what-is lying "equally in the bounds" gives us a picture of the contained, unchanging, complete character of what-is; the bounds are a metaphorical device for indicating that what-is cannot wander away into what-is-not, nor can what-is-not invade the proper sphere of what-is.

Lines 42–49 liken the perfection or completeness of what-is to the bulk or expanse of a sphere, and as has been often noted, this is a comparison rather than an assertion that what-is is a sphere, or that the *kosmos* is spherical.[74] That the comparison is apposite has also been noted, for a sphere is the only one of the regular solids that presents the same appearance no matter from what angle we view it.[75] This is also a mark of what-is; to be a genuine instance of what-is, a thing must be always the same, no matter how we consider it, no matter from what direction we contemplate it. Being completely what it is, what-is "lies equally in the bounds"; that is, it is ungenerably, indivisibly, unchangingly, perfectly, just what it is. For if it failed to be any of these things, there would be the gaps and imperfections that this proof rules out. Thus, the proof of completeness provides an apt summing up and gathering together of the various signs of what-is that have been discussed through B8. Likewise, the image of the sphere illustrates the predicational monism that Parmenides has argued for throughout B8.

3. Difference, Division, and Monism

So far, nothing in the proofs and discussions of B8 suggests that Parmenides adopted numerical monism. Indeed, as we have seen, the arguments of B8 seem to be aimed at a discussion of what it is to be the nature of something (or what it is to be a basic entity), showing that being the nature of *F* implies that that thing be all, only, completely, and unchangingly *F*. But there is a last possibility for numerical monism, for it might be argued that if there are a plurality of entities, each of which satisfies the criteria for what-is, they must be different from each other. And, it may be argued, insofar as they are different, each is not what the other is, and so what-is-not appears. This, it might seem, is exactly what Parmenides is arguing against when he asserts that what-is is indivisible because it is all alike (οὐδὲ διαιρετόν ἐστιν, ἐπεὶ πᾶν ἐστιν ὁμοῖον B8.22).

Predicational monism asserts that each thing that genuinely is can hold only a single predicate and must hold it in an extremely strong way; all claims of the form "*X* is *F*" are claims about what *X* is by its nature, so that no internal divisions are possible. Thus, no claim that could have the form "*X* is by nature not-*F*" is allowed. Suppose now that there is a plurality of such basic beings (*F* and *G*). *F* is all and only, and completely *F*, for it is *F* by nature. *G* is all and only, and completely *G*, for it is *G* by nature. Yet they are two, not one, and so they are different, and so *F* is not *G* and *G* is not *F*. Does it not follow from this that *F* is not and that *G* is not, and so that in trying to explain what it is to be *F* and what it is to be *G*, we have wandered

[74] See Tarán, *Parmenides*, pp. 150–60 for a full discussion of the issue.

[75] See Mourelatos, *Route*, pp. 124–30.

off the route of what-is onto the route of what-is-not? Is this not a violation of the claim "is or is not" (ἔστιν ἢ οὐκ ἔστιν)? In answering this question, we must distinguish between whether or not Parmenides took something to be a problem for his view and whether or not that thing actually is a genuine problem for a theory. While I think that there is a possible difficulty for a theory such as Parmenides' lurking here, I do not think that Parmenides or any other Presocratic thinker saw a problem here. In not seeing that potential difficulty, the later Presocratics did not misunderstand Parmenides' theory (nor did he misunderstand his own).

Parmenides' focus was on the issue of what it is to be a genuine entity. Given that concern, he is primarily interested in the internal structure of each thing and whether or not an account of what that thing is avoids the negative route of inquiry. In such an inquiry, there can be no commitment, either explicitly or implicitly, to negative internal predications. Seeing that such an account of what a thing genuinely is must be whole, complete, unchanging, and cohesive, Parmenides had a powerful weapon against earlier metaphysical theories; moreover, he was able to formulate criteria that future metaphysical and cosmological theories must meet. Later Pluralist theories, such as those of Empedocles and the Atomists, adopted Parmenides' criteria for an acceptable theory, without either seeing or addressing the issue of difference. For instance, Empedocles in B17 stresses that each of his roots is equal to the other, and yet each has its own character.[76]

> πῦρ καὶ ὕδωρ καὶ γαῖα καὶ ἠέρος ἄπλετον ὕψος·
> νεῖκός τε οὐλόμενον δίχα τῶν, ἀτάλαντον ἁπάντῃ,
> καὶ φιλότης ἐν τοῖσιν, ἴση μῆκός τε πλάτος τε·
> . . .
> ταῦτα γὰρ ἶσά τε πάντα καὶ ἥλικα γένναν ἔασι,
> τιμῆς δ' ἄλλης ἄλλο μέδει, πάρα δ' ἦθος ἑκάστῳ,
> ἐν δὲ μέρει κρατέουσι περιπλομένοιο χρόνοιο.
>
> (Empedocles B17.18–20; 27–29)

> Fire and water and earth and unbounded height of air;
> and destructive strife apart from these, equal in every way,
> and love among them, equal in length and breadth;
> . . .
> For all these [the roots] are equal and of like age and origin,
> but each has a different prerogative and each its own character
> and they hold sway in turn as time goes around.

Empedocles nowhere suggests that differences in character among the four roots (and between them and Love and Strife) vitiates the special and strong being that each has. Indeed, in the lines immediately following B17.29

76 See, for instance, Wright, *Empedocles*, p. 171.

(quoted above), he reasserts that nothing else comes to be or passes away in addition to these things that are, stressing the fundamental character of the roots (B17.30–35). So Empedocles, while adopting a Parmenidean framework, adopts a pluralism that is committed to differences among the fundamental entities, without thinking that these differences commit him to a negative characterization of each thing that is. The available evidence suggests that the same is true of Atomism. According to Aristotle, atoms differed from one another in shape as well as in arrangement and position (*Metaph.* 985b14; 67A6); Theophrastus reports (*Sens.* 66; 68A135) that differences in taste are the result of different atomic shapes: bitter taste comes from small, smooth, round atoms; salt taste results from large atoms that are not round (and sometimes uneven or rough). Again, there is no evidence that the Atomists worried that these differences among atoms would jeopardize their status as the basic entities and realities of the theory by importing a negation into their natures. Parmenides is committed to and argues for the internal unity of each thing that is (so there can be no internal differences in each thing that is), but he also allows for a numerical plurality of such things (thus allowing for external differences between things that are). The question is whether external differences entail internal differences (and thus internal negations) of the sort that Parmenides does not allow. Neither Parmenides nor any of the pluralists or atomists that I discuss raise or deal with this issue. So it seems that Parmenides did not think that external differences cause internal differences.

The last great response to Parmenides, working within Parmenides' own criteria and account of the nature of what-is, was Plato's Theory of Forms. In the middle period dialogues, in which the Theory was formulated and refined, there is no evidence that Plato thought that a plurality of different Forms, each with its own nature, posed any difficulty. The *Phaedo* lists a number of Forms that are not only different from one another (for instance, the Equal, the Beautiful, the Good, the Just, the Holy are all mentioned at 75c10–d2), but also pairs of opposite Forms as well (Largeness itself and Smallness itself appear at 102d6–7; they also appear at 75d9 as "the larger and the smaller"). Given the evidence of the *Symposium* (210e6–211b5), we can infer that Plato thought that each of these Forms satisfied the Parmenidean criteria for what-is, and that their differences from one other were no obstacle to the success of the theory. But, as Plato himself showed in the *Parmenides*, this confidence was misplaced. For in the First Hypothesis, in exploring the claim that the One is the same as itself and different from other things, Plato shows that, if one adopts the strong Parmenidean claim that the only way something may hold a predicate is as part of that thing's nature, claims of difference simply cannot be made.[77] The arguments at *Parmenides* 139c3–d1 show that The One cannot be different because it can be only what it is in virtue of itself,

[77] I discuss these arguments in "Problems of Unity."

and in virtue of itself it is neither different nor the same. Were it different, the One could not be one; and being one, it cannot be different. It is worth noting that Plato does not actually argue that difference entails what-is-not or not-being. Rather, he argues that on the Parmenidean view of what-is only what a thing is in virtue of itself can be properly predicated of it. Relations among the things that are simply cannot be accommodated on this view. But the arguments here and in the later hypotheses of the *Parmenides* (especially those involving being and not-being) eventually lead to the arguments of the *Sophist*, with the testing of the words of Father Parmenides and the overthrow of the Eleatic notion of what-is. This difficulty is, according to Plato, inherent in Parmenides' account of what-is; Plato seems to indicate that he is the first to have discovered it.

I conclude, then, that the Parmenidean rejection of division and difference within what-is does not force us to interpret Parmenides as a numerical monist, and that the most natural reading of B8 and the other fragments of the *Alētheia* supports the claim that Parmenides' interest was in exploring the nature of theoretically basic entities and in formulating the criteria that must be met by an account of what a thing really is. To be a basic entity is to meet these criteria. Such an entity must be a predicational unity, but Parmenides' theory leaves open the question of how many such entities there are or may be.

III

Doxa and Deception

CHIEF AMONG the mysteries of Parmenides' poem are the relation between its two main parts, the *Alētheia* and the *Doxa*, and the proper interpretation of the *Doxa* itself.[1] The two issues are connected, for no claim about the relation of the two parts can be made without an analysis of the message of the *Doxa*. How should the *Doxa* section of Parmenides' poem be interpreted?[2] Is it utterly deceptive, as some have thought,[3] or does it illustrate the best

[1] I count as the *Doxa* fragments B9 through B19, plus those lines of B8 (B8.53–61) that follow the goddess's announcement (at B8.50–52) that she is ceasing her trustworthy account. This includes both the goddess's analysis of human error and the remaining details of the cosmogony. What survives of the *Doxa* has been estimated by Diels (in *Parmenides*) to be about one-tenth of the original text. In contrast, thanks to Simplicius, we have what Diels estimates to be about nine-tenths of the *Alētheia*. Gallop (*Parmenides*, p. 29n.8) notes that Diels provides no basis for his estimate and that "the question of length remains a matter for speculation," although on p. 21 and in n. 63 Gallop agrees that the *Doxa* was probably much longer than the *Alētheia*. The division into sections called *Alētheia* and *Doxa* was not made by Parmenides himself.

[2] Even the ancient writers seem unsure about the purpose of the *Doxa* or its proper relation to *Alētheia*. Aristotle seems undecided about Parmenides' purpose. At *Ph.* I.2 (185a17–18) Aristotle asserts that the monists (referring to Parmenides and Melissus) were not writing about nature (this echoes his claim at 184b25–185a4 that "the consideration of whether what is is one and immovable is not part of an examination of nature"). Later in Book I (in Chapter 5 at 188a20–22) he says that Parmenides agreed that opposites are principles of nature. So, according to Aristotle, Parmenides was not interested in nature even though he gives principles of nature. The apparent paradox is resolved by Aristotle's interpretative claim that, in the end, Parmenides "being forced to follow the *phainomena*, . . . posits two causes and two principles" (*Metaph.* I.5 986b31–34 = A24). Aristotle notes in the *Metaph.* passage that Parmenides says that what is is one in definition but "more than one according to sensation" (τὸ ἓν μὲν κατὰ τὸν λόγον, πλείω δὲ κατὰ τὴν αἴσθησιν ὑπολαμβάνων εἶναι). Other ancient commentators echo Aristotle's view: Plutarch claims that *Alētheia* deals with the realm of the intellect, the *Doxa* with appearance (*ad. Col.* 1114D = A34); see also [Plutarch] *Strom.* 5 = A22. Simplicius echoes this account: "He calls this account seeming and deceptive, not as false without qualification, but because the sensibles have fallen out of the world of the intellect into appearing and seeming" (*in Ph.* 39.10–12). Aristotle seems to be groping toward an explanation of the relation between the two parts of the poem when he says that "what is one in definition can appear many through sensation," but there is no attempt to connect the two parts in Plutarch or Simplicius.

[3] This view of the *Doxa* is taken by Mourelatos (*Route*), by Owen ("Eleatic Questions"), and Barnes (*PP,* vol. I, p. 157). Nevertheless, Barnes claims that "the goddess, by describing the Way of Opinion and thereby indicating its flaws, will ensure that Parmenides does not succumb to its meretricious temptations" (p. 157). Barnes does not explain how this description, in all

possible false account that can be given of the world of appearance?[4] Does it depict the minimal error that infects all mortal attempts to explain the sensible *kosmos*;[5] or is it a supplement to *Alētheia*, giving an account of the world as perceived by human beings?[6] This chapter explores the problem of the *Doxa* and offers an account of it that is consistent with the claims of *Alētheia* and that at the same time explains why Parmenides included it in the poem.[7] I shall argue that, while there is deception in the *Doxa* (though not

---

its detail, will save Parmenides from all mortal theories. I tentatively endorsed this negative account of the *Doxa* in "Parmenidean Monism" and rejected it in "Deception and Belief." Here I develop the view I explored in the latter article. A summary and discussion of many of the views that have been advanced concerning the *Doxa* may be found in Clark, "Parmenides and Sense-Perception," pp. 23–24.

4 See, for instance, A. A. Long, "Principles." Long argues that while the *Doxa* is the best version of mortal error, it is nevertheless in error and cannot be correct. This view is also adopted by E. L. Minar, Jr., in "Parmenides and the World of Seeming."

5 See Tarán (*Parmenides*). Nussbaum ("Eleatic Conventionalism," p. 73) describes the *Doxa* as "the simplest version of the basic error of mortals." Stokes (*One and Many*, pp. 148–49) also endorses this account of the *Doxa*.

6 Simplicius seems to adopt this view when he interprets the move from *Alētheia* to *Doxa* as a shift from the intelligible to the sensible world (See n. 2, above and *in de Caelo* 557.19–24). It is the view taken by Chalmers ("Parmenides and the Beliefs of Mortals"), who argues that the *Alētheia* and the *Doxa* describe the same world, the one from the point of view of eternity, the other from the point of view of time. A version of this account of the *Doxa* is to be found in Coxon (*Fragments*), who suggests that Parmenides argues against those who "believe in an empirical reality" (p. 183); at the same time, Coxon argues that the *Doxa* proposes a dualistic account of the sensible world that avoids the errors exposed in the *Alētheia*. It is not an account of truth and reality but is rather "an analysis of human experience in terms of elements which are themselves given in experience" (p. 221). On Coxon's view, Parmenides agrees with Xenophanes (see 21B1 and B34) that while human beings cannot know the truth, right belief about such things is possible. A similar account is adopted by Nehamas ("On Parmenides' Three Ways"): "[Parmenides'] refutation consisted in arguing that cosmology only touches appearance and not the world of reality. . . . He writes the *Doxa* because its falsehood consists not in its being a *wrong* description of appearance but in its being only a description of *appearance* and in its apparent claim to describe reality" (p. 108). A similar account is also suggested by Robinson's remarks in "Parmenides and Heraclitus," p. 165. See also Calvo, "Truth and Doxa," who does not present the contrast as between epistemic states but "between two contrasting forms of language" (p. 246). Finkelberg argues that the contrast between *Alētheia* and *Doxa* illustrates the differences between divine and mortal views of the universe (see "Material and Logical Monism" and " 'Like by Like' "). The difference between this type of account of the *Doxa* (which sees it as an account of the perceived world) and Long's (see note 4) is that this account interprets Parmenides as granting a measure of legitimacy to the *Doxa*, while Long argues that the *Doxa* "demonstrates that the appearances thought by ordinary men to fill reality are totally false" ("Principles," p. 98). There is also the ancient view, endorsed by Aristotle and supported by the evidence from Aetius, that Parmenides intended the *Doxa* as a serious cosmology, "following the *phainomena*" (see *Metaph.* 986b27–28 = A24). On the strength of B16, Aristotle includes Parmenides among those who think that the truth about what-is can be found in the sensibles (*Metaph.* 1010a1–3).

7 For a summary of views concerning the *Doxa* held earlier in the century, see Verdenius, *Parmenides*, pp. 45–49.

in the goddess's account of it), nonetheless the *Doxa* does not in principle renounce beliefs about the sensible world. For, although Parmenides argues that the sensible world alone cannot be the source of knowledge, he does not reject it completely.[8] The problem for mortals is that they suppose that the world reported by the senses is the only reality there is and that coming-to-be, passing-away, and change are therefore real; but Parmenides' diagnosis of this problem does not entail that the world reported by the senses is therefore to be rejected entirely. While Parmenides himself does not give a complete and trustworthy account of the world reported to us by the senses, the poem does not claim that a story about the sensible world that is consistent with the metaphysical and epistemological principles of the *Alētheia* cannot be told. Thus, while I agree with those who argue that the particular view of the nature of things given in the *Doxa* is incorrect, I also agree with those who see the *Doxa* as having something positive to say about mortal belief.[9] I shall suggest that Parmenides supposes a trustworthy cosmology may be possible and that he discloses what such a theory might be like and how it could be tested. After considering some of the difficulties faced by a number of interpretations of the *Doxa*, I discuss the problems of deception and mortal belief and then turn to a positive account of the *Doxa*.

1. Puzzles

At B8.50–52 the goddess announces that she has completed her account of what-is:

ἐν τῷ σοι παύω πιστὸν λόγον ἠδὲ νόημα
ἀμφὶς ἀληθείης· δόξας δ' ἀπὸ τοῦδε βροτείας
μάνθανε κόσμον ἐμῶν ἐπέων ἀπατηλὸν ἀκούων·

[8] While this apparently aligns my view with those of Coxon and Nehamas, there are, as will be seen, important differences. For instance, I argue that the content of the *Doxa*, as it appears in the poem, is not offered as an account of what the senses report which is correct in all details. Rather, coming to understand what is wrong in the *Doxa* can help us to construct an acceptable theory of the sensible world. Moreover, I do not claim that the *Doxa* is meant merely as an account of appearance; rather, I argue that Parmenides conceives the possibility of an explanation of the content of sense perception that is grounded in what-is. While there is a difference between appearance and reality, there is the possibility of a relation between the two. A possible objection to my account is the announcement in B1.30 that there is no "true trust" (*pistis alēthēs*) in mortal beliefs. I deal with this issue below, in Section 4.

[9] I agree with de Rijk (in "Did Parmenides Reject the Sensible World?") that there are both positive and negative aspects to the story the goddess tells about mortal beliefs. We agree that the goddess not only warns against the opinions of mortals but also explains what is wrong with the hope that we should come to have correct views about mortal beliefs. But our views diverge sharply in the accounts that we give of the nature of the mistake and the positive lessons to be learned.

> Here I make an end for you of my trustworthy speech and thought
> about truth; from here on learn mortal beliefs
> listening to the deceptive order of my words.

Here is a warning that the goddess is about to say something untrustworthy. The deceptive character of the goddess's accounting of the *Doxa* raises a number of problems (some of which share a common difficulty).

First, if, as many have supposed, the *Doxa* is wholly deceptive, why should Parmenides have included it at all? The answer comes at B8.61: there the goddess tells the *kouros* that the account is related "so that no thought of mortals shall ever overtake you" (ὡς οὐ μή ποτέ τίς σε βροτῶν γνώμη παρελάσσῃ). But the varieties of mortal error are, we might suppose, limitless. Why should hearing this particular incorrect account allow us to evaluate (and reject) all possible erroneous mortal beliefs?[10] How, exactly, are we to evaluate other accounts? Does the likely-seeming story told by the goddess include an account of the criteria to be used in judging *doxai*? Are they the same criteria that were enumerated in the signs and arguments of B8? Those criteria allowed for distinguishing between truth and falsity, between what-is and what-is-not. What would be needed here in the *Doxa* are criteria for judging falsehoods with respect to one another. What are these criteria?

Second, in the *Alētheia*, the goddess repeatedly tells her hearer to judge, to ponder, to consider, to test by reflection (B2.1, B6.2, B7.2, B7.5). Why does Parmenides instruct us to assess critically the claims of *Alētheia* while at the same time allowing us to accept passively a false account and a "deceptive ordering" in the *Doxa*? But if we are supposed to judge and to ponder the *Doxa* so that we shall not be outrun by the beliefs of mortals, and we know the *Doxa* to be false, we are back at the problem of criteria already raised.

Third, if the cosmology of the *Doxa* is false but also "the best possible account" of the world of sense experience that can be given,[11] what does "best" mean here?[12] How can one false cosmology be better than another

[10] The goddess's words suggest that hearing her account will arm the *kouros* against all varieties of mortal error; against both those theories that have already been proposed and those that he will come across in the future. It is difficult to see how the details that she gives (even if we consider there are many details of the *Doxa* that have been lost to us) can do this, unless the *kouros* is simply to learn this account and repeat that any theory that deviates from it must be false. But this is not teaching the *kouros* understanding; it is indoctrinating him and seems at odds with the goddess's pedagogical methods in the *Alētheia*, and especially her injunction to "judge by *logos*." If the error lies in embracing change as real, we have no need of the *Doxa*, for that lesson has been learned in the *Alētheia*.

[11] See Long, "Principles," p. 96.

[12] Mackenzie questions whether "unequivocally *wrong* views of the world can be rank-ordered" ("Parmenides' Dilemma," pp. 10–11). One might order theories depending on how close to the truth they come and on the nature of their errors, but given the interpretation of the *Doxa* under consideration here, that would not seem to be possible.

false cosmology? To suggest that this is possible is to claim that there are criteria for comparing false beliefs included in the account. One might, for instance, suppose that one cosmology is better than another because it gives a more coherent account of our sense experience or because it fits the phenomena more closely. But this presupposes that a coherent account or a better fit are desirable and known to be desirable, and thus that there are well-recognized (or well-argued-for) criteria for ranking cosmologies with respect to coherence and correspondence to appearances. What are these criteria? On the view that the *Doxa* is entirely false, the only genuine criteria given in the poem are those for what-is, given in the *Alētheia*; and on this interpretation nothing in the *Doxa* is acceptable by those criteria (and we do not need the details of the *Doxa* to know this). Moreover, we have no evidence that Parmenides claimed that earlier theories failed to account for appearances (from his standpoint, their downfall lies in not being genuine accounts of what-is).

Fourth, we might wonder if all mortal opinion is to be rejected. B1.30 announces that there is no true trust or fidelity (*pistis alēthēs*) in mortal opinions. Does this mean that they are all to be repudiated? B6 and B7 warn against a route "on which mortals wander, two-headed, knowing nothing" (ἣν δὴ βροτοὶ εἰδότες οὐδέν πλάττονται, δίκρανοι B6.4–5). But does this imply that any belief held by a mortal is false? If so, this error can be detected easily and there is no apparent need for the elaborate constructions that constitute the *Doxa*. What of the *kouros*, to whom the goddess narrates her story? Does his knowledge, obtained from the goddess (but augmented by his own judging and pondering) somehow move him beyond the category of "mortal"? Does the goddess perhaps mean something quasi-technical by the term *mortal,* implying a particular sort of belief, perhaps trust in the reality of coming-to-be and passing-away, that all "mortal" opinions share?

Fifth, and finally, where is the deception in the goddess's account? Clearly, deception by the goddess is not the issue. If I know that you are about to tell me a falsehood, you cannot deceive me simply by telling it.[13] The goddess may be saying that mortal *doxai* are not knowledge but merely opinions. But what is deceptive about this? There is no deception involved in claiming that something is a matter of appearance rather than reality. The deception might come from thinking the *Doxa* to be true when it is not, but the goddess who narrates the poem explicitly warns against thinking that. So the deception must lie in the "likely-seeming" story told by the goddess. There is apparently something in that story to which we should pay particular attention, something that may deceive us into accepting falsehoods as true if we are not careful. But it cannot simply be that this is a story about sense experience. Is there then something deceitful in the content of the particular story that is told? This would be consistent with the goddess's assertion that

[13] See Clark, "Parmenides and Sense Perception," and Mourelatos, *Route*, pp. 225–28.

the arrangement or ordering (*kosmos*) of the account she gives in the *Doxa* is deceptive.

This suggests that those who claim that the *Doxa* contains an unacceptable account of the world as experienced by the senses are correct. But if there is no truth in the *Doxa,* we are left with the perennial question: Why should Parmenides have included it in the first place?[14] If the particular story that the goddess tells is false, must it follow that any such story is inadmissible? I shall argue that the goddess's account in the *Doxa* is deceptive, but that this does not entail that all aspects of the *Doxa* or all accounts of human beliefs and explanations of sense experience are to be rejected. In other words, the story that is told is wrong in part, but it is not wrong to tell such a story. Discovering the mistake in the view of things held by Parmenides' mortals will help in determining what the correct account should be.[15] That determination must be made by reflecting on the story, testing it by applying the criteria of trustworthiness from *Alētheia*, and reaching a decision about the very possibility of coherent mortal belief.[16] Thus, a hearer's response to the *Doxa* must be the same as the response to the claims of *Alētheia*: there we are exhorted to judge by *logos* what we are told.

The *Alētheia* presents a contrast between mortals and the *kouros* to whom the goddess tells her story. Mortals appear as passive creatures who wander along a vague, backward-turning route, with empty eyes and echoing tongues and ears, while the *kouros* learns to judge, ponder, and consider.[17] The end of B7 contains a warning that the *kouros* must avoid allowing habit to force

[14] According to Barnes (*PP*, vol. I, p. 156), Parmenides "says unequivocally that the Way of Opinion is a path of falsehood and deceit"; yet Barnes adds that it is not "unusual for a philosopher to describe, at length, views with which he vehemently disagrees." But there is usually a purpose in such descriptions: pointing out errors, suggesting amendments to a theory, and so on. Barnes makes no such suggestions about Parmenides' purposes in the *Doxa*, although he adds (without explanation) that the purpose of the *Doxa* is to help Parmenides avoid error (see note 3, above).

[15] It follows from this that although Parmenides does not give a completely correct cosmological account, he does not say that no such account can be given. Indeed, he partially demonstrates what such an account might be like. This is consistent with the practice in *Alētheia:* there Parmenides gives and argues for the criteria for an acceptable account of what-is, but he himself does not give that account.

[16] Such a view may be implicit in the comments of Heidel ("Certain Fragments"). For Heidel, the notion of *pistis alēthēs* is to be compared to the demonstration of forensic evidence, "and πίστις ἀληθής is just this demonstration of proof." Parmenides' objection to the beliefs of mortals is that "they do not carry the force of logical or dialectical evidence, or that such evidence is against them" (p. 719). Heidel does not explore the issue of whether all mortal belief is necessarily untrustworthy, or if some such belief might "carry the force of evidence" and hence pass the test.

[17] Lesher ("Parmenides' Critique," p. 25) has pointed out that the chariot ride of B1 pictures a submissive passenger; but once the goddess begins her account, "the situation changes, as [the *kouros*] is issued a steady stream of commands: come, attend (or carry away) my word, reflect on these things, keep away your thoughts, judge, keep in mind, etc."

him along the mortal route; rather he must judge and consider with care the arguments he is given and embrace them, not because he is given them by a goddess, but because he himself has judged them, using the tests that appear in B8. The *elenchos* (testing) is *poludēris* (rich in strife) because it must repeatedly fight against habit and experience; it is a battle to be won over and over. Those tests themselves, as we have seen, are grounded in the fundamental *krisis* "is or is not" and so can be seen to be the appropriate method of testing a claim about the nature of something. It would be strange were the goddess to allow the *kouros* to become passive just at the point when he will learn the truth about mortal beliefs, a truth that will, apparently, prevent his ever falling into or being taken in by mortal error (B8.61). This suggests that the story of the *Doxa* must itself be put to the test. Hearing the *Doxa* is only the beginning; an evaluation of it must follow.[18]

2. *Doxa*: Opposite Forms

So far, I have suggested that there is a problem in determining what is deceptive in the goddess's account of the *Doxa*, and that Parmenides warns that the story told there should be regarded critically. I now turn to the *Doxa* itself.[19] The basic principles of the *Doxa* are given in B8; at line 50 the goddess announces that she is ceasing her trustworthy account.

> ἐν τῷ σοι παύω πιστὸν λόγον ἠδὲ νόημα
> ἀμφὶς ἀληθείης· δόξας δ' ἀπὸ τοῦδε βροτείας
> μάνθανε κόσμον ἐμῶν ἐπέων ἀπατηλὸν ἀκούων·
> μορφὰς γὰρ κατέθεντο δύο γνώμαις[20] ὀνομάζειν,
> τῶν μίαν οὐ χρεών ἐστιν—ἐν ᾧ πεπλανημένοι εἰσίν—
> ἀντία[21] δ' ἐκρίναντο δέμας καὶ σήματ' ἔθεντο
> χωρὶς ἀπ' ἀλλήλων, τῇ μὲν φλογὸς αἰθέριον πῦρ,

[18] Those who argue that the *Doxa* is inherently unacceptable because it is an explanation of human sense experience will argue that the *Doxa* must fail any test from the *Alētheia* that it undergoes. But this is to prejudge the issue (see n. 26, below).

[19] In what follows I shall be more concerned with the originating principles that generate the cosmology of the *Doxa* and rather less with the particular details of that cosmology. For recent accounts of the content of the *Doxa*, see Finkelberg, "Cosmology"; Laks, " 'The More' and 'the Full' "; and Bollack, "La Cosmologie." For an attempt to link the accounts of the *Alētheia* and the *Doxa*, see Tarrant, "Conclusion."

[20] For γνώμαις rather than γνώμας, see Furley, "Notes," pp. 30–33. Furley is followed by Gallop (*Parmenides*); but see also Woodbury, "Parmenides on Naming." Woodbury suggests that "the proposed reading is not congenial in archaic verse" (p. 2) but also says that if it were to be accepted its sense would be "they established in their purposes two forms for naming," drawing on a parallel in Pindar *N*. X 89. I take the line to mean that mortals decided to name two forms; on this interpretation, Woodbury's comments do not undermine Furley's reading.

[21] See Long ("Principles," pp. 93–94) on *antia*.

ἤπιον ὄν, μέγ' ἐλαφρόν, ἑωυτῷ πάντοσε τωὐτόν,
τῷ δ' ἑτέρῳ μὴ τωὐτόν· ἀτὰρ κἀκεῖνο κατ' αὐτό
τἀντία νύκτ' ἀδαῆ, πυκινὸν δέμας ἐμβριθές τε.
τόν σοι ἐγὼ διάκοσμον ἐοικότα πάντα φατίζω,
ὡς οὐ μή ποτέ τίς σε βροτῶν γνώμη παρελάσσῃ. (B8.50–61)

Here I make an end for you of my trustworthy speech and thought
about truth; from here on learn mortal beliefs
listening to the deceptive order of my words;
for they laid down in their minds two forms for naming,
of which it is not right to name one[22] —in which they have gone astray—
and they distinguished opposites in body and established signs
separate from each other, here the ethereal flame of fire,
being mild and greatly light, in every way the same as itself
and not the same as the other; and then too, that one by itself
in contrast, dark night, a dense and heavy body.
This whole likely-seeming ordering I declare to you
so that no opinion of mortals shall ever run past you.

The goddess reports that mortals begin with two principles, Light and Night, which are the *archai* of a cosmology. At the same time, she points out that there is a fundamental error in the naming or positing of these two forms.[23] At B8.57–8 the apparent independence of Light from Night is stressed; both appear as complete and self-sufficient, which would, one might think, allow them to qualify as genuine entities according to the criteria of the *Alētheia*. But the passage makes explicit (at B8.55 and again at 59) that Light and Night are opposites. The *Doxa* is not simply a pluralism that happens to include two independent elements but is rather a dualism of a special sort.

The pervasive dualism of the whole poem has often been pointed out.[24] Yet the account of the routes in *Alētheia* makes it clear that only one alternative is a genuine path of inquiry. The truth of the correct route rules out the legitimacy of any other. Additionally, the proofs of B8 show that whatever there is must be one. The signs and arguments stress the internal predicational unity of any real entity (that is, of anything that constitutes the nature of a thing); but they do not rule out the possibility of a plurality of such entities. The dualism of the *Doxa*, if it is interpreted simply as a plurality of

[22] The proper translation and interpretation of this line is one of the most disputed issues in Parmenides studies. How I take this line and the one preceding will become clear in the discussion that follows.

[23] Long ("Principles") argues that the two opposites, Light and Night, are not to be identified with the two forms, which he takes to be Being and Not-Being. Thus, for Long, naming forms and distinguishing opposites are two different operations, the latter made possible by the former.

[24] See, for instance, Mansfeld, *Offenbarung*, and Mourelatos, *Route*, on the issue of the dualistic nature of the poem. Nehamas argues that "the overall structure of the poem is dualistic with a vengeance" ("Parmenides' Three Ways," p. 102).

theoretically fundamental entities, is thus not in principle incompatible with the arguments of *Alētheia*. But Light and Night do not just form a pair; they are a dualism of opposites. Parmenides' analysis of the problem with mortal thought lies, I suggest, in this dualism that is at the center of the cosmology. This is not an entirely new suggestion.[25] But I wish first to stress the nature of Parmenides' conception of the dualism of the *Doxa* and the unacceptable consequences of such a dualism, and then to argue that a truly pluralistic (i.e., non-dualistic) cosmology could perhaps win support from Parmenides. Mortal thought or cosmology as such is not ruled out *a priori* by Parmenides; the foundations of mortal opinion must be examined and tested, and some cosmological theories might well pass the test. The deception in the *Doxa* lies not in its being the thought of mortals (any mortals), but rather in its particular content, and especially in the ontological assumptions necessitated by the nature of the two principles that serve as its *archai*. The problem is not plurality in general, but dualism of a special kind.[26]

In the lines of B8 in which Light and Night are introduced, the goddess says that mortals "set up signs separate from one another" (σήματ' ἔθεντο χωρὶς ἀπ' ἀλλήλων B8.55–56). The reference to signs (*sēmata*) is reminiscent of those other signs at the beginning of B8: those on the way to what-is. The description of Light at B8.57–8 as "in every way the same as itself and not the same as the other" (ἑωυτῷ πάντοσε τωὐτόν, τῷ δ' ἑτέρῳ μὴ τωὐτόν) appears thoroughly positive and suggests that Light meets the test for what-is given at B8.29–31. There, in the proof for immobility, what-is is described as "remaining the same and in the same" (ταὐτόν τ' ἐν ταὐτῷ τε μένον); moreover, "it lies by itself (καθ' ἑαυτό τε κεῖται) and remains there steadfast: for mighty necessity holds it in the limits of a bond, which holds it in all around." But the characterization of Light and Night as opposites indicates that they are not as separate as they might seem nor as separate as they must be if they are truly or genuinely to be. First, Light is described in 8.58 as "in every way the same as itself and not the same as the other." As just noted, this appears positive: Light is set apart as uniform and in isolation from all else, so there are apparently no internal negations or divisions to be found in it. But "the other" is clearly Night, and "in every way not the same as the other" suggests that whatever characteristic we attribute to Light we

25 It is the basis of Mourelatos's account of the deceptive nature of the *Doxa* (in chap. 9 of *Route*) and of Coxon's reading of its constructive character (*Fragments*, pp. 13–17 and commentary on fragments B8.50-B19). See also Mourelatos, "Alternatives." My account of the nature of the dualism and the lesson to be learned from mortal error differs from these.

26 It is possible that no plurality will pass. Parmenides is not, I think, writing with the idea of justifying a particular cosmological theory. Any cosmology or mortal theory must be put to the test. I am arguing that Parmenides is not offering a sweeping denunciation of any and all cosmological theories (nor is he restricting his attack to philosophers). The target is those who offer explanations but either do not know or do not care that there are criteria and tests for the acceptability of their accounts.

must deny to Night and *vice versa*.[27] B8.56 describes the first form, "ethereal flame of fire, being mild and greatly light" (φλογὸς αἰθέριον πῦρ, ἤπιον ὄν, μέγ' ἐλαφρόν). At line 59 Night is given the opposite qualities, and these are expressly described as opposites or in contrast (*tantia*): Night is "dark (obscure), a dense and heavy body" (νύκτ' ἀδαῆ, πυκινὸν δέμας ἐμβριθές τε). To be Light is to be airy, mild, and very light; to be Night is to be dense-bodied, obscure, and heavy. For each aspect of the character of Light there is a corresponding and opposite aspect of the character for Night.[28]

It is helpful to think of Parmenides' conception of these opposites in terms of the present-day notion of enantiomorphism or incongruent counterparts. Enantiomorphs are objects that are mirror images of one another; and so they cannot be made congruent.[29] Such enantiomorphic objects as right and left hands cannot fit exactly into the same region of space. We can borrow this notion and say that enantiomorphic opposites exclude one another from the same conceptual or ontological space, because each of a pair of enantiomorphic opposites is defined in terms of what the other is not.[30] Right and left hands are enantiomorphic objects or incongruent counterparts; right-handedness and left-handedness are enantiomorphic opposites. Any complete account of the one includes, necessarily, a reference to and account of the other; and the account of the other will be in negative terms, no matter how positive such terms may seem at first glance. Thus any account of the being of left- or right-handedness will include irreducible references to the ways the other is not. In speaking of enantiomorphic opposites, we are not concerned with left and right as attributes of some underlying thing, but with left-handedness and right-handedness themselves.[31] This phenomenon appears in the opposites up and down or light and dark: to

[27] Finkelberg claims (in "Between Material and Logical Monism") that lines B8.57–58 are meant to refer to Light only and do not include Night at all. But that leaves no reference for "the other" in 58, nor does it take account of the parallel descriptions of Light and Night in B8.56–57 and 58–59, with the phrase ἑωυτῷ πάντοσε τωὐτόν, τῷ δ' ἑτέρῳ μὴ τωὐτόν between and linking the two descriptions. Moreover, in the introduction of the two forms (at B8.55–56), they are said to be separate or apart from each other (χωρὶς ἀπ' ἀλλήλων), which can be taken as indicating that each "is not the same as the other." (This would be true whether or not the forms are identical with the opposites.)

[28] See the discussion of the contrasting characteristics of Light and Night in Mourelatos, *Route*, chap. 9, especially Table 5A on p. 245.

[29] See Frederick, "Introduction to the Argument of 1768." "Enantiomorphs" are the same as "incongruent counterparts"; see Bennett, "Difference."

[30] We might think of the large and the small in the *Phd.* (101b3–103a2). In a sensible particular, the small withdraws at the approach of the large because the large and small cannot both occupy the same "space" in a particular (the same thing cannot be both large and small in the same way with respect to the same thing). But because the Forms Largeness and Smallness each have their own independent character, Socrates is able to explain the puzzles. Simmias can have both largeness and smallness in him, but not with respect to the same thing.

[31] Left and right as attributes (like up and down or hot and cold) may simply be relative. As Plato points out in the *Phd.*, the same thing may have contradictory attributes: Simmias

be up just is to be not-down, and *vice versa*; to be light is to be not-dark, and *vice versa*. The same is true of the *Doxa*'s two forms, Light and Night. Parmenides' argument is that despite their apparent separation and independence, and the insistence that they are opposite forms, the account of them in B8 makes it clear that the natures of the two are intertwined in exactly the way that enantiomorphic opposites are related.[32] There is an especially subversive aspect to these particular enantiomorphic opposites in the role they play in the cosmology of the *Doxa*, for lines B9.3–4 assert that all is full of Light and Night. There is no part of the *kosmos* that is neither light nor night and thus not infected with enantiomorphic opposition. Thus, Parmenides' complaint is that because the ultimate principles of mortal cosmology have enantiomorphic natures, they are an illegitimate mix of what-is and what-is-not.[33] If to be Light is to be not-Night and to be Night is to be not-Light, then this is a conception of the *kosmos* that accords precisely with Parmenides' characterization of mortals in B6 as "two-headed ... by whom to be and not to be have been thought to be the same and not the same" (δίκρανοι ... οἷς τὸ πέλειν τε καὶ οὐκ εἶναι ταὐτὸν νενόμισται κοὐ ταὐτόν). This suggests that Parmenides well understands the implications of the Heraclitean unity and identity of the opposites. For Heraclitus, opposites must both be and not be the same. Knowledge of one opposite must include knowledge of how it both is and is not the other. This is part of what allows Heraclitus to speak of the unity of opposites and to use the road up and the road down as an example of this unity.[34]

It might be objected that this account of the problem with enantiomorphic opposites will succeed only so long as we are restricted to the linguistic description or definition of such an opposite. We might be able to show

may be taller than Socrates but shorter than Phaedo; he may be to the right of Socrates and to the left of Phaedo, and so on. Parmenides' concern here is not with such relative attributes but with the ontological status of opposites (or basic entities whose nature is given in terms of opposites). See also Plato's *Parmenides* 129a2–c2, where Socrates remarks to Zeno that there is nothing amazing in *his* having opposite characteristics (through participation in the appropriate form), but it would indeed be a portent if the Forms themselves were characterized by their opposites. Socrates' claim depends on the Platonic distinction between being and having a character.

[32] Light and Night are not, after all, linguistic or logical opposites, as day/night and light/dark are.

[33] See Austin, *Being*, pp. 109–10 for a similar view: Fire and Night "mimic being and are not depicted as having come to be ... [they] are yet opposed to each other in terms of contraries which are true one at a time (one per entity) and all the way through in the sense that the other contrary is not represented anywhere except in the other" (italics omitted).

[34] Heraclitus B60; see also B8 and B51. For a discussion of the traditional notion of opposites and its development in Presocratic thought, see Kahn, *Anaximander*, Essay II: "Elements and Opposites: The Members of the World" (pp. 119–65, esp. pp. 130–33). See also Lloyd, *Polarity*. Lloyd's account of polar opposites supposes an opposition weaker than that which I see in enantiomorphic opposites. I discuss the role of the opposites in the thought of Parmenides' predecessors in Section 4, below.

or demonstrate the nature of such an opposite by pointing to it.[35] But this objection overlooks the issue of the nature of a thing—what it is in itself—that we are concerned with here. The problem is whether Light and Night are legitimate entities, and thus capable of being pointed to in the relevant sense at all. If they are things that involve the intermingling of what-is and what-is-not to the extent that I have suggested, then Parmenides would argue that they are pseudo-entities and cannot be pointed at. The problem with attributing a negative or mixed nature to a thing is shown in B2.7–8: "for you could neither know what-is-not (for it is not to be accomplished) nor could you single it out (οὔτε γὰρ ἂν γνοίης τό γε μὴ ἐόν [οὐ γὰρ ἀνυστόν] οὔτε φράσαις).[36] The arguments about what-is in the *Alētheia* show that the intertwined natures of Light and Night disqualify them as genuine cosmological principles. Because the dualism Light-Night is one that claims that to be and not to be are the same and not the same, it is, of necessity, a backward turning (*palintropos*) and forever incomplete account.[37]

While the story of the two forms may look plausible or likely (B8.60), the seeming independence of Light and Night is the core of the deception of which the goddess has warned, for Light and Night, with their intertwined natures, are not independent entities; rather, they are enantiomorphic and so the nature of each is to not be the other. Thus, the goddess's diagnosis of mortal error in B8.53–54 turns out to be instructive on two levels; and consideration of both levels is necessary for understanding the goddess's message. On the first level, the mistake is not the laying down of two forms, but the positing of enantiomorphic opposites. So, at first, it looks as though only one of the two should be named, because the other, as an opposite of the first, is not a legitimate form at all. On this level, it seems not to matter which of the two is jettisoned. But this is only the first tier of an analysis of the error. Because Light and Night are enantiomorphs, refusing to name one while naming the other would be just as serious an error. Even if the other opposite goes unnamed, it will, as it were, be left lurking in logical space. So, at the second level, B8.53–54 says that neither of the two, described as they are, should be named at all. The proper translation of B8.54 (τῶν μίαν οὐ χρεών ἐστιν [ὀνομάζειν]) has long been a crux of Parmenidean scholarship. This analysis of the strategy of this part of the poem suggests that two of the several translations and interpretations suggested may both be partially correct, since each concentrates on a different layer of analysis. Suppose we read line 54 as "one of which it is not right to name."[38] This gives the first level of analysis:

35 See, for instance, M. Curd, "Showing and Telling."

36 On this interpretation, see Mourelatos, "*Phradzo*."

37 Consider how one might try to give such a complete account of the natures of left- and right-handedness. The loop of inter-relatedness would just go on and on. Such a project is "not to be accomplished" (B2.7: *ouk anustos*).

38 As in Burnet, Barnes (*Early Greek*, p. 136), Gallop, (*Parmenides*, pp. 10–11 and 75), Guthrie (*HGP*, vol. II, p. 50; with a discussion of earlier scholarly opinion), and Mourelatos

the two forms are opposites; naming both of them entails negations in the natures of the two, so one of the two ought not to be named. But, moving on to a second possible translation, because the two are enantiomorphs, they cannot be named apart from one another; further, they cannot qualify as genuine entities, so neither should be named: "not one of which is it right to name."[39] Thus, two of the possible translations and interpretations of the line are both in a sense correct, though neither is so completely.[40] Having set up Light and Night as principles of their cosmology, mortals must attempt to give an account of the natures of these opposites. They will go astray quite literally if they attempt to do so. As suggested in B6, they take a route of inquiry that is vague, incomplete, and backward-turning. If Light and Night were indeed truly equal (as B9 claims) and independent, then both might be retained, for in neither would there necessarily be internal division and negation. But insofar as this theory insists on naming enantiomorphic opposites as its very basis, it cannot succeed. Mortals go astray here, at the very beginning, laying down two forms, neither of which they ought to name.

The two opposite forms having been posited, the rest of the cosmology unfolds. But the story of that cosmology is misleading, because it rests on a theoretically unacceptable foundation. It may be internally consistent, but the cosmology fails, because it is based, finally, on an illegitimate mixing of what-is and what-is-not, and thus, on what-is-not, for any mixture of what-is-not with what-is puts an inquiry on the negative route. The problem and deception lie, apparently, not in the attempt to give a cosmological account, but in the ontological failings of this cosmology.[41] The goddess is entitled to say that she has given a likely ordering of things (διάκοσμον ἐοικότα ... φατίζω), but she is also right to warn of the deceptive ordering of her words (*kosmos apatēlos*). The warning is heeded by putting the *Doxa* to the test. The failure of the two fundamental forms to pass the tests of the *Alētheia* show that the story of the *Doxa* is untrustworthy, and that it lays out a route of inquiry from which no tidings can come.

(*Route*, pp. 80–85). Long ("Principles," pp. 90–91) also adopts this translation, but it must be kept in mind that Long takes the referents of *morphai* to be what is and what is not, rather than Fire and Night.

39 See, for instance, Furley, "Notes," pp. 30–33.

40 A third alternative is that B8.54 rejects the possibility that the two can be named together as a unity. This alternative can be found in Croissant, Schwabl ("Sein und Doxa"), Tarán (*Parmenides*), and Mansfeld. Tarán translates "a unity of which it is not necessary" (*Parmenides*, p. 86; discussion pp. 217–26). I do not think that this is the correct account: the goddess does not suggest that mortals intended the two forms to be a unity. For full discussions of these issues, see Mourelatos, *Route*, pp. 80–85 and Woodbury, "Parmenides on Naming." Coxon (*Fragments*) translates "of which it is wrong to name only one." I do not see how the "only" is to be gleaned from the text.

41 It is perhaps worth noting again that the ontological failings are not the result of the plurality of the supposed fundamental entities of the cosmology. It is not plurality itself but opposition that is at the root of the problem.

3. The Lessons of Mortal Beliefs

While the details of the beliefs of mortals are given in the fragments that follow B8.53, there are a number of formal characterizations of mortal belief in both the proem and the *Alētheia*. Lines B1.28–32 provide the first contrast between the trustworthy account of "the unshaking heart of well-persuasive truth" (B1.29) that the *kouros* will learn from the goddess, and the beliefs of mortals "in which there is no true trust" (ταῖς[42] οὐκ ἔνι πίστις ἀληθής B1.30). The contrast between the trustworthiness of the account of what-is in *Alētheia* and the questionable status of mortal beliefs occurs again at B8.50–53, the point where the goddess leaves off her proclamation of the truth and turns to the details of the *Doxa*. The *Alētheia* is worthy of trust while the *Doxa* can inspire no genuine confidence.[43] The dangers of mortal belief are further explored in B6 and B7. Those taking that path of inquiry know nothing, wandering two-headed (B6.4–5). The wandering of the *noos* of mortals is contrasted with the straight path taken by a traveler on the route of what-is. For the latter there is a direct connection between thought and what-is; in contrast, mortals are represented as drifters and vagrants who meander and circle, getting nowhere (for them "the path of all is backward-turning" B6.9).

What is mortal belief about? Is all mortal belief to be condemned? As far as can be told from the surviving fragments, the *Doxa*, as a recitation of mortal belief, is a cosmology, describing and explaining the world as experienced by the senses. Does it follow, then, that any cosmology is to be classed as having "no true trust" (B1.30) simply because it is an account of what is reported by the senses? If that is so, then we are faced with the sort of puzzles discussed in Section 1; for how does the goddess's recitation of the particular cosmology that she gives help arm the *kouros* against all beliefs of mortals, as B8.61 promises? Why does she not simply tell the *kouros* that any account of sense experience, regardless of its details, fails to count as knowledge and must be relegated to a lesser epistemic state? The particular cosmology given may the best account of sense experience possible.[44] But if this is the goddess's aim, the two main parts of the poem teach in quite different ways. The *Alētheia*, with its account of what-is and its signs and criteria for trying candidates for the nature of a thing, is quite formal, giving the *kouros* the outline of a procedure to follow in determining what-is. By contrast, the *Doxa* turns out to be a lesson of cosmological details apparently to be learned by rote, and simply repeated when faced with a rival cosmology.

[42] DK, Owen ("Eleatic"), Tarán (*Parmenides*), Mourelatos (*Route*), and Gallop (*Parmenides*) follow the texts of Sextus, Clement, and Simplicius, which read ταῖς. Coxon (*Fragments*) prints τῇς, translating "which comprise no genuine conviction."

[43] For an interesting twist on the notions of trust and persuasion, see Blank, "Faith and Persuasion."

[44] As noted in section 1, this view of the *Doxa* has found considerable favor. See note 6.

Is the insistence on judging and testing that is so prevalent in the *Alētheia* lacking here?

Perhaps judging and testing are present after all. In B1 there is a hint that the recitation of mortal beliefs may contain a lesson for the *kouros*. At B1.28 the goddess asserts that the *kouros* "must learn all things" (χρεὼ δέ σε πάντα πυθέσθαι): her promise is apparently fulfilled when she has related both the details of *Alētheia* and the account in *Doxa* that will guarantee that the *kouros* can avoid all mortal error (B8.61). But this guarantee cannot be the claim that the content of the *Doxa* alone will protect the *kouros* from mortal belief. I have suggested that the fault of the *Doxa* is merely hinted at, not explicitly stated. As a result of applying the testing methods of the *Alētheia*, one can know that the enantiomorphic opposites Light and Night are illegitimate cosmic principles. But the *Doxa* might have further lessons, for it might illuminate the proper nature and function of cosmological principles in a complete and acceptable system. In this sense the particular mortal beliefs the *kouros* hears may indeed be inadmissible. But there may be other cosmological principles that he does not hear. If these could pass the tests of B8, they will be acceptable.

Suppose that Light and Night were indeed the whole, complete, and independent entities suggested at first glance by lines B8.56–59; as such they might indeed form the basis of a cosmology. The details of such a revised *Doxa* might include a number of entities, each of which satisfies the criteria for Parmenidean predicational monism and which might mix and separate, just as the goddess suggests, so as to account for the phenomena related by sense experience.[45] Could such a theory be trustworthy? The goddess shows how to evaluate it: put it to the tests of B8. Any cosmological theory that survives such testing might be quite different from any account then current.[46] But habit must not be the guide here (B7.3); rather, cosmology must become rational in the sense that it meets the criteria given in B8.

Images of trust and persuasion fill Parmenides' poem.[47] The goddess promises that the *kouros* will learn "the steadfast heart of persuasive truth" (πυθέσθαι . . . ἀληθείης εὐπειθέος ἀτρεμὲς ἦτορ B1.28–29) and describes her own account as trustworthy (*pistos logos* B8.50) while asserting that in the beliefs of mortals there is no "true trust (or fidelity)" (*pistis alēthēs* B1.30). This same *pistis alēthēs* has driven out coming to be and perishing (B8.27–28), while mortals have attempted to give to what-is all names "trusting

45 Such a theory might seem quite similar to that of Empedocles or the Atomists; it would also be akin to the account of Anaxagoras. More detailed discussions of this issue appear in Chaps. IV and V.

46 I have in mind the Pythagorean and Milesian cosmologies. Our almost complete lack of knowledge of pre-Parmenidean Pythagorean theories makes it difficult to suggest what such a Pythagorean theory might be. But see English ("Parmenides' Indebtedness") and Coxon (*Fragments*) for a discussion of Pythagorean theories and influences on Parmenides.

47 See Mourelatos, *Route*, chap. 6, pp. 136–63, for a discussion of these issues.

them to be true" (πεποιθότες εἶναι ἀληθῆ B8.39). The notion here is that of reliability; relying on the goddess's account, we will not be led astray. Those mortals who go wrong believe their own theories and do so because they seem to be reliable, although they are not. The apparent trustworthiness of the reports of the senses lies in the pervasiveness of the world that the senses report, as the goddess points out in B1.31–32.

In lines B1.28–32 the goddess mentions three things that the *kouros* will learn, while using two different words for that learning:

> . . . χρεὼ δέ σε πάντα πυθέσθαι
> ἠμὲν ἀληθείης εὐπειθέος ἀτρεμὲς ἦτορ
> ἠδὲ βροτῶν δόξας, ταῖς οὐκ ἔνι πίστις ἀληθής.
> ἀλλ' ἔμπης καὶ ταῦτα μαθήσεαι, ὡς τὰ δοκοῦντα
> χρῆν δοκίμως εἶναι, διὰ παντὸς πάντα περ ὄντα.[48] (B1.28–32)
>
> . . . it is right that you learn all things,
> both the unshaking heart of well-persuasive truth
> and the beliefs of mortals, in which there is no true trust.
> But nevertheless you shall learn these things, too, how it were right that
> the things that seem be reliably, being indeed the whole of things.

The goddess begins by saying that it is right that the *kouros* learn all things, including here both the persuasive truth and the beliefs of mortals (the two are signaled and linked by *ēmen* and *ēde*). Lines 31–32 add something new. In addition to an enumeration of those mortal beliefs, the *kouros* will learn "these things" (ἀλλ' ἔμπης καὶ ταῦτα). The referent of *tauta* may be the mortal opinions of line 30, but it seems rather to point to the next clause: ὡς τὰ δοκοῦντα κτλ.[49] In that case the goddess, after telling the *kouros* that he must learn (*puthesthai* from *punthanomai*) both truth and opinion, adds that in addition he will learn (*mathēseai* from *manthanō*) something new and different concerning mortal belief. The use of the two verbs of learning is significant: while there may be a large area of overlap between the two (both may, after all, be translated as "learn"), there is also a difference between them. *Punthanomai* suggests that one takes in information or learns by experience, while *manthanō* suggests learning and understanding acquired

[48] Reading περ ὄντα rather than περῶντα. See Owen, who notes ("Eleatic," pp. 5–6) that περῶντα appears in only one manuscript of Simplicius, a manuscript that is "particularly given to literal and accentual errors and improvements." See also n. 52, below.

[49] See Stokes, *One and Many*, p. 302n.27. (Stokes's argument is concerned with B6.3 rather than B1.31.) Stokes points out a parallel at Herodotus I.125. *Houtos* normally refers backward. In the first sentence of §125, there are three occurrences of *tauta*; the first goes back to §124; the other two refer forward to the remainder of 125. See also Kühner-Gerth II, 646ff. The examples in Herodotus I.125 show that it is not grammatically impossible that the reference be forward. Compare the English, "Listen to this!" followed by the referent of "this."

by performing an act of judgment.[50] It is clear that the *kouros* is going to learn something about the things that appear, and what he learns is "how the things that seem had to be reliable, being indeed the whole of things." Lines B1.31–32 thus seem to suggest that the *kouros* will learn something about mortal beliefs in addition to hearing from the goddess what those beliefs are (as is promised in line 30).[51]

Lines B1.31–32 suggest why mortals think that what appears to the senses (including coming-to-be and passing-away) must have genuine reality: what appears to the senses seems to be all that there is.[52] Mortals take it that such appearances constitute the whole of things, and so must be the reliable objects of knowledge. They thus miss the fact that what-is, which is available to thought but not to perception, is the fundamental level of explanation, at which will be found the true or genuine natures of things and thus the proper metaphysically basic entities. But if there were a cosmology that was based on entities that pass the tests of B8, Parmenides might well be willing to count it as acceptable if it both explained sense experience and was grounded in what-is. Mortal beliefs might then pass the appropriate tests. If this is so, then Parmenides excoriates mortal thinking because it can be corrected. Mortals may be habitually two-headed (as in B6 and B7), but this tendency can be overcome by taking control of *noos* and applying the lessons learned from the goddess. "Thinking like a mortal" is a bad habit, but one that can be broken.

Thus, the *Doxa* contains within itself the means for determining what is deceptive in the goddess's account of it.[53] Furthermore, the cosmological

[50] The etymologies suggest two different lexical routes, the nuances of which may still be present in Parmenides' uses of the two words. See Chantraine, *s.v. manthanō* (p. 664) and *punthanomai* (pp. 954–55); and Hofman, *s.v. manthanō* (p. 189) and *punthanomai* (with *peuthomai*, p. 266). See also LSJ on *manthanō* and *punthanomai*. It might be objected that Parmenides is simply led by rhyme, metre, and a desire to avoid repetition to use two different verbs. This may be the case; but the two verbs are in the text as the result of the choice to place each in just the spot where it is.

[51] At B8.51–52 in the midst of the goddess's turning from *Alētheia* to *Doxa*, and her warning about the deceptive ordering of her words, the word is again *manthanō*: δόξας δ' ἀπὸ τοῦδε βροτείας μάνθανε κόσμον ἐμῶν ἐπέων ἀπατηλὸν ἀκούων. The implication seems to be that the *kouros* must both listen and judge what he hears. This is consistent with the notion that hearers of the *Doxa* must test what is heard rather than accepting passively the story told by the goddess.

[52] Owen argues persuasively that *dokimōs einai* is to be genuine or reliable, and Mourelatos bolsters his arguments. See Owen, "Eleatic Questions," pp. 6–8, and Mourelatos, *Route*, p. 211–12. The notion of genuineness connects with the idea of trustworthiness. The reading διὰ παντὸς πάντα περ ὄντα in B1.32 is adopted on the basis of Owen's arguments in "Eleatic Questions," but the reading περῶντα adopted by Tarán (*Parmenides*) and Coxon (*Fragments*) will give the same sense. Mortals believe that the things that appear have to be genuine because they "pervade all things" (Tarán's translation); that is, the appearances are all that there is.

[53] In the context of the *Doxa*, "deceptive" and "deceitful" may not mean "false." (See Simplicius *in Ph.* 39.10–12). Rather, the *Doxa* is unreliable, untrustworthy. The reliance on enantiomorphic opposites in the scheme of the *Doxa* is the source of its untrustworthiness.

structure suggested in the *Doxa* might be acceptable, if genuine entities formed the basis of the cosmology. I now turn to a discussion of this second proposal, particularly in consideration of the *Doxa*'s apparent commitment to the reality of coming-to-be, passing away, and mixing. Can these processes be part of a cosmology that is based on Parmenidean unities?

At B8.38–41 there is a specific caution against linking what-is with what changes. At B8.34–38 the goddess stresses the connection between thought and what-is; she claims that "nothing else either is or will be besides what-is, since Fate shackled just this to be whole and unchanging" (οὐδὲν γὰρ ⟨ἤ⟩ ἔστιν ἢ ἔσται ἄλλο πάρεξ τοῦ ἐόντος, ἐπεὶ τό γε Μοῖρ' ἐπέδησεν οὖλον ἀκίνητόν τ' ἔμεναι). She then adds:

> ... τῷ πάντ(α) ὀνόμασται[54]
> ὅσσα βροτοὶ κατέθεντο πεποιθότες εἶναι ἀληθῆ,
> γίγνεσθαί τε καὶ ὄλλυσθαι, εἶναί τε καὶ οὐχί,
> καὶ τόπον ἀλλάσσειν διά τε χρόα φανὸν ἀμείβειν.
>
> ... with respect to this have all names been given
> as many as mortals laid down, trusting them to be true,
> to come to be and to pass away, to be and not to be
> to change place and to exchange bright color.

Mortals try to attribute these characteristics to what-is, and in doing so they suppose themselves to be naming what-is. But mortals misuse these names, for they fail to attach to what-is and thus fail to name. Because it is shackled and held by fate to be immovable, what-is cannot change and so cannot be named by names that entail change. But the *Doxa* describes a world in motion and that undergoes change: there is coming-to-be and passing away; there is birth and death.[55] How can a cosmology that includes such processes pass the tests of B8?

The cases of change in fragments B9 through B19 are instances of coming-to-be, passing away, or growth; these are the processes of change that are forbidden to what-is in B8.6–22. But it is worth noting that in none of the extant fragments of the *Doxa* nor in the testimonia about the *Doxa* section of the poem, is there evidence that Night and Light themselves are subject to coming-to-be or passing away. Aside from their unstable and impossible natures as opposites (known to one who has learned the lessons of the *Alētheia*), they would seem to be permanent aspects of the *kosmos* used, perhaps, by the "goddess who steers all things" (δαίμων ἣ πάντα κυβερνᾷ; B12.3). There is indeed mixing, but it is not identified as being the same process as coming-to-be, which B8 had condemned as

[54] For ὀνόμασται here, see Chap. II, n. 66.

[55] Birth and coming-to-be: B10.3, B11.4, B12.4, B19.1; birth is certainly implied in B18. Passing away: B10.2 ("the destructive works"), B19.2 ("they will come to an end"). Growth: B10.6, B19.3.

involving what-is-not. Plutarch, in the *Reply to Colotes* (1114B = context B10), claims that Parmenides made a cosmic order (*diakosmon pepoiētai*) by the "mingling of the light and dark as elements" (καὶ στοιχεῖα μιγνὺς τὸ λαμπρὸν καὶ σκοτεινόν). The language (of elements, for instance) is late, but Plutarch's report seems consistent with the extant fragments of the *Doxa*. Although Night and Light are mixed, they do not cease to be and presumably retain their character, which allows them to function as the basis for the cosmology. If only Light and Night were genuine entities rather than interdefined opposites, Parmenides' cosmology would give an account of the world as experienced that did not presuppose the reality of coming-to-be and passing-away, and that would pass tests based on the fundamental *krisis*, "is or is not."

4. Objections: Mortal Beliefs and Accounts of Experience

The interpretation presented here sees the *Doxa* as having two purposes, one positive and one cautionary. The positive aspect of the *Doxa* lies in its providing a model for an adequate explanation of the reports of sense experience, using the notion of the genuine nature or character of a thing developed in the *Alētheia*, and rejecting coming-to-be and passing-away as real parts of the physical world, relying instead on mixture and separation. Parmenides' account of experience serves as an example to Anaxagoras, Empedocles, and the Atomists. In its negative role, the *Doxa* warns against adopting a "mortal" model of explanation, one that begins with metaphysically basic entities that are enantiomorphic opposites. One who would learn from the *Doxa* must disentangle the deceptive threads of the goddess's story, separating the negative from the positive lessons.

There are two objections that could be lodged against such an interpretation. First, it might be argued that no predecessor of Parmenides actually adopted a cosmology that depends on enantiomorphic opposites.[56] The lack of a genuine target for the goddess's criticism, as it has been presented here, vitiates the interpretation that has been offered. Second, the account I have proposed suggests that Parmenides might be willing to treat an account of sense experience as metaphysically well-grounded. But, it may be objected, the whole point of the arguments in *Alētheia* is to deny that the reports of

56 See, for instance, Long, "Principles," p. 90, who claims that it is "a little difficult to understand the fundamental error of mortals as the naming of two specific opposites, Fire and Night. No system known to us held just this view. And since Parmenides is making a general statement (B8.53–54), even though the cosmogony is his own, we should expect something less cryptic." Long makes the comment in the context of arguing that the fundamental error mortals make is not the naming of Fire and Night but rather the naming of Being and Not-Being. These, according to Long, are the two *morphai* referred to in B8.53. I think his remark is relevant to the interpretation I am presenting here. The objection, in the form I have presented it, was made to me by David Furley.

sense-experience can ever be so grounded. The *Doxa* is simply an account of sense experience and as such it can have no claim to truth or to "true trust." The deception in the goddess's story lies in the fact that it is a story about sense experience. It may explain the content of sense experience but it can never be trustworthy.[57] I shall consider each of these objections in turn.

We know of no Presocratic cosmogony that begins with Light and Night; but we should not let that blind us to the fundamental role of opposites in the theories of Parmenides' predecessors.[58] As I shall show, opposites and opposition are crucial parts of the theories of Anaximander, Anaximenes, Alcmaeon, and Heraclitus. Were Parmenides to choose a pair of opposites that had figured prominently in the theory of a predecessor, he might appear to be limiting his criticism to that theory rather than to beliefs of mortals in general. By choosing a pair of opposites that have not figured in any particular earlier theory, Parmenides can focus philosophical attention on the idea of opposition itself; and this is just what he does in the lines of B8 that introduce and characterize Light and Night (B8.53–59). Thus, although it is true that there is no one target of his objections that made the specific error noted in the *Doxa*, the type of error was widespread among Parmenides' contemporaries and predecessors.

Although Anaximander and Anaximenes are often classified as "Milesian Monists" because they begin with a single stuff (*apeiron* in the case of Anaximander and *aer* in Anaximenes), the extant fragments and testimonia show the importance of opposites in their theories. Pseudo-Plutarch reports (*Strom.* 2 = 12A10) that "something productive of hot and cold" separated off from the *apeiron* at the formation of this *kosmos*:

> φησὶ δέ τι[59] ἐκ τοῦ ἀιδίου γόνιμον[60] θερμοῦ τε καὶ ψυχροῦ κατὰ τὴν γένεσιν τοῦδε τοῦ κόσμου ἀποκριθῆναι καί τινα ἐκ τούτου φλογὸς σφαῖραν περιφυῆναι τῷ περὶ τὴν γῆν ἀέρι ὡς τῷ δένδρῳ φλοιόν. ἧστινος ἀπορραγείσης καὶ εἴς τινας ἀποκλεισθείσης κύκλους ὑποστῆναι τὸν ἥλιον καὶ τὴν σελήνην καὶ τοὺς ἀστέρας.

[57] This criticism is implicit in the interpretations discussed in n. 6 above, which argue that the *Doxa* is acceptable as an account of the reports of sense-experience and fails to be trustworthy, not because it gives an unacceptable account of experience but simply insofar as it is an account of experience.

[58] It might be thought that Parmenides' target here is Hesiod. Fränkel, for instance suggests that "with his choice of 'fire' and 'night' as basic constituents Parmenides put himself in line with tradition" (*Early Greek*, p. 360) and mentions Hesiod's use of night as a "principle of negativity" in a note to this claim. But I do not think that Hesiod develops a cosmology along Presocratic lines; he may have been a target of Parmenides' arguments, but he is not, I think, to be singled out from the others considered in this section as a special victim.

[59] For τι rather than τό here, see Hölscher, "Anaximander," p. 290; Kahn, *Anaximander*, p. 57n. b.

[60] Kahn suggests that the word *gonimon* "may have been used by Theophrastus, but probably not by Anaximander" (*Anaximander*, p. 57).

> He says that something productive of hot and cold was separated off from the eternal during the genesis of this world and from this a sphere of flame grew around the air around the earth like the bark around a tree. When this was broken off and closed up in some circles the sun and the moon and the stars came to be.

Despite some difficulties in interpretation,[61] Pseudo-Plutarch's report says that what first separates from the *apeiron* (here identified as "the eternal") is something that produces hot and cold. Hot and cold then seem to be responsible for the formation of the heavens and "this world."[62] The role of hot and cold in the production of the *ouranos* is supported by a report in Aetius (II 11 5 [Diels, DG, p. 340]; 12A17a). Under the heading Περὶ οὐρανοῦ τίς ἡ τούτου οὐσία, Aetius reports that for Anaximander it is the mixture of hot and cold that is responsible for the existence of the heavens (Ἀναξίμανδρος ἐκ θερμοῦ καὶ ψυχροῦ μίγματος). So the action of the opposites is a crucial part of Anaximander's cosmogony. The opposites figure prominently in the Anaximander fragment (12B1) as well. The things that "give justice and pay recompense to one another for their injustice according to the order of time" (διδόναι γὰρ αὐτὰ δίκην καὶ τίσιν ἀλλήλοις τῆς ἀδικίας κατὰ τὴν τοῦ χρόνου τάξιν) are surely the opposites, for it is they who have the power of encroaching on one another in the manner supposed by the fragment.[63] In addition, the Anaximander fragment and testimonia suggest that the action of the opposites may have been responsible for coming-to-be and passing-away, the reality of which Anaximander accepted as well.

In Anaximenes we find a similar reliance on opposites. Condensation and rarefaction operate on the basic entity air to determine the form it takes—rarefied air is fire, fully condensed air is stone; see 13A7, e.g.—but there is a fundamental connection between condensation and rarefaction on the one hand, and cold and heat on the other. Plutarch gives the example of people using their breath to both cool and heat things: condensed breath is cool; more rarefied air is warm (13B1). What is not entirely clear is Anaximenes' view of the relation between the processes of condensation and rarefaction and the opposites cold and hot. Does the change in density cause the change in temperature? Or does the action of heat and cold produce

61 See Hölscher, "Anaximander," pp. 290–294; Kahn, *Anaximander*, pp. 57–58, 86–88.

62 Kahn argues that 12A17a provides evidence that the discussion of the roles of hot and cold in the formation of this *kosmos* goes back to Theophrastus (*Anaximander*, p. 57). Hölscher seems unwilling to attribute to Anaximander a theory of opposites. But see Kahn, *Anaximander*, pp. 119–65 for a discussion of the relation between so-called elements and opposites in early Greek thought.

63 See Kahn, *Anaximander*, pp. 166–96 for a full discussion of the fragment, especially the issue of the extent of Anaximander's own words. See also Hölscher, "Anaximander," pp. 295–301. As noted above, Hölscher is unwilling to countenance a theory of opposites in Anaximander. For a full discussion of the fundamental role of the opposites in Anaximander, see Freudenthal, "Theory of the Opposites."

rarefaction and condensation? Plutarch, in the report in 13B1, seems to opt for the former view. He says that breath is cooled by the compression of air through the lips; but "when the mouth is slackened it escapes and becomes warm because of its looseness." So here, it is compression and looseness that cause hot and cold. But Plutarch notes that hot and cold seem to be important for Anaximenes; he says that for Anaximenes hot and cold "supervene upon changes" (ἐπιγιγνόμενα ταῖς μεταβολαῖς). Hippolytus (13A7) opts for the latter view: having run through the progression from the most rare to the most dense (fire to stone), he then asserts that the opposites hot and cold are the most important things in coming-to-be (τὰ κυριώτατα τῆς γενέσεως ἐναντία εἶναι, θερμόν τε καὶ ψυχρόν). It is only in Hippolytus that we find the clear statement that hot and cold are fundamental sources of coming-to-be and passing-away, but Hippolytus's description of the various stages of condensation and rarefaction, the particular examples he gives, and their order, is the same as that which appears in Simplicius's quotation from Theophrastus on Anaximenes (13A5; Simplicius *in Ph.* 24.26 = Theophrastus, *Phys. opin.* fr. 2; Diels 476–77). So Hippolytus may have had access to Theophrastus's account and it may have been from there that he took the notion of the importance of hot and cold. But even if hot and cold are not the sources of rarefaction and condensation, there are still opposites at work in Anaximenes' system; for the dense and the rare are themselves opposites. According to Pseudo-Plutarch (13A6), it is the action of the dense and the rare that turns air into the earth, from which are generated the sun, the moon, and all the other heavenly bodies, perhaps through the rarefaction or heating of moist exhalations that rise from the earth as it is condensed or cooled (this is Hippolytus's account in 13A7). So here again a predecessor of Parmenides espouses a theory that accepts the basic reality of coming-to-be and passing-away and depends fundamentally on the naming of opposite forms.

The evidence for pre-Parmenidean Pythagoreanism is sketchy. We do not know the origin of the table of opposites given by Aristotle (*Metaph.* I.5 986a22ff.), but as Aristotle distinguishes the table from other Pythagorean material that he discusses, it seems that the table was not found in Philolaus.[64] It may be that it goes back to Pythagoras himself or to his early followers, and given the persistent identity of the opposites with Pythagoreanism, and the reliance on opposites in Philolaus, it is reasonable to suppose that an early version of it, or the basic idea of opposition that later gave rise to the table, was a part of the earliest versions of Pythagorean theory.[65] But, despite this possibility, the evidence for Pythagoras himself does not deal with

[64] For the view that most of Aristotle's views about Pythagorean philosophy can be traced back to Philolaus, see Huffman, *Philolaus*, pp. 28–32.

[65] See, for instance, Kahn, "Pythagoras," pp. 180–85. Kahn is cautious here but admits that there is no hard evidence to support his surmise that "there is some reason to believe" that "the generation of the numbers and cosmos from a primitive opposition of Limit (or Limiting) and Unlimited, and from a One that 'breathes in' the void" and the reliance on *harmonia* "were

opposites. Moreover, Burkert has suggested that the table has connections with the Academy, although he also recognizes the possibility (suggested by Aristotle at *Metaph.* 986a22) that it may go back at least to Alcmaeon.[66] Philolaus makes the existence of the whole *kosmos* depend on limiters and unlimiteds (44B1), and limited and unlimited stood at the head of the table as reported by Aristotle. But Philolaus may have introduced limited and unlimited as a response to Parmenides himself.[67] So despite the tantalizing possibility that Parmenides himself received Pythagorean training and thus would have been familiar with the theories of his philosophical neighbors, caution demands that we ought not to rely on any claims about opposites in early Pythagoreanism that may be a target of Parmenides' arguments.

There is very little evidence for Alcmaeon of Croton, and none at all that could be called cosmogonical or cosmological.[68] Yet the evidence we have indicates the importance of opposites to his theories. Aristotle compares Alcmaeon with the Pythagoreans, noting that both rely on opposites or contrarieties, contrasting Alcmaeon's "chance" opposites with the Pythagorean table of ten opposites (*Metaph.* 986a22ff. = 24A3).[69] According to Aristotle, Alcmaeon claimed that "most human things are paired" (φησὶ γὰρ εἶναι δύο τὰ πολλὰ τῶν ἀνθρωπίνων). Aristotle mentions pale and dark, sweet and bitter, good and bad, large and small. Further examples occur in 24B4, which indicates that Alcmaeon believed health to be preserved by maintaining equilibrium among the powers (ἰσονομία τῶν δυνάμεων); he names wet, dry, cold, hot, bitter, and sweet.[70] Whatever the exact details of the theory (which are lost to us), it is clear that the opposites are of fundamental importance in maintaining the proper state of the body. It is reasonable to think, then, that these same opposites are at work in making up the physical world of which the body is a part. Both Diogenes Laertius (24A1) and Aristotle

---

(or ... easily might have been) formulated in the time of Pythagoras" (p. 183). In contrast, Huffman claims that these doctrines are probably post-Parmenidean, having originated with Philolaus.

66 Burkert, *Lore*, pp. 51–52.

67 This is Huffman's suggestion (see *Philolaus*, Part II, section 1). I am grateful to Professor Huffman for discussing with me the problem of opposites and early Pythagoreanism.

68 The chronology here is difficult; I think that Alcmaeon's work preceded Parmenides', although Huffman suggests that it is later.

69 Aristotle further speculates about the possibility of influence (*Metaph.* 986a27–29): Did Alcmaeon get his view from the Pythagoreans or did they get theirs from him?

70 Alcmaeon's use of the opposites to account for health is reminiscent of the use of the opposites in the medical tradition. It is difficult to date the early Hippocratic material, but the discussion of opposites in *On the Sacred Disease* is similar to Alcmaeon's and the reliance on the opposites (as well as on what might be called elements) is criticized in *On Ancient Medicine*. For a discussion see Lloyd, "Ancient Medicine." See also Coxon, *Fragments*, p. 39, for the scanty (but tantalizing) evidence at ancient Elea for the tradition that Parmenides was himself a medical man: a statue purporting to be Parmenides and an inscription. Photographs of the headless statue with its inscription may be seen on pp. 306–7 of the *Illustrated London News* for August 31, 1963.

(A12) attribute to Alcmaeon the view that the soul is immortal; Aristotle attributed to Alcmaeon the notion that "men die because they are not able to fasten the beginning to the end." Aristotle admits to being puzzled about this enigmatic claim, but here again we have opposites coming into play.

Finally, there are the opposites in Heraclitus. Heraclitus's universe is a world of ordered change: 22B30 asserts that "the *kosmos*, the same for all, neither god nor man made, but it was always and is and will be fire ever living, kindling in measures and being extinguished in measures."[71] The turnings of fire in 22B31a and B31b illustrate the role of opposites in Heraclitus's cosmology.[72] Moreover, it is the opposites that make possible the changes that characterize the Heraclitean universe. 22B80 asserts that "one must know that war is common and that strife is justice and that all things come to be and are ordained (?) by strife."[73] This universal strife that leads to the claim that war is king of all (22B53) is probably best understood as change between opposites, change that is governed by the universal *logos* (22B1, B2). From Parmenides' point of view, there are two aspects of Heraclitus's theory of opposites that are most important. The first is the claim that there is a unity of opposites; the second is the role of the opposites in accounting for coming-to-be and other sorts of changes. These two aspects are related, because it is the unity of the opposites that allows for ordered change.[74] The opposites are inherently unstable. Their natural tendency would be to shift back and forth into each other; this is the source of change, birth, and death.[75] The unity of opposites appears in Heraclitus's denigration of Hesiod (and those who set him up as a learned man) in fragment 57: "The teacher of most is Hesiod; they know he knows most things; he who did not know day and night; for they are one." Hesiod fails to recognize the unity between the opposites and so fails to grasp the true nature of day/night. It follows that he cannot give a proper account of them, nor account correctly for the changes between day and night.[76] This unity in opposites is also found in B8, where Aristotle paraphrases a Heraclitean claim, "what opposes

[71] Kahn (*Art and Thought*, p. 44) argues for the omission of *tonde*, which comes, he claims, "from an inferior variant found in Simplicius and Plutarch."

[72] The turnings of fire in 22B31a and 31b seem to depend on temperature changes, as fire goes through various stages; these stages are at least part of what is referred to in the way up and the way down in 22B60 and in the changes of B36 and B76. (For a discussion of the variations on B76 and the textual issues, see Kahn, *Art and Thought*, pp. 153–55.)

[73] I follow Kahn in accepting the manuscript reading χρεώμενα here, also recognizing with Kahn that the translation "are ordained" is rather tenuous. For other suggestions, see Marcovich, pp. 132 and 138–40. See also Kirk, pp. 239–41 for a defense of Diels's suggested χρεών.

[74] I have discussed these issues in "Knowledge and Unity."

[75] See, for instance, 22B10, B36, B62, B76 (even if B76 is not authentic, it seems to express a genuinely Heraclitean sentiment), and B88.

[76] For a discussion of 22B57 (which differs from that offered here), see Mackenzie, "Heraclitus," pp. 18–20.

unites."[77] The ceaseless change that characterizes the Heraclitean *kosmos* (as illustrated in the river fragments[78] 22B12, 49a, and 91) is not capricious, but ordered according to the principle Heraclitus calls the *logos*. According to B126, "Cold heats up, warm cools off, moist dries out, dry is wetted." Here change is cyclical and regular. The same principles of orderly change and unity of opposites are at work in B88: "the same . . .[79] living and dead, and the waking and the sleeping and the young and the old; for these changed are those and those changed again are these." What keeps these changes regular and within bounds is that they occur between pairs of opposites. Moreover, these opposites seem to be conceived of as enantiomorphic: each end of a pair of opposites is exactly what the other is not, yet because change runs between the members of a pair, Heraclitus says that the two are unified. An example is 22B60, "the road up and down is one and the same." While it is true that the way up and down is the same, it is not the case that anything on the way is going both directions at once: something is either on the way up or the way down (an example would be the turnings of fire in B31a and b). So both Heraclitus's cosmology and his theories of change require a metaphysical connection between opposites. What is particularly significant from the Parmenidean standpoint is the connection between opposites and change, a connection that is stressed in the extant Heraclitean fragments on opposites.

This brief survey shows that none of Parmenides' predecessors constructed a cosmology dependent on Light and Night, and to that extent the criticism with which this section began is correct. But what has become clear is the near universality of opposites in early Presocratic theories. A reason for that ubiquity appears in Heraclitus, where an intimate connection between the opposites and change is made quite clear. It seems likely that this connection is part of the reason for the widespread role of opposites in pre-Parmenidean thought. But not only are the opposites present in many theories; in Heraclitus, the metaphysical standing of opposites receives attention. Parmenides expands that metaphysical analysis, but unlike Heraclitus he is not complacent about the place of opposites in a physical theory. Even though hot and cold or limited and unlimited may appear to be separate entities, Heraclitus had shown that there is a crucial connection between them, a connection that allows for the possibility of change but which, Parmenides argues, depends on an opposite's both being and not being just what it is. The *Alētheia* has already rejected the inclusion of what-is-not in the nature of a thing. The account of the natures of the opposite forms

77 B8 is almost certainly an Aristotelian paraphrase of a Heraclitean thought. See Kahn, *Art and Thought*, p. 193 for a discussion of the textual issues this fragment raises.

78 Mackenzie ("Heraclitus," pp. 1–4) argues that all three river fragments should be accepted. Her discussion provides accounts of the texts of all three.

79 I follow Kahn in omitting τ' ἔνι here. For other suggestions, see Marcovich, pp. 216–17 and 218; Kirk, pp. 136–38.

Parmenides gives in lines B8.55–59 show that, despite the appearance of two separate entities, each of which has its own positive and complete nature, a system of enantiomorphic opposites actually imports what-is-not into the very heart of a cosmological system. Despite thinking that they are on the positive route of inquiry, all theorists who depend on opposites and who insist that coming-to-be and passing-away are real (and this includes most of Parmenides' predecessors) are actually on the negative route, a route that leads nowhere, from which no tidings ever come.

The account of the *Doxa* offered here allows the possibility that Parmenides might accept an explanation of the world reported to us by the senses as rational and metaphysically well-grounded. On the view I have defended, the arguments of the *Alētheia* explore what constitutes the nature of a thing, and one or more metaphysically basic entities that meet the requirements of the *Alētheia* might well function as the foundation of a cosmology. But it might be objected (and this is the second criticism mentioned at the beginning of this section), this view blurs the distinction between the *Alētheia* and *Doxa* sections of the poem, disregarding Parmenides' claim that the *Doxa* is deceptive, and the pronouncement that there is "no true trust" in the beliefs of mortals. The *Doxa* is an account of sense experience, and, as such, no matter its details, it cannot be rationally well-grounded or meet the criteria for what-is formulated in the *Alētheia* and especially in B8. We may be able to rank accounts of sense-experience, and Parmenides may have intended that the cosmogony of the *Doxa* is the best explanation that can be given, but no such account can be true or trustworthy, sure or certain.[80] This is a serious objection, for the distinction between the *Alētheia*, which describes a realm of what-is that is available only to rational thought, and the *Doxa*, which deals exclusively with a world reported by our senses, seems clear; moreover, there is strong textual support for this traditional interpretation of the relation between the two main parts of the poem.[81]

While the objection is serious, it does not undermine the interpretation offered here. I begin with the textual evidence. Throughout the poem, the goddess condemns what she calls beliefs of mortals, or the route taken by mortals. These condemnations of, and warnings against, both the route followed by mortals and actual mortal beliefs occur at B1.30–32, B6.4–9, B8.38–41, B8.51–52. Additionally, B7 contains a warning to the *kouros* against letting habit force him along a route that is to be identified with

[80] I have raised questions about the possibility of ranking deceptive accounts of sense experience above, in Section 1. The objection will be even stronger if one claims that the *Doxa* is entirely deceptive and that there is no positive lesson to be learned from it.

[81] The main evidence is B8.50–52, where the goddess explicitly claims that she is ceasing her trustworthy account: ἐν τῷ σοι παύω πιστὸν λόγον ἠδὲ νόημα ἀμφὶς ἀληθείης· δόξας δ' ἀπὸ τοῦδε βροτείας μάνθανε κόσμον ἐμῶν ἐπέων ἀπατηλὸν ἀκούων. These lines echo B1.30, which asserts that there is no "true trust" in the beliefs of mortals. The inadequacy of mortal belief is reiterated in B6 and B7 and in B8.39–41.

the route of inquiry taken by those who hold mortal beliefs. It is worth asking just what Parmenides means by a mortal belief. It cannot be that any belief held by a mortal human being is to be disqualified. Such a criterion for the truth or falsity of a belief makes truth depend on the holder, rather than on the content, of the belief. Within the context of Parmenides' own poem, the *kouros* is both mortal and in possession of the sure and certain truth. His new beliefs about what-is are surely not to be ruled out just because he, the bearer of them, is mortal.[82] Thus, it seems likely that "beliefs of mortals" is a shorthand way for Parmenides to refer to some particular set of beliefs or philosophical views.[83] In the poem, it is striking that two themes appear and reappear when details of mortal beliefs are given. They are, first, that mortals believe that what-is-not can be, and second, that change, coming-to-be, and passing-away are real. The belief in the reality of what-is-not appears in the castigation of two-headed mortals in B6, in the route that the goddess warns against in B7, and in the list of things that mortals believe to be real and named by "what-is" at B8.38–41, which includes εἶναί τε καὶ οὐχί. But the belief that what-is-not is real is connected with the belief in the reality of change, for the arguments against change in B8 turn on the impossibility that what-is-not is. So the reality of change presupposes the reality of what-is-not, and it is the reality of change (and especially the reality of coming-to-be, passing-away, and other sorts of change) that particularly characterizes the beliefs of mortals. At B8.38ff. the goddess catalogues what mortals accept as real:

> . . . τῷ πάντ(α) ὀνόμασται
> ὅσσα βροτοὶ κατέθεντο πεποιθότες εἶναι ἀληθῆ,
> γίγνεσθαί τε καὶ ὄλλυσθαι, εἶναί τε καὶ οὐχί,
> καὶ τόπον ἀλλάσσειν διά τε χρόα φανὸν ἀμείβειν.
>
> (B8.38–41)

> . . . with respect to this have all names been given
> as many as mortals laid down, trusting them to be true,
> to come to be and to pass away, to be and not to be,
> to change place, and to exchange bright color.

82 Nor, even more strongly, should we think that Parmenides' own philosophical views are to be ruled out *a priori* simply because he is mortal. Within the context of the poem, it might be argued that the imparting of these views to the *kouros* by the goddess gives them divine sanction. But it must be remembered that the goddess insists that the *kouros* must not accept these views passively; he must test them himself.

83 In Chap. I (n. 66) I suggested that "mortals" could refer both to the ordinary run of persons and to philosophers, for Parmenides' philosophical predecessors seemed to be trying to formulate theories that would account for the world as experienced by ordinary persons. (This holds even of Heraclitus, with his contempt for the usual run of persons, for his argument seems to be that they misinterpret the information available to them about the world as it is experienced. See fragments 22B1 and B2.)

These are names that mortals have attempted to attach to what-is, and it is significant that Parmenides describes mortals as "trusting them to be true," thus, both echoing the reference to "no true trust" in B1.30's reference to the beliefs of mortals, and showing how these mortal beliefs mimic the character of that genuine route of inquiry which is "the path of Persuasion, for it attends upon truth" (Πειθοῦς ἐστι κέλευθος [ἀληθείῃ γὰρ ὀπηδεῖ] B2.4). Of the four names that are canvassed, three refer to various sorts of change: change of place, exchange of color, and coming-to-be and passing-away; the fourth refers to the purported reality of what-is-not that is the basis for claims about the possibility of change. It is such change that characterizes our experience of the perceived world and that the *physikoi* who preceded Parmenides had attempted to explain. The fundamental entities of these theories were capable of undergoing such changes as those mentioned in B8.40–41, and indeed the cosmological theories of the Milesians, Xenophanes, and Heraclitus required such changes. Moreover, theories based on change could find in the opposites an easy way to explain both the regularity and measured order of such changes. So I suggest that we understand by "mortal belief" the assertion (or tacit assumption) of the reality of change and the ability of fundamental entities to undergo change. Certainly this provides the proper contrast with the arguments of the goddess in the *Alētheia*, where what-is is whole, complete, perfected, and unchanging.

If mortal beliefs are those that assert the reality of change and what-is-not, then not all cosmology as such is condemned by Parmenides' arguments. An account of the world as perceived by the senses that denies the reality of change and ensures that its fundamental principles do not allow for what-is-not could be allowed. Moreover, such a theory would not be the subject of the goddess's attacks in the Proem and the *Alētheia*, for such a theory would not count as "mortal."[84] Such a theory would have to account for the appearance of change but could do so through the mixing of its fundamental entities, without committing itself to the reality of any sort of change. The objection under consideration here denies the possibility of a cosmology acceptable to Parmenides, a rational cosmology, as I have called it. But the separation of so-called mortal beliefs from other possible explanations of the world reported by the senses allows for just this possibility. There is no true trust in mortal beliefs, because no theory that asserts the reality of what-is-not and of change can be trustworthy or reliable, for it would fail the tests of the arguments of the *Alētheia*. Indeed, there are no criteria by which it could be regarded as acceptable.[85] On any version of the *Doxa* that claims that no

84 Might it be that Parmenides chooses to call beliefs in the reality of coming-to-be and passing-away "mortal" because it is their susceptibility to destruction and what-is-not that distinguishes mortals from gods? See the discussion of *brotos* in Chantraine, vol. I, pp. 197–98.

85 It might be argued that such a theory can be judged by how well it accounts for our experience. But as I noted in Section 1 of this chapter, there are difficulties in maintaining this view coherently.

cosmological story could be true (no matter whether different stories may be better or worse than one another), the account offered there by the goddess simply exists in isolation, with no way to check or correct it, and no way to connect it with the story told in *Alētheia*. Such a cosmology cannot be justified and could never be called rational. It is difficult to see how the *kouros*'s commitment to such a theory could guarantee that he will never be overtaken by mortal belief.

But if the *Alētheia* and the *Doxa* work together, with the *Alētheia* providing criteria for what counts as the genuine nature of an entity that plays a fundamental role in a cosmology, and the *Doxa* offering a model of a cosmology (though a deceptive one that must be studied carefully), the poem becomes a coherent whole, with a consistent story to be told throughout. The argument of Chapter I was that Parmenides is concerned to argue for the criteria for a genuine nature of a thing; the *Doxa* provides one reason why he is so concerned to do this. Ontologically sound, theoretically basic entities in a cosmology will be those that pass the tests of the *Alētheia*. Such entities then will mix and separate as do Light and Night (which are not ontologically sound) in the deceptive *Doxa* so as to account for the world reported to us by our senses. Such a theory would have its origin in the deceptive ordering of the goddess's story but would be an improvement based on what has been learned from that story. It could explain and account for what is reported by the senses ("mortal belief") but it would pass the tests of the *poludēris elenchos*. It would, finally, be a rational cosmology. It could serve as a model for later cosmological theories (such as those of Empedocles and the Atomists), which stress the unreality of coming-to-be and passing away while insisting on the reality of the fundamental entities of the theories. If this is the case, those who followed Parmenides learned as much from the *Doxa* as they did from the *Alētheia*.

IV

Pluralism after Parmenides

THE PREVIOUS CHAPTERS have argued that although Parmenides is not a typical *physiologos*, his views are firmly in the tradition of Presocratic physical thought. Rather than constructing his own account of what there is, both at the fundamental metaphysical level and at the level of cosmology, he criticizes earlier theories of the nature of things and offers criteria for the genuine constitution of a thing by concentrating on the character of what-is (Chap. I). The criteria for what-is that are explored in B8 indicate that Parmenides is a monist of a particular sort. He argues that what-is cannot be subject to coming to be or passing away, and is whole of a single kind, unshaking and complete.[1] The key notion here is that of being a whole of a single kind, for this secures the unchanging nature of what-is, as is indicated in lines B8.5–6: "nor was it once nor will it be, since it is now altogether one, continuous" (οὐδέ ποτ' ἦν οὐδ' ἔσται, ἐπεὶ νῦν ἐστιν ὁμοῦ πᾶν ἕν, συνεχές). The single-natured character of what-is prevents any change, whether qualitative change, coming-to-be, or passing-away. Parmenides' arguments do not indicate that there must exist only one thing; rather, he argues that whatever is a genuine entity must be one in kind, or, as I have called it, predicationally one (Chap. II). The importance of predicational unity in an entity that functions as the nature of something appears in Parmenides' account of mortal error, the *Doxa*. The goddess warns that the story she will tell in the *Doxa* is deceptive (B8.51–52: δόξας δ' ἀπὸ τοῦδε βροτείας μάνθανε κόσμον ἐμῶν ἐπέων ἀπατηλὸν ἀκούων), and I have argued (Chap. III) that the deception lies in the account of Light and Night, which treats them as genuine entities underlying a cosmology, even though, as enantiomorphic opposites, neither can be a predicational unity (a whole of a single kind) of the sort that the *Alētheia* has shown a genuine entity must be. Nevertheless, the *Doxa* has a positive story to tell in addition to its deceptive account of Light and Night. Parmenides constructs a cosmology based on entities that do not shift or change in themselves (or at least would not if they were genuine entities rather than enantiomorphic opposites), but that can mix and separate to form the phenomena reported to us by our senses. In this chapter I turn from Parmenides to two of his successors, examining

[1] These "signs" on the route "that it is" set out the character of what-is that later lines of B8 will argue for: ὡς ἀγένητον ἐὸν καὶ ἀνώλεθρόν ἐστιν, οὖλον μουνογενές τε καὶ ἀτρεμὲς ἠδὲ τέλειον (B8.3–4).

the Pluralist theories of Anaxagoras and Empedocles, in order to explore the influence of Parmenides on these later thinkers. I argue that this influence appears in two fundamental aspects of their theories: in their conceptions of the fundamental entities that are the genuine beings of their cosmologies, and in the form (mixture and separation of the basic entities) these cosmologies take. I begin with a short discussion of the question of Pluralism itself and then turn first to Anaxagoras and then to Empedocles.[2]

1. The Question of Pluralism

After Parmenides, any theory that attempts to provide a rational, metaphysically well founded cosmology must satisfy two conditions. First, it must be based on entities that meet Parmenides' criteria for what-is. Second, it must find a way for those entities to account for and explain the world that is reported to us by our senses without violating Parmenides' strictures against coming-to-be and passing-away. I shall argue that both Anaxagoras and Empedocles set out to meet those conditions. But what evidence is there that Anaxagoras and Empedocles were at all concerned with Parmenidean criteria in their theories? Perhaps either or both of them simply ignored his arguments and continued in the pre-Parmenidean tradition of cosmology without pausing to worry about Parmenides' metaphysical and epistemological critique of earlier theories.[3] The evidence of the surviving fragments shows that it is unlikely that Anaxagoras and Empedocles were not aware of

[2] I am here assuming that Anaxagoras wrote earlier than Empedocles and that Melissus was perhaps rather later than both. For a discussion of the issues of chronology, see Introduction, Section 2.

[3] Schofield suggests that Anaxagoras "does not feel obliged to refute [Parmenides'] monism or his argument against the possibility of change" (*Essay*, p. 82), although Schofield acknowledges that Anaxagoras is influenced in some ways by Parmenides. Barnes rejects the notion of Eleatic influence on Anaxagoras's claim that "all things come from all things" (*PP*, vol. II, pp. 30–31). O'Brien discusses the Parmenidean influence on Empedocles in *Cosmic Cycle*, pp. 239–49, concentrating on issues of rest and motion. O'Brien sees in the alternations of rest (at the triumph of Love) and motion in the cosmic cycle an attempt to reconcile what he sees as Parmenides' two worlds, that of being (which is at rest) and of sense perception (which is in motion). Millerd claims that "Eleatic criticism made necessary the abandonment of the single element of the early Ionians" (p. 33), but she sees no difficulty in opting for Pluralism in the face of these arguments. Inwood claims that Parmenides' "lack of a clear argument against plurality" shows that "Empedocles need not argue for plurality" but is justified in asserting it in the face of the numerical monism that Inwood attributes to Parmenides (*Empedocles*, pp. 23–24). Wright says that Empedocles accepted Parmenides' rejection of what-is-not and the subsequent denial of coming-to-be and passing-away but from there "began to reason independently" in positing that "what exists . . . comprises four 'things.' " She argues that the claim that each root has its own character and prerogative is a "new application" of the "Eleatic argument for self-consistency" (Wright, *Empedocles* pp. 29–30). Osborne claims that Empedocles accepts from Parmenides the notion that the One must be undifferentiated, and then goes on to explain

and influenced by Parmenides. There are, in those fragments, both verbal echoes of Parmenides' poem and doctrinal claims that can be traced back to Parmenides. For instance, in fragment 3 Anaxagoras claims that there is no least (but always a lesser) and offers as his reason τὸ γὰρ ἐὸν οὐκ ἔστι [τὸ] μὴ οὐκ εἶναι[4] (for it is not possible that what-is not be), a claim that is reminiscent of Parmenides B6.1–2. In Empedocles we find similar verbal echoes: B17.26 urges Pausanias to "hear the undeceptive ordering of [my] account" (ἄκουε λόγου στόλον οὐκ ἀπατηλόν), which is both a reminder of the goddess's instruction to the *kouros* in Parmenides B8.51–52 to "learn the beliefs of mortals, hearing the deceptive order of my words" (δόξας ... βροτείας μάνθανε κόσμον ἐμῶν ἐπέων ἀπατηλὸν ἀκούων) and a warrant that Empedocles' own account of the world reported by the senses is reliable. Empedocles again mentions deception at B23.9; in a fragment that explains that the roots mix to account for the coming-to-be of "mortal things" just as painters create by mixing colors, he warns against letting "deception (*apatē*) overcome your mind" about the source of mortal things. Both Anaxagoras and Empedocles explicitly deny the reality of coming-to-be and passing-away, while acknowledging that such changes are apparent to the senses. In 59B17 Anaxagoras claims that talk of coming-to-be and perishing is misleading:

> τὸ δὲ γίνεσθαι καὶ ἀπόλλυσθαι οὐκ ὀρθῶς νομίζουσιν οἱ Ἕλληνες· οὐδὲν γὰρ χρῆμα γίνεται οὐδὲ ἀπόλλυται, ἀλλ' ἀπὸ ἐόντων χρημάτων συμμίσγεταί τε καὶ διακρίνεται. καὶ οὕτως ἂν ὀρθῶς καλοῖεν τό τε γίνεσθαι συμμίσγεσθαι καὶ τὸ ἀπόλλυσθαι διακρίνεσθαι. (B17)

> The Greeks incorrectly recognize coming-to-be and perishing; for no thing comes to be or perishes, but rather it is mixed together and separated from the things that are. And so they would rightly call coming-to-be being mixed together and perishing being separated.

Similarly, Empedocles rejects coming-to-be and passing away as unreal in 31B8 (which rejects growth—*physis*—and death), B12, and B11:

---

the apparent differences in the world reported by sense perception by the action of Strife in breaking up the sphere; the cause is "sin"("Recycled," p. 50).

[4] For the text, see Schofield, *Essay*, p. 80 and n. 15 (pp. 156–57). See also Lanza, pp. 198–99, and Jöhrens, pp. 18–21. Zeller suggested τομῇ οὐκ εἶναι, and this is accepted by Sider and Teodorsson, among others (see Sider, *Fragments*, pp. 56–57 for a discussion of the proposal). Raven, in KR/KRS, accepts the manuscript reading in the printing of the fragment but finds Zeller's suggestion "attractive" (KRS p. 362). The suggestion depends, I think, on reading B3 as a specific answer to Zeno (although Sider connects it with Parmenides B4). The evidence about the relation of Anaxagoras and Zeno is too uncertain a hook on which to hang the proposal, especially when a coherent interpretation can be found without it. Sider also connects the reading with Anaxagoras's own B8, but the uses of cutting are quite different in the two fragments: B8 is concerned with the impossibility of a pure, unmixed instance of a thing, B3 with the possibility of unlimited smallness.

νήπιοι· οὐ γάρ σφιν δολιχόφρονές εἰσι μέριμναι,
οἳ δὴ γίγνεσθαι πάρος οὐκ ἐὸν ἐλπίζουσιν,
ἤ τι καταθνῄσκειν τε καὶ ἐξόλλυσθαι ἁπάντῃ. (B11)

Fools—for their meditations are not far-reaching,
those who expect that was not before comes to be
or that something dies and is in every way destroyed.

Like Anaxagoras, Empedocles notes the conventional uses of coming-to-be and passing-away (in both B8 and B9). Although he claims that this mode of speech is wrong (οὐ θέμις ᾗ καλέουσι (following Wilamowitz) B9.5), unlike Anaxagoras, Empedocles assents to the convention and follows it (B9).[5] So it is clear that there are Parmenidean echoes and influences in the views of Anaxagoras and Empedocles about coming-to-be and change.

Monism is the major issue over which Anaxagoras and Empedocles are traditionally seen as differing with Parmenides. Often, they are described as postulating an original plurality of entities, thus contradicting Parmenides' numerical monism, while at the same time accepting his strictures against the reality of change or coming-to-be. Their failure to accept numerical monism is usually treated as unimportant; the reason most often given is that because Parmenides either fails to argue for monism or argues badly for it, the Pluralists are justified in ignoring that part of his theory.[6] I have argued that although Parmenides is indeed a monist, he does not adopt numerical monism. Rather he argues for what I have called predicational monism. It does not matter how many real entities there are; what matters is the nature of those entities. Each must be an internal unity (what Parmenides calls "a whole of a single kind"), not subject to coming-to-be, passing-away, or any other sort of change. Such internal unity ensures the completeness or perfection of the thing and guarantees that what-is cannot become what-is-not and that what-is-not cannot be. On this view, there is nothing to be explained away in the Pluralists' response to Parmenides: as long as each of the basic entities in the theories (Anaxagoras's *chrēmata* or Empedocles' roots and Love and Strife) is itself a Parmenidean unity (an issue to be explored in this chapter), not subject to what-is-not, the theory can legitimately be said to be working within a Parmenidean framework. That the Pluralists clearly accept and work within Parmenidean strictures on what there is, yet adopted Pluralism without explanation or apology indicates that they did not take pluralism itself to be inconsistent with or a deviation from Parmenides' own views. Those who attempt to explain away the lack of argument have missed the point: the Pluralists' silence on the issue of the number of their

[5] Having marked the conventional use and stressed that coming-to-be and passing-away are not real events but only the result of mixture and separation, Empedocles uses the notions of generation, growth, and destruction quite often in the fragments.

[6] See note 3, above.

theoretically basic entities is not a problem to be explained, but a confirmation that numerical pluralism is not the target and numerical monism is not the point of Parmenides' arguments.

Indeed, there is some reason to think that numerical monism could not work as a response to Parmenides, if that monism were combined with an attempt to explain the world reported to us by our senses. The only post-Parmenidean Presocratic monist is Diogenes of Apollonia. Diogenes takes great care to argue that a plurality of entities, each with its own nature, cannot provide an account of the sensible world. In fragment 64B2, he argues that if each thing is entirely different from every other, "being different in its own peculiar nature" (ἕτερον ὂν τῇ ἰδίᾳ φύσει), then things "could in no way mix with each other, or benefit or harm come from one to another, nor plants grow from the earth, nor animals or anything else come to be."[7] But in order that these phenomena, which are obvious to the senses, should arise from a single entity (air, in the case of Diogenes of Apollonia), that entity must itself alter and change. Diogenes recognizes this in the same fragment: in the opening of B2 he claims that "all the things that are are alterations of the same thing" (πάντα τὰ ὄντα ἀπὸ τοῦ αὐτοῦ ἑτεροιοῦσθαι).[8] Later in the same fragment Diogenes repeats that if there were not a single thing that "is changed in many ways and altered" (τὸ αὐτὸ ἐὸν μετέπιπτε πολλαχῶς καὶ ἡτεροιοῦτο) impossible consequences would follow. But to alter so as to become other things is to change in a way that Parmenides would disallow (see B8.26–31, for instance). It was, as we have seen, just such change in the air of Anaximenes or the *apeiron* of Anaximander that seems to have been Parmenides' target in his poem. So Diogenes of Apollonia, in returning to a pre-Parmenidean monism that requires change and alteration in the one entity, constructs a theory subject to the same objections Parmenides had already lodged against his predecessors. Anaxagoras and Empedocles, in contrast, in adopting numerical pluralism, are not open to the same sorts of objections, as long as they can guarantee the unchanging nature of the original entities themselves. This, I shall argue, is just what their theories indeed ensure.

2. Anaxagoras

2.1. Anaxagoras and the Indefinitely Many Things

According to Simplicius and Diogenes Laertius, Anaxagoras's book opened with these words:[9]

[7] For the text of Diogenes of Apollonia, I follow Laks, *Diogène*.

[8] The alterations of air are explored in B5.

[9] Simplicius claims that B1 was the opening of Anaxagoras's book at *in Ph.* 155.26, 164.15, 460.26, and at 608.21 of *in de Caelo*. Diogenes Laertius discusses the opening of Anaxagoras's work at I.4. For further discussion see Sider, *Fragments*, pp. 42–43.

> ὁμοῦ χρήματα πάντα ἦν,[10] ἄπειρα καὶ πλῆθος καὶ σμικρότητα· καὶ γὰρ τὸ σμικρὸν ἄπειρον ἦν. καὶ πάντων ὁμοῦ ἐόντων οὐδὲν ἔνδηλον ἦν ὑπὸ σμικρότητος· πάντα γὰρ ἀήρ τε καὶ αἰθὴρ κατεῖχεν ἀμφότερα ἄπειρα ἐόντα· ταῦτα γὰρ μέγιστα ἔνεστιν ἐν τοῖς σύμπασι καὶ πλήθει καὶ μεγέθει.[11]
>
> (59B1)

> All things were together, unlimited both in multitude and in smallness, for the small, too, was unlimited. And all things being together, none of them was manifest because of smallness; for air and aether covered all things, both being unlimited. For these are the greatest among the whole of things both in multitude and in size.

This description apparently represents the state of things in some unspecified beginning, before the mass is set in motion by *Nous* (Anaxagoras adopts the Attic spelling of *noos*). "Beginning" is somewhat of a misnomer: because nothing comes to be or passes away, there could be no genuine beginning of the whole, although there can be various cosmogonical stages within it. It is the beginning of the cosmic whirl to which Anaxagoras refers here. Anaxagoras insists that all things (*chrēmata panta*) were together. This raises the question of what Anaxagoras means by "things" and the range of "all things." Does he mean to include all natural objects as well as artifacts, or only natural objects; or is *chrēmata* perhaps a technical term that is restricted to a particular range of items?

Anaxagoras uses the term "thing" (*chrēma*) throughout the fragments. There is no indication that he restricts it to a technical use, and in B17 it seems to be used both of objects available to sense experience (some of which are the result of the mixture or separation of other things) and of the fundamental entities that are not subject to coming-to-be and passing-away. Whatever the range of the things (*chrēmata*), it is clear that they are the basic entities of Anaxagoras's system. They are not subject to coming-to-be or passing away and are unchanging in themselves, though they may separate out from the original mixture and combine with other things (as claimed in

10 Following the word order in Sider, *Fragments*. For the argument in support, see Rösler.

11 Text as in Sider, *Fragments*, but I follow most editors in including the last clause of B1 (from ταῦτα γὰρ μέγιστα) as part of the quotation. Sider has argued that the last clause is not part of the fragment but belongs to Simplicius's commentary (*Fragments*, pp. 49–51). His argument is threefold: (1) that the *gar* clause explains the *kateichen* clause, and that it is Simplicius who "felt the need" for further explication; (2) that the plural *sumpasi* is "suspicious" (Sider claims that Anaxagoras elsewhere prefers the singular); and (3) that Anaxagoras prefers the accusative rather than the dative of respect and that such datives "are characteristic of later Greek." (Sider is followed by Wright, in *Presocratics*.) In a review of Sider, Schofield rejects Sider's suggestion; "[Sider] has not seen that A. here supplies just that reason for making ἀήρ and αἰθήρ dominate the original mixture which he himself offers as a guess" p. 189). Verdenius, in another review, responds to Sider's philological arguments, suggesting that *sumpasi* "forms the natural sequel to the plural πάντα" and argues (with examples) that "the dative of respect is very common in early Greek" (p. 404).

B17). A further characteristic of the *chrēmata* is that none of them actually occurs in a pure or unmixed state. Not only is it the case that "all things were together" at the cosmogonical beginning; so too, now, in some sense, "all things are together." While the separation from the original mix may result in a local predominance of one thing or another, the separation is never complete. This follows from Anaxagoras's dictum "in everything a share of everything," which appears in B4a, B6, B11, and B12. In modern scholarship, there are three views current about the range of the *chrēmata*. First, there is the claim that when Anaxagoras says "all things" he means this literally. Whatever is to emerge from the original rotation or from the further mixture of things that come out of that rotation is already present in the original mixture. There is disagreement over the status of artifacts: some artifacts are clearly ruled out (computers, e.g.), while others, such as bronze, are not.[12] Another possibility is that the range of the *chrēmata* is restricted: the ultimate "things" of which everything is constructed through mixture and separation are the opposites.[13] Finally, there is a third view, proposed by C. Strang, which takes a wide view of the range of the *chrēmata*, but according to which there is a distinction to be drawn between the common occurrences of a thing in our experience, and the elemental occurrences of those things that are their ingredients.[14] According to Strang, the elemental things are (in principle) unmixed, although they never actually exist in isolation.

Before we decide among these interpretations, it will be helpful to list the fragments in which things that are or might be *chrēmata* are mentioned:

B1: when all things were together "*aer* and *aether* pervaded all things" (πάντα ... ἀήρ τε καὶ αἰθὴρ κατεῖχεν) because both were unlimited.

B2: *aer* and *aether* separate out of the surrounding multitude (καὶ γὰρ ὁ ἀήρ τε καὶ ὁ αἰθὴρ ἀποκρίνονται ἀπὸ τοῦ πολλοῦ τοῦ περιέχοντος[15]).

B4a: "many and varied things are present in all the things being mixed" (πολλά τε καὶ παντοῖα ἐν πᾶσι τοῖς συγκρινομένοις); there is a mention of seeds "of all things" (σπέρματα πάντων χρημάτων).

B4b: "the mixture of all things prevented [discrimination of characteristics or whatever], of the moist and the dry and the hot and the cold and the bright and the dark, there being much earth and seeds unlimited in amount" (ἀπεκώλυε γὰρ ἡ σύμμιξις ἁπάντων[16] χρημάτων, τοῦ

[12] See, for instance, Furley ("Anaxagoras in Response"), Furth ("Philosophical Hero"), Kerferd, ("Anaxagoras"), Raven (in both "Basis" and KR/KRS), and Stokes ("Anaxagoras"). Barnes (*PP,* vol. II, pp. 18–20) rejects typewriters and benches (though he accepts cheese) as genuine *chrēmata*; he does not mention alloys such as bronze.

[13] This is the view adopted by, for instance, Tannery, Cornford ("Theory of Matter"), Vlastos ("Physical Theory"), Schofield (*Essay*), and Inwood ("Infinite Divisibility").

[14] See Strang, "Physical Theory," esp. pp. 361–65.

[15] Text as in DK, but see Sider, *Fragments*.

[16] Ibid.

τε διεροῦ καὶ τοῦ ξηροῦ καὶ τοῦ θερμοῦ καὶ τοῦ ψυχροῦ καὶ τοῦ λαμπροῦ καὶ τοῦ ζοφεροῦ, καὶ γῆς πολλῆς ἐνεούσης καὶ σπερμάτων ἀπείρων πλῆθος).

B8: "The things in the one *kosmos* have not been separated from each other, nor have they been cut off with an axe, neither the hot from the cold nor the cold from the hot" (οὐ κεχώρισται ἀλλήλων τὰ ἐν τῷ ἑνὶ κόσμῳ οὐδὲ ἀποκέκοπται πελέκει οὔτε τὸ θερμὸν ἀπὸ τοῦ ψυχροῦ οὔτε τὸ ψυχρὸν ἀπὸ τοῦ θερμοῦ).

B10: "for how could hair come from not-hair, and how could flesh come from not-flesh?" (πῶς γὰρ ἂν ἐκ μὴ τριχὸς γένοιτο θρὶξ καὶ σὰρξ ἐκ μὴ σαρκός;).[17]

B12: the stars, sun, moon, air, and *aether* are produced by separation because of the rotation of the original mixture; there is also mention of the separation from each other of rare and dense, cold and warm, dark and bright, and moist and dry.

B15: "The dense and the moist and the cold and the dark came together here where the earth is now; the rare and the warm and the dry ⟨and the bright⟩ moved out into the far reaches of the aither." (τὸ μὲν πυκνὸν καὶ ⟨τὸ⟩ διερὸν καὶ τὸ ψυχρὸν καὶ τὸ ζοφερὸν ἐνθάδε συνεχώρησεν ἔνθα νῦν ⟨ἡ⟩ γῆ,[18] τὸ δὲ ἀραιὸν καὶ τὸ θερμὸν καὶ τὸ ξηρὸν ⟨καὶ τὸ λαμπρὸν⟩ ἐξεχώρησεν εἰς τὸ πρόσω τοῦ αἰθέρος.)

B16: a discussion of the progress from clouds to water to earth to stones. Stones are said to be compacted from earth by cold.

No one supposes that the sun, moon, and stars are in the original mixture. They are formed by further separation and mixture from items that separate from the original mix (Anaxagoras says that the heavenly bodies are stones that are ignited and thrown upward by the whirl, in A42, A71). So, leaving the astronomical objects aside, the items mentioned in the extant fragments are air, aether, earth, seeds, flesh and hair (if B10 is genuine), clouds, stones, and the opposites moist and dry, hot and cold, bright and dark, dense and

[17] Schofield, "Doxographica," questions the authenticity of B10, arguing that it is heavily influenced by Aristotle's interpretation of Anaxagoras and concluding that Eudemus is the author of the scholium that is the source of the fragment. In the later *Essay*, Schofield says "the ultimate author of the scholium may ... preserve Anaxagoras's own words in his repudiating question; even if he does not, his account of Anaxagoras's theory of growth may be based in part upon his own consultation of Anaxagoras's book" (p. 140). Schofield rejects the view that he thinks the scholium suggests, that the main impetus for Anaxagoras's theory is his observation of nutrition and growth.

[18] DK print ⟨ἡ γῆ⟩; a large literature has appeared debating the merits of the supposed emendation. This has now become moot since the publication of Sider's discovery that all of the manuscripts of Simplicius that he examined read γῆ, and that the printing in DK was a mistake. Sider does not add ⟨ἡ⟩. See Sider, "Confirmation" and *Fragments*, p. 115.

rare. This is a rather parsimonious (and eclectic) list of basic items; any view about the range of the *chrēmata* will have to assume that the items mentioned in the fragments stand in for others, and will make some additions to the list.

The first interpretation of the *chrēmata* takes the widest possible view of Anaxagoras's claim: whatever is in the world has emerged from the mixture and so must have been in the original mixture in the first place.[19] There are two difficulties with this. First, if, as Anaxagoras asserts, "everything is in everything," we shall have difficulties identifying anything. At the close of fragment 12, Anaxagoras asserts that "each one thing is and was most manifestly those things of which there are the most in it" (ἀλλ' ὅτων[20] πλεῖστα ἔνι, ταῦτα ἐνδηλότατα ἓν ἕκαστόν ἐστι καὶ ἦν). But if everything is in everything, it is difficult to determine just what anything is. For if we take a lump of coal, we may say coal predominates. But what is the coal that predominates? It itself is a mixture in which coal predominates. And what is the predominating thing? Coal, which is a mixture in which coal predominates; and so on. It is impossible to explain what coal itself actually is.[21] So, far from having a theory in which an entity is stable and neither comes to be or passes away, Anaxagoras seems to have a theory on which there are no genuine entities with stable identities at all.[22] A second problem with the wide interpretation is the question of organisms.[23] If what emerges from the original mixture is, in all cases of natural objects, supposed to have

[19] I shall assume that those holding this view would accept Guthrie's version of it: "every natural substance" is in the original mix (Guthrie, *HGP*, vol. II, p. 281).

[20] Here I follow DK, rather than Sider who, with the manuscripts, reads ὅτῳ.

[21] A clear statement of the problem appears in Strang, p. 361: using gold as his example, he says, "it is gold because gold predominates in it as an ingredient; and we can ask the same question about the ingredient of the ingredient, and so on, *ad infinitum*. But this will not do, for it will be impossible to say what is physically distinctive about gold as opposed to any other substance. It will be possible to say only that gold is the substance whose predominant ingredient is the substance whose predominant ingredient is the substance whose predominant ingredient is . . .; and the answer to the same question about any other substance whatever will be identical" (ellipsis in original). There is also a version of the regress in Cornford (see "Anaxagoras," pp. 309–11). Vlastos ("Anaxagoras") argues that Cornford's account of the regress is not vicious (pp. 335–36 with n. 75). He disagrees with Strang about the proper interpretation of the last lines of B12 and argues that the regress would be vicious only if the explanation of manifest characteristics entailed explanation at every level. Schofield agrees with Vlastos that the regress is not vicious (*Essay*, p. 75, with n. 9, where Schofield quotes Vlastos). Schofield ties the regress to the particulate theory of matter, rather than to the problem of analyzing manifest characters. But the problem of analysis is Strang's target; one cannot explain manifest gold, on Strang's interpretation, until one had reached some level of "pure" or as Strang calls it, elemental, gold. This problem would hold whether or not one thinks Anaxagorean matter is particulate.

[22] This problem is not peculiar to the wide interpretation of *chrēmata* but would seem to infect any interpretation of Anaxagoras's views which does not mark a distinction between a mixture and an ingredient. I shall have more to say about this distinction below.

[23] This is Furley's formulation of the problem; see "Anaxagoras in Response," pp. 50–51.

been already in the mixture, what are we to say of a dog? The blood, bone, skin, and hair, and so on are easily imagined as included in the mixture, but what of the dog itself? There seems to be no provision for it in the mixture.[24] One response is to invoke Anaxagoras's seeds; if they are interpreted in the most natural way, they are the biological beginnings of organisms.[25] Another response would be to claim that organisms, as mixtures that are not eternal, were not intended by Anaxagoras to be in the original mix at all but are accounted for by the mixing and separating mechanisms of B17. But this second response has now narrowed the range of the original *chrēmata* and recognizes a difference in status between ingredients and the things composed of them that the wide interpretation was supposed to deny.

A second account of Anaxagorean *chrēmata* is that they are to be identified with an unlimited range of opposites; everything else is then the result of the mixing of these opposites.[26] According to this view everything in the world reported to us by our senses can be accounted for through references to opposites.[27] A major advantage of the opposites analysis of the *chrēmata* is that it allows a distinction, which its proponents find in the fragments, between ingredients and manifest objects (Schofield refers to

24 It is this, I think, that accounts for Aristotle's claim (which has proved troublesome to commentators) that Anaxagoras makes the homoeomeries elements (*Gen. Corr.* I.1 314a18–20). For flesh, blood, bone, and even, I suppose hair, count as homoeomerous on Aristotle's view. Furth claims that for Anaxagoras "the whole world is Blood and the whole world is also Boar. . . . Anaxagoras is not clear about [the] . . . difference between Blood and Boar" ("Philosophical Hero," p. 113n.27). See also Graham, "Postulates," pp. 81–83; 101–12.

25 This is Furley's view ("Anaxagoras in Response," pp. 55–58); see also Barnes, (*PP*, vol. II, p. 21). Mann rejects this account of the seeds; on his account of the biological interpretation of seeds, "consistency requires that the seeds of men be homunculi" (p. 236). Mann apparently takes this as a *reductio* of the biological interpretation. Mann himself claims that human beings, trees, and organisms in general are not *chrēmata* because they are not eternal and fail to meet his analysis of homoeomerity. Vlastos suggests that *seed* is a technical term in Anaxagoras ("Physical Theory," pp. 323–29). He suggests that "Anaxagoras was the first cosmologist to use this term not in [a] vague and general fashion, but as a precise and technical concept" (p. 343n.12). Vlastos suggests a technical use for *seed* based on his account of Anaxagoras's fundamental entities (that they are the opposites only; so each seed contains all the opposites) and then argues that Anaxagoras was the first to use the term in this way. Depending as it does on the claim that the *chrēmata* are to be identified with the opposites, this account is not, I think, successful. I shall return to the issue of seeds below, but I think that the ordinary biological sense can account for the two occurrences of *sperma* in the extant fragments (one mention in 4a and one in 4b).

26 As mentioned above (note 13), several scholars have adopted this view (for summaries and discussions of various views about the opposites and the wider interpretation, see Teodorsson, pp. 25–43); the most recent and most detailed version is that of Schofield, and it is on his interpretation that I shall concentrate.

27 See Schofield, *Essay*, pp. 116–17. "The sensible world can be described completely and adequately in terms solely of opposites; . . . any other ways of describing the world—e.g., by using sortals and mass terms—are parasitic on the vocabulary of opposites and are to be treated as introducing nothing but epiphenomena, or logical constructions out of opposites" (p. 116).

the latter as "substances"[28]). Once the original mass has been set in motion by *Nous*, the opposites begin to separate out of the original mixture; it is their subsequent mixture and separation that account for the apparent coming-to-be and passing-away of sensible objects, just as B17 suggests. There is evidence in the texts for this view. Both B2 and B15 suggest that Anaxagoras recognized a distinction between ingredients and what those ingredients make up. In B2 Anaxagoras claims that air and aether separate out of the surrounding multitude; B15 provides a model of how this might occur on the opposites model. There, it is claimed, "the dense and the moist and the cold and the dark came together here where the earth is now" (τὸ μὲν πυκνὸν καὶ ⟨τὸ⟩ διερὸν καὶ τὸ ψυχρὸν καὶ τὸ ζοφερὸν ἐνθάδε συνεχώρησεν ἔνθα νῦν ⟨ἡ⟩ γῆ).[29] Similarly, B4b, which mentions earth, lists primarily opposites and seeds as being in the mixture before separation; it could be read as referring to what the opposites make up (earth) rather than as a reference to earth as a fundamental entity in the mixture. The distinction between ingredients and opposites is further explored in B16. Read as meteorological rather than cosmogonical, B16 presents a cyclical pattern of change, accounting for it by a rearrangement and redistribution of the ingredients (which are opposites) that make up first clouds, then water, then earth, and finally stones.[30] An advantage of the opposites account of the *chrēmata* is that it gives Anaxagoras a much less complicated system. According to Schofield, who rejects the view that Anaxagoras was primarily interested in questions of growth and nutrition, Anaxagoras's system, if interpreted in terms of ingredients and objects, and those ingredients identified as opposites, explains both why there is quite diverse change and differentiation in the world while at the same time there is "but a single order of things."[31]

While the opposites account of the *chrēmata* is attractive, it does not, I think, ultimately succeed. There are three difficulties with the view. First,

[28] I am unwilling to follow Schofield's terminology here, because "substance" seems to suggest a real and permanent entity. This is just what the objects made up of the opposites are not.

[29] Schofield accepts the inclusion of ⟨ἡ⟩ in B15 (see note 18, above). If Sider's suggestion of omitting ἡ is accepted, the text may provide even stronger support for the view that the *chrēmata* are to be identified with the opposites, for then we would have a general "recipe" for earth. Of course, if all earth is concentrated on the earth, it does not matter which version of the text is accepted.

[30] Stokes argues that B16 is meteorological ("On Anaxagoras," p. 229–44); he is followed in this by Schofield.

[31] Schofield, *Essay*, p. 121. B10 poses an apparent difficulty for the opposites view. If it is authentic or even reports a claim that Anaxagoras made (Schofield's later view; see note 17, above), it seems to suggest that the coming-to-be problem can only be solved by including anything that emerges at any later time in the original mixture. But one could avoid this conclusion. In the larger context of the fragment, the Scholiast is discussing seeds. This suggests that hair and flesh are included in seeds, which themselves could be

although it can provide consistent interpretations for the extant texts of Anaxagoras, and while there is, as we have seen, not a great variety of things mentioned in those texts, the interpretations are bought at the price of having to explain away or reinterpret certain of Anaxagoras's claims. While many texts discussing the *chrēmata* mention the opposites, there are also references to earth, air, and aether. These texts would seem to read most naturally as suggesting that earth, air, and aether are on the same footing with the opposites, thus implying that they are in the original mixture. Further, it becomes difficult to give an account of seeds. If a seed is, as Vlastos suggests, a simple congeries of opposites, then either the Scholiast's repudiating question (in B10) goes unanswered, or the repudiating question raises no special difficulty and refers to all cases of apparent coming-to-be.[32] If a seed is a biological unit, containing all that is necessary for an organism, there still remains the question of the growth of that organism. If it grows by addition of like to like, then flesh and hair must be added to it, and they must have been in the original mix somehow. Second, if the regress that arose on the wide view of the *chrēmata* is vicious (as I believe that it is), then the opposites themselves are subject to it. For the "portion of everything in everything" principle must apply to the opposites as well. So the hot will be that in which the predominant ingredient is hot, which is that in which the predominant ingredient is ... and so on. Indefinite divisibility and the principle of "every thing in every thing" must apply to the opposites as to anything else.[33] Finally, and, I think, most importantly, while the opposites account gives Anaxagoras a slimmed-down metaphysics, it fails to account for what seems to be Anaxagoras's main motivation: making cosmology consistent with Parmenidean principles, and especially dispensing with coming-to-be and passing-away.

The distinction between ingredients and mixed objects is itself unobjectionable on Parmenidean terms, as long as the fundamental metaphysical status of the ingredients is guaranteed by the theory. In the *Doxa* Parmenides

composed of opposites, or which each contain the stuff that will produce a certain sort of plant or animal life. Vlastos adopts the former view, Schofield the latter. For Schofield's arguments against Vlastos's view (arguments which are, I think, successful), see *Essay*, pp. 126–30.

32 This is the case whether or not we assume Anaxagoras's primary interests to be cosmological and metaphysical or biological. Even if B10 is not authentic (and I suspect that it is either authentic or close to something Anaxagoras himself said), the problem raised by the question remains. For B17 shows that Anaxagoras denied that there is any real coming-to-be or passing away, and so the question of the apparent coming-to-be of hair or flesh is a legitimate one.

33 This is the case even if we identify the opposites as ingredients rather than emergent things, unless some move is made to distinguish, on the lines Strang suggests, between common opposites and elemental opposites. I do not think that Schofield makes such a distinction or would wish to.

himself provides a model cosmology that marks just such a distinction.[34] But Anaxagoras does not seem to say anything that would show that the opposites, as ingredients, have the special status of fundamental entities in his theory, or that their metaphysical status is different from that of the objects they produce through separation or mixture. Strang suggests that Anaxagoras's term for the things that are metaphysically derivative is *ta apokrinomena*, "the things separated off" (as, for instance, in B16);[35] but this fails to mark a distinction between opposites as ingredients and the things composed of these ingredients. For B12 shows that opposites (Schofield's ingredients) themselves are separated out from the original mixture: "and the dense is separated out from the rare and the hot from the cold and the bright from the murky and the dry from the moist" (καὶ ἀποκρίνεται ἀπό τε τοῦ ἀραιοῦ τὸ πυκνὸν καὶ ἀπὸ τοῦ ψυχροῦ τὸ θερμὸν καὶ ἀπὸ τοῦ ζοφεροῦ τὸ λαμπρὸν καὶ ἀπὸ τοῦ διεροῦ τὸ ξηρόν). So the opposites themselves may be said to be *ta apokrinomena*. Moreover, in B17, just where one might expect the distinction to be marked, there is no mention of *ta apokrinomena*; rather, Anaxagoras twice uses forms of *diakrinō* rather than forms of *apokrinō*. The two terms are obviously related, but if *ta apokrinomena* is supposed to serve as a technical term, it is odd that Anaxagoras does not use it here. B17 indeed marks a distinction between ontologically basic entities and ephemeral, changing objects. But it does so by remarking on the differences between things that apparently come to be or pass away and the "things that are" (*eonta chrēmata*):

> τὸ δὲ γίνεσθαι καὶ ἀπόλλυσθαι οὐκ ὀρθῶς νομίζουσιν οἱ Ἕλληνες· οὐδὲν γὰρ χρῆμα γίνεται οὐδὲ ἀπόλλυται, ἀλλ' ἀπὸ ἐόντων χρημάτων συμμίσγεταί τε καὶ διακρίνεται. καὶ οὕτως ἂν ὀρθῶς καλοῖεν τό τε γίνεσθαι συμμίσγεσθαι καὶ τὸ ἀπόλλυσθαι διακρίνεσθαι. (B17)
>
> The Greeks incorrectly recognize coming-to-be and perishing; for no thing comes to be or perishes, but rather it is mixed together and separated from the things that are. And so they would rightly call coming-to-be being mixed together and perishing being separated.

The metaphysical work in this passage is done by the verb "to be"; Anaxagoras uses "thing" (*chrēma*) indiscriminately between things at the metaphysically basic level ("things that are") and things at the level of apparent coming-to-be and passing-away ("no thing comes to be or perishes").[36] The

[34] Keeping in mind that the *Doxa* as presented is deceptive, although the model it uses may not be.

[35] Strang, p. 362; see also Schofield, Essay, p. 110.

[36] It might be argued that the clause οὐδὲν γὰρ χρῆμα γίνεται οὐδὲ ἀπόλλυται (no thing comes to be or perishes) refers to fundamental entities, but the rest of sentence makes clear that it does not. Anaxagoras discusses the phenomena of coming-to-be and passing-away and his argument is that any "thing" that seems to come to be or pass away is actually a mixture

important point about the things that are mixed together and into which things separate is that they are entities that deserve the epithet "thing that is." But Anaxagoras does not, at least in the extant fragments, provide a complete list of the "things that are." In contrast with Anaxagoras, Empedocles stresses the fundamental status of the four roots and Love and Strife: at 31B17.30–35 he discusses coming-to-be and passing-away, asserting that "just these things are, and on account of running through one another they show themselves different at different times and yet are always and ever the same." The emphasis on the basic nature of the roots and their accounting for other things by their "running through" each other is repeated at B21.13 and at B26.3. In all three of these passages, Empedocles claims "that these very things are," using the verb "to be" to mark off their metaphysically basic status. In B21 (at lines 9–11) Empedocles contrasts the roots with the things that are the result of their mixture: "trees, and men and women, beasts and birds and 'water-nourished' fish, and long-lived gods." Here in Empedocles there is a determined marking of the difference between real entities and phenomenal objects. But there is no such marking in Anaxagoras; and aside from a problematic remark in Aristotle, there is no evidence of such a distinction in the doxography.[37] So it looks as though there is nothing in the fragments to support the chief pillar of the opposites interpretation, the distinction between ingredients and objects. Further, the texts do not seem to support an ontological distinction between opposites and other things; all things were together in the original mixture: earth, air, aether, opposites, and seeds.

The third interpretation, that of Strang, distinguishes between what Strang calls "common" and "elemental" instances of a thing.[38] Insofar as this is a version of the "ingredients" view that is also part of the opposites account of the *chrēmata*, which requires that there be a metaphysical distinction between ingredients and the mixtures of such ingredients, I do not think it can succeed, because as we have seen, there is no strong textual support for such a distinction. But Strang's account of the elemental substances is interesting in its own right and suggests what I take to be the proper interpretation of the *chrēmata*. Strang takes a wide interpretation of "things" in Anaxagoras's claims about the original state, and he believes that the regress of analysis discussed above is vicious. To halt the regress, he suggests a distinction between the common occurrence of something and

---

"from the things that are." In the vocabulary of ingredients and objects, "thing" marks both ingredients and mixed objects in this fragment.

[37] Aristotle twice says that earth, air, water, and fire are conglomerations of "the elements," which he identifies with the homoeomeries (*Gen. Corr.* 314a28–b1; *de Caelo* 302a31–b3). I think that this is a mistaken interpretation of Anaxagoras; nevertheless, it offers no comfort to those who wish to restrict the *chrēmata* to the opposites, for Aristotle is quite clear that he takes fire, air, earth, and water to be mixtures of basic things that he takes to be homoeomeries (flesh, bone, etc.) and not opposites.

[38] Strang, pp. 361–62.

its elemental occurrence. The common occurrence of a thing (a C-substance, as he calls it) has many ingredients; indeed, a portion of everything is in each thing. But an elemental occurrence (an E-substance) is an instance of the pure thing. There is no use asking for its ingredients, for it has none.[39] An important, indeed fundamental, aspect of Strang's theory is often overlooked: "an E-substance is one which cannot be isolated, which never παντάπασιν ἀποκρίνεται (B12)."[40] Strang notes that there is little direct evidence for his account in the fragments of Anaxagoras since the theory demands that Anaxagoras's "substance words, both particular and generic, are systematically ambiguous. Anaxagoras himself evidently had no ready means of marking the distinction."[41] Strang's view is basically a theory of metaphysically basic ingredients and metaphysically dependent things made up from these ingredients; and it has the virtue of stopping the regress of analysis that has proved troublesome. But as we have seen, there is little evidence in the fragments to support the view that there are two metaphysically distinct levels of entity in Anaxagoras's system (other than those things which are the result of mixing natural objects—an example would be the mixing of copper and tin to form bronze, or the building of houses as in B4a[42]). Although Strang's view is unsuccessful insofar as it depends on two sorts of occurrence for each thing (an elemental and a common instance of each), it does suggest what is needed to provide Anaxagoras with a coherent account that is not subject to the regress of analysis: what is required is a way to grasp what a *chrēma* really is, in and of itself; a way to understand its nature. Such a grasp or understanding of a thing would allow for the intellectual analysis of coal, or earth, or the hot. There would be no need for ontologically different levels of these things, so we would not have to resort to a difference between ingredients (however understood) and common or phenomenal instances of things. Each instance, at whatever level, would share the same nature. Can the fragments of Anaxagoras support such a view? The answer is to be found in one of the more enigmatic aspects of Anaxagoras's system: the nature and role of *Nous*.

2.2. Anaxagoras: **Nous** *and the* **Chrēmata**

Both Plato and Aristotle denigrated Anaxagoras's account of Mind (*Nous*), arguing that *Nous* had no serious role to play in the Anaxagorean system. Plato, according to the claims he puts into the mouth of Socrates in the

39 Ibid.

40 Ibid.

41 Ibid.

42 B4a makes it clear that artifacts do not have the status of *chrēmata*: there Anaxagoras claims that human beings build cities and make or construct various works.

Phaedo, at 97b8ff., seems to have wanted *Nous* to play a teleological role in Anaxagoras and was disappointed by finding no such role in the theory. Aristotle, too, finds fault with Anaxagoras's use of Mind: he claims that it appears as a stopgap, whenever Anaxagoras "is in difficulty about the cause" of something (*Metaph.* 985a18–21). Eudemus, quoted by Simplicius (*in Ph.* 327.26), echoed Aristotle's criticism. One problem is that, aside from originating the motion that sets off the rotation of the original mixture, it is unclear just what Mind's role is. In *de Anima* Aristotle complains that Anaxagoras has not explained how mind can know at all. One response to the lack of evidence about thought and *Nous* is simply to deny that *Nous* has any intellectual role at all in Anaxagoras and to claim that it is simply a principle of movement; but, as Laks has shown, this suggestion will not do.[43] The language of 59B12 clearly attributes some sort of understanding and intellectual power to *Nous*: there Anaxagoras insists that *Nous* "holds every judgment about everything and has the greatest strength" (καὶ γνώμην γε περὶ παντὸς πᾶσαν ἴσχει καὶ ἰσχύει μέγιστον).[44] B12 further claims that "Mind knew all things, both the things being mixed and the things being separated and the things being distinguished" (καὶ τὰ συμμισγόμενά τε καὶ ἀποκρινόμενα καὶ διακρινόμενα πάντα ἔγνω νοῦς). So what does *Nous* actually know and what does it do?

Laks has suggested that, as knowing or judging (*krinein*) is itself a kind of distinguishing or separating out, Mind's knowing and its role as the instigator of motion in Anaxagoras are the same; for, as the rotation goes on, more and more things are separated out and thus become more like *Nous*, which is itself the only pure and unmixed entity in Anaxagoras's system (B12). *Nous* sets the cosmic rotation going in order "to identify [things] properly."[45] But, according to Laks, *Nous* can never succeed in this task, for the things that were originally mixed together never separate out completely: "in everything there is a portion of everything" (B6, B11). Moreover, according to Laks, the identities that seem to emerge through the rotation are only quasi-identities. They appear at the level of sense perception, but what sense reports as an identity or nature is only a mixture in which "quantitative superiority" masquerades as identity.[46] Lesher has argued that there are textual and philosophical problems with Laks's

[43] Silvestre, in "Significato" and "Simplicius' Testimony," argues that "*nous* is no more than that which gives motion to everything" ("Simplicius' Testimony," p. 373). Laks argues decisively against her account in "Mind's Crisis," pp. 26–27.

[44] Lesher translates "*gnōmē*" as "decision" ("Mind's Knowledge," p. 139); see pp. 137–40 for his discussion of the translation.

[45] Laks, "Mind's Crisis," pp. 30–31.

[46] Ibid., pp. 31–33; "In some sense at least, Anaxagoras's cosmic νοῦς has worked in vain. And so would our νοῦς, if it claimed, as the senses suggest, to know what things are in their ultimate identity, pure gold or white snow. For there is no such thing as an ultimate identity" (p. 32).

view.[47] While I agree with Lesher's criticisms, there is another problem with Laks's account, one that Lesher has not addressed in detail and that begins to expose the heart of the issue of Mind's knowledge and its role in Anaxagoras's metaphysical and cosmological views. In a note Laks suggests that Mind will indeed have to know the basic constituents of the original mixture: "Of course νοῦς will have to 'know' the primary constituents, namely their properties, in order to have them interact in the proper way."[48] I am unsure how to interpret the scare quotes on "know" here, but this comment seems to suggest both that there is indeed an identity (as Laks puts it) for each thing that Mind is well able to grasp even while things are mixed and separating and that, indeed, Mind must grasp the true identities of things in order to arrange and control things in the *kosmos*.[49] But Laks's official view rules this out: something can have an identity and *Nous* could know that identity only if the thing is entirely separated out, so there is an inconsistency here. Further, I do not see how mind can order all things and have all discerning judgment about them if they are unknown to it. Anaxagoras's claims in B12 do not constitute a promissory note of what Mind will (perhaps) know; rather, these are claims about Mind's power now. I shall return to this issue of Mind's grasping of things in the original mixture after considering Lesher's account of Mind's knowledge.

Lesher proposes that the crucial passage in understanding the role of Mind in Anaxagoras is in B12: as he translates, *Nous* "holds every decision concerning everything." This captures the notion that Mind is a governing

[47] Lesher has four criticisms of Laks ("Mind's Knowledge," pp. 129–30). First, "Many of the elements in Laks's account of Anaxagoras's epistemology require us to go beyond anything actually said in the fragments or reported in any of the ancient testimonia." According to Lesher there is no evidence that Mind wants to know all things, or that Mind wants to make things like itself. Further, there is no evidence for Laks's claims that things must be separate individuals for them to be like Mind and so known by *Nous*, or that Mind sets the rotation going in order to accomplish this goal. Second, Laks himself points out ("Mind's Crisis," p. 24) that Anaxagoras is unlikely to have accepted the view that like is known only by like. So it seems odd to claim that Mind must make things like itself in order to know them. Third, B12 provides evidence that Mind knows things even when they are not separated out: καὶ τὰ συμμισγόμενά τε καὶ ἀποκρινόμενα καὶ διακρινόμενα (the things being mixed and the things being separated and the things being distinguished); so the motivation for the cosmic separation has disappeared. Finally, according to Lesher, "if Mind were to decide to set out on an individuating enterprise that could not possibly succeed, it would clearly not be the supremely intelligent being Anaxagoras makes it out to be. Since Mind possesses 'all discerning judgment or understanding . . . concerning everything' it would have to know better than to attempt to know things in some impossible way." Finally, although Lesher does not mention this, it is odd that Anaxagoras should make epistemological success depend on a cosmological process.

[48] Laks, "Mind's Crisis," p. 36n.58.

[49] In a private communication, Laks suggested to me that Mind's knowledge before the separation remains "in some sense deficient." But it is still unclear to me why this must be so, except on the basis of an interpretation of the "like is known by like" principle that claims that unmixed things can be known only by an unmixed thing. This seems to be a dubious version of "like by like," and not one to which Laks himself need be committed (see note 47).

force in the *kosmos*; for everything that happens (beginning with the initiation of the rotary motion of the original mixture) is a result of Mind's decision-making and its power to accomplish those decisions.[50] Lesher's main concern is exploring Mind as a decision maker, and so he says little about the content of Mind's knowledge. He suggests that the later assertion in B12, that Mind "*egnō* all things, both the things being mixed and the things being separated and the things being distinguished" (καὶ τὰ συμμισγόμενά τε καὶ ἀποκρινόμενα καὶ διακρινόμενα πάντα ἔγνω νοῦς), should be understood as "Mind decides or determines[51] everything," taking *gignōskō* in its sense of "judging or determining" and interpreting the clause as a statement about Mind's decision about "how the individual portions get distributed." According to Lesher, Anaxagoras's stress in his account of *Nous* is on how Mind works to order and control the cosmos, rather than on Mind's knowing or understanding the *kosmos*.[52] So (aside from a brief mention in the last paragraph of his paper), Lesher leaves open the issue of what it is that Mind actually knows; moreover, his comments suggest that it is not knowledge *per se* that Lesher conceives of Mind as having. Lesher's account of the role of *Nous* has much to recommend it; but I think that the issue of the content of Mind's knowledge is more important than either Lesher or Laks has indicated. Lesher is right that *Nous* has an important role in deciding the order of the *kosmos*, but as I indicated above, such decision-making cannot be intelligent unless *Nous* has complete knowledge about each thing in the *kosmos*, for only if it has such knowledge can its decisions about "the things being mixed and the things being separated and the things being distinguished" be genuine intelligent decision-making rather than the whim of the moment or a hopeful decision made on the basis of inadequate or incomplete information.

So, while Lesher is correct that the claims about Mind's *gnōmē* should be understood as a discussion of Mind's decision-making power and capacity to enact those decisions, I think that Anaxagoras's claim that *Nous egnō* all things should be understood in the stronger sense of "know." The things that Mind *egnō* are enumerated in three stages: "the things being mixed (*summisgomena*), the things being separated (*apokrinomena*), and the things

[50] According to Lesher, "It would be difficult . . . to imagine a more appropriate premiss to find at the heart of Anaxagoras's account of how a supremely powerful intelligence controls and orders the cosmos than the assertion that whatever happens in the cosmos results from Mind's decision making powers"; "Mind's Knowledge," p. 139.

[51] Lesher argues that *egnō* is a gnomic aorist, and thus a universal generalization.

[52] According to Lesher, "The 'γνώμη concerning all things' Anaxagoras attributed to his cosmic Mind should not, therefore, be understood as a matter of its possessing all γνῶσις or σύνεσις—full knowledge or complete understanding of the cosmic order, but rather as the same wise or intelligent decision-making Anaxagoras's predecessors had detected at work throughout the cosmos imposing an order on the natural realm and setting limits to its processes of change" ("Mind's Knowledge," p. 140; italics omitted).

being distinguished (*diakrinomena*)." B12 is about the character and activities of *Nous*. It begins by asserting that *Nous* is unmixed with anything else, although all other things have a share of all things; it then explores the issues of why *Nous* must be unmixed. Anaxagoras then returns to an enumeration of the characteristics of Mind: it is the finest of all things and the purest, it holds every decision about all things, and has the greatest strength. It controls all things that have soul, and it "controlled the whole rotation, so that it rotated in the beginning." There is a short description of the rotation, and then comes the claim that Nous *egnō* "all things, the things being mixed, the things being separated, and the things being distinguished." Laks and Lesher take the passage as referring to processes that are going on now, rather than as a claim that Mind knew, or distinguished, or determined all things in the beginning.[53] But as the process of rotation is continual, and as the original state was a mixture (*summixis*, B4b), it must be the case that, whatever translation of *egnō* we settle on, Mind *egnō* things in the original mix as well as in the present state of mixture and partial separation. This suggests to me that we should adopt the stronger translation: Mind knew all things, whether they were or still are in the mixture, or whether they are in the process of separating out and being distinguished. Without such knowledge, Mind cannot be an intelligent decision-maker.[54] B12 stresses that Mind has powers of control, and suggests that Mind controls well. But knowledge of what things are, and thus how they will behave when in motion after Mind begins and maintains the rotation that begins the process of separation, is prior to such power, and, I suggest, a condition of it. To know the things in the mixture, and the things separating out, and so on, would be to know what each of them really or genuinely is. It is to know what Laks calls their identity, and what I would prefer to call their nature or character. Each emergent thing is still a mixture, as Anaxagoras reminds us at the opening of B12, and again at the end. Each thing, no matter how manifestly separate it seems to be, is but a mixture, whose character is indicated by the predominating ingredient: "each one thing is and was most manifestly

[53] Laks, "Mind's Crisis," p. 36n.58; Lesher, "Mind's Knowledge," pp. 129–30. Lesher recognizes (pp. 130, 131) that the passage includes the claim that *Nous egnō*, mind knows, or decides, things even before they are separated out of the mixture.

[54] According to Lesher, "any power capable of overseeing the operations of the whole cosmos would most naturally be assumed to possess the greatest amount of wisdom" ("Mind's Knowledge," p. 141). But Lesher is not specific about what *Nous* actually knows. He says (p. 142) that it "must have enjoyed some degree of awareness of individual entities as it went about its work" and further suggests that intelligence "is capable of grasping the identity of the elements in their pure state." But he does not explain further just what it is that *Nous* grasps, and denies that this grasping should be understood as *gnōsis* or *sunesis* (p. 140n.54); nor does he link this grasping with the metaphysics of Anaxagoras's system (a topic outside of the main focus of his article). So it is unclear to me just what the capacity for the "grasping of an identity of an element in its pure state" is supposed to be on Lesher's view. I shall argue that *Nous* actually knows the natures of the *chrēmata*.

those things of which there are the most in it" (ἀλλ' ὅτων πλεῖστα ἔνι, ταῦτα ἐνδηλότατα ἓν ἕκαστόν ἐστι καὶ ἦν). But unless there is something that each ingredient actually is, and that can be known to be such, Anaxagoras's claim here makes no sense. Unless there is a nature of gold or coal that can be known, we cannot justifiably claim that it is the predominance of gold or coal in a particular emergent mixture that warrants giving that mixture the name that it has. Anaxagoras's insistence on an original mixture in which nothing is manifest can blind us to the fact that the original mixture is a mixture of things, of entities that maintain their nature throughout. If they did not, then coming-to-be and passing-away would be real or genuine, something that Anaxagoras is at pains to deny, and which he thinks would violate the Parmenidean strictures against the not-being of what-is.[55] Plato and Aristotle complained that *Nous* plays only a mechanical role in Anaxagoras's *kosmos*. But, if the account suggested here is correct, they were wrong. *Nous* has an important role to play in the metaphysical foundations of Anaxagoras's system. The regress of analysis that was explored earlier (in Section 2.1) is stopped if we see that there are natures of each of the *chrēmata* and that *Nous* has knowledge of the nature of each thing. Mind knows the nature of gold or coal. That is, *Nous* understands what it is to be gold, or what it is to be coal, even though gold or coal never have been or never can be in a pure, unmixed state. Although there are no physically unmixed *chrēmata*, their natures can be known by *Nous* through a process of intellection.[56] There is no need to claim, as Strang does, that Anaxagoras distinguishes between elemental and common occurrences of these natural materials (although Strang takes care to point out that E-substances can never be isolated), or otherwise to mark a metaphysical distinction between ingredients (as opposites, perhaps) and substances; for Anaxagoras does not make such a distinction.[57] But he does allow for the knowability of his *chrēmata*: the

[55] This claim is supported by B17 and B3. One consequence of B3 (of the small there is no smallest but only a smaller) is that we can never reach a physically unmixed state. The principle of no smallest is clearly said to follow from the principle that what-is cannot not be. The link between Parmenides and Anaxagoras's conception of the *chrēmata* is rightly stressed by Furth ("Philosophical Hero"). See his n. 27, p. 113: "... the *khrēma* must be thought of as a *single* nature spread throughout the entirety of the cosmos; the various 'large' and 'small' 'portions' of it ... are merely local protuberances or recessions, where it is prominent or hidden."

[56] I briefly discussed this issue in an earlier version of this chapter, presented at a conference on the Presocratics at Princeton University in December 1992. At the same conference David Furley made a similar point about Mind's knowledge of individual entities in his paper "Anaxagoras and the Naming of Parts." The same point is suggested in his "From Anaxagoras." See now both Lesher, "Mind's Knowledge," and Graham, "Postulates," p. 87n.26: Graham claims that Anaxagoras's "primitive substances," which he calls "elements," are "conceptually distinguishable (though not, apparently, physically separable) as the basic stuffs of which all phenomenal objects are composed." Graham does not discuss the role of *Nous* here.

[57] This should not be taken to suggest that the *chrēmata* never occur as ingredients. It is obvious that they do, especially in artifacts and in organisms (whose status is not quite clear

nature of each thing is available to cosmic *Nous*, although *nous* in us may be unable to work out those natures.[58] B21 indicates that the senses are "feeble"; because of this we are not able to determine the truth: ὑπ' ἀφαυρότητος αὐτῶν οὐ δυνατοί ἐσμεν κρίνειν τἀληθές. Pure cosmic *Nous*, which is not hampered by sense perception, would have no difficulty, since its grasping of the *chrēmata* would be an act of pure intellection. Nevertheless, there is for *nous* in us some access to the real nature of things: B21a asserts that phenomena are a glimpse of the unseen (ὄψις τῶν ἀδήλων τὰ φαινόμενα). *Nous* in us allows us to have some understanding of how things are, though we may never have the complete understanding that Mind has. It makes no difference whether *Nous* considers a *chrēma* in its present mixed state or in the original mixture; in both cases Mind could and would know its essential nature.

2.3. Anaxagoras and the Problem of Large and Small

The natures of the *chrēmata* must be permanent, unchanging features of the *kosmos*, as there is no coming-to-be or passing-away. There may be temporary mixtures (an artifact, or an organism such as a human being, say) that are subject to separation, as B17 suggests. But these temporary mixtures are made up of the *chrēmata* that remain just what they are, no matter how emergent, or thoroughly mixed, or large, or small, they are. The issue of largeness and smallness is a vexed one in Anaxagoras, and numerous interpretations have been suggested.[59] Smallness is evidently a crucial notion (as important as the principle that "all things were together"), for it is mentioned right at the beginning of the book, in B1.[60] Anaxagoras says more about smallness in fragment 3:

> οὔτε γὰρ τοῦ σμικροῦ ἔστι τό γε ἐλάχιστον, ἀλλ' ἔλασσον ἀεί (τὸ γὰρ ἐὸν οὐκ ἔστι [τὸ] μὴ οὐκ εἶναι)[61] · ἀλλὰ καὶ τοῦ μεγάλου ἀεί ἐστι μεῖζον· καὶ

---

in Anaxagoras, given the problem of interpreting seeds). So the view I offer here has some points in common with Strang's. But I would claim that the *chrēma* as ingredient in the mix is exactly the same as the *chrēma* in its common occurrence, as both share a common nature. The nature that *Nous* grasps will, on Strang's view, be an elemental occurrence, but I see no need to draw a distinction between the elemental and common levels, as Strang does; moreover, I would deny any metaphysical difference between the status of the *chrēmata* as ingredients and as occurring in mixtures.

58 For discussion of some of the differences between cosmic and individual *Nous*, see Graham, "Postulates," pp. 114–15.

59 Both Mann and Konstan rightly stress that largeness and smallness are cognate terms in Anaxagoras; both must be analyzed together, and whatever account is given for the one must, *mutatis mutandis*, apply to the other. For a brief discussion of various recent interpretations of large and small in Anaxagoras, see Graham, "Postulates," n. 58, pp. 107–8.

60 Quoted on p. 132.

61 On the text, see n. 4.

ἴσον ἐστὶ τῷ σμικρῷ πλῆθος. πρὸς ἑαυτὸ δὲ ἕκαστόν ἐστι καὶ μέγα καὶ σμικρόν.

For of the small there is indeed no smallest, but always a smaller (for it is not possible that what-is not be); but also of the large there is always a larger; and it is equal to the small in number. In relation to itself each thing is both large and small.

Anaxagoras here makes two claims, both of which are crucial to his theory: there is no smallest part or portion (however small a part or portion of something there is, a smaller part or portion is always available); similarly, there is no largest (however large a part or portion of something one takes, there is always possible a larger part or portion). The importance of the principle of unlimited smallness becomes clear with B6, in which Anaxagoras argues from unlimited smallness and the equality in multitude of small and large, to the claim that everything is in everything. Together, the "everything in everything" principle and the principle of unlimited smallness guarantee that there is no genuine coming-to-be or passing away; for if everything is in everything, coming-to-be will be a matter of separating out and mixture (just as B17 claims), and unlimited smallness will ensure that nothing ever genuinely ceases to be: no matter how small a thing is, it will always remain just what it is.

B1 and B3 have suggested to many commentators a particulate reading of Anaxagoras, and an interpretation of unlimited smallness as infinite divisibility.[62] Everything is an aggregate of particles of everything, and there is no particle of anything so small that it cannot be divided into even smaller particles. But each of these particles must contain further particles of everything else, and so on. Commentators have found difficulties with the particulate view.[63] One problem with any interpretation of the combination and division of Anaxagoras's *chrēmata*, whether they are understood as particles, portions, or droplets, is that the extant fragments are quite vague on this issue; it is just not obvious from the text how we are to think of the *chrēmata* when they are mixing and separating, nor is there anything in the text that would force the particulate account.[64] Another difficulty lies in seeing how to

62 Barnes notes the connection between the particulate view of matter and the principle of infinite divisibility; see *PP*, vol. II, pp. 22–23.

63 The problems of the particulate view have been widely discussed; see, for instance, Barnes, *PP*, vol. II, pp. 21–23; Schofield, *Essay*, pp. 68–80; Mann, pp. 243–47; Inwood, "Infinite Divisibility." Furth ("Philosophical Hero") and Inwood have argued that "larger" means "more emergent" and "smaller" means "less emergent." One recent view that reinterprets but does not reject the particulate view is that of Graham; see "Postulates," pp. 102–5. Graham considers Barnes's objections, noting that they are not very strong, but he does not discuss other objections, notably Schofield's.

64 Schofield stresses the lack of textual support for the particulate view (*Essay*, pp. 73–74). He points out that one might interpret "seed" in Anaxagoras as "small particle" and

make sense of the manifest character of anything if there are infinitely many particles of every kind in everything. According to the end of B12, "Each one thing is and was most manifestly those things of which there are the most (*pleista*) in it." But what sense can be made of this if there are infinitely many particles (even very small particles) of everything in everything? For every particle of gold in a given particle of gold, there will be a particle of coal, and of air, and of aether, and so on. Suppose we were able to break down this particle of gold into its composite particles and then further divide those composite particles, putting the gold particles we extract in one bowl, the coal particles in another bowl, and so on.[65] We continue with this process and then at some point begin drawing particles out of the bowls. If gold was the "most" in the original particle, the heap of particles in the bowl containing the gold should be larger than the others. Yet when we draw particles out, given the particulate view and infinite divisibility, each particle of gold will be matched by a particle from each of the other bowls; and because the small is unlimited (interpreted by the particulate view as there is always a smaller and smaller particle possible), the process of matching gold and coal particles will be unlimited: for every particle of gold drawn from the larger bowl, there will be a particle of coal drawn from the smaller. There will not be a "most" in anything, if "most" means "most particles of that type."[66] So, on the particulate interpretation, it seems impossible that any character can be manifest by being "most." But this is clearly what

indeed many commentators do so (see for instance Graham, "Postulates," pp. 105–6, and Furth, "Philosophical Hero"). But if a "seed" is a small particle, why is it, too, not indefinitely divisible? What role does a seed now play in the theory? These worries suggest that Peck, Furley, Barnes, and Schofield are right in thinking of the seeds as normal biological seeds that account for the structures of organisms. They can then contain everything and still retain their role in the system. See Schofield, *Essay*, pp. 121–32. For a summary of scholarly views on the seeds, and his own view, see Teodorsson, pp. 45–64, 80, and 89–91. See also Mourelatos, "Quality," pp. 155–57.

65 For purposes of illustration, I am assuming that we can recognize the particles that a particular particle of gold will break into.

66 A similar worry is raised by Furth, "Philosophical Hero," p. 120 with n. 49. Cornford discusses the problem in "Theory of Matter," pp. 297–99; 309–11; he attempts to avoid the difficulty by relying on seeds and opposites. Guthrie also briefly considers the issue in *HGP*, vol. II, pp. 290–91. It is not clear to me that reinterpreting particles as droplets, as Graham does, avoids this difficulty. He challenges Barnes's argument against the particulate view, rightly noting that it depends on a homoeomerous interpretation. But the objection I raise here is not grounded in thinking of particles of something as homoeomerous; rather it arises from noting that the "everything in everything" and the "infinite divisibility" interpretation of "indefinite smallness" together seem to have this unwanted conclusion. Graham rejects Barnes's claim that "every piece of S is a piece of S;" regarding it as a commitment to homoeomereity. But Anaxagoras's claim that "of the small there is no smallest, only a smaller" (B3) seems to guarantee that every piece of S (gold, say) must be S (gold). The problem is that any piece of S (gold) will itself be a mixture, apparently of the same sort as S itself. If this is the case, I do not see that Graham has successfully refuted Barnes's argument. It might be that "most" must mean something like "largest particles." But it is unclear that there is any support for

Anaxagoras claims; I conclude that the particulate interpretation was not what Anaxagoras had in mind.

It is, I think, more helpful to think of Anaxagoras's *chrēmata* as masses of varying concentration or density, thoroughly mixed together so that no mass is pure but always contains some percentage of everything else. Thus, for instance, no mass of gold is pure gold, for it will always contain what might be referred to as impurities by someone interested in making gold coins or jewelry. These impurities are not particulate bits of flesh or coal (which can be further subdivided into ever smaller bits, as on the particulate view), but varying concentrations of flesh or coal distributed continuously, evenly blended into the gold, as salt is distributed continuously in sea-water, or resin in wine. To the extent that the impurities in the gold have a much lower density (amount of stuff per unit volume) than the gold, the lump will give the manifest appearance of being gold. The concentration of gold can be increased by refinement, but the impurities can never be entirely eliminated. Just as there is no upper limit to the density of gold, so there is no lower limit to the concentration of all those other things in the gold that are called impurities. "In everything there is a portion of everything" does not imply that every portion of gold contains equal concentrations of everything: that is why it is gold; it may contain coal, or flesh, or salt (and each of these will themselves contain everything else), but the density of each of these impurities is smaller than the density of gold. In some wine, there will be some of everything, but of certain of the *chrēmata* there will be greater densities: of grape essence, of water, of the dark as opposed to the pale, of the hot as opposed to the cold, and of the sweet as opposed to the bitter: thus, according to the principle stated at the end of B12, there will be warm sweet red wine—a warming posset, perhaps. The varying degrees of density are referred to as portions; but there is nothing here that forces us to adopt the particulate interpretation.[67] The largeness or smallness of a thing refers to its density—there is no limit to how large or small a density is possible; and the higher densities (in comparison with other things in the local area) will be those that are manifest or apparent to sense perception.[68] But no matter

interpreting *pleista* in terms of size; *pleista*, particularly as the plural form, seems to have to do with quantity, not mass. We might suppose that "most" in B12 refers to weight: the different-sized particles might have different weights. But if we determine that something is a particle of gold by comparing the overall weights of the various *chrēmata* in it, we have moved rather far away from the particulate interpretation.

67 I assume that what I am referring to here as "concentrations" or "densities" are what Schofield refers to as "proportions" (see *Essay*, pp. 75–79) and Barnes calls "portions." Schofield links his account of proportions with Barnes's view (see *PP*, vol. II, pp. 22–24) but rightly notes the difficulty of interpreting unlimited smallness in B1 on Barnes's account, which reads "large" and "small" as referring to the total amount of each *chrēma* in the original mix.

68 Thus, I think that the suggestions of Inwood ("Infinite Divisibility") and Furth ("A Philosophical Hero") that "large" and "small" in Anaxagoras refer to manifestness and latency

how small or great the density, each instance of a particular *chrēma* will have the same unchanging nature as any other instance, and this nature is known by *Nous*, as argued above in Section 2.2.

2.4. Anaxagoras and the Opposites

Mind's knowledge of the nature of each thing is also helpful in understanding Anaxagoras's treatment of the opposites in his theory. The fragments make it clear that the opposites are *chrēmata*, with the same metaphysical status as all the other basic entities of Anaxagoras's theory. Fragment 4b provides a brief account of the original mixture:

> πρὶν δὲ ἀποκριθῆναι ταῦτα πάντων ὁμοῦ ἐόντων οὐδὲ χροιὴ ἔνδηλος ἦν οὐδεμία· ἀπεκώλυε γὰρ ἡ σύμμιξις ἁπάντων χρημάτων, τοῦ τε διεροῦ καὶ τοῦ ξηροῦ καὶ τοῦ θερμοῦ καὶ τοῦ ψυχροῦ καὶ τοῦ λαμπροῦ καὶ τοῦ ζοφεροῦ, καὶ γῆς πολλῆς ἐνεούσης καὶ σπερμάτων ἀπείρων πλῆθος οὐδὲν ἐοικότων ἀλλήλοις. οὐδὲ γὰρ τῶν ἄλλων οὐδὲν ἔοικε τὸ ἕτερον τῷ ἑτέρῳ. τούτων δὲ οὕτως ἐχόντων ἐν τῷ σύμπαντι χρὴ δοκεῖν ἐνεῖναι πάντα χρήματα. (B4b)

> Before these things were separated out, all things being together, not even any color was manifest; for the mixture of all things prevented it, of the damp and the dry and of the hot and the cold and of the bright and the murky, and much earth being present also and seeds unlimited in number, in no way resembling each other. For of the others none is like another. These things being so, it is right to think that all things were in the whole.

Here, three pairs of opposites are on the same footing with other things (earth and seeds) that are mentioned as being present in the original mixture. That the opposites have the same metaphysical standing as the other *chrēmata* is made clear by the opening claim that "all things" (*panta*) were together in the original mix, and by Anaxagoras's summation at the end of the fragment, which repeats that one must think that "all things" (*panta chrēmata*) were in the original mix. The middle lines illustrate the principle enumerated at the beginning and the end, and the three pairs of opposites, earth, and seeds seem to serve as stand-ins for all things, which are too many to be enumerated separately. So the opposites are clearly basic entities, part of the

---

(Furth's terms) or to being separated out and so distinguishable or mixed and indistinguishable (Inwood's account) have merit. On the view suggested here, a larger density in a given area will be more separated out and thus more manifest than other things, a smaller density (in relation to the surroundings) will be more mixed and less manifest. A small (sized) lump of gold will have a lower density than the surrounding air, but in relation to other *chrēmata* (such as coal, flesh, etc.) in the immediate vicinity, it will have a larger density or concentration of gold and thus will be more manifest (more separated out) than the (very small) density of coal that is undoubtedly mixed in the gold (along with unlimited other *chrēmata*).

original mix, and among the "things that are" (*eonta chrēmata*) from which the things that appear to come to be and pass away are mixed and into which they are separated (B17).

Given the equivocal status of opposites within the Parmenidean system, it might seem odd that Anaxagoras counts them as genuine entities. In Parmenides' *Doxa*, each of the opposites, Light and Night, was described as "the same as itself and not the same as the other" (B8.57–58), indicating that there is no character shared by the two. Such a conception of opposites treats them as enantiomorphic, completely excluding and repelling one another. The problem with Parmenides' opposites, Night and Light, is that although they seem to be independent entities they actually fall short of being so, because they fail to meet the criteria for what-is argued for in B8. Their intertwined, Heraclitean characters guarantee that they cannot be genuine entities, although mortals err in believing them to be such. It is impossible to conceive of Light and Night independently, for each is what the other is not. That Anaxagoras conceives of opposites rather differently is indicated in B8:

> οὐ κεχώρισται ἀλλήλων τὰ ἐν τῷ ἑνὶ κόσμῳ οὐδὲ ἀποκέκοπται πελέκει οὔτε τὸ θερμὸν ἀπὸ τοῦ ψυχροῦ οὔτε τὸ ψυχρὸν ἀπὸ τοῦ θερμοῦ.[69] (B8)
>
> The things in the one *kosmos* have not been separated from each other, nor have they been cut off with an axe, neither the hot from the cold nor the cold from the hot.

The original state was one of universal mixture, and that original state continues to a certain extent even now, because even now "all things are together" (B4a, B12). But, as we have seen, that mixture is not incompatible with there being a genuine nature that each thing (*chrēma*) has and that can be known by *Nous*. B8 provides an illustration of the fundamental claim that nothing can be genuinely separated so as to be "itself by itself" (except *Nous*), and it is suggestive of his view of them that Anaxagoras should choose the opposites to illustrate his point. Each of the *chrēmata* in Anaxagoras's system has its own nature, yet each is thoroughly mixed with, and inextricable from, all others. Thus, each can be conceived as a separate, independent entity, though none in actuality is like this. And Anaxagoras's treatment of the opposites indicates that in this respect they are no different from any of the other *chrēmata*. Anaxagoras seems then to reject both Heraclitus' claim that the opposites are "one" and Parmenides' conception of opposites as

[69] Sider suggests (*Fragments*, p. 86) that the words that immediately follow the passage in Simplicius, at *in Ph.* 175.14, might be part of the quotation: οὐ γὰρ ⟨ἔστιν⟩ εἶναί τι εἰλικρινὲς καθ' αὑτό (for it is not possible for anything to be pure by itself). The line does not appear in Simplicius's second quotation of B8, at 176.29 (nor are hot and cold mentioned in the second instance). Whether or not the line is actually part of the fragment, it certainly contains an Anaxagorean sentiment (as long as it is kept in mind that *Nous* is excluded, for it certainly can exist "pure by itself").

enantiomorphic.[70] Rather, it is crucial for Anaxagoras that hot and cold (and all the other opposites) have positive and independent natures; each is thus an entity in its own right. Were this not the case, the mixtures apparent to sense perception could not be as they are.[71]

It has been suggested that a special problem for Anaxagoras is the explanation of intermediate states between the opposites: the lukewarm, the slightly damp, and so on.[72] On a quite strict interpretation of the "everything in everything" principle, Anaxagoras would have to claim that the lukewarm (in all possible degrees) must already be in the original mix and must emerge through separation. This view can garner support from B4a: "It is right to think that there are many things and of all sorts in all the things that are put together, and seeds of all things having forms and colors and tastes of all sorts (χρὴ δοκεῖν ἐνεῖναι πολλά τε καὶ παντοῖα ἐν πᾶσι τοῖς συγκρινομένοις καὶ σπέρματα πάντων χρημάτων καὶ ἰδέας παντοίας ἔχοντα καὶ χροιὰς καὶ ἡδονάς)." Further, one might extend B10 in support: "How," one might ask, "can what is lukewarm come from what is not lukewarm?" On this account the hot and the cold would be the extremes of a continuum of genuine entities. In response, it may be said that there seems to be no reason to suppose that Anaxagoras would require that the lukewarm (in all its various manifestations) be a genuine entity on the same footing with earth, air, or hot and cold. B17 makes it clear that there are some things that are the result of mixing and compounding of the things that are real, and there is no reason to suppose that this is not the case here.[73] Experience suggests that the lukewarm just is the result of the temporary mixing of the hot and the cold, each of which is a genuine, permanent entity. Hot and cold water are mixed to reach the appropriate temperature for bathing; the hot (as fire) is applied to a pot of cold soup in order to reach the proper temperature for eating. The lukewarm is itself a phenomenal entity (rather

[70] See for instance Descartes, *Meditations on First Philosophy*, Meditation III. Descartes there contrasts the idea of an infinite substance as a real thing with the ideas of rest and darkness. According to Descartes "my conceptions of rest and darkness are arrived at by negating movement and light" (translation by Cottingham, Stoothoff, and Murdoch II.31 = Adam and Tannery VII.45); he makes the same assertion about the idea of cold. In the Fourth Objections, Antoine Arnauld disputed this characterization of the idea of cold: "What is the idea of cold? It is coldness insofar as it exists objectively in the intellect. But if cold is an absence, it cannot exist objectively in the intellect by means of an idea whose objective existence is a positive entity. Therefore, if cold is merely an absence, there cannot ever be a positive idea of it" (translation CSM, CSM II, 145 = AT VII.206). Descartes takes a "semi-Parmenidean" view (for he thinks that movement, light, and heat are real), while Arnauld adopts an "Anaxagorean" account of the opposites.

[71] Anaxagoras thus adopts a view that has affinities with Plato's account of the compresence of opposites in sensible things. See Furley, "Naming of Parts."

[72] See Mourelatos, "Quality," pp. 146–52.

[73] This is the answer to Furth's objection against B17, made on pp. 124–25 of "Philosophical Hero," that the view of things being mixed and separated in B17 is at best confusing and at worst incompatible with the rest of Anaxagoras's system.

like an artifact), a temporary emergence as the result of the mixing of the hot and the cold, both of which are basic, genuine entities.[74] Unless hot and cold were each independent, metaphysically basic entities, each with its own nature or character, they could not function in this way. Here again is a case where perception suggests the proper account, where phenomena are a sight of the unseen (B21a). It is because of what it is (its nature) that the hot can warm other things, and because of what it is (its nature) that the cold can cool things. If their natures were intertwined in the manner of Parmenides' enantiomorphic conception of opposites, so that neither had a complete nature of its own, hot and cold would be unable to play this role within Anaxagoras's system.

The influence of Parmenides on Anaxagoras is multifaceted. The most obvious influence is Anaxagoras's rejection of the reality of coming-to-be and passing-away, but there is further influence from both Parmenides' *Alētheia* and *Doxa* to be seen in the metaphysics of the Anaxagorean system. The *chrēmata* themselves, stable and permanent features of the *kosmos*, are entities that meet Parmenidean criteria, each with a fixed and unchanging nature that can be grasped by *Nous*. These *chrēmata* form the basis of Anaxagoras's account of the sensible world, emerging from the original mixture through the whirling motion that *Nous* initiates. The details of Anaxagoras's world may appear to be different from that of Parmenides' *Doxa*, where there is mixture and separation of two basic entities, Light and Night. But there are important similarities. The separating out of things from the original mix is a first step, for they then also combine—not just hot and cold to form lukewarm, but also in the processes of nutrition and growth. Various parts of an organism separate from the food taken in and then combine in the process of growth, so hair is added to hair and flesh to flesh. Likewise, separation occurs in natural processes of decay in artifacts and organisms.[75] Similarly, the reciprocal changes catalogued in B16 further involve separation and combination. So, although the number of basic entities is vastly larger, the model of Parmenides' *Doxa* is maintained, while the Parmenidean requirements about the unified, whole, unchanging, complete nature of the fundamental things are also satisfied.

[74] See Inwood "Infinite Divisibility" p. 25n.29. Inwood applies this analysis to "all macroscopic phenomenal entities," holding that only the opposites are genuine basic entities. I have already indicated that I think the range of the *chrēmata* to be wider than simply the opposites. Mourelatos considers this account of the lukewarm ("Quality," p. 149; it is his option [d]), and he objects to the account because he thinks it commits Anaxagoras to the coming-to-be of the lukewarm. But, as we have seen, temporary mixtures that satisfy the requirements of B17 are not genuine cases of coming-to-be.

[75] Even if Schofield is correct (as I believe he is) that the consideration of biological phenomena was not the basis of Anaxagoras's system, the explanation of those phenomena is a fundamental part of the theory.

3. Empedocles

3.1. Empedocles and the Roots of All Things

There can be little doubt of the Parmenidean influence on Empedocles; the verbal and doctrinal echoes of Parmenides in the extant fragments have often been noted.[76] Like Anaxagoras, Empedocles accepts and repeats Parmenides' banishment of coming-to-be and passing-away:

> ἄλλο δέ τοι ἐρέω· φύσις οὐδενός ἐστιν ἁπάντων
> θνητῶν, οὐδέ τις οὐλομένου θανάτοιο τελευτή,
> ἀλλὰ μόνον μίξις τε διάλλαξίς τε μιγέντων
> ἐστί, φύσις δ' ἐπὶ τοῖς ὀνομάζεται ἀνθρώποισιν. (B8)
>
> And I shall tell you another thing; there is growth of none of all
> mortal things, nor is there any end in baneful death,
> but there is only mixing and interchanging of what is mixed.
> and growth is the name given these by human beings.
>
> ἐκ γὰρ τοῦ μὴ ἐόντος[77] ἀμήχανόν ἐστι γενέσθαι,
> καί τ' ἐὸν ἐξαπολέσθαι ἀνήνυστον καὶ ἄπυστον·
> αἰεὶ γὰρ τῇ γ' ἔσται[78] ὅπῃ κέ τις αἰὲν ἐρείδῃ. (B12)
>
> For it is impossible that there should be coming to be from what is not,
> and that what is should be destroyed is not to be fulfilled and is unheard of;
> for wherever one may ever set it, there in truth it will always be.

Also like Anaxagoras, Empedocles recognizes that if there is to be a rational account of the things that appear to the senses that is consistent with the injunction against coming-to-be and passing-away, then there must be a fundamental entity or a set of fundamental entities that form the basis of that explanation. These have fixed and settled natures that are not in themselves subject to change; no matter what combinations and permutations of them occur, these entities remain the same. As Empedocles says, "wherever one may ever set it, there in truth it will always be."[79] Empedocles posits six basic entities: the roots Earth, Water, Air, and Fire, and the motive forces Love

[76] See n. 3, above.

[77] Here I follow the text of Wright and Inwood; see Wright, *Empedocles*, p. 173. Bollack prints ἐκ τοῦ γὰρ μὴ ἐόντος; DK: ἔκ τε γὰρ οὐδάμ' ἐόντος.

[78] This is the text of DK, followed by Inwood and by Wright in her translation. Bollack prints θησεῖται.

[79] See also B16: "For they are as they were and shall be, and never, I think, shall endless time be empty of these two" (ἔ⟨στ⟩ι γὰρ ὡς πάρος ἦν τε καὶ ἔσσεται, οὐδέ ποτ' οἴω τούτων ἀμφοτέρων κενεώσεται ἄσπετος αἰών; following the text of Wright who accepts a proposal by Lloyd-Jones; Inwood follows Wright; Bollack: ἦν γὰρ καί). While the context of the fragment in Hippolytus (*Haer.* VII.29.9–10) makes it clear that the subjects here are Love and Strife, there is no doubt that Empedocles would be committed to the same claim for the four roots. As fundamental entities, Love and Strife and the four roots are on the same metaphysical footing.

and Strife. Under the forces of Love and Strife, the four roots combine and separate to make up the *kosmos* as we know it.[80] In the reliance on mixture and separation as the mechanisms operating within the *kosmos*, and in the use of Love as a principle of combination, Empedocles is following the model that had appeared in Parmenides' *Doxa*.[81]

Preceded by a guarantee, a description of the roots, Love, and Strife occurs at B17.27–29. As if to stress both the Parmenidean character of these entities and the trustworthiness of his account, Empedocles inverts Parmenides B8.51–52. There the goddess had warned her listener about the *Doxa*: "from here on learn mortal beliefs, listening to the deceptive order of my words" (δόξας δ' ἀπὸ τοῦδε βροτείας μάνθανε κόσμον ἐμῶν ἐπέων ἀπατηλὸν ἀκούων). But at B17.26 Empedocles reassuringly bids Pausanias, "but you listen to the undeceptive progress[82] of my account" (σὺ δ' ἄκουε λόγου στόλον οὐκ ἀπατηλόν). B17 is a long discussion of Empedocles' "double tale"; during its course he introduces the roots and Love and Strife, stressing their independent natures and their equality to each other, while asserting that these six alone are genuine entities.

ὡς γὰρ καὶ πρὶν ἔειπα πιφαύσκων πείρατα μύθων,
δίπλ' ἐρέω· τοτὲ μὲν γὰρ ἓν ηὐξήθη μόνον εἶναι
ἐκ πλεόνων, τοτὲ δ' αὖ διέφυ πλέον' ἐξ ἑνὸς εἶναι,
πῦρ καὶ ὕδωρ καὶ γαῖα καὶ ἠέρος ἄπλετον ὕψος·
νεῖκός τε οὐλόμενον δίχα τῶν, ἀτάλαντον ἁπάντῃ,
καὶ φιλότης ἐν τοῖσιν, ἴση μῆκός τε πλάτος τε·
τὴν σὺ νόῳ δέρκευ, μηδ' ὄμμασιν ἧσο τεθηπώς·
ἥτις καὶ θνητοῖσι νομίζεται ἔμφυτος ἄρθροις,
τῇ τε φίλα φρονέουσι καὶ ἄρθμια ἔργα τελοῦσι,
Γηθοσύνην καλέοντες ἐπώνυμον ἠδ' Ἀφροδίτην·
τὴν οὔ τις μετὰ τοῖσιν ἑλισσομένην δεδάηκε
θνητὸς ἀνήρ· σὺ δ' ἄκουε λόγου στόλον οὐκ ἀπατηλόν.
ταῦτα γὰρ ἶσά τε πάντα καὶ ἥλικα γένναν ἔασι,

[80] The claims that I am making about the metaphysical status of the roots and Love and Strife, and the role of Parmenidean influence on Empedocles will hold regardless of the exact details of Empedocles' cosmic cycle. For details of the traditional interpretation of the cycle, see O'Brien, *Empedocles' Cycle*; Wright, *Empedocles*; and Graham, "Symmetry." For revisionist views of the cycle, see Bollack, Hölscher ("Welt Zeiten"), and Solmsen ("Love and Strife"; "Eternal and Temporary"), along with Long, "Empedocles' Cycle." O'Brien reaffirms his account of Empedocles in "Revisited." I am inclined to think that the traditional view is correct.

[81] The goddess who rules over birth and mixture in Parmenides B12 and who is identified with Love in B13 is probably a forerunner of Empedocles' Love, although Love in Parmenides has been "devised" and is thus to be contrasted with Love in Empedocles, which has no birth or death.

[82] "Progress" is Wright's translation of *stolos*; it connects Empedocles' views with the journey motifs that pervade Parmenides' poem.

τιμῆς δ' ἄλλης ἄλλο μέδει, πάρα δ' ἦθος ἑκάστῳ,
ἐν δὲ μέρει κρατέουσι περιπλομένοιο χρόνοιο.
καὶ πρὸς τοῖς οὐδ' ἄρ τι ἐπιγίγνεται οὐδ' ἀπολήγει·
εἴτε γὰρ ἐφθείροντο διαμπερές, οὐκέτ' ἂν ἦσαν.
τοῦτο δ' ἐπαυξήσειε τὸ πᾶν τί κε, καὶ πόθεν ἐλθόν;
πῇ δέ κε κήξαπόλοιτο, ἐπεὶ τῶνδ' οὐδὲν ἐρῆμον;
ἀλλ' αὔτ' ἔστιν ταῦτα, δι' ἀλλήλων δὲ θέοντα
γίγνεται ἄλλοτε ἄλλα καὶ ἠνεκὲς αἰὲν ὁμοῖα.[83] (B17.15–35)

For as I said before, making manifest the limits of my story,
I will tell a double tale; for at one time they grew to be one alone
from many, and at another again they grew apart to be many from one,
fire and water and earth and boundless height of air;
and destructive strife apart from them, equal in every way,
and love among them, equal in length and breadth;
you look at her with your mind, and do not sit with amazed eyes;
and she is thought by mortals to be inborn in their joints,
and by her they think loving things and accomplish friendly deeds,
calling her by the names of Joy and Aphrodite;
no one of mortal men has seen her whirling among them.
but you listen to the undeceptive progress of my account.
For all these are equal and of like age in their origin,
but each has a different prerogative and each its own character,
and they hold sway in turn as time goes around.
And in addition to these nothing comes to be or passes away;
for if they continuously passed away, they would no longer be.
And what would increase this whole, and from where would it come?
And how could it be destroyed, as nothing is bereft of them?
But there are just these things, and on account of running through one another
they become different at different times and yet are ever and always the same.

There are a number of things to note in this important passage. First, there is an imitation of Parmenides' language in the introduction of the roots and Love and Strife as genuine entities. Empedocles asserts, in lines 30–35, that there is nothing in addition to these, and, in the manner of Parmenides B8.6–10, stresses this through the use of repudiating questions. "What would increase the whole? From where would it come? How could the totality of what there is be destroyed?" Next, although Empedocles occasionally uses different personifications and terms for the roots, here he is quite straightforward: they

[83] I follow the text printed by both Wright and Inwood, following DK. In line 33 Bollack prints κε κῆρ' ἀπόλοιτο.

are fire and water and earth and air.[84] Importantly, Empedocles emphasizes that each of the four has its own nature: "each has a different prerogative and each its own character" (τιμῆς δ' ἄλλης ἄλλο μέδει, πάρα δ' ἦθος ἑκάστῳ). He here says nothing about these characters, but they must account for the different qualities present in mixtures of the roots in different proportions. Rather more is revealed about Strife and especially about Love. Love and Strife are the equals of the four roots: they, too, are genuine and basic entities, not subject to coming-to-be or passing-away. Strife, as we might imagine, is "destructive." Love is constructive and is the agent of unifying works and friendly thoughts.[85] While maintaining their own characters, the four roots "run through" each other so as to become different at different times (lines 34–35). This is the mixture and separation that results in the changes that are, according to B8, called growth and death. Yet the roots remain always the same. In the closing lines of the fragment, Empedocles contrasts the "becoming" of the roots as they mix with their permanent characters. No matter how different they may "become" through mixing with each other, they always remain the same, thus preserving their prerogatives and characters throughout the processes of mixture and separation.

The extant fragments do not say much about the particular "prerogatives and character" of the four roots. In B6 they are given the names of gods and goddesses: "shining Zeus" (fire; also called Hephaistos in B96 and B98), "life-bringing Hera" (air), Aidoneus (earth), and "Nestis who dampens with tears mortal springs" (water).[86] Although Empedocles uses these names, the elasticity of his references and the paucity of evidence make it difficult to discern particular marks of character (other than the obvious connection of "shining" with fire and tears with water) in the choice of names. B21 contains some discussion of the characters of the various roots, although it needs to be kept in mind that the "witnesses" are phenomenal earth, air, fire, and water, which are partially mixed versions of the pure roots:

> ἀλλ' ἄγε, τόνδ' ὀάρων προτέρων ἐπιμάρτυρα δέρκευ,
> εἴ τι καὶ ἐν προτέροισι λιπόξυλον ἔπλετο μορφῇ,
> ἠέλιον μὲν λαμπρὸν ὁρᾶν καὶ θερμὸν ἁπάντῃ,[87]

[84] For a chart detailing the different names and terminology used of the roots, see Wright, *Empedocles*, p. 23 (see also note 86).

[85] Thus the force of Love separates things that cling to their own kind and brings together things that are unlike, while Strife pulls apart such mixtures and brings together likes.

[86] These are the attributions that have now become standard, although there was disagreement about them even in the ancient commentators. There is a discussion of the divine names of the roots in Guthrie, *HGP*, vol. II, pp. 144–46. Kingsley discusses the various terms for the roots in *Ancient Philosophy* and in "Interpreters." But on the latter, see Mansfeld's response in "Critical Note."

[87] In this line I follow the text printed by Inwood; at *in Ph.* 33.8 and 159.15, Simplicius (followed by Bollack) has θερμὸν ὁρᾶν καὶ λαμπρόν; Aristotle (who is followed by DK and Wright) has λευκόν.

ἄμβροτα δ' ὅσσ' εἴδει τε καὶ ἀργέτι δεύεται αὐγῇ,
ὄμβρον δ' ἐν πᾶσι δνοφόεντά τε ῥιγαλέον τε·
ἐκ δ' αἴης προρέουσι θελεμνά[88] τε καὶ στερεωπά.

(B21.1–6)

But come, look on this witness to my earlier discourse,
if anything in my earlier (words) was defective in form:
the sun, brilliant to look on and hot in every way,
the immortals, drenched in heat and in shining light,
rain, in all things dark and chilling;
and from earth flow out things rooted and solid.

Unfortunately, there are several difficulties in the text at this point, and Empedocles has further complicated matters by using several words in the description of his roots that appear nowhere else in the extant Greek corpus. Simplicius quotes B21 twice in his commentary on the *Physics* (at 33.8–11 and at 159.13–18), both times saying that the passage is Empedocles' characterization of the roots. What seems clear from Simplicius's silence on any passages other than B21 that discuss the particular characters of the roots is that this is as specific as Empedocles was on this issue. Although there is some ancient evidence (from Stobaeus) that the roots were made up of the opposites (A33), I think that this is unlikely. In the *Laws* (at 889b1-c6) the Athenian discusses a theory that is probably Empedocles' and connects the mixing of the four with the "blending of opposites" (889c1), while Stobaeus suggests that the "elements" (as he calls them) are compounded from the opposites (A33). But there is no mention of this in Aristotle, who would probably have mentioned a forerunner of his own view that each of the simple bodies is made up of a characteristic pair of opposites (*Gen. Corr.* 330b1–7). It is possible that the connection of the roots and opposites was made in order to explain their mixture, though influence from Aristotle's own views on the connection of the elements and the opposites may also be at work here. In the recipes for mixture that survive, there is no evidence that Empedocles thought of the combining of the roots as just the mixing of opposites, for he is precise in his mention not of opposites, but of the roots as Earth, Water, Air, and Fire or of specific substantial forms of them such as rain, sun or aither (see B71, 73, and especially B96 and 98). He does not seem to think of them as capable of being broken down into the more basic opposites. Indeed, such compounded natures of the roots would be inconsistent with his characterization of them as real or genuine entities. He stresses that each of them is; I take it that he thought that each of them is an instance of what-is in the full sense explained in Parmenides B8. Thus each will be permanent and unchanging, but each will also have a

[88] Here I follow Wright, but see O'Brien (*Cosmic Cycle*, pp. 266–67) on the possibility of θέλυμνα and an overview of editorial decisions.

monogenous character that cannot be separated or divided into constituent parts. Fire is hot and bright, but these are consequences of its character as *fire*, rather than separate constituents of brightness and hotness that mix together to become fire.

Because the roots are not fundamentally composed of, nor characterized by, the opposites as such, they are not naturally antagonistic to one another.[89] Rather, it is through the influence of Love and Strife that they mix and separate as they do.[90] In the fragments and testimonia that contain recipes for the mixing of the roots, there is no evidence that any of the roots refuses to combine with any other, or that there is any special difficulty in getting the roots to blend, although there are problems in the combinations of certain compounded things; B91 suggests that water is more easily mixed with wine than with oil. But, as the B98 recipe for blood (and other forms of flesh) shows, the four roots seem to combine easily with one another: blood is composed of the four roots mixed in "more or less" equal parts. It might be that B26.1 suggests an antagonistic nature for the roots, in saying that "they hold sway in turn as the cycle goes around" (ἐν δὲ μέρει κρατέουσι περιπλομένοιο κύκλοιο), but this is a reference to the point in the cycle when the roots are completely separated and constitute a many, that is, at the moment when Strife is in full ascendancy; the line does not claim that "each holds sway in turn," but that they, the four together, do so.[91] In B17 the same line follows the claim that the four are all equal, though each has a different character, and in B26 the line is followed by a description of their mixture and separation. There is no reason to think that Empedocles does not mean what he says in claiming that the roots are genuine entities and that it is they who are responsible for the "mortal things" whose coming-to-be and passing-away are simply the mixture and separation of these roots. There is no hidden commitment to opposites as the basis of what there is.

There is an apparent difficulty with the attribution of a permanent character to each of the roots. What happens to them as they are completely mixed into

89 Guthrie suggests that the roots are by nature mutually hostile in his comment (*HGP*, vol. II, p. 171) that "under the unchallenged influence of Love . . . all their [the roots'] otherwise antagonistic characteristics have become subdued and indeed annihilated in an ineffable harmony."

90 Aristotle indicates at *Ph.* 196a21–24 and *Gen. Corr.* 334a1–7 that there is no natural place associated with each of the roots, but that they seem to be governed by chance, although in the latter passage he indicates (quoting B54) that fire may naturally move upward and aether downward. There is not enough evidence to settle the issue conclusively.

91 Another text that might seem to suggest that the roots are naturally antagonistic is B22.6–9. But I think that Wright is correct in saying that the "reference here is to *thnēta* in general"; she links B22 with B20, which seems to offer illustrations of the phenomena discussed in B22; the examples are all of mixed things rather than the roots themselves. See Wright, *Empedocles*, p. 193.

the single sphere when Love has achieved complete ascendancy? B26.7 says that when they grow together into the whole they are subdued (ἓν συμφύντα τὸ πᾶν ὑπένερθε γένηται). This is the state opposite to their "holding sway" when Strife is ascendant; here in the sphere they are completely mixed together by love. But if they are so thoroughly combined, can they still retain their individual characters, or have they ceased to be just what they are? Philoponus seems to have thought that the latter is the case:

> πρὸς μὲν γὰρ τὰ φαινόμενα ἐναντία λέγει ἀναιρῶν τὴν ἀλλοίωσιν ἐναργῆ οὖσαν, πρὸς ἑαυτὸν δὲ διότι λέγει μὲν ἀμετάβλητα τὰ στοιχεῖα, καὶ αὐτὰ μὲν μὴ γίνεσθαι ἐξ ἀλλήλων τὰ δὲ ἄλλα ἐκ τούτων, πάλιν δέ φησι τῆς Φιλίας κρατούσης τὰ πάντα ἓν γίνεσθαι καὶ τὸν Σφαῖρον ἀποτελεῖν ἄποιον ὑπάρχοντα, ὡς μηκέτι μήτε τὴν τοῦ πυρὸς μήτε τῶν ἄλλων τινὸς σῴζεσθαι ἐν αὐτῷ ἰδιότητα, ἀποβάλλοντος ἑκάστου τῶν στοιχείων τὸ οἰκεῖον εἶδος.
>
> (*in GC* 19.3–9 = A41)

> He speaks contrary to the phenomena, doing away with qualitative change which is obvious; and contrary to himself because he says that the elements are unchanging and that they do not come to be from each other but that other things come to be from them; but again he says that during the rule of Love all things come to be one and make the Sphere, which is qualityless, since neither the particular [quality] of fire nor of any of the others is any longer preserved in it, each of the elements throwing off its own form.

Philoponus is here commenting on and echoing Aristotle's complaint in *On Generation and Corruption* I.1 (315a3–19) that Empedocles contradicts himself, because, while claiming that the elements (as Aristotle calls the roots) do not come to be out of each other, they do come to be out of the One (the Sphere). Aristotle argues that the differentiae (*diaphorai*) of the roots are taken away as they go into the Sphere (for, he says, "it is possible that they be taken away, since they came to be" εἰσὶ γὰρ ἀφαιρεταὶ γενόμεναί γε 315a12); thus just as they can be said to be generated from the One, so they can be generated from one another. Aristotle's argument is actually not very good. First, it depends on the existence of differentiae of the roots that operate just as Aristotelian differentiae do (a questionable assumption). Second, he suggests that these differentiae are taken away, and the reason he gives is that they are added when the roots came to be. But the generation and destruction of the roots is exactly what is at issue. If the roots do not lose their character when they enter the Sphere, then there is no difficulty about their re-emergence, for they simply come out of a mixture, rather than coming to be from the Sphere. So the crucial issue here is Aristotle's claim that while they are merged into the Sphere the roots simply disappear, having no special character of their own while in the one Sphere (οὐ γὰρ δὴ πῦρ γε καὶ γῆ καὶ ὕδωρ ὄντα ἓν ἦν τὸ πᾶν 315a18–19). Philoponus's comment stresses that the Sphere is supposed to be devoid of qualities. For, on his view, unless the

Sphere has no qualities that could be attributed to the presence of the roots, Aristotle's claim that they come to be out of it, rather than simply emerging from being thoroughly mixed or subdued in it, would be groundless.[92] Are Aristotle and Philoponus correct? Do the roots "disappear" into the Sphere by "throwing off" their own forms and hence ceasing to be when they are in the Sphere?

It is unlikely that this is Empedocles' considered view. After all, B8, 9, 11, and 12 all record his rejection of the claim that anything actually comes to be or passes away, and it is a cornerstone of his theory that the roots are themselves unborn, while being the source of all "mortal things" through their mixture and separation.[93] An alternative view is that Empedocles conceived of the Sphere as a very fine mixture of all the roots such that although nothing is manifest the roots still retain their character (as in the original mixture of Anaxagoras). If the roots are blended uniformly throughout the Sphere, none would be visible (not even to "the eye of Lynceus," cf. *Gen. Corr.* 328a15). The resulting mixture would be analogous to the mixtures that produce mortal things: in many of them the individual roots are not discernible, yet there is no question of their having lost their characters.[94] Moreover, in such a complete mixture of the roots, the Sphere itself would have a uniform character, so that nothing could be distinguished in it.[95] Love, after all, is responsible for the mixture of unlike with unlike. What could better exemplify the utter triumph

[92] Both Wright and Longrigg discuss the arguments of Aristotle and Philoponus. Wright (*Empedocles*, pp. 35–36) agrees with Aristotle and Philoponus, relying on B27.1 for evidence (a text I shall examine presently). She suggests that "Empedocles wanted to say both that the roots are individual and immortal and that in the sphere under Love there is a mingling of minute particles of the component roots such that no one root could in any part be picked out as distinct from another" (p. 36) and claims that these assertions are incompatible: "later it was recognized that one of these two assumptions would have to be sacrificed." Longrigg ("Roots") denies that there is a contradiction: Empedocles' conception of the roots as occurring in very small particles mixed in the Sphere means that they can maintain their character. He takes B27.1 to refer to the sun itself and not to the root, fire. Certainly, as Wright phrases it, a "mingling of minute particles" does not entail that the Sphere is literally qualityless; there is no incompatibility in the two assertions she attributes to Empedocles.

[93] See for instance B7, a report of Hesychius, *s.v.* ἀγέννητα: στοιχεῖα παρ' Ἐμπεδοκλεῖ (text as in Wright and Inwood). Even if B7 is not an actual quote from Empedocles, there is evidence in the fragments themselves that he certainly conceived of the roots as "unborn."

[94] This is not true of all mortal mixtures: earth, air, fire, and water as we perceive them seem to be mixtures rather than pure instances of the roots, yet retain much of the character of the pure root (as in the use of visible earth, water, air, and fire as "witnesses" to the truth of Empedocles' claims about the roots in B21). See also B22, although it is not clear what stage of the cycle is being discussed here; see Wright, *Empedocles*, pp. 192–93.

[95] Millerd (p. 61) argues that we simply cannot tell from the existing fragments whether or not the Sphere was "homogeneous in the strict sense of that term because Empedocles had evidently not faced the problems involved in it." Millerd asserts that Empedocles either "evaded" or did not recognize the problems involved. Her claim rests on her further assertion that Empedocles did not appreciate the problems of unity and plurality explored by Parmenides: "The searching

of Love than a mixture of the four roots so complete than none is discernible? But the roots' being indiscernible in a mixture is not the same as their losing their distinctive characters altogether. B27.1 has been treated as support for the claim that the roots lose their character in the Sphere; but it is not clear that the fragment actually makes this strong claim. Two versions of the line occur, one in Plutarch *de Facie in orbe lunae* 926D, the other in Simplicius *in Ph.* 1183.28ff.[96] Simplicius quotes the line as an example of how things are under the predominance of Love in the Sphere; Plutarch quotes it as exemplifying the state of things while Strife (and thus complete separation) is in control. Certainly in the latter case there is no question of the roots failing to have their individual characters, and so the reference must be to the sun itself rather than to sun as a synonym for fire. Given Empedocles' predilection for repeating himself *verbatim* or with small changes, as in this case, a repetition that mirrors the cycles of change, it is not surprising that the same line should appear in descriptions of both the Sphere under the control of Love and the state of things during the absolute rule of Strife. Just as under the complete control of Strife, under Love no sun is discernible in the homogenous mixture of the roots that comprises the Sphere. If we insist on reading B27.1 as a reference to fire, the same claim would hold: no fire is visible under the complete sway of Love (although the parallel would be broken). There is some evidence that Empedocles conceived of the roots as occurring in very small particles (see A43 and A43a),[97] and in the Sphere the particles of all the roots would be so small and the blending so complete that nothing separate is discernible in the mix. The state of things under Love would then resemble the original state in Anaxagoras when "all things were together" and nothing

Eleatic criticism of the problem of the 'one and the many' was really passed by without being comprehended." I think that Millerd rather underestimates Empedocles' appreciation of Parmenides' arguments. Osborne (in "Empedocles Recycled") argues that Aristotle's criticisms are reasonable and must have been based on evidence in Empedocles that "things [the roots] come into being out of something without any of these differentiae" (p. 44). But she does not say why this must be the case. (Aristotle is certainly capable of attributing the view to Empedocles without evidence.) She says that unless the roots lose their characters in the sphere it "would then be simply a huge 'mortal' " (p. 44n.84). She adds that such a view fails to appreciate Empedocles' distinction between one and many and the sphere's status as divine. Its use in B17 suggests that the term *mortal* seems in Empedocles to be restricted to those phenomenal objects that come to be and pass away in the mixed periods between the times of the total ascendancy of Love or Strife. There is no question that Empedocles would not have thought of the Sphere as mortal (even though it is broken up by Strife and so comes to an end). But on any view, the homogenous sphere is "made of" the roots (that is, it comes into being as the roots are mixed into it by the force of Love), so I do not think that Osborne's objection holds. See also note 99, below.

[96] Diels (in DK) thought the two were different versions of the same fragment; Bollack, Wright, and Inwood all treat the versions as separate fragments. Simplicius's version: "There the fleet limbs of the sun are not distinguished" (ἔνθ' οὔτ' ἠελίοιο διείδεται ὠκέα γυῖα); in Plutarch the line reads "There the shining form of the sun . . ." (*agalaon eidos*).

[97] I shall return to the issue of the particulate structure of the roots below.

was manifest because of the smallness of the *chrēmata* and the completeness of the mixture. Empedocles nowhere claims that the roots are "lost" in the mixture, but that "it [the Sphere] is fixed in the dense covering of harmony" (ἁρμονίης πυκινῷ κρυφῷ ἐστήρικται B27). B28 and 29 describe the Sphere in language that is similar to Parmenides (B8.43–44) but whereas Parmenides used the sphere ("nicely circular from every side" *pantothen eukuklou*) as a simile for the perfection, completeness, and perspectival neutrality of what-is, Empedocles envisions an actual sphere. But the Parmenidean influence is there, for Empedocles says that the Sphere is "equal from every side" (*pantothen isos* B28[98]). The equality referred to is no doubt the result of the equal radii of a sphere, but as in Parmenides' use of the image, there is also the implication of uniformity of the contents of the sphere, caused by the completeness of the mixture. I conclude that Aristotle's criticism of Empedocles and his claim that the roots are characterized by differentiae that they lose in the Sphere are unwarranted; there is no genuine coming to be of the roots from the Sphere, but simply their re-emergence from the complete, rather Anaxagorean mixture that constitutes the state of things under Love.[99]

3.2. Empedocles: Particles and Pores

A crucial issue remains. Are the roots meant to be particulate in structure? The "small particles" interpretation of the roots provides an answer to the Aristotelian criticism but may raise problems of its own in considering the "running through" one another of the roots as they mix and separate in the

98 On the problem of the texts of B28 and B29, see Wright, *Empedocles*, pp. 189–90.

99 Why does Aristotle make this criticism of Empedocles? Cherniss claims that Aristotle is simply reading his own views back into Empedocles (p. 121–22), and there may be something to this criticism. It is an important part of Aristotle's own theory that the four elements can be produced from each other (*Gen. Corr.* II.4), and it is fundamental to this that the elements be characterized by hot, cold, wet, and dry as differentiae. That which is hot and dry (fire) can change into that which is hot and wet (air) by having the hot serve as matter for the change while wet changes to dry, with each element exchanging one of its two characterizing differentiae in the process (this preserves the model of change adumbrated in *Ph.* I). But it is not at all clear that this Aristotelian picture of an underlying substance with various differentiae represents Empedocles' conception of his roots. It is important that they not be capable of being broken down into constituent elements, and that they retain their characters throughout the cosmic cycles. I think that Aristotle may have failed to appreciate the Parmenidean character of the roots, as he so often fails to appreciate the role Parmenides played in influencing the later Presocratic thinkers. The issues of change and internal unity that so exercised those thinkers and Plato no longer seemed to be troublesome. I do not think that Aristotle willfully misunderstood Empedocles; rather he simply does not address the particular problems (generated by the Parmenidean arguments) that Empedocles faced and with which he was dealing. Moreover, Aristotle's concern in this passage from I.1 of the *Gen. Corr.* is whether Empedocles begins with one principle or many. The Sphere seems to be a one, but unless the roots disappear altogether in the Sphere, it is not, according to Aristotle, a genuine unity. But this need not have been Empedocles' view.

production of "mortal things"—those phenomena whose so-called "coming-to-be" and "destruction" (see B9) are explained by the action of the roots. Empedocles asserts three times that the four roots "run through" each other while at the same time stressing that they are genuine entities. At B17.34–35 the claim is that "there are just these things, and on account of running through one another they become different at different times and yet are ever and always the same" (ἀλλ' αὔτ' ἔστιν ταῦτα, δι' ἀλλήλων δὲ θέοντα γίγνεται ἄλλοτε ἄλλα καὶ ἠνεκὲς αἰὲν ὁμοῖα); B21.13–14 explains the "becoming different at different times" in terms of changes of shape through mixture: "these things are, and running through each other they become different shapes, for the mixing changes them" (αὐτὰ γὰρ ἔστιν ταῦτα, δι' ἀλλήλων δὲ θέοντα γίγνεται ἀλλοιωπά· τὰ γὰρ διὰ κρῆσις ἀμείβει[100]). Finally, B26.3–4 spells out the change of shape; as the roots mix, they become humans and animals: "for these things are, and running through each other, they become humans and the other kinds of animals" (αὐτὰ γὰρ ἔστιν ταῦτα, δι' ἀλλήλων δὲ θέοντα γίγνοντ' ἄνθρωποί τε καὶ ἄλλων ἔθνεα θηρῶν). "Running through each other" is clearly Empedocles' term for the mixture of the roots, and the changes that result from this are the so-called mortal growth and destruction that B8 refers to:

> ἄλλο δέ τοι ἐρέω· φύσις οὐδενός ἐστιν ἁπάντων
> θνητῶν, οὐδέ τις οὐλομένου θανάτοιο τελευτή,
> ἀλλὰ μόνον μίξις τε διάλλαξίς τε μιγέντων
> ἐστί, φύσις δ' ἐπὶ τοῖς ὀνομάζεται ἀνθρώποισιν. (B8)

> And I shall tell you another thing; there is growth of none of all
> mortal things, nor is there any end in baneful death,
> but there is only mixing and interchanging of what is mixed.
> and growth is the name given these by human beings.

But "running through" may be more than a metaphor for the mixing of small particles of the roots. Some ancient authorities suggest that the mixture of the roots with one another was effected by pores. Both Aristotle and Theophrastus assume that there are pores, and that the mixture is controlled by the size and smoothness or roughness of the passages in the things being mixed. At *de Generatione et Corruptione* 324b34–35 (= A 87) Aristotle reports that "he says that only those things whose pores are commensurate with one another can mix" (μείγνυσθαί φησιν ὅσων οἱ πόροι σύμμετροι πρὸς ἀλλήλους εἰσίν). Similarly, Theophrastus says that "in general he makes mixture through a commensurability of pores. On account of this, oil and water do not mix, but other liquids do, as indeed do many others whose particular mixings he lists" (ὅλως γὰρ ποιεῖ τὴν μίξιν τῇ συμμετρίᾳ

[100] Here I follow the text as in Wright and Inwood. "τὰ γὰρ διὰ κρῆσις" is Wright's conjecture. DK, followed by Bollack, print τόσον διὰ κρῆσις.

τῶν πόρων· διόπερ ἔλαιον μὲν καὶ ὕδωρ οὐ μείγνυσθαι, τὰ δὲ ἄλλα ὑγρὰ καὶ περὶ ὅσων δὴ καταριθμεῖται τὰς ἰδίας κράσεις *Sens.* 12 = Diels 502.28–503.2 = A86.12).[101] Theophrastus's reference to oil and water is no doubt to B91; other fragments also give accounts of fitting together, although in the fragments themselves there is no mention of pores in discussions of the mixing of the roots.[102] B71 includes a general claim that "from the mixing of water, earth, and aether and sun came to be the colors and forms of mortals, which have now come to be, fitted together by Aphrodite"; while B107 asserts that "all things have been fitted together and formed" from the four roots. B96 gives a formula for bone, made from the fitting together of two parts water and four parts fire in the "well-built"[103] channels of two parts of earth, while the B98 recipe for blood "and other kinds of flesh" calls for equal parts (more or less) of the four roots mixed "in the perfect harbors of *Kypris*." Love and Strife are the motive forces, but the character of the roots would account for the particular structures and qualities in the emergent mortal mixtures.[104]

Are the roots themselves characterized by pores? The testimonia certainly suggest that compound bodies have pores, but it is less clear that the roots do. It may be that the further mixture of the compounds is a reflection of the mixture of the roots themselves. B91 contrasts the easy mix of water and wine with the more difficult mixture of oil and water, and Theophrastus refers to the fragment in his discussion of the commensurability of pores. It is unclear whether the water mentioned here is elemental water (the root) or a mixture that contains a high proportion of the root, nor is it clear that all compounded bodies have pores; the contrast seems to be between oil and wine, rather than oil and water. According to Philoponus, "As Aristotle said in *On Generation and Corruption*, Empedocles said that there are pores and solid parts (*nasta*) mixed together in all the sublunary bodies, such as water, oil, and the others, the pores he called 'hollow' and the solid bits 'dense' " (*in GA* 123.13–16 = A 87). The reference to "sublunary bodies" is intriguing, for it suggests that the heavenly bodies, which are equally constructed by the mixture of the roots, do not have pores.[105] In any case there are certain metaphysical difficulties in attributing pores to the roots. First, suppose there are pores

101 See also *Sens.* 7. On pores in Empedocles see also Long, "Thinking"; Mourelatos, "Quality"; and Longrigg, "Philosophy and Medicine."

102 *Poros* occurs three times in the extant fragments: at B3.7, at B35.1, and at B100.17; none of these mentions of the word is in a context relevant to the mixing of roots.

103 Reading εὐτύκτοις with Inwood and Sider, "Empedocles B96." DK, Bollack, and Wright read εὐστέρνοις.

104 Mourelatos argues that "the theory of *poroi* makes it possible for Empedocles to determine and to explain by a sort of mechanical calculus salient facts concerning events of mixture: the ease or the difficulty of mixing; the character of the outcome; the stability of the outcome" ("Quality," p. 172).

105 As indicated above (note 102), *poros* does not appear in this context in the extant fragments themselves, but only in the testimonia. This, by itself, decides nothing, of course, as those

in the roots. What is in them? Are they empty when the roots are unmixed? If so, is Empedocles committed to the existence of void? Second, the doctrine of pores suggests internal divisions and differences within the structure of the root.[106] But if, as Empedocles seems to insist, the roots are supposed to satisfy the Parmenidean criteria for what-is, they cannot be subject to such internal divisions.[107]

Philoponus says at least twice that there is no void in the pores. First, he claims that "the pores differ from void, because those introducing pores did not say that there is void" (διαφέρουσι δὲ τοῦ κενοῦ οἱ πόροι, διότι οἱ τοὺς πόρους εἰσάγοντες κενὸν εἶναι οὐκ ἔλεγον *in GC* 154.5–6 = A87). The issue here is whether Philoponus means to claim that Empedocles denied that there was void; simple silence from Empedocles on the issue is not enough here. At 178.2–5 in the same commentary, Philoponus claims that the empty spaces are "filled with some very fine-particled body such as air. For they differed in this way from those positing void" (πεπληρωμένους λεπτομερεστέρου τινὸς σώματος οἷον ἀέρος. ταύτῃ γὰρ διέφερον τῶν τὸ κενὸν ὑποτιθεμένων. = A87). This latter account will not, of course, answer the question of what is in the pores of the roots in their unmixed state, for there could not be "some fine body such as air" in the pores of unmixed water or earth.

Several testimonia give an alternate account of the mixing, an account that does not rely on pores at all but rather characterizes Empedocles' roots as particulate in structure, with the construction of mortal things from the roots being rather like the construction of a stone wall.

> ἐκείνοις τε γὰρ τοῖς λέγουσιν ὡς Ἐμπεδοκλῆς τίς ἔσται τρόπος; ἀνάγκη γὰρ σύνθεσιν εἶναι καθάπερ ἐκ πλίνθων καὶ λίθων τοῖχος· καὶ τὸ μεῖγμα δὲ τοῦτο ἐκ σῳζομένων μὲν ἔσται τῶν στοιχείων, κατὰ μικρὰ δὲ παρ' ἄλληλα συγκειμένων· οὕτω δὴ σὰρξ καὶ τῶν ἄλλων ἕκαστον.
>
> (Aristotle, *Gen. Corr.* 334a26–30 = A43)

> For what will be the manner of it [the production of things from the elements] for those who argue as Empedocles does? It is necessary that it be combination,

---

fragments that discuss pores may have been lost. But it remains true that not one of the commentators who discuss pores supplies an illustrative quotation. Philoponus merely reports that Empedocles used the terms *hollow* and *dense.* There is a mention of pores at B100.17, in the discussion of the mechanism of breathing and the comparison with the clepsydra. But this will not help decide the issue of pores in the roots. Long, in "Thinking," suggests that the roots do not have pores, for he says, "the πόροι are channels which interpenetrate all compound bodies" (p. 260). But I am not certain that he means to deny that there are pores in the unmixed roots, given his discussion of perception (which is the main focus of the article).

[106] The point is made by Inwood, *Empedocles,* p. 24 with n. 54

[107] They may be divisible—that is, there could be several instances of earth separated from each other, as long as each instance is itself all, only, and completely earth. The problem lies in thinking that some of earth may be not-earth, or that there are two structures for earth: pore-earth and dense-earth. This would mean that there are two ways to be earth, rather than one.

just as a wall [comes to be] out of bricks and stones. And this mixture comes to be out of elements that are preserved, and they will be put alongside one another in small bits. And this is the manner for flesh and each of the others.

κἀκεῖνος γὰρ ἐκ μὲν τῶν αὐτῶν στοιχείων ... γεγονέναι φησὶν ἡμᾶς τε καὶ τὰ ἄλλα σώματα πάντα τὰ περὶ τὴν γῆν, οὐ μὴν κεκραμένων γε δι' ἀλλήλων ἀλλὰ κατὰ σμικρὰ μόρια παρακειμένων τε καὶ ψαυόντων.

(Galen, *Commentary on Hippocrates' "The Nature of Man"* 27.22 = A34)

For he [Empedocles] said that from the same elements ... we and all the other bodies on the earth have come to be, but not through the elements being blended with each other, but on account of them being laid side by side in small parts and touching.

On these accounts, the roots are particulate and mortal things are constructed from these particles, which lie together. This "particles side-by-side" account seems, on the face of it, incompatible with the "running-through-by-means-of-pores" account. Either the roots interpenetrate one another by means of pores and channels, or they lie side by side as in a stone wall. Can the metaphor of running through be reconciled with the accounts of mechanical mixture and separation by means of small particles?[108]

The salient feature in the "particles-side-by-side" account is that the particles retain their character. The particulate interpretation is one way to preserve the crucial identity of the roots as they mix and separate. Thus, although they may be very small particles, they will not disappear into the mixture so completely that we can no longer understand them to be genuine entities. B11 illustrates Empedocles' insistence on this point:

νήπιοι· οὐ γάρ σφιν δολιχόφρονές εἰσι μέριμναι,
οἳ δὴ γίγνεσθαι πάρος οὐκ ἐὸν ἐλπίζουσιν,
ἤ τι καταθνήσκειν τε καὶ ἐξόλλυσθαι ἁπάντῃ.

Fools—for their meditations are not far reaching—
are those who expect that what was not before comes to be,
or that something dies and is in every way destroyed.

If the mixture required by the pore theory results in the destruction or genuine disappearance of the roots, Empedocles' theory would fail on its own

[108] Oddly, the two interpretations seem to mirror a difficulty in the interpretation of B23. Empedocles there illustrates the mixture of the roots by referring to painters who mix their colors to produce images. The problem is to understand exactly what we are being told in this example. Did the painters mix pigments to produce new shades (suggested by Mourelatos, "Quality," pp. 141n.15; 180–84) or were shades and figures built up by laying washes of color together or over one another (as Wright suggests, *Empedocles*, pp. 38–39)? I suspect that Wright is correct here. See also Longrigg, "Roots of All Things," pp. 431–32.

grounds, for he insists that the roots do not come to be or pass away. The fragments include descriptions and metaphors that would seem to envisage a literal running (or flowing) through and fitting together of the roots; not only in the three occurrences of "running through" in the texts, but also in the references to channels and receptacles of earth, and the mentions of bolts, glues, and fittings together.[109] The importance of the pore theory is the insistence on the joining together of the roots so that there is a real fit and a resultant structure, rather than a mere mingling. But there are no real bolts or glues present: there are only the four roots plus the activity of Love and Strife.[110] There are two alternatives here. Either the roots themselves have pores or they do not. If they do not, then the pores and dense bits in mortal things are the result of the lying side by side of the particles of roots, which themselves are not penetrated by pores. The roots maintain their own characters but combine in particles (the same particles that survive in the Sphere). In mixing and combining to produce mortal things, they lie next to each other (likes bricks in a wall, as Aristotle puts it) and the differences in the character of the particles constitute the pores in mortal objects through which animals and humans breathe and sense.[111] Theophrastus suggests (at *Sens.* 7 = A86) that water and fire will result in different sorts of pores: "the pores [of the organ of sight] are arranged alternately of fire and water; we come to recognize pale things through those of the former, and dark things through those of water." On the view that the roots themselves, in their pure and unmixed states, do not have pores, Theophrastus means that when fire and water combine in the construction of eyes, their method of combining, together with differences in the character of the discrete particles of fire and water, will result in pores of varying size and character. This account is supported by a comment from Philoponus (at *in GC* 160.3–7 = A87). He attributes to Aristotle the claim that Empedocles must say that some part of a body must be solid and indivisible; otherwise the whole body would be pore. Philoponus can be read as applying this principle to the roots as well as to the sublunary bodies he mentions in the commentary on *de Generatione Animalium* 123.13–16. On the other hand, if

[109] On this issue see Mourelatos, "Quality," pp. 174–75.

[110] Philolaus seems to have objected to just this aspect of Pluralist theories. The lack of structure in the accounts of Anaxagoras and Empedocles may be a motivation for his claim that what is cannot simply be unlimited; there must be a place for the limiters which give structure as well. See Philolaus B1, B2, and especially B3. See Huffman, *Philolaus*, for full discussions of these fragments and the role of limiters in giving structure to unlimiteds.

[111] If the roots are like liquids or pastes, they can easily combine and could generate structure through their combination. Consider combining milk and lemon juice: the thick, curdled liquid that results has a structure that differs from both but results from the combination of the two. Empedocles himself gives the example of rennet and milk in making (I suppose) cheese, in B33. It must be noted that the particulate view of Empedocles' roots is based on Aristotle's claim of what someone who adopts a view like Empedocles' "must" say, and on reports that are clearly grounded in Aristotle's account of Empedocles.

the roots do have pores, we are faced with the metaphysical problems posed above, although their force may be lessened if we see that the particular texture of each root just is part of its basic nature and character. Parmenides B8.42–49 (the simile of the sphere) argues that what-is must be perspectivally neutral. A particular, and characteristic, texture for earth (and for each of the other roots) would satisfy that demand, for all bits of earth would have the same specific nature and would be characteristically earthy.[112] It would, I think, be preferable if Empedocles did not conceive of the roots as having pores, but the issue must, I think, remain open. The evidence is too scanty to be sure just what Empedocles' view actually was.

But suppose that Empedocles conceived of the roots as very small particles or droplets that mix and separate. When Strife is in the ascendancy, all the particles of earth are together, as are all the particles of water, and so on. At other times they mix with each other in various proportions; and when Love is triumphant, they are all mixed together so thoroughly that no particular character can be ascribed to their mixture: nothing is perceptible in it. Aëtius links Empedocles, Anaxagoras, and Democritus with Epicurus and others "who make the *kosmos* through the gathering together of fine-particled bodies" (ὅσοι κατὰ συναθροισμὸν τῶν λεπτομερῶν σωμάτων κοσμοποιοῦσι I.24.2 = A44), also claiming that there are minimal particles of the roots that are, as it were, "elements prior to elements" (πρὸ τῶν τεττάρων στοιχείων θραύσματα ἐλάχιστα I.13.1 = A43). Aëtius repeats the claim at I.17.3 (also A43), saying that the elements are combined from "very small masses" (ἐκ μικροτέρων ὄγκων) and saying again that these are minimal particles. This might suggest that the smallest parts of the Empedoclean roots were atomistic. But Aristotle is careful to distinguish Empedocles' view from that of the atomists. At *de Caelo* III.6 305a1–4 (= A43a), he contrasts the atomists and Empedocles: for the atomists the separating of the elements stops at an indivisible body. But Empedocles "wishes to say" that the body will be "divisible yet nonetheless not ever divided" (διαιρετὸν μέν, οὐ μέντοι διαιρεθησόμενον οὐδέποτε).[113] Thus, while the smallest parts of the roots can apparently become even smaller, thus corresponding to Anaxagoras's

[112] Parmenides B8.22–25 (lines which argue that what-is must not be divided: οὐδὲ διαιρετόν ἐστιν, ἐπεὶ πᾶν ἐστιν ὁμοῖον) might seem to militate against this possibility. But as I read the lines, they argue against the internal division of what-is such that parts of it are *f* and parts not-*f*. But if the particular character of a root is such that it must have a certain texture and if that texture just is the pattern of pores, then a root with pores would not seem to be inconsistent with Parmenides' demands.

[113] Another comparison with the atomists is at *Gen. Corr.* I.8 325b15ff. There is no mention of divisible but undivided bodies as in *de Caelo*, but the *men* . . . *de* construction (*men* at 17, introducing the discussion of indivisible bodies, *de* at 19) gives a contrast with the indivisible bodies of the atomists. It is not clear what text of Empedocles Aristotle had in mind in making this claim.

notion, Empedocles apparently thought that there comes a point where, as a matter of fact, diminution comes to an end.[114]

The exploration of these issues dealing with the metaphysical status and the nature of Empedocles' roots makes clear how great is his debt to Parmenides. That the roots are conceived as Parmenidean unities, each of which satisfies the criteria of B8 is, I think, beyond question. But there is no commitment to a plurality of entities in the face of Parmenidean numerical monism, as the traditional views have held. Instead, as with Anaxagoras, the reliance on a plurality of basic entities as well as the model of mixture and separation is quite in line with Parmenidean claims in both the *Alētheia* and the *Doxa*. The accounts of Anaxagoras and Empedocles that I have offered here are, for the most part, similar to the traditional views, although I have attempted to explore more thoroughly the metaphysical nature of the *chrēmata* and the roots. But my account differs from the traditional views in seeing Anaxagoras and Empedocles as understanding and whole-heartedly accepting Parmenides' teachings in both the *Alētheia* and the *Doxa*. Further, because I reject the traditional account of Parmenides as a numerical monist, there is no need to explain away the unargued-for assumption of Pluralism in Anaxagoras and Empedocles, nor to explain why they accept some of the arguments of B8 but not all. Indeed, the lack of argument for Pluralism in Anaxagoras and Empedocles is evidence for the view that I argue for. Anaxagoras and Empedocles do not see Pluralism as such as a deviation from the Parmenidean principles about what there is, and this is evidence that Parmenides was not concerned to argue for numerical monism. I have tried to show that the characters of the *chrēmata* and the roots are thoroughly Parmenidean, completely in line with the signs and arguments given in Parmenides B8, and that the model cosmology of the *Doxa* has been accepted, and its "deceptive" lessons learned. Rejecting the assumption that Parmenides is a numerical monist and seeing him instead as concentrating on the criteria for any genuine entity in an account of what-is makes it easier to see the important connections between Parmenides and the Pluralists, connections that hold because of, rather than in spite of, Parmenides' own views.

4. Zeno and Some Problems of Divisibility

Both Plato and Aristotle linked Zeno's arguments with those of Parmenides.[115] In the *Parmenides*, Plato represents Zeno as a faithful servant

[114] An important difference is that Empedocles does not adopt the Anaxagorean claim that "everything is in everything." Thus, the problem of distinguishing what a thing actually is does not arise in Empedocles.

[115] In addition to the discussion in the *Prm.*, Plato connects Zeno with Parmenides at *Sph.* 216a3–4. Aristotle links Parmenides and Zeno at *S.E.* 182b26 and *Metaph.* 1001b7.

of Parmenides' views, responding to those who found Parmenides' claims absurd with the retort that even more ridiculous consequences follow from their own theories (128b7–e4). Plato's version of the relation of Zeno and Parmenides and of the purport of Zeno's arguments has served as a model for most later accounts.[116] Plato does not name Zeno's target; the evidence that survives suggests no good candidates, and there is no indication that Anaxagoras or Empedocles found Parmenides' views laughable.[117] Indeed, the contention of this chapter is that they took both the *Alētheia* and the *Doxa* as models to be followed, not ridiculous claims to argue against or to dismiss. It is, therefore, worth considering Zeno's quarrel with plurality, to try to determine what aspects of the Pluralism of Anaxagoras and Empedocles, as discussed here, fall prey to his arguments.[118] Exploring these issues may also shed some light on the question of whether Zeno is a wholehearted monistic Eleatic whose arguments, undertaken in the defense of Parmenides, affect only pluralism, or whether he also attacked certain aspects of Parmenides' own views.

116 Bicknell ("Zeno's Arguments") and Solmsen ("Zeno") raise doubts about the traditional view, as does Barnes (*PP*, vol. I, pp. 231–37). Solmsen argues that Zeno, rather than being the faithful follower of Parmenides, is instead a dialectician, opposing with equal relish both the One and the Many (Barnes agrees with this assessment). Vlastos, in "Plato's Testimony," disagrees with Solmsen's conclusions but he does not challenge Solmsen's important claim that the later tradition's linking of Parmenides and the One can be traced through Plato's remarks about Parmenides and Zeno in the *Parmenides* (although Dillon has suggested that Proclus had a treatise by Zeno available to him, independent of the *Prm.*). Vlastos argues that Plato's remarks about Zeno in the *Phd.* and the *Alc.* I are not relevant to our knowledge of Zeno or his intentions. For a thorough discussion of similarities and differences between Parmenides and Zeno, see Cordero, "Zénon."

117 Vlastos, who accepts the traditional view but has subjected it to considerable scrutiny, offers no candidates as Zeno's targets; see "Plato's Testimony," n. 12, p. 138. On this issue he says (in the same note), "the surviving fragments do not contain a single word which would suggest that the views they combat are anything but those of common sense—common to all non-Eleatic philosophers and to non-philosophers alike." Gorgias, who undertook to prove that nothing is, as neither what-is nor what-is-not is, might be a candidate, for he uses (or parodies) Parmenidean arguments in his proof. He does argue that if what-is is one it must be a quantity, or something continuous, or a magnitude, or a body; in any of these cases, it will turn out to be many (Sextus, *M*. VII.73 = 82B3). But Gorgias does not quite fit the profile Plato gives of those against whom Zeno argues.

118 My purpose here is not primarily to analyze Zeno's arguments; there is a vast literature that does just that (see, for instance, the bibliographies in Barnes, *PP*, and Mourelatos, *Pre-Socratics*). Rather, my concern is the worries Zeno raises about the viability of pluralism as it appears in Anaxagoras and Empedocles. I do not discuss the arguments against motion here. While those arguments interested Aristotle, they do not seem to have been of serious concern to other Presocratic philosophers of Zeno's time. The obvious possibility of motion (as reported by the senses) provides evidence that Zeno's arguments are unsound. But the problems and paradoxes generated by the divisibility of a unified basic entity are less obvious. As this comment indicates, I do not take Zeno to have been arguing strictly against a numerical plurality of things that are, but rather against the predicational divisibility of these things.

Two arguments about plurality are preserved in the B fragments of Zeno; a third is reported by Simplicius, who gets it from Porphyry. Although Simplicius reports that Porphyry attributed the argument to Parmenides, he thinks that Alexander was right to credit it to Zeno.[119] I begin with the argument Simplicius says is reported by Porphyry; he calls it an argument from dichotomy and claims that it shows that "what is is one thing only, and partless and indivisible" (τὸ ὂν ἓν εἶναι μόνον καὶ τοῦτο ἀμερὲς καὶ ἀδιαίρετον):

> εἰ γὰρ εἴη, φησί, διαιρετόν, τετμήσθω δίχα, κἄπειτα τῶν μερῶν ἑκάτερον δίχα, καὶ τούτου ἀεὶ γενομένου δῆλόν φησιν, ὡς ἤτοι ὑπομενεῖ τινὰ ἔσχατα μεγέθη ἐλάχιστα καὶ ἄτομα, πλήθει δὲ ἄπειρα, καὶ τὸ ὅλον ἐξ ἐλαχίστων, πλήθει δὲ ἀπείρων συστήσεται· ἢ φροῦδον ἔσται καὶ εἰς οὐθὲν ἔτι διαλυθήσεται καὶ ἐκ τοῦ μηδενὸς συστήσεται· ἅπερ ἄτοπα. οὐκ ἄρα διαιρεθήσεται, ἀλλὰ μενεῖ ἕν. καὶ γὰρ δὴ ἐπεὶ πάντῃ ὅμοιόν ἐστιν, εἴπερ διαιρετὸν ὑπάρχει, πάντῃ ὁμοίως ἔσται διαιρετόν, ἀλλ' οὐ τῇ μέν, τῇ δὲ οὔ. διῃρήσθω δὴ πάντῃ· δῆλον οὖν πάλιν ὡς οὐδὲν ὑπομενεῖ, ἀλλ' ἔσται φροῦδον, καὶ εἴπερ συστήσεται, πάλιν ἐκ τοῦ μηδενὸς συστήσεται. εἰ γὰρ ὑπομενεῖ τι, οὐδέ πω γενήσεται πάντῃ διῃρημένον. ὥστε καὶ ἐκ τούτων φανερόν φησίν, ὡς ἀδιαίρετόν τε καὶ ἀμερὲς καὶ ἓν ἔσται τὸ ὄν. (Simplicius, *in Ph.* 139.27–140.6)

For if, he says, it is divisible, let it have been cut in two, and then each of the parts in two, and as this goes on forever, it is clear, he says, that either some last least and uncuttable magnitudes will remain, unlimited in number, and the whole will be made up of an infinite number of these least things; or it will vanish and it will indeed have dissolved into nothing, and it will be made up of nothing; but these [consequences] are absurd. Therefore it will not be divided but it will remain one. Moreover, as it is everywhere alike, if it is indeed divisible, it will be everywhere alike divisible, and not on the one hand here but not there. Let it now have been divided everywhere; it is then clear that again nothing will remain, but it will have vanished, and if indeed it is made up [of parts], it will again be made up of nothing. For if something remains, it will not yet have come to be divided everywhere. So that, he says, it is clear from these considerations that what-is will be undivided and partless and one.

[119] Simplicius quotes B3 in the discussion of whether the "Porphyry argument" is to be attributed to Zeno; they may be two versions of the same argument. Owen ("Zeno," p. 48n.10) points out the similarity of Porphyry's report to Aristotle's argument at *Gen. Corr.* 316a14–34. Among modern commentators, Fränkel rejected a Zenonian origin ("Zeno's Attacks" p. 129 n. 16: "the style is completely un-Zenonian"); but Vlastos ("Note on B1," p. 183n.9 and "Zeno," pp. 371–72), Owen ("Zeno," p. 48n.10), Barnes (*PP*, vol. I, pp. 246–47), and Makin (*Indifference*, pp. 26–27) all accept the argument as Zenonian. Vlastos had argued (in the 1957 "Zenonian Argument") that the argument is not Zeno's and should perhaps be ascribed to Melissus; in his later work he describes the argument as Zenonian.

The argument proceeds in two main steps.[120] Suppose something to be divisible. Divide it and keep dividing each part until the division is complete. There are only two possible results.[121] Either we reach some atomic (uncuttable) parts, which are claimed to be infinite in number,[122] or we reach a point where our divisible thing simply disappears. These parts are supposed to make up the whole—so either we have a whole made up of infinitely many small particles, or something made up out of nothing. These results are said to be impossible. Why? It is easy to see how any object (whatever is divided up) cannot be made out of a multitude of nothings. But why should not something be made of an infinite number of indivisible particles? Zeno seems to suppose that if that were the case, the thing put together from those particles would be infinite in size, and thus larger than it was before the division began. But, as a matter of fact, the first alternative turns out to be impossible; and here is the second main step of the argument. For suppose our divisible thing to be all alike. Then there is no reason why it should not be everywhere divisible, and thus it will be divided everywhere and disappear into nothing.[123] If what is divided is all alike, there can be no smallest indivisible bit to stop the infinite division.

Two questions arise at once. Why not simply stop the regress at the beginning and say that what is being considered here is all alike indivisible? And at whom is the argument aimed? The answers to these questions are related. It is generally assumed that the Pluralists Anaxagoras and Empedocles (or at least one of them, depending on the view taken of the chronology) are the targets of the argument because they claim that there are a plurality of things. It is, I think, clear that the views of Anaxagoras and

120 For thorough analyses of the argument, see Vlastos, "Zenonian Argument" and Makin, "Zeno on Plurality."

121 Makin is, I think, right to note that the stress is on the products of the division rather than the task of division itself; see "Zeno on Plurality," p. 226. He focuses on the second part of the argument in this comment, but I think that it holds equally for both parts. For a discussion of an alleged fallacy in this aspect of the argument in the second part of the Porphyry report, see Forrester, "Porphyry Text."

122 On this passage, Vlastos says that Zeno is assuming an infinite number of divisions "for nothing less than an infinite number of divisions is required to produce an infinite *number* of these atoms from a single original thing; but that 'final' terms do result would also entail that the series of divisions is *not* infinite. This is a muddle, the worst I have encountered in this inquiry" (Vlastos, "Zenonian Argument," p. 140n.40; italics in original). Makin counters that if what is being divided is homogeneous then the division will be infinite (from the second part of the argument, beginning at 140.1). So if the division is infinite but results in indivisible magnitudes, there must be an infinite number of such magnitudes (Makin, "Zeno on Plurality," pp. 229–31).

123 For a discussion of the use of an indifference argument here, see Makin, *Indifference*, pp. 24–27. Makin suggests that the indifference argument in the second part (140.1–6) provides the reason why the cutting in the first part must be infinite and not finite. That would account for the claim that the product of the cutting is an infinite number of indivisible particles.

Empedocles are under attack here.[124] But it is not just the simple plurality of things that is Zeno's target; it is their divisibility. Anaxagoras had asserted that each of the *chrēmata* must be indefinitely divisible (B3), and Zeno here shows that this assertion leads to absurd consequences. Empedocles, according to Aristotle, wanted to say that each root is indefinitely divisible, though perhaps not actually so divided (*de Caelo* III.6 305a1–4 = A43a). Again, Zeno claims that the assumption leads to absurdities. The theories of Anaxagoras and Empedocles required that mixture and separation take place between things or roots. Such mixture or separation entails that the things or roots be divisible. Anaxagoras needs the divisibility of the *chrēmata* to make sense of the "everything in everything" (B11 and B12) and "each thing is that in which there is most" (B12) claims. (Ironically, Anaxagoras claimed in B3 that "of the small there is no smallest" because "what is cannot not be.") Empedocles' account requires that the roots mingle and separate in clumps or particles of different sizes, down to the tiny particles that are all joined together in the Sphere. Zeno claims that this sort of divisibility entails that, as a matter of fact, each bit of a root or a thing can be divided away to nothing.[125]

Similar arguments appear in the surviving fragments of Zeno. What seems clear from the arguments is that it is not plurality *per se* that is under attack. Although he is quoted as saying that inconsistencies follow from the claim that there is a many, the details of the arguments seem to indicate that Zeno is rather arguing that whatever is extended and divisible, yet still supposedly one, actually turns out to have contradictory characteristics. Thus the basic entities of Anaxagoras and Empedocles are especially vulnerable, for they have just the properties of homogeneity and divisibility that Zeno attacks. Fragments B2 and B1 together argue that such things must be both large and small—"so small as to not have magnitude, so large as to be infinite" (μικρὰ μὲν ὥστε μὴ ἔχειν μέγεθος, μεγάλα δὲ ὥστε ἄπειρα εἶναι), as B1 puts it. B2 argues that what has no magnitude is nothing. Simplicius says (*in Ph.* 139.18–19) that Zeno shows that it has no magnitude by claiming that "each of the many is the same as itself and one" (ἕκαστον τῶν πολλῶν ἑαυτῷ ταὐτὸν εἶναι καὶ ἕν), but he does not explain how the argument goes. What

124 There may be a Pythagorean target, but it is difficult to be sure about this.

125 Makin argues that infinite divisibility is not a premise of any of Zeno's arguments, but that divisibility is rather always introduced as a conditional ("Zeno on Plurality" and *Indifference*, pp. 18ff.). I am inclined to think that he is correct that Zeno does not assume infinite divisibility in the arguments that have come down to us. But I disagree with Makin's views about how Zeno gets the divisibility claims from plurality. I suspect that, as I have argued here, they are part and parcel of the Pluralist claims about what there is. Would the arguments work against a monist such as Diogenes of Apollonia, who claims that there is one basic entity, air? Insofar as air "becomes" different things, it will be divisible in the sense of having different characters and so would be vulnerable to the "sameness and difference" argument that appears in Plato, *Prm.* (at 127e1–3). On the issue of types of divisibility (especially with respect to atoms), see Chap. V, n. 20.

Simplicius means is presumably explained in his reference to Themistius, who, he claims, says that Zeno's argument proves that what-is is one "because it is continuous and indivisible"; for, according to Themistius, division entails plurality.[126] If something were one and the same and yet had magnitude it would, according to Zeno's other arguments, be divisible, and thus no longer one. But a thing with no magnitude turns out to be nothing, because, as B2 shows, if such a thing were attached or detached from something there would be no change in size effected.[127] Thus the supposed unit of a pluralist theory is "so small as to have no magnitude" at all. But, further, it is also infinitely large. B1 is, I think, best read (as Vlastos suggests) in terms of contiguous parts of an extended magnitude, each of which has parts, each further part having yet more parts, and so on.[128] Thus, B1 argues that if the magnitude is extended it will have an infinite number of parts each with some magnitude, and, as we have seen, Zeno believes that the sum of an infinite number of parts with finite magnitude is infinite. So, on Zeno's assumptions, a unit of a pluralist theory (an Anaxagorean *chrēma* or an Empedoclean root, for instance) turns out to be contradictory in character.

B3 further explores problems of plurality and divisibility:

> εἰ πολλά ἐστιν, ἀνάγκη τοσαῦτα εἶναι ὅσα ἐστὶ καὶ οὔτε πλείονα αὐτῶν οὔτε ἐλάττονα. εἰ δὲ τοσαῦτά ἐστιν ὅσα ἐστί, πεπερασμένα ἂν εἴη. εἰ πολλά ἐστιν, ἄπειρα τὰ ὄντα ἐστίν· ἀεὶ γὰρ ἕτερα μεταξὺ τῶν ὄντων ἐστί, καὶ πάλιν ἐκείνων ἕτερα μεταξύ. καὶ οὕτως ἄπειρα τὰ ὄντα ἐστί. (B3)

> If there is a many, it is necessary that they be as many as they are and no more and no fewer. If they are as many as they are, they will be limited. If there is a many, the things that are are unlimited; for there are always others between the things that are, and again others between them. And in this way the things that are are unlimited.

The first part of the argument assumes that being the same as oneself (in number in this case) amounts to being limited or finite. Zeno does not spell out the premises in his argument; perhaps he took it as obvious that being just what one is, no more and no less, is a way of being limited. The claim that each is no more and no less than it is plays an important role here, for it is that which generates the claim that what-is is limited, which here seems to have the sense of "definite" or "circumscribed" or "held within

[126] See Vlastos ("Zeno," p. 369) and Prior (Zeno's First Argument," p. 251), who accept this as a premise in the argument of B1. See also Fränkel ("Zeno's Attackers"), pp. 110–11.

[127] On "attached" and "detached" instead of "added" or "subtracted," see Vlastos, "Zenonian Argument," pp. 120–21, and esp. n. 15, p. 138. On the claim that what does not change the size of a thing when attached or detached is nothing, see Vlastos, "Zenonian Argument," p. 121–22; "Note on B1"; and "Zeno," p. 370.

[128] Vlastos, "Note on B1," pp. 178–82.

limits."[129] But such a thing is also unlimited or indefinite; for if we distinguish two parts of it, there will always be a third part that separates the two. But then there must be things between the third part and the first two, and so on. Consider an extended bit of a pluralist entity, a bit of earth, say. Even if that bit of earth is monogenous, two parts of it can be distinguished (what is here and what is there, for instance). But if they are genuinely two parts, Zeno will claim that there must be something to distinguish them, which he takes as separating them in some sense. But that third part must itself be distinguished by having further parts between it and the first two parts, and so on. Thus our original bit of earth becomes indefinitely many, while at the same time being definite (just as many as it is, no more and no less). The key to the second part of the argument is, I think, divisibility. Parts can be distinguished within the thing, and those parts are divided from one another in thought if not in actuality.[130] Once again, it appears that the pluralist conception of the various basic entities as divisible plays a fundamental role in Zeno's argument.[131]

Do Zeno's arguments threaten Parmenides as well as the Pluralists? If Parmenides' account entails that what-is is incorporeal, then Zeno's arguments fail to affect it.[132] But a possible difficulty appears for Parmenides' claims on the interpretation that I have offered here. On my view, Parmenides' model is accepted by the pluralists, who base their pluralities of unified beings on the views of both the *Alētheia* and the *Doxa*. But, as we have seen, the account of each basic entity as physically divisible has raised the specter of incoherence for their theories. We do not know how Parmenides envisaged the mixture of the basic entities in the *Doxa*, but it may have been along the lines of the mixture in Empedocles' theory. If this is so, then Parmenides' own views are vulnerable to Zeno's arguments.

[129] For an analysis of the argument that stresses the role of "no more and no less" and that interprets *peperasmena* as "finite," see Peterson, "Zeno's Second Argument."

[130] See Makin, *Indifference*, pp. 23–24. Makin claims that the argument applies to a plurality of distinct units, arguing that each unit fails to be a unity. But there is no real need to begin with a plurality of units.

[131] Fränkel suggests that once divisibility is accepted nothing can be genuinely one. See "Zeno's Attacks," esp. n. 41, p. 133, which canvasses ancient texts on the issue of divisibility and unity.

[132] I argued for this claim in "Eleatic Monism," with respect to an argument that Simplicius gets from Eudemus via Alexander of Aphrodisias. In that argument (Simplicius, *in Ph.* 138.38–139.3 = 97.13–16) Alexander took Zeno to be "confuting the one," a claim that Simplicius disputes. At the time that I maintained that Simplicius was right that Parmenides' account of what-is is immune from Zeno's arguments, I had a different view of Parmenides' *Doxa* than the one I have defended in this book. I now think the issue is more complex than I did at the time of the earlier paper, although I still maintain that so long as what-is is held to be incorporeal, Zeno's arguments do not apply to it. Mourelatos, Vlastos, and Coxon (*Fragments*, pp. 214–15) all argue that what-is in Parmenides is not bodily. On the view that Parmenides' claim is that what-is is corporeal, but is unaffected by Zeno's arguments, see Makin, "Zeno on Plurality."

Parmenides' *Alētheia* concentrates on the metaphysical requirements for a thing to qualify as the nature of a thing, as the notion appears, for instance, in Heraclitus B1. Such a thing cannot be divisible in the sense of being two things: whatever it is, it must be all and only that thing, not subject to division into two sorts or kinds of thing. Parmenides' proof of indivisibility (B8.22–25) corresponds to the sign *mounogenes* (B8.4): what-is is of a single kind, monogenous. This, as argued in Chapter II, is consistent with there being more than one thing. Moreover, as a requirement for what it is to be the nature of a thing, metaphysical indivisibility appears to be consistent with the physical divisibility of such an entity. Empedoclean fire is always fire, always having the same character, whether it is in one contiguous mass (as when Strife is in the ascendancy) or divided into many bits (in the mixtures that constitute mortal things or the complete mixture that occurs in the Sphere under Love). The case is similar for the Anaxagorean *chrēmata*. Zeno's arguments do not attack the metaphysical nature of these things. Rather, he concentrates on the physically divisible character that such basic entities must have to function in the pluralist theories. In essence he asks: can a metaphysically single nature be physically divisible?[133] Zeno has not shown that there are actually metaphysical difficulties with this; rather he shows that there are paradoxical consequences that follow from thinking that a single nature can be in two places at once. The arguments attack not so much the plurality of entities themselves, as the consequences of requiring that each of these must be divisible. In this way the arguments about plurality are like the arguments about motion: both show that reasonable and even well-grounded assumptions generate paradoxical results.

If what I have suggested here is correct, what does it tell us about Zeno's relation to Parmenides? Recent debates about Parmenides and Zeno have offered us two opposing images. First, in the picture derived from Plato's *Parmenides*, and upheld by Simplicius the late Platonist, there is the Zeno who is a faithful servant of the One. This Zeno would never attack Parmenides' own views and works only to show that those who find Parmenides' views absurd face even greater absurdities themselves. This account assumes that Parmenides himself was a numerical monist and that Zeno's arguments are aimed at numerical pluralism. Second, there is Zeno the Sophist, happily attacking all comers, Parmenides as well as the Pluralists. This Zeno is a pure dialectician, caring little for truth, but only for the force of paradoxical argument. But there might be room for a third picture of Zeno.

[133] The issue may be compared to Parmenides' questions to Socrates about the nature of participation in the *Prm*. If the whole of the form is in many things, it will turn out to be divided and no longer one, as in a sail spread over many. Each of the many can claim a part of the sail; similarly, each of the many participants will have a part of the form and it will no longer be one but many (131a8–c10).

This Zeno is convinced by the metaphysical arguments of the *Alētheia*; and to that extent he is a conscientious Eleatic. But he is also a serious philosopher, who will follow an argument where it leads, and this means that he may well have discovered and raised difficulties about Parmenides' views that Parmenides himself had not yet seen.[134] The issues Zeno raises about the divisibility of a basic entity are serious philosophical problems with which Plato and Aristotle will both wrestle. This Zeno is an Eleatic but he is also an independent agent; if this is the real Zeno, then our view of the relations among the Eleatics must be revised, allowing that Eleaticism is not a monolithic philosophical view, but one that allows for differences of shade and even of doctrine.

[134] Again a comparison with the *Prm.* may be relevant. As I read the *Prm.*, Plato there explores difficulties that had been part of the Theory of Forms since it was formulated—difficulties whose seriousness he has now come to appreciate.

V

Atoms, Void, and Rearrangement

LIKE THE PLURALISTS, the Atomists try to give a rational account of how things are, and also like the Pluralists, the Atomists work within an Eleatic framework (a framework complicated by the arguments of Zeno and, perhaps, Melissus).[1] In this chapter I examine the atomist claims about the nature of atoms and about void and argue that both atoms and void satisfy the Parmenidean criteria for what-is (despite the Atomists' calling void "not-being" or "what-is-not"). But I also explore the possibility that the atomist theory is vulnerable to the arguments of Melissus.

Zeno had argued that a theory of what-is that includes a divisible basic entity is plagued with contradiction and paradox. The Atomists responded to the Zenonian challenge by beginning with a plurality of indivisible entities that, with void, were the fundamental principles of sensible objects.[2] Although there are direct quotations from Democritus that assert the reality of atoms and void (68B125, for instance), no extant fragments explain their natures. For that we must rely on Aristotle and others, and even that evidence is sketchy.[3]

> Λεύκιππος δ' ἔχειν ᾠήθη λόγους, οἵτινες πρὸς τὴν αἴσθησιν ὁμολογούμενα λέγοντες οὐκ ἀναιρήσουσιν οὔτε γένεσιν οὔτε φθορὰν οὔτε κίνησιν καὶ τὸ πλῆθος τῶν ὄντων. ὁμολογήσας δὲ ταῦτα μὲν τοῖς φαινομένοις, τοῖς δὲ τὸ ἓν κατασκευάζουσιν ὡς οὐκ ἂν κίνησιν οὖσαν ἄνευ κενοῦ, τό τε κενὸν μὴ ὂν καὶ τοῦ ὄντος οὐθὲν μὴ ὄν φησιν εἶναι· τὸ γὰρ κυρίως ὂν παμπλῆρες ὄν. ἀλλ' εἶναι τὸ τοιοῦτον οὐχ ἕν, ἀλλ' ἄπειρα τὸ πλῆθος καὶ ἀόρατα διὰ σμικρότητα τῶν ὄγκων. ταῦτα δ' ἐν τῷ κενῷ φέρεσθαι (κενὸν γὰρ εἶναι), καὶ συνιστάμενα μὲν γένεσιν ποιεῖν, διαλυόμενα δὲ φθοράν.
>
> (Aristotle, *Gen. Corr.* I.8 325a23–32 = 67A7 = Luria 146)

[1] For problems in placing Melissus in the chronology of post-Parmenidean thinkers, particularly with respect to the Atomists, see the Introduction, Section 2. References to "the Atomists" should be understood to include both Leucippus and Democritus. What evidence there is suggests that there were no fundamental differences between the theories of the two.

[2] Zeno's arguments will succeed against any divisible entity, but they are particularly destructive when aimed against such a theoretically basic entity as an Anaxagorean *chrēma* or an Empedoclean root.

[3] Because of the absence of direct quotations about atoms and void, we are, in the case of the Atomists, even more dependent than usual on Aristotle, his commentators, and other doxographical sources.

> Leucippus thought that he had arguments saying things agreeing with perception that would not do away with coming to be or passing away, or motion and the plurality of things that are. Conceding, on the one hand, these things to the phenomena, but on the other hand, conceding to those who support the one that there could not be motion without void, he says that the void is not being and that nothing of what is is not being; for that which is strictly is quite full. But this sort of thing is not one but unlimited in number and invisible because of the smallness of its bulk. These are carried about in the void (for there is void) and coming together they produce coming-to-be and separating they produce destruction.

> Λεύκιππος δὲ καὶ ὁ ἑταῖρος αὐτοῦ Δημόκριτος στοιχεῖα μὲν τὸ πλῆρες καὶ τὸ κενὸν εἶναί φασι, λέγοντες τὸ μὲν ὂν τὸ δὲ μὴ ὄν, τούτων δὲ τὸ μὲν πλῆρες καὶ στερεὸν τὸ ὄν, τὸ δὲ κενὸν καὶ μανὸν τὸ μὴ ὄν (διὸ καὶ οὐθὲν μᾶλλον τὸ ὂν τοῦ μὴ ὄντος εἶναί φασιν ὅτι οὐδὲ τοῦ κενοῦ τὸ σῶμα[4]), αἴτια δὲ τῶν ὄντων ταῦτα ὡς ὕλην.
>
> (Aristotle, *Metaph.* I.4 985b4–10 = 67A6 = Luria 173)

> Leucippus and his associate Democritus say that the full and the empty are elements, calling the one being and the other not-being; of these, being is full and solid, not being is empty [void] and rare. This is why they say that being is no more than not being, because body is no more than void. These are the material cause of the things that are.

Aristotle's reports indicate that there are an infinite number of solid (or full) atoms, and that they and void are the basic realities of the atomic system. It is through the combination and separation of atoms that what are called coming-to-be and passing-away take place, for like Anaxagoras and Empedocles the Atomists deny that generation and destruction are genuine phenomena, if by that is meant the generation of something from nothing or the destruction of something into nothing at all. Rather, what seems on the level of sense perception to be coming-to-be or passing-away is simply the combining or separating of atoms, while alteration is their rearrangement:

> Δημόκριτος δὲ καὶ Λεύκιππος ποιήσαντες τὰ σχήματα τὴν ἀλλοίωσιν καὶ τὴν γένεσιν ἐκ τούτων ποιοῦσι, διακρίσει μὲν καὶ συγκρίσει γένεσιν καὶ φθοράν, τάξει δὲ καὶ θέσει ἀλλοίωσιν.
>
> (Aristotle, *Gen. Corr.* I.2 315b6–9 = 67A9 = Luria 240)

[4] Reading τοῦ κενοῦ τὸ σῶμα with Ross (following Schwegler) in line 9. Jaeger had suggested that leaving the text as it is reported in the manuscripts can also give the right sense; but Ross disputes this, claiming that the passages Jaeger cites in support "are to be otherwise explained" (p. 139). KRS follow DK in accepting Zellers's τὸ κενὸν ⟨ἔλαττον⟩ τοῦ σώματος. The Ross reading makes the phrase consonant with B156 as reported by Plutarch. The fragment is discussed in Section 2, below.

> Having made the shapes, Democritus and Leucippus make alteration and generation from them; coming-to-be and passing-away through separation and combination, alteration through arrangement and position.

Despite the fundamental importance of atoms in the theory, the extant fragments of Democritus and the testimonia concerning Leucippus and Democritus provide little information about them. Even less is said about void. The evidence shows that atoms are full, solid, homogeneous, hard, probably small, indivisible, and differ in shape.[5] Void is empty or rare. Further, and perhaps most importantly, atoms are called being or what-is (*to on*) while void is called not-being or what-is-not (*to mē on*). Aristotle and Simplicius suggest that the designation of void as what-is-not or not-being actually goes back to Leucippus and that Democritus followed him in applying this name to void.[6] Calling void "not-being" is clearly provocative, as Parmenides had banned what-is-not and Melissus had explicitly extended the Parmenidean proscription to void.[7] The Atomists compound the affront to Eleatic claims by asserting that void is; given the essential identification of void and what-is-not, this comes to the stark declaration, in the face of Eleatic arguments to the contrary, that what-is-not is.

Parmenides had insisted that what-is-not cannot be; for he had maintained that what-is-not cannot be said or thought; and he had announced that attempts to show that something is not (in the particular sense under

[5] Aristotle seems convinced that Leucippan or Democritean atoms were very small, certainly too small to be sensed. See for instance *On Democritus* = Simplicius, *in Cael.* 295.5–6 = 68A37 = Luria 227; *Gen. Corr.* 325a30 = 67A7 = Luria 205; see also Simplicius, *in Ph.* 925.15 = 67A13 = Luria 113. The small size and thus imperceptibility of atoms is part of the justification for two kinds of *gnōmē* in Democritus B11 = Luria 83. This can, I think, be deduced from the evidence of B11 no matter what we take to follow the break-off point ("*leptoteron*") in Sextus's discussion that forms the context of the fragment. Aetius asserts that Democritus claimed that there could be an atom as large as the *kosmos* (I.12.6 = 68A47 = Luria 207). Makin suggests that while the atoms that make up phenomenal things are, indeed, very small, the indifference arguments used by Democritus in discussing size do not rule out very large atoms indeed. These would not be available to human senses because of the mechanism of perception in Democritus's system. Moreover, according to Makin, larger atoms would be at the center of cosmic whirls and thus also imperceptible (Makin, *Indifference*, pp. 62–65, esp. p. 64).

[6] See Aristotle *Metaph.* I.4 985b4–10 = 67A6 = Luria 173 (quoted above) and Simplicius, *in Ph.* 28.12–15 = 67A8 = Luria 147.

[7] I do not see Parmenides himself as specifically concerned with void; the explicit discussion of void as such seems to enter Eleatic thought with Melissus, for Zeno's arguments about motion do not depend on the impossibility of void. On the issue of Parmenides and void, see Kirk and Stokes, "Parmenides' Refutation" with response by Bicknell ("Implication"). Stokes replies to Bicknell in *One and Many*, p. 312n.6. Barnes claims that Melissus's linking of the impossibility of void with the impossibility of motion "is original with him" (*PP*, vol. II, pp. 217–18) and asserts that Melissus's arguments against motion are superior to those in Parmenides (p. 222). As with all the Presocratics in this period, fixing the chronology is very difficult. It is just possible that some tenets of atomism were formulated before Melissus wrote B7; on this issue, see Klowski.

consideration) would fail. The route taken by mortals, who turn out to be seeking what-is-not (even if this is not how they themselves would conceive of their search[8]) is a backward-turning path (28B6.9) from which no tidings ever come (28B2.6). Melissus had extended those claims by asserting that what is empty or void (*kenon*) is nothing and thus subject to the prohibition of what-is-not (30B7). So, in claiming that the fundamental parts of their theory are atoms and void or being and not-being, if the Atomists simply assert that what-is-not is, they flatly contradict Parmenides. This may, indeed, be their strategy, but there is good reason to doubt that their method is simple assertion in the face of the Eleatic prohibition of what-is-not. First, like the Pluralists, the Atomists accept Parmenides' arguments against coming-to-be and passing-away; those arguments are firmly grounded in the rejection of what-is-not. The arguments of Parmenides B8 show that the rejection of *genesis* depends crucially on the impossibility of what-is-not:

> . . .τίνα γὰρ γένναν διζήσεαι αὐτοῦ;
> πῇ πόθεν αὐξηθέν; οὔτ' ἐκ μὴ ἐόντος ἐάσσω
> φάσθαι σ' οὐδὲ νοεῖν· οὐ γὰρ φατὸν οὐδὲ νοητόν
> ἔστιν ὅπως οὐκ ἔστι. (B8.6–9)

> . . . for what birth of it will you seek out?
> How, and whence grown? Neither from what is not shall I allow
> you to say or think; for it is not to be said or thought
> that it is not.

> οὐδέ ποτ' ἐκ μὴ ἐόντος[9] ἐφήσει πίστιος ἰσχύς
> γίγνεσθαί τι παρ' αὐτό· τοῦ εἵνεκεν οὔτε γενέσθαι
> οὔτ' ὄλλυσθαι ἀνῆκε Δίκη χαλάσασα πέδῃσιν,
> ἀλλ' ἔχει· ἡ δὲ κρίσις περὶ τούτων ἐν τῷδ' ἔστιν·
> ἔστιν ἢ οὐκ ἔστιν· κέκριται δ' οὖν, ὥσπερ ἀνάγκη,
> τὴν μὲν ἐᾶν ἀνόητον ἀνώνυμον (οὐ γὰρ ἀληθής
> ἔστιν ὁδός), τὴν δ' ὥστε πέλειν καὶ ἐτήτυμον εἶναι. (B8.12–18)

> Nor will the force of trust permit anything to come to be from
> what is not alongside it. On account of this neither coming to be
> nor perishing would Justice allow, loosening the fetters,
> but holds fast. And the decision about these is in this:
> is or is not; and it has been decided, just as is necessary,
> to leave the one unthinkable and unnamed (for it is not a true
> route), and the other to be and to be genuine.

Insofar as the Atomists accept the arguments against coming-to-be and passing-away, they are committed to the Parmenidean rejection of the reality

[8] On the nature of mortal error, see Chap. I, Section 3.
[9] For the text here, see Chap. II, n. 33.

of what-is-not. Aristotle's report at *On Generation and Corruption* I.8 (325a23–25 = 67A7 = Luria 146) might, at first glance, seem at odds with the claim that the Atomists indeed accept the Parmenidean exclusion of what-is-not, for there Aristotle claims that "Leucippus thought that he had arguments saying things agreeing with perception that would not do away with coming to be or passing away, or motion and the plurality of things which are." But later in the same passage he clarifies his claim. Leucippus did not say that there actually is coming-to-be in the sense proscribed by the Eleatics, for he explained coming-to-be and passing-away as the mingling and separation of atoms, and no atom is itself generated or destroyed. So Leucippus (and Democritus with him) accepted the Eleatic denial of generation. But if this is true, the Atomists cannot merely assert that what-is-not is, for that would undermine their own claims about the unreality of coming-to-be and destruction. Thus, it is reasonable to look for arguments used by the Atomists to justify the claim that what-is-not, in the form of void, is. That there were such arguments seems likely, and the reports of Aristotle and Simplicius, together with a fragment of Democritus, bear this out. There seem to have been two sorts of argument, each doing a different job in justifying the reality of void. First, arguments about the non-divisibility of atoms point out the need for void;[10] second, a version of an *ou mallon* (no more) argument shows that void has a claim to what-is, for atoms are no more real than void.[11] It is to these arguments that I now turn.

1. Atoms and Void

Atoms are called "full" and what-is. Simplicius reports (*in de Caelo* 569.6 = 68A61) that all atoms have the same nature (τὰς ἀτόμους πάσας ὁμοφυεῖς οὔσας ... φασί). Atoms are unchangeable in themselves, always the same, and one in nature; thus they each qualify as a Parmenidean entity. According to Aristotle they differ from one another in shape (*schēma*), arrangement (*taxis*), and position (*thesis*) (*Metaph.* I.4 985b14–15). Various combinations of atoms differing in these ways result in the multiplicity of objects reported by the senses. Again according to Aristotle, they bring about compound objects by combining and becoming entangled with one another (*in Gen. Corr.* 325a32–34).[12] Compound objects have the characters they do because of the properties of the atoms of which they are composed and the relations

[10] Aristotle, *Gen. Corr.* 316a13–b13.

[11] Aristotle, *Metaph.* 985b7–9 = 67A6 = Luria 173, Simplicius, *in Ph.* 28.11–13 = 67A8 = Luria 147, Plutarch, *Adv. Colot.* 4.1109A ff. = 68B156 = Luria 7.

[12] Aristotle's reference to entanglement is puzzling, for if atoms are separated from one another by void, they do not touch, and it is difficult to see how they can become entangled. Philoponus, commenting on Aristotle's remark here, says that atoms do not actually touch one

of those atoms to one another. Because all atoms are made of the same monogeneous stuff, differences in compound objects must be attributable to some other feature of atoms.[13] Theophrastus says that the tastes of things differ according to the shapes of the atoms that make them up; thus "he [Democritus] makes sweet that which is round and quite large, astringent that which is large, rough, polygonal and not rounded" (*CP* VI.1.6 = 68A129 = Luria 497). According to Simplicius, things composed of sharp and very fine atoms in similar positions come to be hot and fiery; those composed of atoms with the opposite character come to be cold and watery (*in Ph.* 36.3–6 = 67A14 = Luria 247). So atoms differ at least in size and shape. Simplicius, following Aristotle and Theophrastus, attributes to Democritus the claim that some atoms are heavier than others (*in de Caelo* 569.5–9 = 68A61 = Luria 368), while Aetius says that the view that weight is a property of atoms is due to Epicurus (I.3.18 = 68A7 = Luria 157). Aristotle says that "those who say the primary bodies are solid" can say that the larger is heavier (*de Caelo* IV.2. 309a1 = 68A60 = Luria 368); but he goes on to note difficulties in this view, saying that they should say that it is the presence or absence of void in compound bodies that accounts for their lightness or heaviness. But at *On Generation and Corruption* 326a9 = 68A60 = Luria 368, he reports that according to Democritus larger atoms are heavier. Theophrastus follows this, saying that Democritus "distinguishes heavy and light by size" (*Sens.* 61 = 68A135 = Luria 369), but Theophrastus also attributes the heaviness of lead to the fact that it has less void than do other compounds (*Sens.* 62 = 68A135 = Luria 369).[14]

In most of Aristotle's discussions of atomism, including the fragment from *On Democritus* that survives in Simplicius, he simply reports the Atomists' commitment to the existence of void. In these passages no reference is made to any argument in Leucippus or Democritus for the need for void, or for any reasons why they insisted on the atomic or uncuttable nature of their basic entities. But there is an argument for atomic entities in I.2 of *On Generation and Corruption* (at 316a13–b16 = 68A48b = Luria 105). There

another but are always separated by void; rather they are said to be in contact when they are quite close to one another (*in Gen. Corr.* 158.26–159.3 and 160.10 = 67A7 = Luria 236). Godfrey (in "Democritus") considers the ancient atomist view in the light of modern discussions of the possibility of collisions in "completely mechanistic physics."

[13] Aristotle reports that Democritus held that there is a single atomic matter at *Ph.* 184b21 = Luria 223 and *de Caelo* 275b31–276a1 = 67A19=Luria 261.

[14] Barnes claims that "it is evident that Aristotle and Theophrastus are preferable to Aetius. . . . The thesis that atoms have weight or mass is an obvious corollary of the central tenets of atomism" (*PP*, vol. II, p. 63). Barnes does not note the Aristotelian and Theophrastean claims about presence or absence of void accounting for weight in compound objects. O'Brien maintains both that atoms differ in weight in proportion to their size and that the weight of compound bodies is determined by the amount of void they contain (*Theories of Weight*, I, pp. 345–46). I return to the issue of the role of void in determining the character of compound objects in Section 3.

Aristotle rehearses arguments against the supposition that "a body (that is, a magnitude) is divisible everywhere and that this division is possible" (εἴ τις θείη σῶμά τι εἶναι καὶ μέγεθος πάντῃ διαιρετὸν καὶ τοῦτο δυνατόν). If such a division were to be carried out, the result will be nothing at all. If some magnitude remains, there has not been division through and through, and if no magnitude remains, nothing at all is left. The conclusion (at 316b14–16) is that "if it is impossible that magnitudes are made of contacts or points, it is necessary that there must be indivisible bodies and magnitudes" (εἴπερ ἀδύνατον ἐξ ἁφῶν ἢ στιγμῶν εἶναι τὰ μεγέθη, ἀνάγκη εἶναι σώματα ἀδιαίρετα καὶ μεγέθη). Aristotle does not endorse the argument, nor does he explicitly say in the course of it with whom it originated, but he seems to attribute it to Democritus (at 316a13) as a reason why the Atomists postulated indivisible bodies. If this is an atomist argument, it is a direct response to Zeno, who had claimed that a body divisible through and through would disappear into nothing.[15] Postulating an ultimate indivisible body that neither comes to be nor passes away would avoid Zeno's argument while giving the Atomists a basic entity that could combine and separate as in the cosmological model proposed by Parmenides in the *Doxa* and adopted by Anaxagoras and Empedocles.[16] If a sensible body were composed of a multitude of indivisible entities, then an explanation of why that particular body is divisible to a certain point but no further could be given. Void or emptiness separates the indivisible bodies and allows for division; to the extent that a body contains void, it is to that extent divisible.[17]

This argument, relying on void, implies that atoms are not divisible, for composite bodies can be divided only where there is void. The doxographers are not completely clear about the cause of the indivisibility of atoms. Simplicius says (at *in Ph.* 82.1–3 = Luria 212) that atoms are characterized by both solidity (*nastotēs*) and hardness (*sterrotēs*). At *in de Caelo* 242.18–20 = 67A14 = Luria 214, Simplicius claims that atoms are impassable (*apathē*) because of their solidity, without mentioning hardness.[18] He also asserts (*in Ph.* 925.14–15 = 67A13 = Luria 113) that Leucippus and Democritus maintain that atoms are indivisible because they are small and partless in

[15] The argument reported by Aristotle is strikingly similar to one reported by Simplicius who follows Alexander in attributing it to Zeno (*in Ph.* 139.27–140.6). See Chap. IV, Section 4.

[16] See n. 20, below, on the problem of the various sorts of indivisibility that have been attributed to atoms, and the problems of theoretical indivisibility.

[17] See Makin, *Indifference*, chap. 3 (esp. pp. 49–55), for a full discussion of the use the Atomists might have made of the argument that Aristotle reports at 316a13–b16. Makin acknowledges that Aristotle does not anywhere explicitly attribute the argument to the Atomists, but he thinks that this is not a serious objection to treating it as an atomist argument. See also Makin, "Indivisibility."

[18] See Makin, *Indifference*, p. 55 with nn. 30, 31, 32, and 33. Makin argues that an atom that is soft yet homogeneous would prove to be indivisible, if the atomist argument for indivisibility is generated by an indifference argument in the style of Zeno. I take it that by "homogeneous" Makin means that an atom is single in kind or nature.

addition to being impassable. All this suggests that the doxographers were in considerable confusion about just why atoms are indivisible, and also that neither Leucippus nor Democritus pointed out a single positive character of atoms themselves that is responsible for this indivisibility. What appears to be crucial is the absence of void in an atom; as Simplicius says, "they said that division comes to be because of the void in bodies" (τὴν ... διαίρεσιν κατὰ τὸν κενὸν τὸ ἐν τοῖς σώμασιν ἔλεγον γίνεσθαι).[19] So, in the atomic theory, void explains divisibility: physical bodies may be divided wherever there is void, and as there is no void in atoms, they are indivisible.[20]

Void plays another, yet related, role: it is that which separates things. First, void, separates atoms and prevents the existence of only a single, undifferentiated object in the *kosmos*.[21] The nature of atomic stuff is the same in every case,[22] so if there were no void to separate the atoms the *kosmos* would be a plenum of atomic stuff. At *de Caelo* I.7 275b31–276a1 (67A19 = Luria 261) Aristotle says that the atoms "are differentiated by shapes; they say that the nature of them is one, just as if each were a separated piece of gold" (διώρισται μὲν γὰρ τοῖς σχήμασιν· τὴν δὲ φύσιν εἶναί φασιν αὐτῶν μίαν, ὥσπερ ἂν εἰ χρυσὸς ἕκαστον εἴη κεχωρισμένον). Just as gold has

[19] Simplicius, *in de Caelo* 242.20–21 = 67A14 = Luria 214. See also Theophrastus's account of the differences between iron and lead on the atomic view (*Sens.* 62 = 68A135 = Luria 369). Lead has less void than iron and so is heavier, but its atoms are arranged evenly. It is thus easier to cut (i.e., is softer), presumably because the areas of void are more contiguous and provide a straight and easy path for division.

[20] Commentators disagree about whether the indivisibility of the atoms is limited to physical indivisibility or also includes theoretical indivisibility. Furley argues for both physical and theoretical indivisibility in *Two Studies*, pp. 85–101 and in *Greek Cosmologists, Vol. I*, pp. 124–31; see also Baldes, "Divisibility" for a similar view. Barnes (*PP*, vol. II, pp. 50–58) concludes that the evidence on theoretical indivisibility is unclear: "the verdict must be *non liquet*" (p. 57). Guthrie, in *HGP*, vol. II, provides a clear discussion of the issues and accounts of the views of scholars up to the middle of the 1960s; he opts for both physical and theoretical indivisibility. Sorabji claims that Democritus did not distinguish between physical and theoretical indivisibility (*Time*, pp. 354–57). Makin ("Indivisibility" and *Indifference*, pp. 53–62) agrees with Sorabji that the distinction between physical and theoretical indivisibility is not clear in Democritus. Makin goes further and argues that the distinction itself is not clearly drawn. He argues that because it was the Zenonian indifference arguments concerning divisibility that underlie Atomism, it is atomic homogeneity that is important for their indivisibility. According to Makin, an atom made of homogeneous atomic stuff will necessarily be indivisible, and that is all Democritus need claim. Given the evidence of difference in atomic shapes, and that (according to Makin) there is no reason to attribute partlessness to Democritean atoms, Makin thinks it reasonable to conclude that atoms are physically indivisible yet are not partless.

[21] Aristotle reports this function of void (as well as its role in making motion possible) at *Gen. Corr.* 325a4–6. Bollack, following Natorp and Luria, argues that the passage in which this report occurs is actually based on a Leucippan account of the origin of Atomism (Bollack, "Deux figures," p. 35). Bollack's view is successfully criticized by de Ley in "Leucippan Fragment?" On the separation issue, see Stokes, *One and Many*, pp. 221–22; Furley, *Greek Cosmologists I*, pp. 118–19; and Makin, *Indifference*, p. 24.

[22] Aristotle says that atoms are one in kind and differ only in shape: *Ph.* I.2 184b21 = 67A6 = Luria 173.

the same nature no matter whether it is in a very large lump or separated into pieces of varying size, so the nature of every atom is the same. Atoms differ in shape and size, but not in their essential nature. This is crucial to the atomic theory, which both follows the Parmenidean requirement that what-is be one in its nature, and claims that it is the arrangement of atoms of varying sizes and shapes that constitute the world reported by the senses. Thus the coming-to-be and passing-away of the multiple things in the sensible world can be explained simply by the rearrangement of atoms rather than by referring to ingredients having different natures. But this similarity of nature requires that, if there are indeed an unlimited number of atoms, there must be void. For, if there were no void separating the various occurrences of atomic stuff, there would simply be a single (very large) atom.[23] Second, void also separates composite objects from one another. This capacity to separate atoms and objects is a further aspect of void's divisibility function, for atoms grouped into two apparently distinct composite bodies are simply atoms separated from one another by first smaller and then larger areas of void. A dense composite body is made up of atoms separated by small areas of void, or in which void is arranged in particular patterns; if the composite body is quite separate from other composite bodies, that is because there is a large area of void (or of void and a small number of atoms) between it and the other bodies.

These arguments show that the atomic theory requires the reality of void. But they do not show that void is, as a matter of fact, real. That task is complicated by the Atomists' identification of void with what-is-not, or nothing. They must provide an argument that what-is-not can be, or at least give a good reason to think that what-is-not is as much as what-is. That argument is reported in Democritus B156 and in those testimonia that refer to an argument that what-is is no more (*ou mallon*) than what-is-not. But it is not entirely clear how the *ou mallon* argument is supposed to justify the claim that void is, or is real.

2. Void, Being, and the *ou mallon* Arguments

Aristotle reports the Atomists' use of an *ou mallon* argument in *Metaphysics* I.4 (985b4–9), attributing it to both Leucippus and Democritus: "Leucippus and his associate Democritus say that the full and the empty are elements, calling the one being and the other not-being; of these, being is full and

[23] Considering the possibility of such a large atom and the role of void in separating atoms, one can understand why the Atomists begin with an indefinite plurality of atoms. If atoms are by nature indivisible, a universe that began with a single undifferentiated atom would remain in that state, because such an atom could not divide and separate into smaller bits of atomic stuff.

solid, not being is empty [void] and rare. This is why they say that being is no more than not being because body is no more than void" (διὸ καὶ οὐθὲν μᾶλλον τὸ ὂν τοῦ μὴ ὄντος εἶναί φασιν ὅτι οὐδὲ τοῦ κενοῦ τὸ σῶμα). In his commentary on the *Physics*, Simplicius also reports an *ou mallon* argument, apparently attributing the first atomist use of it to Leucippus, and noting that Democritus concurred with Leucippus in calling void "not-being":

> ἔτι δὲ οὐδὲν μᾶλλον τὸ ὂν ἢ τὸ μὴ ὂν ὑπάρχειν, καὶ αἴτια ὁμοίως εἶναι τοῖς γινομένοις ἄμφω. τὴν γὰρ τῶν ἀτόμων οὐσίαν ναστὴν καὶ πλήρη ὑποτιθέμενος ὂν ἔλεγεν εἶναι καὶ ἐν τῷ κενῷ φέρεσθαι, ὅπερ μὴ ὂν ἐκάλει καὶ οὐκ ἔλαττον τοῦ ὄντος εἶναί φησι. παραπλησίως δὲ καὶ ὁ ἑταῖρος αὐτοῦ Δημόκριτος ὁ Ἀβδηρίτης ἀρχὰς ἔθετο τὸ πλῆρες καὶ τὸ κενόν, ὧν τὸ μὲν ὄν, τὸ δὲ μὴ ὂν ἐκάλει.
>
> (Simplicius, *in Ph.* 28.11–17 = 67A8 = 68A38 = Luria 147)

> Further, [Leucippus says] that what-is is no more than what-is-not, and that both equally are causes for the things that come to be. For, supposing that the substance of the atoms is compact and full, he says that they are being and are carried about in the void, which he called not-being and says is no less than being. Likewise, his associate, Democritus of Abdera, made the principles the full and the empty, of which he called the one being and the other not-being.

Finally, Plutarch gives the argument in perhaps its best-known form:

> [Δημόκριτος] διορίζεται μὴ μᾶλλον τὸ δὲν ἢ τὸ μηδὲν εἶναι, δὲν μὲν ὀνομάζων τὸ σῶμα, μηδὲν δὲ τὸ κενόν, ὡς καὶ τούτου φύσιν τινὰ καὶ ὑπόστασιν ἰδίαν ἔχοντος. (Plutarch, *Adv. Colot.* 4.1109A = 68B156 = Luria 78)

> . . . when [Democritus] declares that the thing is no more than the nothing, he is calling thing body and nothing void, and declaring that this too [void] has some nature and existence of its own.

Although these reports seem to indicate that there was indeed an argument for the reality of void, there is little discussion by modern commentators of what the form or the significance of the argument might have been.[24] To begin, there is the strange word *den*, which occurs only in Alcaeus and Democritus B156 (along with the reports on Democritus that are influenced by B156).

24 See, for instance, Barnes, *PP*, vol. II, pp. 101ff. and 251–57; McKirahan, pp. 313–17; Guthrie mentions the fragment twice (*HGP*, vol. II, pp. 34 and 392) and quotes it in full once (p. 461), but he does not offer a separate discussion of it. Matson ("Democritus") suggests that the argument is a joke, but see the response by McGibbon ("Atomists and Melissus"). Makin, who has devoted a book to indifference arguments, says only that "use of the expression *ou mallon* functions here as a vivid way of expressing the Democritean position and endorsing the existence of atom and void" (*Indifference*, p. 98). He notes that the phrase "p no more than q" is an indication of an underlying indifference argument but he does not discuss what Democritus's argument might have been.

Leucippus apparently used *to on* and *to mē on* rather than Democritus's *to den* and *to mēden*. A. C. Moorhouse has surveyed the use of *den* and he concludes that any similarity between Alcaeus and Democritus is accidental.[25] Whether or not Democritus knew of Alcaeus's use of the term, it must have seemed a natural way to make the point that body (thing, *to den*) and void (nothing, *to mēden*) are equally fundamental parts of the atomist theory. There is not, I think, anything significant in the differences in terminology chosen by Leucippus and Democritus.[26] Just as *to den* seemed an appropriate term for "what-is," given the parity in reality that the Atomists claim for what-is and what-is-not, so an *ou mallon* argument seems the perfect procedure for showing the parity. But how, exactly, does the argument show this? More crucially, what do the Atomists mean in claiming that what-is-not is a fundamental part of the theory? As with most other issues in Presocratic thought, there is little unanimity among commentators. Almost all agree in thinking that the inclusion of void is a direct response to Melissus's arguments against motion. But apart from this minimal accord (which is not universal), there is disagreement. Before turning to an analysis of the argument and its significance, I shall consider two accounts that, though raising issues crucial to a correct understanding of the argument, are, finally, less than satisfactory.

Jonathan Barnes interprets Democritus in B156 as claiming only that "nothing, no less than existent things, exists."[27] On the face of it, this is a contradiction, and so Barnes suggests that Democritus and Leucippus intended to draw a distinction between two senses of "exist"; although Barnes claims that there is no evidence that Democritus thought *einai* to be ambiguous, he was nevertheless "feeling towards such an insight."[28] The distinction Barnes sees Democritus making is between "there are" and "are real."[29] For example, there are unicorns, yet unicorns are not real. So, when the Atomists identify atoms with what-is and void with what-is-not yet claim that what-is is no more than what-is-not, they are, on Barnes's analysis, claiming that there are atoms and atoms are real, and also that, while there is void, void is not real. Barnes further explicates the distinction by claiming that to exist in the fullest sense (to be real) is to be a "space-filler" (Barnes's term). So, as atoms are bodies and thus fill space they are necessarily real in

25 Moorhouse, "ΔEN," p. 238. In an addendum, Moorhouse reports a possible use of *den* in Aristophanes, at *Thesmophoriazusae* 1197, but he doubts that this is a genuine occurrence.

26 If we knew that Leucippus wrote before Melissus, there might be some significance in the terms chosen by Leucippus and Democritus. We might then read Melissus B7 as a rejection of Leucippus's claim that there is void, and Democritus B156 as a response to Melissus's argument that the void or empty is nothing. But the chronology is far too uncertain to be sure about this. Like almost all other writers on the subject, I reject Matson's claim that the argument is a merely facetious reply to Melissus's claim that nothing cannot be. See especially McGibbon on this point.

27 Barnes, *PP*, vol. II, p. 101.

28 Ibid.

29 "Are real" corresponds to Barnes's exist_1, while "there are" is Barnes's exist_2.

the fullest sense. Void, on the other hand, as bodiless, fails to fill space and is necessarily unreal while still existing in the weaker sense that there are empty spaces.[30] But although Barnes is willing to countenance a double sense of "existence" in the Atomists, he is unwilling to read the *ou mallon* argument as the claim that, as he puts it, "the void is just as existent as the atoms are." This reading, he claims, would entail a commitment to the peculiar notion that one thing can be "more existent" than another.[31] Rather, Barnes reads the argument as asserting that "there is no more reason for" the existence of atoms than for that of void. Barnes finally concludes that, in this form, the *ou mallon* argument reported in B156 fails, for the Atomists give no reason for the equipollence of "there are atoms" and "there is void" (or, in Barnes's terms, for the equipollence of the claims that there is occupied space and that there is unoccupied space). Melissus had certainly given reasons why what-is is and void is not, and the Atomists, on Barnes's view, fail to answer Melissus adequately.[32] Like McGibbon, Barnes suggests that the *ou mallon* statement simply points to the Atomists' argument rather than being that argument itself.[33]

McGibbon and Barnes are, I think, correct on the last point. The *ou mallon* claim is less an argument in itself than the summary or conclusion of an argument. But there are a number of problems with Barnes's interpretation of the Atomists' claims here. First, it is difficult to accept the attribution to the Atomists of a distinction between different senses of existence. Barnes's claim that both of the senses he concentrates on "can be put across by the verb 'exist'" is dubious:[34] surely it is part of the point in marking a distinction between "there are" and "are real" that there is something quite odd in asserting that unicorns exist, especially if one means that they don't *really* exist in the full-bodied sense in which horses, for example, exist. While it may indeed be the case that the Greek *einai* can capture both notions, it is strange that neither Aristotle, who had a sharp ear for distinctions and differences in sense, nor Simplicius mention this at all in their references to the *ou mallon* argument.

[30] A similar interpretation of the *ou mallon* argument as depending on different senses of being is implicit in McGibbon's comments at the end of his paper ("Atomists and Melissus"; see also n. 4 on pp. 250–51). McGibbon suggests that the *ou mallon* argument is actually the summary of a now-lost argument, probably a *reductio*, based on the need for both atoms and void to account for phenomena. He seems to take void as empty space, as Barnes does. Though he interprets what-is and what-is-not as "substance and non-substance," I take him to be claiming that to be a substance is to be a body that occupies space.

[31] Barnes, *PP*, vol. II, p. 103.

[32] Ibid., p. 256.

[33] It is unclear to me whether Barnes thinks that this further claim vitiates his evaluation of the *ou mallon* argument as unsatisfactory. Does he think that the Atomists could not have given a satisfactory answer to Melissus? Or is he merely claiming that if we take the *ou mallon* claim as the whole of the Atomists' response to Melissus, it is unsatisfactory as an argument on its own?

[34] Barnes's claim is on p. 101 of *PP*, vol. II.

Indeed, Aristotle's silence on the possibility that the Atomists meant to rely on different senses of "is" in the *ou mallon* claims tells strongly against Barnes's interpretation. Barnes argues that his construal, which relies on different senses of "exist," is the only one that saves the Atomists from contradicting themselves in the argument. But the oddity of the reading "more existent" that Barnes first suggests and then seeks to avoid is evidence that the claims of the *ou mallon* argument ought not to be taken as primarily existential.[35] Second, having called on the existential sense of *einai* to explain the difference between the being of atoms and the being of void, Barnes abandons it to explain the "is no more" part of the *ou mallon* claim. Thus, on Barnes's interpretation in the short claim μὴ μᾶλλον τὸ δὲν ἢ τὸ μηδὲν εἶναι (the thing is no more than the nothing) there are three senses of "is" at work, together with an unstated but assumed reference to reasons for existing. Surely, a more natural reading of the line is that *to den* and *to mēden* are on an equal footing with respect to being, whatever that footing is.[36] Third, despite his rejection of the notion that one thing may be "more existent" than another, it is just this to which Barnes's reading of the argument commits him. To say that there is void yet it is not real is to posit a hierarchy of things that are. Yet Barnes insists that *einai* be read as existence; thus he has created a hierarchy of existence in which things are first said to exist (there are X's) and then ranked or assigned one degree of existence or another depending on whether they are or are not real. Finally, it is not clear that the distinction between atoms and void is to be cashed out solely in terms of filling or not filling space.[37] There is, I think, an interpretation of the argument that can save the Atomists from contradiction and that does not rely on Barnes's odd and anachronistic distinction between senses of existence. But before discussing that interpretation, I consider a different account of the Atomists' conception of void.

David Furley stresses that for the Presocratic Atomists, atoms and void are both "elements" (as Aristotle will later call them) because both are fundamental to the theory.[38] For Furley, void plays two roles in the theories of

[35] I have already argued (in Chaps. I and II) that the existential interpretation of *einai* is usually not the most appropriate in interpretations of Parmenides and indeed of Presocratic philosophy in general. The difficulty generated by attempting to read the *ou mallon* claim as purely existential provides more evidence for this view. As I have noted already, there is an existential component in Presocratic claims about what-is, but most claims about what there is are not primarily existential.

[36] Sedley argues that Barnes's interpretation cannot stand, because one of the points of the *ou mallon* claim is the assertion that both atoms and void are real. This is just what Barnes's version of the argument denies. Sedley, "Two Conceptions"; pp. 181–82.

[37] Sedley argues in "Two Conceptions" that this is not the only way to conceive the difference between atoms and void. Algra raises objections to Sedley's position in *Concepts of Space*, p. 42n.36, pp. 48–52. I discuss Sedley's interpretation and Algra's objections below, in Section 3, n. 66.

[38] Furley's fullest discussion of void is in *The Greek Cosmologists, I*, pp. 117–22.

Leucippus and Democritus. First, it separates atoms from one another, allowing for plurality; second, it makes motion possible. Like Barnes, Furley sees B156 and the other *ou mallon* claims as the key to understanding the Presocratic atomist conception of void. But Furley does not find a distinction between two senses of existence here; rather he sees the Atomists as "accepting [Melissus's identification of void with nothing] and then making a distinction within the concept of 'nothing.' "[39] He identifies a sense of "nothing" or "not-being" in which it negates what is said. " 'I hear nothing' means 'I am not hearing anything' or 'no hearing is being accomplished by me.' "[40] Mourelatos has called this the existential sense of "nothing."[41] This existential sense is contrasted with another sense of "nothing," in which what is meant is a negative predicate. On Furley's previous example, "I am hearing nothing" in this sense means, "I hear sounds, but I hear nothing in particular." This is what Mourelatos has called the characterizing sense of "nothing."[42] According to Furley, Democritus does not claim that void is non-existent when he says that it is nothing; rather "it is *not anything in particular*."[43] Void is a real, existent thing; it just is not any particular thing. Having presented this account of void, Furley then poses an important question: Once the Atomists admit not-being, or what-is-not, in the form of void, why do they not then also simply reject all of the Eleatic arguments about what-is-not? Why should they any longer be concerned to stay within the Eleatic limits on coming-to-be and passing-away, including changes in qualitative characteristics? In answering this question, Furley says more about his understanding of the atomist conception of void. He argues that the fundamental Eleatic claim is epistemological and is formulated in Parmenides B2.7–8: what-is-not cannot be known, thought, or uttered. According to Furley, in positing void, the Atomists do not reject this fundamental principle "but only modified it, in such a way that the dependent arguments still appeared to hold."[44]

Nevertheless, according to Furley, the Atomists did reject some of Parmenides' claims about what-is-not:

> They [the Atomists] would have been compelled to deny some expressions of the premiss, such as "Never shall this prevail, that things that *are not*, *are*" (fr. 7.1), since that is precisely what did "prevail" in their conception of the void. But some force would still remain in "you cannot know what *is not*." What *is not*—the

39 Furley, *Greek Cosmologists, I*, p. 119.

40 Ibid., pp. 119–20.

41 Mourelatos, "Nothing," p. 60.

42 Ibid., pp. 320–21; see also Moorhouse, "A Use of ΟΥΔΕΙΣ." It should be noted that although Mourelatos accepts many of Moorhouse's claims, he dissents from certain of his conclusions.

43 Furley, *Greek Cosmologists, I*, p. 120; emphasis in original.

44 Ibid., p. 122.

> void—is still only the negation of whatever properties belong to what *is*: it is without properties of its own.[45]

On Furley's account, then, void is not non-existent; but while it exists, it has no positive properties and can be known only indirectly, by negating the properties of what-is, the atoms. As the separator of atoms and that which makes motion possible, void turns out to be empty space and to be a nothing in the characterizing sense.

Furley is right to emphasize that the Atomists accepted Parmenides' arguments and to focus on the question of the nature of what-is-not at work in the atomist assertions that void is not-being or what-is-not and that being is no more than not-being. His application of the characterizing sense of nothing to void, thus focusing on a predicational rather than an existential sense of *einai* at work in the claim that void is what-is-not, is helpful. But there are difficulties in his further account of void. In claiming that void is to be characterized completely negatively—as "the negation of whatever properties belong to what is," Furley saddles the Atomists with exactly what he says they want to avoid: the claim that what-is-not is neither knowable nor sayable. For if void is just the negation of everything that being or what-is is, then we are immediately faced with the problem of how to know what is nothing at all. If no properties or nature can be attributed to void, it is difficult to grasp what it is about void that makes it knowable and sayable. Because it lacks a nature, it just is unknowable and unsayable.[46] The completely negative nature of void as Furley envisions it thus cannot be made consistent with Parmenides B2.7–8. Further, it is not clear that B7.1 ("never shall this prevail, that what-is-not is") is a version of the fundamental claim of Parmenides B2 (that what-is-not cannot be known, said, or thought) as Furley claims. For if the Atomists can legitimately claim that B2.7–8 is true while B7.1 is false, the latter cannot be a version of (or equivalent to) the former. And if B7.1 is a consequence of the claims of B2 (rather than a version of it), then it cannot be denied without denying the claims of B2.7–8. Furley claims that the Atomists "modified" the premise that what-is-not cannot be known or uttered, but he does not explain what these modifications are. On his view, it looks as though the Atomists rejected rather than modified the crucial Parmenidean claim. Thus, Furley's version of the Atomists' account of void is not satisfactory, although it improves on Barnes's view by stressing a predicational rather than an existential understanding of what-is-not in considering void, and avoiding a commitment to an ambiguity in *einai*.

[45] Ibid., p. 122; emphasis in original.

[46] One might think that void can be known, even though it has no character of its own. For one could simply negate the nature of atoms and thus grasp void. But this sort of "negative nature" and "negative knowledge" is ruled out by Parmenides' arguments in B8. See Section 3, below.

The analyses of Barnes and Furley suggest several points that are desirable in an account of void and of the *ou mallon* statements. First, Barnes is right in thinking that the *ou mallon* claim is probably the conclusion or summary of a longer argument that has been lost. Second, Furley is correct in emphasizing the Parmenidean basis of the Atomist claims, and in arguing that a predicational reading of what-is-not in an analysis of void is preferable to an existential understanding. Third, an interpretation of the argument that depends on attributing different senses of *einai* to atoms (being, what-is) and void (not-being, what-is-not) should, if possible, be avoided. Finally, some way must be found to make sense of the *ou mallon* claim itself, so that it becomes clear just how what-is and what-is-not are shown to be equivalent.

In the usual form of the *ou mallon* argument, what-is, or being (*to on, to den*) is said to be no more than what-is-not, or not-being (*to mē on, to mēden*).[47] There is an interpretive point to be gained from this formulation.[48] Parmenides and Melissus had given a number of reasons to think that what-is-not is not real at all; according to them, then, being is more than not-being. Leucippus and Democritus respond with the claim that, as a matter of fact, being is no more than not-being. There is an argument hidden in the claim. Suppose that Leucippus had said that "not-being is no more than being." This would be surprising, as no one had thought that not-being is at all, much less that it is more than being is. Given the Eleatic arguments about what-is, the point of phrasing the *ou mallon* claim as it appears in Plutarch's report becomes clear. The force of the claim is the following: Parmenides and his followers have shown what it is to be; according to them, what-is-not fails to meet the criteria for what-is, so what-is is more than what-is-not (for what-is-not is not at all); being is more than not-being. But the Atomists can respond by showing that what-is-not, too, meets the criteria for what-is. Thus being is no more than not-being, for whatever arguments we have for thinking that being is are equally reasons for thinking that not-being is as well.

The claim that what-is-not cannot be occurs in Parmenides B2. There the path of what-is-not is ruled out as a route for inquiry because it is "wholly inscrutable"; according to B2.7–8, "you could not know what-is-not (for it is not to be accomplished), nor could you point it out (οὔτε γὰρ ἂν γνοίης τό γε μὴ ἐόν [οὐ γὰρ ἀνυστόν], οὔτε φράσαις).[49] The characteristics of what-is, those that guarantee its reality, appear in the signs of B8.2–4. There Parmenides claims that the signs on the route that it is show that what-is

[47] Matson takes the claim that what-is is no more than what-is-not as a clue in his argument that the *ou mallon* argument is meant as a facetious response to Melissus. According to Matson, when it is put this way, the claim reduces what-is to the level of what-is-not.

[48] Barnes denies that there is any significance in the formulation. According to Barnes, "We need not delay over the order of the phrases in this quotation: '*a* exists no more than *b*' and '*b* exists no more than *a*' both mean no more than *a* and *b* alike exist; the relative order of *a* and *b* has at most a stylistic point" (*PP*, vol. II, p. 101).

[49] For a fuller discussion of these issues, see Chap. 1.

is "ungenerated and imperishable, whole, of a single kind, unshaking and complete" (ὡς ἀγένητον ἐὸν καὶ ἀνώλεθρόν ἐστιν, οὖλον μουνογενές τε καὶ ἀτρεμὲς ἠδὲ τέλειον[50]). Whatever meets the criteria adumbrated by these signs is a genuine entity; failing to satisfy them disqualifies a putative entity. Thus, while enumerating the characteristics of what-is, the signs also function as tests that anything that truly is must meet. On Parmenides' account, what-is-not, which can be neither said nor thought, must fail to meet the criteria. So, when Leucippus and Democritus insist that being is no more than not-being, they are not only echoing the Eleatic identification of void with what-is-not, but also recalling the Eleatic understanding of what it is for something to be. Thus, to justify their claim, they must argue that void—the empty, what they call not-being—can itself satisfy the Parmenidean signs and is both sayable and thinkable. Void must, on their view, qualify as a genuine entity. This would put it on the same footing with what-is and make it true that "being is no more than not-being."

That this may have been the Atomists' argument is suggested by Plutarch's report of Democritus's use of the *ou mallon* claim. Plutarch is responding to Colotes, who, according to Plutarch, has misunderstood Democritus's uses of the "no more" claims and has thus falsely accused Democritus of "throwing life into confusion" in the Protagorean manner. Plutarch not only accuses Colotes of misunderstanding Democritus; he also charges him with being insufficiently familiar with the texts. Plutarch's specific complaint is that Colotes has misread our fragment B156, and to prove his point, Plutarch both quotes and explains the relevant bit of text. Ironically, it is likely that Colotes had in mind not B156, but rather whatever text it was that later allowed Simplicius to make the report that has come to us as 67A8 = 68A38 = Luria 2: the shapes of atoms are no more like this than that. If this was actually something that Leucippus rather than Democritus said, it would account for Plutarch's difficulty in tracing the source of Colotes's claim. But it is lucky for us that Plutarch misinterpreted Colotes, for it means that B156 was preserved.[51]

> ... when [Democritus] lays it down that the thing is no more than the nothing (μὴ μᾶλλον τὸ δὲν ἢ τὸ μηδὲν εἶναι), by thing he means body and by nothing void, and that this too [void] has a sort of nature and existence of its own (ὡς καὶ τούτου φύσιν τινὰ καὶ ὑπόστασιν ἰδίαν ἔχοντος).
>
> (Plutarch, *Adv. Colot.* 4.1109A = 68B156 = Luria 7)

Plutarch explains that the strange word *den* that appears in the quotation refers to atoms, while by *mēden* Democritus meant "void." But he goes further, clarifying Democritus's point in saying μὴ μᾶλλον τὸ δὲν ἢ τὸ μηδὲν εἶναι.

50 On τέλειον see Chap. II, n. 15.

51 On Plutarch's replies to Colotes' objections to Democritus, see DeLacey, "Colotes' First Criticism."

According to Plutarch, Democritus meant that void had "some nature and existence of its own" (φύσιν τινὰ καὶ ὑπόστασιν ἰδίαν ἔχοντος). While it is clear that the explanation that follows the quotation from Democritus is Plutarch's own (*hypostasis* is a word Democritus is unlikely to have used,[52] but it is a natural way for Plutarch to summarize a Democritean claim that void is or is real), it is probable that he had available some text of Democritus that would justify his claim.[53] While it is useful to have Plutarch's account of the atomist uses of *to den* and *to mēden*, what is particularly striking about his comment is that he thought that Democritus attributed some nature (*physis*) to void.[54] But to claim that void has some nature of its own is to suggest that it indeed has some unchanging character and that we can know what it is. To have such a nature or character is what is needed to satisfy the criteria for what-is that are laid down in the signs and demonstrated in the arguments of Parmenides B8. By claiming or demonstrating a nature for void, the Atomists are responding to the Eleatic requirements for what-is, not simply by asserting the reality of what-is-not in the face of Eleatic arguments to the contrary, but by maintaining that what-is-not, in the form of void, qualifies as something that is, on the Eleatics' own grounds. Plutarch's comment provides some evidence that there was an atomist argument or claim, known to Plutarch, that would support the assertion that void, as what-is-not, indeed satisfied the criteria for what-is and so could legitimately be said to have "some nature and existence of its own."

The *ou mallon* argument, then, reported by both Aristotle (in Book I of the *Metaphysics*) and Plutarch (in the context for 68B156) provides evidence that the Atomists thought that void met the same criteria for what-is as the atoms did. Parmenides B2.7–8 insists that what-is is both sayable and knowable or thinkable. If the Atomists held that void satisfies the Parmenidean strictures about what-is, they would have to argue that void

52 It does not appear in the extant fragments. LSJ's first reported use of the term as meaning "substantial nature" is in Theophrastus, *CP* 5.16.4; they report an occurrence of it as meaning "substance" or "actual existence" in Socrates Scholasticus, *HE* 3.7; and as meaning "to have substantial existence" (*hypostasin echein*), LSJ give Demetrius Lacon, *Herc*. 1055.14.

53 McGibbon has pointed out the folly of Plutarch making assertions about Democritus if he could not substantiate them, especially because Plutarch has just castigated Colotes for attempting to understand statements taken out of context (McGibbon, "Atomists," p. 250).

54 Most modern scholars have found whatever interest they have in the fragment in Plutarch's identification of body (*sōma*) with *to den* and void (*to kenon*) with *to mēden*. As indicated above (n. 24), Guthrie quotes the fragment twice along with Plutarch's interpretation, but he does not comment on that interpretation. Barnes quotes Plutarch's explanation in the course of attributing two senses of "exist" to Democritus (*PP*, vol. II, pp. 100–101) but offers no comment on it. B156 is not quoted at all but appears only as a reference in a footnote in KRS, and Plutarch's further remark is omitted by McKirahan. Makin mentions Plutarch's report of B156 as an example of the atomist argument that void is real; he glosses the argument as "since atoms are what is and void is what is not, both atoms and void exist" (*Indifference*, p. 98); he quotes B156 but not Plutarch's comment (p. 123n.2). Algra (*Concepts of Space*) does not mention the passage at all.

can be said or thought. But that argument would turn on there being a stable nature of void, for it is such a nature that is said and thought when what-is is grasped or uttered.

3. Knowing Void

If the Atomists are to make good their claim that what-is is no more than what-is-not, they must show that what-is-not—void—is something that can be known, thus satisfying the requirements of Parmenides B2 and B3. Furley, it will be recalled, suggested that the Atomists "modified" the claim, presumably to allow for knowledge of void. But what is the sort of knowing that Furley has in mind here? He proposes that when Leucippus and Democritus identify void with not-being or with nothing, they mean that it is something that has no properties of its own: it is simply the negation of all properties of what-is.[55] This means that knowledge of void must be what might be called "negative knowledge"; void is known by first knowing atoms and then negating all their properties. But this is not a modification of Parmenides B2.7–8 and B3; it is a rejection of them. The arguments of Parmenides are aimed against just such negative predications—those that attempt to give the nature of a thing in negative terms, either directly (as here) or indirectly. In fragments B6 and B7, Parmenides catalogues the woes of those who try to know that which is not (or negative natures) by attempting to take a negative path of inquiry. Genuine knowing is grasping the positive, complete, whole, unchanging, and perfect nature or reality of a thing (just as the signs of B8 indicate), and those who confuse what-is and what-is-not, or try to know what-is-not in the sense of knowing a thing by knowing what it is not, are on a path of inquiry that cannot be completed. One can claim to know a thing just in case one can state or express or identify just what something is, that is, just in case one can express its nature.[56] It is a consequence of this view that attempting to understand something that is merely the negation of what-is is a futile task. Unless there is a genuine and positive nature of void, it simply cannot be known.

[55] Furley, *Greek Cosmologists, I*, p. 122.

[56] See Chap. I, where I argued that this account of knowing is common in Presocratic philosophy. It is to be found in Heraclitus, whose fragment B1 announces that Heraclitus will be "distinguishing each thing according to its nature and saying how it is" (κατὰ φύσιν διαιρέων ἕκαστον καὶ φράζων ὅκως ἔχει). Parmenides argues that anything that constitutes the nature of a thing must meet certain criteria so that it can indeed be known. This notion of the knowable nature of a thing is also found in post-Parmenidean thought, underlying Philolaus's claim that all the things that are known have number. Number makes it possible to grasp and understand the nature of a thing; as Philolaus says, "all things that are known have number. For, without this, nothing whatever could possibly be thought or known" (44B4). Further, this notion of knowing as grasping the reality of a thing continues into Plato, who identifies knowing *F* with knowing what it is to be *F*.

A "modification" in this sense of the epistemological side of Parmenides' arguments cannot succeed.

Yet the Atomists apparently claim that void is knowable. Evidence for this comes from a series of fragments quoted by Sextus Empiricus:

> Δημόκριτος δὲ ὁτὲ μὲν ἀναιρεῖ τὰ φαινόμενα ταῖς αἰσθήσεσι, καὶ τούτων λέγει μηδὲν φαίνεσθαι κατ' ἀλήθειαν ἀλλὰ μόνον κατὰ δόξαν, ἀληθὲς δὲ ἐν τοῖς οὖσιν ὑπάρχειν τὸ ἀτόμους εἶναι καὶ κενόν· "νόμῳ" γάρ φησι "γλυκὺ καὶ νόμῳ πικρόν, νόμῳ θερμόν, νόμῳ ψυχρόν, νόμῳ χροιή· ἐτεῇ δὲ ἄτομα καὶ κενόν." (ὅπερ ⟨ἔστι⟩· νομίζεται μὲν εἶναι καὶ δοξάζεται τὰ αἰσθητά, οὐκ ἔστι δὲ κατ' ἀλήθειαν ταῦτα, ἀλλὰ τὰ ἄτομα μόνον καὶ τὸ κενόν.) ... καὶ πάλιν φησίν "ἐτεῇ μέν νυν ὅτι οἷον ἕκαστον ἔστιν ⟨ἢ⟩ οὐκ ἔστιν οὐ συνίεμεν, πολλαχῇ δεδήλωται." ἐν δὲ τῷ περὶ ἰδεῶν "γιγνώσκειν τε χρή" φησίν, "ἄνθρωπον τῷδε τῷ κανόνι ὅτι ἐτεῆς ἀπήλλακται." ... ἐν δὲ τοῖς κανόσι δύο φησὶν εἶναι γνώσεις, τὴν μὲν διὰ τῶν αἰσθήσεων τὴν δὲ διὰ τῆς διανοίας, ὧν τὴν μὲν διὰ τῆς διανοίας γνησίην καλεῖ, προσμαρτυρῶν αὐτῇ τὸ πιστὸν εἰς ἀληθείας κρίσιν, τὴν δὲ διὰ τῶν αἰσθήσεων σκοτίην ὀνομάζει, ἀφαιρούμενος αὐτῆς τὸ πρὸς διάγνωσιν τοῦ ἀληθοῦς ἀπλανές. λέγει δὲ κατὰ λέξιν "γνώμης δὲ δύο εἰσὶν ἰδέαι, ἡ μὲν γνησίη, ἡ δὲ σκοτίη· καὶ σκοτίης μὲν τάδε σύμπαντα, ὄψις ἀκοὴ ὀδμὴ γεῦσις ψαῦσις· ἡ δὲ γνησίη, ἀποκεκριμένη δὲ ταύτης." εἶτα προκρίνων τῆς σκοτίης τὴν γνησίην ἐπιφέρει λέγων· "ὅταν ἡ σκοτίη μηκέτι δύνηται μήτε ὁρῆν ἐπ' ἔλαττον μήτε ἀκούειν μήτε ὀδμᾶσθαι μήτε γεύεσθαι μήτε ἐν τῇ ψαύσει αἰσθάνεσθαι, ἀλλ' ἐπὶ λεπτότερον ⟨...⟩."[57]
>
> (Sextus Empiricus, *M.* VII 135–39)

Democritus sometimes does away with the things appearing to the senses and says of them that none appears in accordance with truth but only in accordance with opinion, truth among the things that are being that there are atoms and the void. For he says, "By convention sweet and by convention bitter, by convention hot, by convention cold, by convention color: in reality atoms and void" [68B125 = B9 = Luria 55]. That is to say, the perceptibles are thought and believed to be, but these things do not exist in truth, but only atoms and void do.... And again he says, "Now, that in reality we do not understand how each thing is or is not has been shown in many ways" [68B10 = Luria 55]. And in *On Ideas* he says, "it is necessary that a person know by this rule that he is separated from reality" [68B6 = Luria 48].... But in the *Rules* he says that there are two kinds of knowing, one through the senses and the other through the understanding. The one through the understanding he calls genuine, witnessing to its trustworthiness in deciding truth; the one through the senses he names bastard, denying it steadfastness in the discernment of what is true. He says in these words, "There are two forms of knowing, one genuine and the other bastard. To the bastard belong all these: sight, hearing, smell, taste, touch. The other, the genuine, has been separated from this" [68B11 = Luria 83]. Then preferring the genuine to the bastard, he

[57] Text as in the (Teubner) Mutschmann and Mau edition of Sextus, rather than DK.

continues, saying, "Whenever the bastard is no longer able to see more finely nor hear nor smell nor taste nor perceive by touch, but something finer..." [68B11 = Luria 83].

The context for Sextus's quotations from Democritus helps to make clear the problem that concerns Democritus. He marks a distinction between what is genuine or real (atoms and void) and what appears to us or is reported by the senses. What appears to the senses seems to be the case but actually is only "by convention." The distinction between what is genuinely true and what is reported and accepted by the senses can be found throughout Presocratic thought, from Anaximenes' claim that the first principle of everything is air (13B1, B2) and its corollary that what appears to the senses to be different sorts of objects is really just air that has been altered by being condensed or rarefied, through Parmenides' own distinction between truth and the opinions of mortals, down to Empedocles' claim that the roots earth, water, air, and fire are genuine beings that "become" other things by running through each other, a process that humans class as "coming-to-be," but which Empedocles insists is not itself real (although he will follow convention in using the terms "coming-to-be" and "passing-away": see 31B8, B9, B11, B12). Democritus is quite clear that atoms and void constitute reality (*eteē*) while everything else is merely the result of the commingling of atoms with one another.[58] We cannot know phenomena because they have no nature as such to be known. We are removed from reality (68B6) because we cannot have direct access to atoms and void. All that we learn through the senses is suspect because the objects reported to us by the senses are literally not real but only conventional. Although we may believe we have knowledge gained through sense experience, that knowledge is not genuine, but bastard, not connected in the proper way with what is real and so not trustworthy.[59] In contrast, understanding (*dianoia* is Sextus's term; we do not know if it was Democritus's) connects with what is real; properly grounded in what is real, it is thus genuine and legitimate. It is understanding that allows us to claim correctly that there are atoms and void. When the senses fail us, because of the smallness and fineness of what is to be perceived, a finer cognitive state (understanding or reason) takes over and corrects the claims of the senses to have genuine knowledge.[60] A similar account of the role of understanding or reason may be found in other Presocratics as well. It is to be found, for

[58] Plutarch's report of the *nomōs/eteē* distinction also includes the claim that combination is by convention. See Wardy, "Eleatic," pp. 139–40.

[59] The connection between what is known and what is real gives genuine knowledge its legitimacy. It is precisely this lack of connection with the genuine that makes the other form of *gnōmē* "bastard."

[60] Democritus's epistemology is a highly controversial topic. See Weiss, "Democritus' Theory" for a non-sceptical interpretation of Democritus. For a rejection of Weiss's account and the claim that Democritus embraced a scepticism similar to that of Sextus, see Asmis,

instance, in Heraclitus's claim that grasping the *logos* is a requirement for genuine understanding, and it is certainly present in Parmenides.

All of this suggests that atoms and void are available to thought or understanding, even if they cannot be grasped by the senses. Just as we can know that there are atoms, and what their character is, so we must also know that void is, and thus its character or nature. As one of the basic realities of the atomist system, void must be knowable in the same way that atoms are; if so, Leucippus and Democritus would be able to claim that the requirements of Parmenides B2 and B3 are satisfied. But important questions remain so far unanswered: just what is the nature of void? How are atoms and void known?

Determining how void is known will aid in understanding the nature of void. The standard view of the development of atomism is that it came in response to Melissus's arguments against motion. That view has been separately challenged by both Barnes and Solmsen.[61] They propose (and I accept their arguments) that the first motivation for the atomist theory was a response to Zeno's dichotomy arguments by positing something that could no longer be cut or broken and so divided. This uncuttable, indivisible thing is the atom.[62] But if there is to be more than one atom, the atoms must be separated from one another, and this is a job done by void. Another job for

---

Epicurus' Methodology, pp. 337–48. Makin (*Indifference*, chap. 3, pp. 65–84) discusses the role of indifference arguments in Democritus's epistemology and argues for a moderately sceptical interpretation of Democritus's views. Taylor, in "Pleasure," argues for a moderate interpretation of Democritus's epistemology but believes that the theory is finally contradictory, both relying on and rejecting the evidence of the senses. For a discussion of the nature of soul and *nous* in Democritus, see Couloubaritsis, "Considérations."

61 Barnes, *PP*, vol. II, pp. 40–75; Solmsen, "Abdera's Arguments"; see also Klowski, "Antwortete Leukipp." Even if Solmsen and Barnes are wrong, and Melissus is prior to the Atomists, it still seems likely that the fundamental impetus for atomism was Zeno's arguments against divisibility.

62 A similar argument about Democritus's arguments for atoms is to be found in Makin, "Indivisibility" and *Indifference*. In *Indifference*, Makin posits two possible Democrituses: Democritus the philosopher and Democritus the scientist (pp. 9–14). The philosophical Democritus is not primarily concerned to formulate a theory of nature in response to Eleatic arguments (that is the business of the scientific Democritus); rather his interest is in exploring the nature and consequences of indifference arguments as used by Zeno. That the atoms and void that result from such exploration can serve as the basis of a theory of nature is a happy but serendipitous consequence of the philosophical Democritus's concerns. Makin seems to think that positing a primarily scientific Democritus saddles Democritus with views that are incomplete or inconsistent (particularly having to do with the status of compound objects), whereas this problem is mostly avoided by positing a philosophical Democritus motivated primarily by concern with Zenonian indifference arguments. Thus, according to Makin, it is more charitable to posit a philosophical Democritus and note that the theory "is going to be flawed in some respect" (*Indifference*, pp. 13–14). In contrast, Sinnige argues that the primary influence on Democritus was Ionian nature theory as reinterpreted by Anaxagoras. Sinnige asserts that the view that the atomic theory was based in Zeno's arguments about divisibility is "an Aristotelian corruption" (*Matter and Infinity*, p. 153), although he offers little evidence

void is to allow for motion and change in general; Zeno had, of course, argued against motion as well, although the arguments that specifically link motion and void occur in Melissus B7. If the Atomists are responding to Zeno, their arguments for atoms are not based on experience ("there are uncuttable things, so there must be atoms") but are instead based on a conception of what an entity that is truly indivisible must be. In the same way the argument for void is not based on experience ("there is motion, so there must be void"); such an argument would beg the question against Zeno who argues, in the face of experience, that motion is not possible.[63] Rather it, too, seems to be *a priori*. This might mean that the theoretical need for something (void) to separate and distinguish atoms from one another might precede the need for something that, it turns out, allows motion.[64] It is an agreeable aspect of the economy of the atomic theory that void performs both tasks, but on the analysis presented here, void as separator of atoms is primary in the theory.[65] Void as a space-occupier, albeit the emptiness in space, as suggested by Sedley, fits this description well. Sedley's interpretation of void turns on his analyses of Melissus's rejection of void in B7 and of Aristotle's identification of void with empty space. Sedley argues that Melissus conceives of void as something mixed in things rather than empty space: because Melissus has demonstrated that what-is has no boundaries, he would have no concern with empty space around what-is; rather he denies that what-is has any void mixed in with it, which would allow it to give way (*hypochōrein*). This interpretation is consistent with the view that void is what allows things to be divided. Sedley notes that Aristotle, in his *Physics* IV discussions of void, attributes to the proponents of void the view that it is unoccupied space or place, naming Democritus as a holder of this view in the fragment *On Democritus*. But Aristotle also attributes to the Atomists the claim that void is what-is-not, and in the historical account in *Metaphysics* I.4 985b4–10, he claims that the full and the empty or rare are elements, "material cause of the things that are" for Leucippus and Democritus. This suggests that in the treatment of void in *Physics* IV and *On Democritus* the identification of void with place is a polemical move in an argument against void rather than an accurate account of what Leucippus and Democritus actually claimed void

---

for this position. Sinnige claims that Democritus's interests were in physics and mathematics rather than in metaphysics (p. 164; on p. 155 he claims that "Democritus' theory was physics not mathematics"). I see no reason to insist on classifying Democritus as being primarily either a philosopher or a scientist. Such a distinction between philosophy and science makes little sense in Presocratic thought, and I think that the difficulties that Makin sees can be avoided.

63 See also Melissus's arguments in B7 against void and thus against motion.

64 Anaxagoras and Empedocles apparently did not see the need for such a separator. On their theories, the various genuine entities are distinguished from one another by their differing characters.

65 This would suggest that void is not primarily considered as empty space in which there are atoms. See n. 66, below.

to be.[66] Sedley's account of void allows it to be treated as an element or principle (*archē*) in the Atomist system, and this understanding of void is

[66] See Sedley, "Two Conceptions," pp. 175–76; 177–79. A similar evaluation of Aristotle's testimony about void and space or place is to be found in Inwood, "Epicurus' Concept" (see also Solmsen, *Aristotle's System,* pp. 140–42). The Sedley-Inwood analysis of Aristotle is rejected by Algra, who also rejects Sedley's account of Democritean void as emptiness in space. Algra assumes that Melissus is prior to both Leucippus and Democritus and attributes to Melissus the view that "not-being takes the guise of empty *extension*, i.e., of the void (p. 42). He then interprets Melissus's argument (in B7) that there is no motion because there is no void this way: if there were void, what-is would move into it. Thus, he says, "it is obvious that *to kenon* here stands for empty *space* or an empty *place* (p. 42). Algra does not respond to Sedley's argument that *hypochōrein* is not a "simple verb of locomotion" (Sedley, p. 178). Algra translates it as "move" while Sedley chooses "retreat." Algra's translation thus prejudges the issue of what Melissus is actually arguing against, making it natural that Algra would see void as "an external void into which what exists would transport itself" (Sedley, p. 178). Algra supports his argument against Sedley by claiming that "at any rate Melissus speaks of 'moving *into* the void' and the essential point seems to be that in order to make it possible for Being to move, there must be some place for Being to move *into*" (p. 43n.36). But Sedley's point is to argue against such an interpretation of void, and Algra's assertion that the interpretation is correct is not a refutation of Sedley's arguments for his own view. Algra admits that the arguments against dense and rare in B7 require a notion of void of the sort that Sedley defends (p. 43), but that would mean that Melissus would have to have two notions of void in mind in the course of eight or nine lines (in DK) of argument. Algra distinguishes three possible conceptions of void and claims that "a number of philosophers used two (or even all three) of these kinds of *kenon promiscue*" (p. 40). Algra does not discuss the roles that void plays in separating atoms and in the arguments for atomic indivisibility, but only its role in motion. This omission makes it easier to suppose that void must be equated with empty place or space or even with space itself. Algra also attacks Sedley's account of Aristotle on early conceptions of void. He claims that when Aristotle identifies void with place in *Physics* IV he could have had no one in mind other than the Atomists, and so the Atomists must have thought void was empty space. But he does not consider that Aristotle may have been attacking Plato's views in the *Timaeus* as well as the Atomists' conception of void. But in his account on pp. 111–13, where he discusses Aristotle's treatment of void in *Physics* IV, Algra argues that Aristotle, treating void as space, must have had the receptable of the *Timaeus* in mind; these are the same passages that Algra had earlier asserted must be concerned with the Atomists' conception of void. Algra here grants that Aristotle probably ran together several notions of void in the course of his discussion. Moreover, the passage in *On Democritus* that Algra quotes in defense of his view does not actually support that view. Aristotle claims that "[Democritus] assumes that underlying these [atoms], there is another thing, place/space (*topos*) which is infinite in extent. And he calls place/space by the following names 'void,' 'nothing,' and 'infinite' " (Algra's translation of 68A37 = Luria 172). But there is nothing in this passage that rules out the possibility that Aristotle means that what Democritus calls void etc., Aristotle himself would call space or place. Aristotle often expresses himself this way. Algra claims that Aristotle need not have made such a move because he had plenty of ammunition against the arguments for void; but he admits that the arguments that are "new" (not directed against place?) are "primarily directed against the conception of an 'internal void' or void as what Sedley called a 'space filler' " (p. 49). But this concedes the point to Sedley. Algra claims that there is "a brief but . . . adequate refutation of Sedley's argument" in Furley, *Greek Cosmologists I*, p. 112n.10. Furley there asserts that *hypochōrein* "is a species of movement after all. The essential point is Melissus' claim that there must be some place where there is no being, if there is to be the possibility of local change in being." First, this simply asserts a claim against which Sedley argues. Second, Melissus's claim is actually that

just what is needed to characterize void as something with "a nature (*physis*) and existence of its own," as Plutarch claimed.[67] Suppose the Atomists to have equated genuine reality with occupying space. Then, as the full and the empty in space, both atoms and void satisfy this criterion. Both are thus equally real, for both occupy space, although their natures differ: to be an atom is to be a full and indivisible occupier of space, to be void is to be that emptiness in space that separates atoms. The reality of void may be compared to the reality of Love and Strife in Empedocles. Love and Strife are genuine entities, on the same ontological level with the four roots, yet they differ importantly from the roots. They are forces under whose control the various parts of the cosmic cycle occur, and under whose aegis the mixing and separating of the roots takes place. While void does not play such a cosmic role in atomist thought, the reality of Love and Strife serves as a precedent: for they are genuine realities yet do not function like the other material entities, the roots.[68] The nature of Love is to bring together unlikes while separating likes; Strife separates unlikes and brings together likes. Each thus has a whole, complete, single, and unchanging nature. Similarly, for the Atomists, void is that emptiness that occupies space between atoms. So, the full is no more real than the empty, as Leucippus and Democritus might say.[69]

But, as far as we know, neither Leucippus nor Democritus claimed that the full is no more than the empty (although Aristotle's report in *Metaphysics* I.4 gives a version of the "no more" claim involving body and void). Rather, what is attributed to them are the claims that being is no more

---

there must be something that is empty if there is to be such local change, and that what is empty is nothing. The issue is what is meant by "empty" and whether the "local change" to which Furley refers must be interpreted as locomotion into empty space, which is what he seems to mean by "a species of motion." Finally, Furley suggests that Sedley can give no account of the difference between space and an occupier of space that is not a body. Sedley suggests that given the particular problems that concerned the Atomists, they simply did not give such an analysis: "questions about the status of place, as also that of time, are higher-order metaphysical questions" that worried the Atomists as little as they seemed to have disturbed Anaxagoras and Empedocles (Sedley, "Two Conceptions," p. 180).

67 Sedley's comment is apt: ". . . anyone equating void with one of these elements should be predisposed to treat it as a movable entity capable of occupying whatever places are occupied by the compound objects of which it is part" (Sedley, "Two Conceptions," p. 177). Sedley claims that void is a "negative substance," a characterization that I would not endorse.

68 Even if Love and Strife are not corporeal in the same manner as the roots, Empedocles seems to think they occupy space, given his comments about the placement of Love and Strife in the center and on the edge of the Sphere (see B35). Void receives a similar treatment in Philolaus: as one of the unlimiteds, void is a real thing, on which limits are set by limiters. See Huffman, *Philolaus*, esp. pp. 43–44. In Philolaus, void also serves as a separator (see Huffman, p. 213).

69 Dumont suggests a more active role for void, claiming that void is both the necessary and the sufficient cause as well as an efficient cause of motion in early Atomism ("Les Abdéritains," p. 46 *et passim*). But his arguments for this claim are, I think, finally unsuccessful.

than not-being and that the thing is no more than the nothing. How is it that void, emptiness in space, comes to be called not-being and nothing? One fundamental difference between atoms and void is the role each plays in what passes (among human beings) for coming-to-be and passing-away. As we know, Democritus claimed that these are not real but are merely the phenomenal result of the motions of atoms. This aspect of Atomism is well attested in Aristotle, Theophrastus, Simplicius, and Plutarch. But it is the rearrangement of atoms themselves that accounts for what is called generation and destruction, and it is the shapes and positions of atoms that account for the features of compound objects. Void has no genuine role to play here, and there is no evidence that the Atomists thought that there could be coming-to-be or passing-away from, or on account of, void. But that from which nothing comes to be is itself nothing. So here is a sense in which void or the empty can be said to be nothing. But because it is an occupier of space and is what it is that separates atoms, this nothing is real, indeed just as real as body or what-is—the atoms.

There are two possible objections to this account. First, it might be suggested that void indeed has a role in phenomenal things, insofar as the amount of void is responsible for the rarity and density of that thing and thus for certain of its qualities. An example of void's role here can be found in Theophrastus's report of the Atomist account of the difference between iron and lead.[70] According to Theophrastus iron is harder than lead but lighter; harder because its atoms are arranged unevenly, lighter because it contains more void than lead. Lead, on the other hand, has less void than iron, but the even arrangement of the atoms makes lead easier to cut or bend. While it is true that the amount of void in a thing determines its density or rarity, what determines whether what we have is lead or iron is the arrangement of atoms themselves, and the shapes of those atoms.[71] It is atoms that take the leading role, for without the atoms there would be no lead or iron at all. Void may play a secondary explanatory role in accounting for certain characteristics of phenomenal things, but in generation it is a passive partner, responsible by itself for nothing. Adding or subtracting void from the compound to change it would seem to make no sense, while adding or rearranging atoms would result in a change in the object. Second, it might seem strange that what accounts for the claim that void is nothing is its role (or non-role) in coming-to-be. If the concern is to account for the permanent nature of a genuine entity, generation and destruction should not be considered at all. Stable characters or natures belong to the realm of what-is rather than to the realm of becoming, and to look to the latter to explain the former seems a serious blunder. This objection misunderstands the point of the reference to void's role in coming-to-be. That role has nothing to do with understanding the

[70] *Sens.* 62 = part of 68A135 = Luria 369.

[71] See Mourelatos, "Δημόκριτος."

nature of void, which is determined by looking at what void itself is, rather than any role it plays in accounting for the world reported to us by our senses. It is only in seeking to understand why Leucippus and Democritus call void "not-being" or "nothing" rather than, say, "the divisible" that generation is considered at all. The determination of the natures of atoms and void, and thus their right to be said to be genuine entities in the atomist theory does not depend on considerations of coming-to-be or passing-away. Thus the Atomists can claim that void is nothing, while claiming at the same time that it is, that what-is is no more than what-is-not.

There is, then, in the claims of Leucippus and Democritus, just as in the Pluralist theories of Anaxagoras and Empedocles, an answer to Eleatic arguments and an attempt to work within an Eleatic framework, rather than a mere retort. But the Atomists remain vulnerable to Eleatic attack, because their theory requires that what-is (the atoms) can be rearranged. Without some commitment to the arrangement and rearrangement of atoms and void, the Atomists cannot account for the world that is reported to us by our senses, for it is the rearrangement of atoms that explains or accounts for what passes for coming-to-be and passing-away in the sensible world. But this whole system is called into question by the arguments of Melissus.

4. Melissus on the One

Melissus criticizes the metaphysical assumptions that underlie Pluralist theories, attacking both the Pluralism of Anaxagoras and Empedocles and the Atomism of Leucippus and Democritus.[72] Melissus argues that what-is must be numerically one and unlimited; his arguments, if successful, undermine central theses of these views. Moreover, it is a fundamental feature of both Pluralism and Atomism that while there is no genuine coming-to-be or passing-away, there can be rearrangement, either through the mixture and separation of the things that are (the *chrēmata* in Anaxagoras or the roots in Empedocles) or through the combination and separation of atoms. The rejection of generation is based, as we have seen, on Parmenidean arguments

[72] As noted both in the Introduction and earlier in this chapter, placing Melissus correctly in the chronological order is difficult. Because the only reliable date we have for Melissus is the Samian defeat of the Athenian navy in 441, we have no way of knowing whether his work pre- or post-dates that of Leucippus and Democritus. (It is most likely that they overlapped one another.) By placing Melissus last in this chapter, I do not intend to beg any questions about chronology. Commentators are divided on whether Melissus's arguments are aimed at Atomism or instead served as a motivation for the atomist theory. If Melissus comes after the Atomists, his assertion that void is nothing and therefore cannot be, begs the question against them, at least on the interpretation that I argue for in this chapter. But if Melissus predates the Atomists, they, while having an argument about void, do not seem to have addressed directly Melissus's argument against rearrangement, although Wardy argues that they responded directly to Melissus on this problem.

for the unchanging nature of what-is, and the natures of the basic entities are reflections of Parmenidean arguments about the nature of what-is. The Pluralists and the Atomists assume that temporary arrangements brought about by the combination and separation of ontologically basic entities are acceptable because they do not involve any change in the natures of these entities. The *chrēmata* and the roots remain just what they are throughout the processes of mixture and separation and so cannot themselves be said to be subject to coming-to-be or passing-away. Melissus will argue that this sort of rearrangement is metaphysically objectionable, and that no theory that attempts to explain the changing world reported by sense experience through an appeal to unchanging entities can be successful. So Melissus's arguments attack the metaphysical foundations of Pluralism and Atomism, as well as the mechanism by which the basic entities of those theories account for the world reported by sense experience.

Melissus's account of what-is differs from Parmenides' in two important ways. First, Melissus argues that what-is must be unlimited, as opposed to Parmenides' claim that what-is is limited, "held within the limits of mighty bounds" (28B8.26, see also B8.30–31). Second, Melissus claims that what-is is numerically one; indeed he calls what-is "The One" (B8).[73] Both of these deviations from Parmenides' view follow from Melissus's commitment to the predicational unity of what-is, for his arguments show that he thought that only by being numerically one can what-is remain predicationally one. A claim reported in *De Melisso Xenophane Gorgia* suggests that Melissus follows both Parmenides and Zeno in arguing for the predicational unity of what-is.

> ἓν δὲ ὂν ὅμοιον εἶναι πάντη· εἰ γὰρ ἀνόμοιον, πλείω ὄντα οὐκ ἂν ἔτι ἓν εἶναι, ἀλλὰ πολλά. (MXG 974a12–14 = 30A5)
>
> Being one, it is entirely alike; for if it were unlike, being several, it would no longer be one but many.

The implication here is clear: the likeness and unlikeness in question is similarity and difference of properties or of character.[74] The "several" rules out any other predicates: something with more than a single predicate will

[73] According to Aristotle, Parmenides claimed that what-is is one in *logos*, while Melissus claimed that it is one in matter, and Aristotle links the claim with Melissus's argument that what-is is unlimited (*Metaph.* 986b18–21). I shall argue that Melissus maintains that what-is can be one in *logos* (that is, predicationally one) only if it is unlimited and thus one in number. Melissus's commitment to numerical monism is remarked on by Schofield in KRS (p. 395): "When Plato and Aristotle represent monism as the principal thesis of the Eleatics . . . , they must be reading Parmenides through Melissan spectacles." This is exactly right.

[74] Barnes (*PP*, vol. I, p. 208) understands *homoion* as "qualitatively similar," arguing that this is implied by the lines that follow. Like Barnes, I accept the *MXG* as Melissan, without claiming that it gives us more than a paraphrase of Melissus's actual arguments. See also Mansfeld, " 'De Melisso.' "

turn out to be unlike (insofar as it has predicates *F* and *G*, and *F* is not identical to *G*) and thus many (because it is both *F* and *G*), in exactly the sense ruled out by Parmenides' arguments in B8.[75] So what-is must be predicationally one. This same type of monism appears in the opening lines of B7. There the claim is that any change in what-is from being all alike will result in its no longer being one. Melissus begins B7 by listing the characteristics of what-is: "it is eternal and unlimited and one and all alike" (ἀίδιόν ἐστι καὶ ἄπειρον καὶ ἓν καὶ ὅμοιον πᾶν). That what-is must be all alike is a requirement taken over from Parmenides; what is unfamiliar is the claim that it is eternal and unlimited, and the associated claim that what-is is numerically one. In the proofs of B8, Parmenides had insisted that what-is has limits, is bounded, and is held in mighty bonds.[76] In Parmenides' arguments, the images of limits and bonds serve to underscore the completeness and stability of what-is; as bound and fettered it cannot gain or lose anything essential to what it is, nor can it be subject to those internal shifts that would be possible if its nature were dual or plural. In Melissus the notion of the unlimited plays a similar role. The arguments that what-is is *apeiron* prevent internal change and affirm the strict single-natured character of what-is.[77] Melissus clearly supposes that having a limit would undermine the strict internal unity of what-is. It is seemingly paradoxical that opposite notions should serve the same purposes in the theories of Parmenides and Melissus. The solution to the paradox lies in Melissus's treatment of the unlimited.

Arguing in B2 that what-is has no beginning and no end, Melissus concludes that it has no temporal limits and is thus both eternal and unlimited.[78] The argument against an end for what-is is curious. Melissus begins by showing that what-is has no beginning. If there were some time at which it began to be, it would have had to come into being from what-is-not. This is impossible (the argument for this is in B1); so there is no beginning for what-is. If it had a beginning, there would also be a time at which it completes its process of *genesis*, and so there would be an end to its coming-to-be. This is the odd step in the argument. One expects Melissus to say that what-is has no end because it would then become what-is-not. But there is no argument against passing-away in the extant fragments (B7 claims that what-is will not perish because

[75] This is consistent with Plato's characterization of Zeno's argument at *Prm.* 127e1–4. It should be kept in mind that the "is" at work in Melissus's argument is the same as that which also appears in Parmenides. It is a predicational *esti* that reveals just what a thing is and thus identifies its nature.

[76] Parmenides B8.42: what-is is complete because there is an outermost limit; B8.26: it is immovable in the bounds of great bonds; B8.30–31: Necessity holds what-is in the limits of a bond; B8.49: what-is lies within the limits; B8.14–15: it is held in mighty fetters.

[77] Unlike Parmenides, Melissus does not explicitly claim that what-is is "of a single kind" (*mounogenes* Parmenides B8.4). But his claim that what-is is "all alike" (30B7) comes to the same thing.

[78] B4 claims that a thing having a beginning and end can be neither eternal nor unlimited.

it would then no longer be one; but there is no argument for this assertion). In a paraphrase of Melissus's arguments (the entire paraphrase occurs at *in Ph.* 103.13–104.15; the relevant lines are 103.20–21), Simplicius reports an argument that what-is cannot be destroyed (οὔτε φθαρήσεται τὸ ὄν) because it cannot change into what-is-not (οὔτε γὰρ εἰς τὸ μὴ ὂν οἷόν τε τὸ ὂν μεταβάλλειν); but Simplicius does not provide a supporting quotation from Melissus, and there is no such argument in the surviving fragments. Having claimed that what-is has no beginning and no end (in the sense of an end of its coming-to-be), Melissus claims that it is unlimited. Then, in B3 he expands the notion to include not only temporal but also spatial unlimitedness: "but just as it always is, in this way too it is necessary that it is always unlimited in magnitude" (ἀλλ' ὥσπερ ἔστιν ἀεί, οὕτω καὶ τὸ μέγεθος ἄπειρον ἀεὶ χρὴ εἶναι).[79] In B6 Melissus connects unlimitedness and numerical unity: "if it were unlimited, it would be one; for if it were two, the two could not be unlimited but would have limits against each other" (εἰ γὰρ ⟨ἄπειρον⟩ εἴη, ἓν εἴη ἄν· εἰ γὰρ δύο εἴη, οὐκ ἂν δύναιτο ἄπειρα εἶναι, ἀλλ' ἔχοι ἂν πείρατα πρὸς ἄλληλα[80]). Starting from the same premise, "is or is not," Parmenides and Melissus arrive at different conceptions of what-is. Parmenides uses the denial of what-is-not to show that what-is must be unchanging and limited, yet the limits he imposes on what-is guarantee only the internal monogeneity of what-is and do not place restrictions on the number of entities that may possess this monogeneity. In contrast, Melissus argues that the rejection of coming-to-be entails that what-is is unlimited and thus numerically one.[81]

Thus, in B7 Melissus can summarize his argument so far: "In this way, then, it is eternal, and unlimited, and one, and all alike" (οὕτως οὖν ἀίδιόν ἐστι καὶ ἄπειρον καὶ ἓν καὶ ὅμοιον πᾶν).[82] As B7 continues, Melissus goes on to claim that what-is "does not perish, nor become larger, nor is it rearranged, nor does it suffer pain or anguish" (καὶ οὔτ' ἂν ἀπόλοιτο οὔτε μεῖζον γίνοιτο οὔτε μετακοσμέοιτο οὔτε ἀλγεῖ οὔτε ἀνιᾶται).[83] He argues that if any of this were true of what-is, "it would no longer be one" (εἰ γάρ τι

79 On this argument see Ross, *Physics*, pp. 470–73; Verdenius, "Notes," pp. 8–10; and Reale, *Melisso*, pp. 66–104.

80 On the text of B6, see Reale, *Melisso*, pp. 380–82.

81 I took a different view of the structure of these arguments in "Zeno and Melissus," p. 12, arguing there that numerical monism is logically prior to the notion of being unlimited in Melissus. I now think that his numerical monism is a consequence of his commitment to the unlimited character of what-is. The denial of void is also connected with numerical monism, for if what-is has extension (even though it has no thickness, as B9 asserts) and if there is no void to act as a separator for what-is, and all of what-is is alike in character, then there can exist only one such thing.

82 Melissus's claim that what-is is eternal is also an addition to the claims that Parmenides had made. See the discussion in Chap. II, n. 38.

83 The denial of pain and anguish to what-is has troubled commentators. See, for instance, Loenen, *Parmenides*, pp. 157 and 160–61. Guthrie makes a valiant effort to explain the claim by treating it "as a timely reminder that in the normal belief of early Greek thought the ultimately

τούτων πάσχοι, οὐκ ἂν ἔτι ἓν εἴη), because "if it alters, it is necessary that what-is would no longer be alike" (εἰ γὰρ ἑτεροιοῦται, ἀνάγκη τὸ ἐὸν μὴ ὁμοῖον εἶναι). Thus Melissus sees a strong connection between ceasing to be alike and ceasing to be one; the former is offered as the reason for the latter. Ceasing to be alike, what-is would have changed its character and would no longer be just what it is; it would have become unlike itself and would no longer be one in character. Here Melissus follows Parmenides' claim that what-is must be of a single kind and cohesive (*mounogenes* and *suneches* Parmenides B8.4–6) and is arguing for predicational and not numerical monism; predicational pluralism would allow what-is to be predicationally many and so not all alike.[84] But the claim that what-is cannot be rearranged does not seem to be adequately supported by an argument that appeals to unity (whether predicational or numerical). And indeed, later in B7 when Melissus gives the full argument against rearrangement, the argument is based on the claim that there is no coming-to-be, passing-away, or alteration, rather than on any assertions about unity:

> ἀλλ' οὐδὲ μετακοσμηθῆναι ἀνυστόν· ὁ γὰρ κόσμος ὁ πρόσθεν ἐὼν οὐκ ἀπόλλυται οὔτε ὁ μὴ ἐὼν γίνεται. ὅτε δὲ μήτε προσγίνεται μηδὲν μήτε ἀπόλλυται μήτε ἑτεροιοῦται, πῶς ἂν μετακοσμηθὲν τῶν ἐόντων εἴη; εἰ μὲν γάρ τι ἐγίνετο ἑτεροῖον, ἤδη ἂν καὶ μετακοσμηθείη. (30B7)
>
> But neither is it feasible that it can be rearranged; for the arrangement that was before is not destroyed nor one that is not come to be. And since nothing comes to be in addition, nor is destroyed, nor alters, how could anything of the things that are be rearranged? For if it became different at all, it would already also be rearranged.

Melissus here takes a given arrangement as something that is, and so subject to the Eleatic requirements on what-is.[85] Thus, it cannot be subject to coming-to-be or passing-away. According to this argument, no shift in the

---

real is divine and alive" (*HGP*, vol. II, p. 114). Barnes comments: "The next sentences [viz. those dealing with pain and anguish] are curiosities.... It is hard to believe that Melissus would have invented those strange theses off his own bat; yet scholars have unearthed no suitable opponent against whom they may have been enunciated" (*PP*, vol. I, pp. 216–17). But Longrigg, who finds a "suitable opponent" in Empedocles, suggests that the argument that feeling pain is incompatible with completeness might be directed against Empedocles, "who seems to have held that pain was caused by the aggregation of elements alien to the composition of a body" ("Elements," p. 113n.44).

[84] There is no reason why that which is only numerically one could not have more than one character, for a single thing may have many properties. See Solmsen, "Eleatic One," esp. p. 141. Solmsen rightly points out that the subject of the arguments is what-is; but because he thinks that the only monism possible is numerical monism, he proposes removing the *hen* from this line in B7 and from Simplicius's summary at *in Ph.* 104.1–2 (see pp. 141–44).

[85] See, for instance, Wardy, "Eleatic Pluralism," p. 130: "Rearrangement of what is contravenes the ban on existential change, if a configuration is a thing over and above, distinct from, the entities constituting it."

arrangement of the Empedoclean roots, the Anaxagorean *chrēmata*, or the atoms is possible. Mixture and separation, fundamental mechanisms for the Pluralist and Atomist theories, are therefore ruled out on the very grounds that the Pluralists and Atomists had used to claim that their fundamental entities could count as what-is and so meet the Parmenidean criteria.[86] Melissus's treatment of rearrangement is thus one of his strongest arguments against the current pluralistic theories.

Melissus's arguments are not simply an echo of Parmenides; he is not an uncritical follower of Parmenides or a mouthpiece for a unified Eleatic position. B7 and B8 show that Melissus is pursuing his own version of monism (a version that includes both numerical and predicational monism) and, at the same time, arguing against post-Parmenidean Pluralist accounts of what-is. B8 argues that a theory based on a plurality of Parmenidean ones cannot succeed in explaining the world as reported by our senses:

> μέγιστον μὲν οὖν σημεῖον οὗτος ὁ λόγος, ὅτι ἓν μόνον ἔστιν· ἀτὰρ καὶ τάδε σημεῖα. εἰ γὰρ ἦν πολλά, τοιαῦτα χρὴ αὐτὰ εἶναι, οἷόν περ ἐγώ φημι τὸ ἓν εἶναι. εἰ γὰρ ἔστι γῆ καὶ ὕδωρ καὶ ἀὴρ καὶ πῦρ καὶ σίδηρος καὶ χρυσός, καὶ τὸ μὲν ζῶον τὸ δὲ τεθνηκός, καὶ μέλαν καὶ λευκὸν καὶ τὰ ἄλλα, ὅσα φασὶν οἱ ἄνθρωποι εἶναι ἀληθῆ, εἰ δὴ ταῦτα ἔστι, καὶ ἡμεῖς ὀρθῶς ὁρῶμεν καὶ ἀκούομεν, εἶναι χρὴ ἕκαστον τοιοῦτον, οἷόν περ τὸ πρῶτον ἔδοξεν ἡμῖν, καὶ μὴ μεταπίπτειν μηδὲ γίνεσθαι ἑτεροῖον, ἀλλὰ ἀεὶ εἶναι ἕκαστον, οἷόν πέρ ἐστιν. νῦν δέ φαμεν ὀρθῶς ὁρᾶν καὶ ἀκούειν καὶ συνιέναι· δοκεῖ δὲ ἡμῖν τό τε θερμὸν ψυχρὸν γίνεσθαι καὶ τὸ ψυχρὸν θερμὸν καὶ τὸ σκληρὸν μαλθακὸν καὶ τὸ μαλθακὸν σκληρὸν καὶ τὸ ζῶον ἀποθνῄσκειν καὶ ἐκ μὴ ζῶντος γίνεσθαι καὶ ταῦτα πάντα ἑτεροιοῦσθαι, καὶ ὅ τι ἦν τε καὶ ὃ νῦν οὐδὲν ὁμοῖον εἶναι, ἀλλ' ὅ τε σίδηρος σκληρὸς ἐὼν τῷ δακτύλῳ κατατρίβεσθαι ὁμουρέων, καὶ χρυσὸς καὶ λίθος καὶ ἄλλο ὅ τι ἰσχυρὸν δοκεῖ εἶναι πᾶν, ἐξ ὕδατός τε γῆ καὶ λίθος γίνεσθαι· ...[87] οὐ τοίνυν ταῦτα ἀλλήλοις ὁμολογεῖ. φαμένοις γὰρ εἶναι πολλὰ καὶ ἀΐδια καὶ εἴδη τε καὶ ἰσχὺν ἔχοντα, πάντα ἑτεροιοῦσθαι ἡμῖν δοκεῖ καὶ μεταπίπτειν ἐκ τοῦ ἑκάστοτε ὁρωμένου. δῆλον τοίνυν, ὅτι οὐκ ὀρθῶς ἑωρῶμεν οὐδὲ ἐκεῖνα πολλὰ ὀρθῶς δοκεῖ εἶναι· οὐ γὰρ ἂν μετέπιπτεν, εἰ ἀληθῆ ἦν· ἀλλ' ἦν οἷόν περ ἐδόκει ἕκαστον τοιοῦτον. τοῦ γὰρ ἐόντος

[86] The argument against rearrangement in 30B7 is followed (after the discussion of pain and suffering) by Melissus's argument that because none of what-is is empty there is no motion. The rearrangement argument also rules out motion, but the two arguments are independent. Indeed, a Pluralist like Empedocles can claim that "of the whole none is empty" (B14; Inwood claims that B14 is a paraphrase rather than quotation; Wright does not include it in her collection) and that his account of mixture and separation (the running through one another of the roots) needs no void. The roots can shift about among themselves without, apparently, needing void. By providing the rearrangement argument against motion, Melissus can thus respond to Pluralist mixture claims without having to invoke the impossibility of void.

[87] The following phrase (ὥστε συμβαίνει μήτε ὁρᾶν μήτε τὰ ὄντα γινώσκειν) is omitted, as it seems to be in the wrong place. Barnes suggests that it is a "marginal gloss written in a later jargon" (*PP*, vol. II, p. 340n.3).

ἀληθινοῦ κρεῖσσον οὐδέν. ἢν δὲ μεταπέσῃ, τὸ μὲν ἐὸν ἀπώλετο, τὸ δὲ οὐκ ἐὸν γέγονεν. οὕτως οὖν, εἰ πολλὰ εἴη, τοιαῦτα χρὴ εἶναι, οἷόν περ τὸ ἕν. (B8)

This argument, then, is the greatest sign that only the One is; yet there are also these signs. For if there were a many, it is necessary that they be just as I say the one to be. For if there is earth and water and air and fire and iron and gold, and something is living and another dead, and dark and light and all the other things, as many as people say to be true, if indeed these things are and we see and hear correctly, it is necessary that each of these should be just as they first seemed to us and must not change or become different, but each must be just as it is. Now we say that we see and hear and understand correctly; but it seems to us that the hot becomes cold and the cold hot, and the hard [becomes] soft and the soft hard, and the living dies and comes to be from what is not living, and that all these things undergo change and that which was and which now is are in no way the same; but iron, being hard is worn down by the touch of a finger, and [so too] gold and stone and anything else that seems to be strong, and earth and stones come to be from water; . . . Now these things do not agree with one another. For we said that there is a many, being eternal and having forms and strength, yet they all seem to us to alter and to change from that which we see each time. So then, it is clear that we do not see correctly nor that those many seem correctly to be; for they would not change, if they were true, but each would be such as it seemed to be. For nothing is stronger than what is true. And if they changed, what is would be destroyed and what is not would come to be. In this way, then, if there were a many, they would have to be just such as the one is.

The opening and closing claim of the argument, that if there were a many, they would have to be such as the One is, might be taken as a recognition on Melissus's part that a plurality of ones (on the model of Pluralism or Atomism) is possible.[88] But the core of the argument shows that this is not Melissus's view. The point of the argument is to undermine any claim that the senses are reliable in pointing to how things really are. The Pluralists may think that they can begin with a plurality of ones and explain the sensible world in a way that makes the world reported by sense experience both subject to rational explanation and a sign of what-is. But Melissus argues that the requirements on what-is are such that no plurality of ones that

[88] See, for instance, Schofield in KRS, p. 400: "This conclusion, intended by Melissus as a *reductio ad absurdum* of belief in a plurality of things, was accepted by the Atomists and made into another fundamental thesis of their system." KR adopted the same view. McKirahan notes the difficulty of reconciling the claim with Melissus's arguments for the uniqueness of the One but claims that a "restricted view of the properties of what is may have played a role in the formation of ancient atomism" (*Before Socrates*, p. 300). Guthrie is sceptical that the Atomists took B8 as a model but concedes the possibility (*HGP*, vol. II, pp. 117–18).

mix and separate can meet them. Suppose that we perceive correctly. No change from our first perception can then be possible, for the "ones" that we perceive cannot, on Melissus's earlier arguments (in B7), be subject to change. But we perceive change (both qualitative change and coming-to-be and passing-away). Then either our senses are untrustworthy or the entities we perceive actually do undergo change and cannot be genuine entities. If so, they fail as a metaphysical basis for the sensible world. Empedocles defends sense experience in B3, and he treats some sensory phenomena as witnesses to the reality and nature of the four roots and of love and strife (in B21), while Anaxagoras thinks that appearances are a sight of the unseen (B21). The Atomist attitude to sense perception is more complex, but Democritus apparently argues for some degree of trust in sense experience, as long as it is recognized that what we sense is "by convention." Questions about the reliability of sense experience aside, the real force of Melissus's claim in B8 is that there can be no rational explanation of the sensible world, if by that is meant an explanation that is ultimately based in genuine, Parmenidean entities, having an unchanging, unified nature.[89] Melissus's argument suggests that were there such an explanation, there would have to be a link between the realm of the permanent entities and the world of change reported by sense experience. But no link is possible that would allow the genuine entities to be unchanged while the sensible world changes. Either both what-is and the world change, or neither changes. But both halves of the disjunct are impossible. The assertion of those who adopt a plurality of ones that the changes in the sensible world are not real but only apparent thus fails; for the apparent change is accounted for by mixture and separation of the basic entities, which contravenes the Melissan argument (in B7) against rearrangement. The claim that "if there were a many, it would have to be as the One is" is destructive of attempts to link the worlds of being and becoming. First, it is crucial to Melissus's arguments that the One not only satisfies Parmenidean criteria for what-is, it is also unique (shown by the arguments that what-is is unlimited in both time and extension[90]); obviously no plurality will satisfy this demand. Second, the argument against rearrangement will prevent the mixing and separating that is crucial to any pluralistic theory.[91]

[89] For an analysis of the argument that stresses its attack on perception, see Barnes, *PP*, vol. I, pp. 298–302.

[90] In addition to arguing that the One must be unlimited in extension, Melissus also argues that it must have no body. If it had thickness, he claims in B9, it would have parts and would therefore not be one. The attributions of both extension and incorporeality to the One have puzzled commentators. I discussed this issue in "Eleatic Monism," pp. 14–18, arguing that the two claims are not incompatible.

[91] The argument against rearrangement would also undermine the cosmology of Parmenides' *Doxa* as well. But insofar as Melissus is committed to both predicational and numerical monism, he would also have other objections to the *Doxa*.

The Pluralists and Atomists attempted to make inquiry into the nature of things consistent with Eleatic arguments about what-is. Anaxagorean *chrēmata*, Empedoclean roots, and the atoms all satisfied requirements for what-is formulated first by Parmenides, and then by Zeno. These theories share not only a commitment to the predicational monism of Parmenides, but also a recognition of the strength of the Eleatic arguments against the reality of coming-to-be and passing-away. It is the latter that motivates the commitment of all three theories to mixture and separation in order to explain what the senses report as generation and corruption. As long as these mixings and separatings do not result in real coming-to-be or destruction or disturb the single, stable natures of the fundamental entities, the Pluralists and Atomists are confident that Parmenidean requirements have been satisfied, while, at the same time, a rational account of the world of the senses can be given. But by claiming that an arrangement of Eleatic entities must itself be considered a thing that cannot be generated or destroyed, Melissus challenges an assumption at the core of Pluralistic theories. If there is to be a rapprochement between Eleatic metaphysics and scientific inquiry, Melissus's arguments must be disarmed.[92]

R.B.B. Wardy has argued that scattered claims in the testimonia show that a disarming response was given by the Atomists.[93] Melissus's rearrangement objection depends on the claim that an arrangement of genuine entities itself counts as something that is generated and destroyed. But there can be no such coming-to-be or passing-away, so there can be no arrangement and rearrangement of the things that are. The argument thus does away with the pluralist and atomist explanations of how it can seem that things come to be and pass away in the world reported to us by the senses. A response to Melissus would be to deny the reality of such arrangements. The Atomists can claim that what seems to be an arrangement of atoms into a sensory object is itself just an arbitrary separation from the background of atoms and void.

[92] There is also the problem of Melissus's commitment to numerical monism. If the Atomists are indeed responding to Melissus, they give no evidence of being threatened by his assertion that there is only one thing. Melissus's argument for the conclusion that The One is the only thing there is depends on his claim that what-is must be unlimited. This claim is in turn grounded in the B2 argument that what-is has no beginning and no end. But that argument is invalid because it equivocates on the notion of an end. Thus the Atomists could avoid Melissus's numerical monism while being seriously concerned about his other arguments about the nature of what-is, which are based on Parmenides' predicational monism about natures (which the Atomists accept).

[93] For a full discussion, including both the metaphysical and epistemological ramifications of this response to the problem of rearrangement, see Wardy's "Eleatic Pluralism." See also Makin, *Indifference*, section 3.3 (pp. 65–84), "Indifference and Epistemology" for a discussion of the epistemological side of the problem. In adopting the view he does of the "by convention" claims in Democritus, Makin does not, I think, allow the rearrangement argument sufficient force. For instance, in his comments on p. 79, he is willing to treat as real certain aspects of atomic cosmology that the view discussed here would treat as conventional.

Such a separation of atoms into a tree, or a dog, or even into earth, air, fire, or water, is, in the Atomists' terminology, conventional. Two testimonia suggest that the Atomists took this step. Diogenes Laertius reports in his summary of Democritus's views that "the first principles of the whole are atoms and void; all the other things are apprehended by belief" (Δοκεῖ δ' αὐτῷ τάδε· ἀρχὰς εἶναι τῶν ὅλων ἀτόμους καὶ κενόν, τὰ δ' ἄλλα πάντα νενομίσθαι Diogenes Laertius, *Lives* IX.44 = 68A1 = Luria 93).[94] And Plutarch gives a version of the "by convention" fragment that includes combination: "color is by convention and sweet by convention and combination by convention" (τὸ γὰρ νόμῳ χροιὴν εἶναι καὶ νόμῳ γλυκὺ καὶ νόμῳ σύγκρισιν Plutarch *adv. Colot.* 8 1110 E = Luria 61).[95] Wardy sees this response to Melissus's argument as the primary motivation for the Atomist theory.[96] But this places too much emphasis on a single argument of Melissus, which is itself based in broad Eleatic concerns about the nature of theoretically basic entities, about coming-to-be and passing-away, and about issues that develop from these fundamental concerns. I suspect that Atomism developed as a response to a cluster of Eleatic problems, including Parmenides' account of the nature of what-is, Zeno's arguments about division, and Melissus's concerns to deny the empty and to challenge Pluralist theories of mixture. There is a sense in which it is not surprising that the Atomists should give such an answer to Melissus's argument. This account of the status of mixture and arrangement

94 Diogenes specifically mentions fire, water, air, and earth as compounded of atoms—ἐξ ἀτόμων τινῶν συστήματα (IX.44). See also Aetius IV.9.8 = 67A32 = Luria 95.

95 Plutarch's comments, and the similar claims about convention reported by Galen (B125) and by Sextus (B9) are usually treated primarily as epistemological claims. But if Democritus were responding to Melissus's argument about arrangement and rearrangement, the epistemological claims would ultimately be based on and secondary to metaphysical principles that are rooted in atomist worries about Eleatic arguments.

96 Wardy is aware of a difficulty in maintaining that this response to Melissus is a primary motivation for Atomism: the dearth of textual evidence. He discusses the problem and concludes that the ancient authorities "fail accurately to express the actual nature of atomic metaphysics and epistemology because they take it very much for granted that the core tenet of Eleaticism, the impossibility of real change, is a dead letter" ("Eleatic," p. 141). While Wardy's comment is apt (and useful to keep in mind when considering later ancient discussions of Parmenides and post-Parmenidean thought), I do not think that it will bear as much weight as it must on his view. But if we see Atomism as a response to a group of Eleatic problems, and not to just a single Eleatic argument, the evidence that Wardy cites shows atomist concern with Melissus's argument about rearrangement as yet another motive for the theory. Wardy does not, apparently, accept that all the Pluralist theories share this feature in their response to Parmenides' arguments in *Alētheia*, although he comes close to adopting this position when he writes that "the mutability of all combinations renders them unreal" ("Eleatic," p. 140). By "all combinations" he seems to mean all combinations of atoms. But the remark could apply equally well to combinations of the roots in Empedocles or to the particular mix of the *chrēmata* in Anaxagoras that is called "a human being." The case of the *chrēmata* is more complicated because they are themselves real. But the unclarity about the status of organisms makes it possible to see such a move in Anaxagoras (though I do not mean to claim that Anaxagoras himself conceived of his claim about mixture and separation in B17 in exactly this way).

is inherent in all pluralistic responses to Parmenidean arguments about the impossibility of coming-to-be and passing-away. Parmenides himself had argued that nothing that is genuinely real can be generated or destroyed, and Melissus's argument is simply a version of that argument applied to the myriad mixtures and separations by means of which the Pluralists attempted to account for the evidence of the senses in a metaphysically responsible way. None of these theories asserts or even requires that these mixtures be real. Indeed the fact that they are temporary guarantees that they cannot be counted as genuine entities. This is inherent in Anaxagoras B17 and Empedocles B8, both of which reject coming-to-be and passing-away and replace them with mixture and separation. If the mixtures are only temporary they cannot count as genuine entities (recognized by Empedocles when he calls the results of such mixtures "mortal things"). But the Pluralist failure to stress this fact about the mixtures, and their readiness to treat the products of such mixture as quasi-entities leaves them vulnerable to Melissus's argument and opens the way for the more radical atomist response.[97]

[97] A virtue of Wardy's account of the atomist response is that a new arrangement of atoms is reduced to spatial changes and "these spatial relations are not themselves ὄντα" ("Eleatic," p. 130). This is an improvement on the Pluralist account, but there is no textual evidence that such a claim was made explicitly by the Presocratic Atomists.

VI

Final Remarks

THIS STUDY has argued that Parmenides positively influenced later Presocratic theories of what there is. His arguments affected two aspects of these theories: the metaphysical principles adopted by the Pluralists and Atomists, and the models of mixture and separation that they postulated to explain what appears as change in the world reported by the senses. These two aspects are closely related. What-is can neither come to be nor pass away, and so what seems to the senses to be such change must, in a rational account of the world, be explained by some other mechanism, such as the mixture and separation of ungenerated and unchanging real entities. I have argued that the metaphysical principles adopted by later Presocratics come from the arguments of the *Alētheia* (and the further arguments based on them developed by Zeno and Melissus), while the model of mixing and separating is based on the cosmology developed in the *Doxa* of Parmenides' poem. Parmenides argued that anything that genuinely is must meet certain criteria, which he elaborates in B8. Such an entity must not be subject to coming-to-be or passing-away, must be unchanging, must be a complete and perfect whole, and must be single in nature (and so indivisible). As I argued in Chapter II, these characteristics of what-is are interrelated, and all follow from the fundamental *krisis* "is or is not?" Something that meets these requirements is a genuine entity and can serve as a basic component in a cosmological theory, or a theory that explains the world as reported to us by the senses.[1] Despite the radical differences between the theories of Anaxagoras, Empedocles, and the Atomists, all share a metaphysical outlook that can be traced back to Parmenides. That theories so different should share metaphysical principles so fundamental is evidence of the great importance of Parmenides, and the strength of his legacy. But that legacy extends further. In this final chapter, I consider two other Presocratic philosophers whose theories were, I think, also affected by Parmenides' arguments: Philolaus of Croton and Diogenes of Apollonia. Finally, I close with some comments on the Eleatic influence to be found in Plato's Theory of Forms, influence that justifies the claim that Plato was the last Presocratic.

[1] Parmenides' claim, as I have interpreted it, is that to be a genuine entity a thing must meet the requirements set out in 28B8. According to the story I have told here, Zeno and Melissus have both argued for certain modifications or interpretations of Parmenides' claims, placing new restrictions on a fundamental entity.

1. Philolaus of Croton and Diogenes of Apollonia

Philolaus and Diogenes were probably contemporaries, belonging to the last generation of Presocratic thinkers, which also included Democritus. They inherited a range of philosophical problems and assumptions that can be traced back to Parmenides, although in the case of Philolaus, the Pythagorean influence is also strong. Carl Huffman has argued that while Philolaus was indeed a Pythagorean, he should also be seen as a traditional Presocratic thinker, whose interests resemble those of other post-Parmenidean philosophers.[2] Huffman argues that Parmenides' influence on Philolaus was primarily epistemological, but I think that metaphysical influences can also be found, and that both work together with Pythagorean doctrine to shape Philolaus's views.[3] Philolaus's fundamental metaphysical claims can be found in fragment 1:

> ἁ φύσις δ' ἐν τῷ κόσμῳ ἁρμόχθη ἐξ ἀπείρων τε καὶ παραινόντων καὶ ὅλος ⟨ὁ⟩ κόσμος καὶ τὰ ἐν αὐτῷ πάντα. (44B1)
>
> Nature in the *kosmos* was fitted together out of unlimiteds and limiters, both the *kosmos* as a whole and all the things in it.

The fundamental things of the cosmos are the limiters and the unlimiteds; it is their "fitting together" that constitutes both the world order of the *kosmos* and everything in that ordered world. Philolaus says little about the limiters and the unlimiteds and gives no specific examples in the extant fragments. But, according to Aristotle, the Pythagoreans claim that "the universe is one and that it drew in from the unlimited time, breath, and void" (Aristotle fr. 201 [Rose] = 58B30). Huffman argues that Aristotle is here referring to Philolaus and makes a good case for thinking that time, breath, and void are examples of unlimiteds.[4] Another possible example of an unlimited is sound, which is limited to produce musical tones. Whatever the exact range of limiters

[2] Huffman, *Philolaus,* esp. pp. 49–53. My account of Philolaus is heavily indebted to Huffman's work, and I follow his texts throughout. I accept Huffman's judgments about which fragments attributed to Philolaus are genuine.

[3] Ibid., p. 67.

[4] Ibid., pp. 43–44. Huffman suggests that B7, which says that "the one in the middle of the sphere, the hearth" was the first thing to be fitted together, refers to the central fire mentioned in A16 and A17 and gives us the example of an unlimited, fire, being fitted together with a limiter, "the middle of the sphere" (ibid., pp. 41–42). Barnes suggests that the unlimiteds are "unformed stuffs" (*PP,* vol. II, p. 86). Huffman points out that Aristotle fr. 201 (Rose) indicates that while stuffs probably are unlimiteds, the class also includes continua, such as time and void. It is unclear just how Philolaus conceived of void, since there are no extant fragments that mention it, and there are few references in the doxography. At *Ph.* 213b24–25 Aristotle claims that the Pythagorean view is that void is a separator, and this is consistent with the atomist conception of void as that which separates atoms and so accounts for the division of sensible bodies.

and unlimiteds, B2 makes it clear that both are necessary as beginning points in the theory, and B6 provides some information about their ontological status:

> περὶ δὲ φύσιος καὶ ἁρμονίας ὧδε ἔχει· ἁ μὲν ἐστὼ τῶν πραγμάτων ἀΐδιος ἔσσα καὶ αὐτὰ μὰν ἁ φύσις θείαν τε καὶ οὐκ ἀνθρωπίνην ἐνδέχεται γνῶσιν πλάν γα ἢ ὅτι οὐχ οἷόν τ' ἦν οὐθενὶ τῶν ἐόντων καὶ γιγνωσκομένων ὑφ' ἁμῶν γεγενῆσθαι μὴ ὑπαρχούσας τᾶς ἐστοῦς τῶν πραγμάτων, ἐξ ὧν συνέστα ὁ κόσμος, καὶ τῶν περαινόντων καὶ τῶν ἀπείρων. ἐπεὶ δὲ ταὶ ἀρχαὶ ὑπᾶρχον οὐχ ὁμοῖαι οὐδ' ὁμόφυλοι ἔσσαι, ἤδη ἀδύνατον ἦς κα αὐταῖς κοσμηθῆναι, εἰ μὴ ἁρμονία ἐπεγένετο ᾡτινιῶν ἂν τρόπῳ ἐγένετο. (44B6.1–9)
>
> Concerning nature and harmony it is like this: the being of things, which is eternal, and nature itself, admit of divine and not human knowledge, except that it was not possible for any of things that are and are known by us, to come to be, without the prior existence of the being of the things from which the *kosmos* was put together, both the limiters and the unlimiteds. And as these principles existed, being neither alike nor of the same kind, it would have been impossible for them to be ordered, if harmony had not come upon them, in whatever way it came to be.

Philolaus begins by asserting that humans cannot have complete knowledge of things that are fundamental. The claim seems to be that we are limited to complete knowledge of only those things within our experience. In this he echoes the views of both Xenophanes (21B34) and Alcmaeon (24B1). Divine things (including the eternal natures of things) are known by divine minds but not human ones. Human knowledge can justifiably extend only to claims about what must be the case in order for the *kosmos* as we can know it to be such as it is. Here Philolaus adopts the same view that Anaxagoras took in 59B21: appearances are a sight of the unseen, insofar as they give us evidence that must be accounted for, and insofar as we can say what must be true in order that the appearances be such as they are. Three sorts of things must have preceded the coming-to-be of this *kosmos*: limiters, unlimiteds, and a principle of harmony that would fit them together. Philolaus's claim that they must have existed before the *kosmos* was "put together" suggests that limiters and unlimiteds (and the principle of harmony itself) are permanent and immutable in themselves, although they may be joined in various ways by *harmonia* to produce the features of the *kosmos*. In this way they are comparable to the roots of Empedocles or the atoms of Leucippus and Democritus and satisfy the Parmenidean requirement that what-is be unborn and unchanging. Yet it may seem that Philolaus departs from the Parmenidean model in one crucial way. In B6 he denies that human minds can grasp the natures of the beginning principles of limiters and unlimiteds: "the being of things, which is eternal, and nature itself admit of divine and not human knowledge." It is a central tenet of the Parmenidean system that the fundamental entities must be knowable; as Parmenides B3 puts it, "the same thing is for thinking and for being." Thus, insofar as Philolaus denies that such knowledge is available to human beings, he seems to stray rather far from Parmenides' basic principles. But this is merely an appearance of difference with Parmenides rather than a genuine disagreement. Philolaus does not commit himself to the claim that the limiters and unlimiteds cannot be known at all. Rather, the basic principles are knowable by the divine, just as Anaxagoras's *chrēmata* are known by *Nous* itself. Human understanding can grasp that there must be such permanent realities, and we must know what it means to be an unlimited thing or a limiter, even if we are incapable of fully understanding their natures. So the Parmenidean requirement that genuine entities must be knowable is met. So far, then, Philolaus is in accord with Parmenidean arguments about what there is.[5]

Nevertheless, there is a departure from Parmenides and the systems based on his principles that have been examined so far. Parmenides had claimed that what-is is knowable or graspable by understanding, and that what is genuinely knowable is what genuinely is. Objects in the world reported to us by our senses are the result of the combination and separation of fundamental and genuine entities, and to the extent that they are grounded in what-is, they are capable of being understood. But these objects are not, strictly speaking, knowable, because they are the impermanent results of mixture. Philolaus suggests that sensible things, resulting from the combination of limiters and unlimiteds according to a principle of harmonia, can be known.

> καὶ πάντα γα μὰν τὰ γιγνωσκόμενα ἀριθμὸν ἔχοντι. οὐ γὰρ ὁτιῶν ⟨οἷόν⟩ τε οὐδὲν οὔτε νοηθῆμεν οὔτε γνωσθῆμεν ἄνευ τούτω. (44B4)

> And indeed all things that are known have number. For without this nothing whatever could be understood or known.[6]

I take it that *ta gignōskomena*, "the things that are known," refers to things that can be known by human knowers. This is supported by B5, which claims

[5] See Huffman's commentary on B6 in *Philolaus,* esp. pp. 124–29. Huffman argues that Philolaus "denies the possibility of any knowledge of an ultimate reality such as the Eleatics were searching for" (p. 127), although he modifies this claim somewhat in arguing that we can know that limiters, unlimiteds, and the principle of *harmonia* must be real. This, I think, does constitute genuine knowledge on the Parmenidean model. Because Philolaus argues that whatever is known must have number, and "pure" limiters and unlimiteds do not, the limiters and unlimiteds could not be known just in themselves, at least by human minds. B6 seems to suggest that a divine mind could grasp the nature of a pure unlimited or limiter.

[6] For the translation of οὔτε νοηθῆμεν οὔτε γνωσθῆμεν as "understood or known," see Huffman, *Philolaus,* pp. 176–77. Huffman argues (convincingly, I think) against Nussbaum that *gignōskein* does not necessarily refer to a successful cognitive activity. See Nussbaum, "Eleatic Conventionalism," with Huffman's comments (*Philolaus,* pp. 116–18).

that there are two "proper kinds" (*idia eidē*; the translation is Huffman's) of number, odd and even, and that "each thing itself" shows this by signs.[7] The things here referred to must be sensible objects, which are the result of the combinations of limiters and unlimiteds according to a certain *harmonia,* which gives a ratio that can be expressed numerically.[8] Because sensible things exhibit numerical ratios that can be grasped by the mind, they are knowable. Understanding something is understanding how it is structured, and the numerical ratio that describes the relations of limiters and unlimiteds in a thing just is that structure. Although the individual thing itself may not be permanent or otherwise meet Parmenidean criteria for what can be known, these mathematical relationships, which constitute the structures of sensible things, do satisfy Parmenides' demands. Thus, knowledge of the world reported to us by our senses can be secured, even though the items in that world are not unchanging complete wholes of a single kind.[9] By linking knowledge of the sensible world to knowledge of unchanging mathematical relations, Philolaus apparently avoids the problem that Melissus had sketched in 30B8.[10] There Melissus had argued that basic entities in any theory must "be such as I say the One is"—yet if the senses are reliable, things in the sensible world change and so cannot be properly linked to unchanging basic entities. Thus, the senses cannot be reliable, and we cannot be justified in our claims about the plurality of things in the world reported to us by the senses. Philolaus responds that, as long as sensible objects "have number," that is, exhibit a rational structure that can be determined mathematically, they can

[7] For a discussion of B5—both its textual difficulties and its interpretation—see Huffman, *Philolaus,* pp. 177–93.

[8] For a thorough discussion of the issue of number and ratio, see Huffman, *Philolaus,* pp. 54–77.

[9] Huffman argues that mathematical relations meet most of Parmenides' criteria: "It seems quite plausible to argue that [they] ... did not come into existence at any point, nor will ... pass away. Similarly, there seems little problem in saying that mathematical relationships are unchangeable. Further, since mathematical relationships are completely determinate, they are perfect in Parmenides' sense of being complete and not deficient" (*Philolaus,* p. 68). Huffman sees difficulties in claiming that a mathematical relationship is *xuneches* (continuous), but suggests that this requirement may be linked with numerical monism and so will be ignored by Philolaus insofar as he wishes to adopt numerical pluralism. But if "continuous" is linked with being a whole of a single kind, there is no problem in seeing mathematical relations as each being of a single kind, because each supposedly has a character that is the same in all cases. Moreover, as we have seen, Pluralism is not a difficulty. For another account of structure in Philolaus, see Schrenk.

[10] If we divide a string on a monochord instrument in two, we produce an octave, which thus has the numerical ratio 1 : 2. Sound can also be divided into other proportions, to produce other musical intervals. When the tuning of the monochord is changed, it might seem that the mathematical relation of 1 : 2 has been destroyed and replaced by some other ratio. But this is not the case. The particular sound produced by that tuning at that time has indeed ceased to be, but the nature of that note (as we might call it), as an instance of the ratio 1 : 2 remains the same and can be reproduced by restoring the ratio.

indeed be known, no matter that they are impermanent.[11] For, although the sensible thing itself is subject to change, the structure is permanent and unchanging in just the right way. Philolaus here uses epistemological principles derived from Parmenides to disarm a conundrum posed by Melissus. So, despite his particular interest in mathematics and structure, and his apparent commitment to the Pythagorean way of life, which distinguish him from the other post-Parmenidean thinkers I have discussed, Philolaus shares with them certain interests in the fundamental nature of the world and the form and limits of human knowledge. In developing these interests he shares with the Pluralists and the Atomists basic metaphysical and epistemological assumptions that can, I believe, be traced to Parmenides and to problems raised by the later Eleatics.

Diogenes of Apollonia would seem to be the later Presocratic most influenced by Eleatic arguments, for he insists that there is but a single basic entity, air, which, by altering, accounts for all the variety reported to us by the senses. Taking monism seriously, Diogenes argues that "all the things that are are alterations from the same thing and are the same thing" (64B2: πάντα τὰ ὄντα ἀπὸ τοῦ αὐτοῦ ἑτεροιοῦσθαι καὶ τὸ αὐτὸ εἶναι).[12] As I have argued throughout, however, Parmenidean monism does

[11] For further discussion of the role of number in Philolaus's theories, see Huffman, "The Role of Number." A related view is given in Zhmud'.

[12] Most commentators do not see Eleatic influence on Diogenes of Apollonia, or if they acknowledge it, see it as minor compared to the strength of the influence of Milesian thought. Barnes, for instance, has this to say: "Diogenes was aware of Eleatic metaphysics, and defended an old Milesian monism in its face. The evidence for the first part of that statement is in fact thin, though it will hardly be imagined that a *phusiologos* writing at the end of the fifth century could have been unaware of Parmenides' writings" (*PP,* vol. II, p. 266). Barnes quotes A1 as support for Eleatic influence. But Barnes's account of Eleatic influence is too weak, on several counts. First, there was not a single "Eleatic position" that influenced Diogenes; rather, he responded to arguments from both Parmenides and Melissus. Second, the "return" to Milesian monism is in fact an attempt to satisfy Melissus's requirements for what-is, and it is Melissus rather than the Milesians who is the primary motivation for material monism in Diogenes. Other commentators see even less influence from Parmenides and Melissus in Diogenes of Apollonia. Guthrie, for instance, argues that the "return to monism" in Diogenes is a response to the Eleatics, but he does not take into account possible Parmenidean or Melissan influence on Diogenes' theory of the nature of air or other aspects of Diogenes' view, and he asserts that Diogenes could feel free to adopt Leucippus's claim that void is real in order to account for condensation and rarefaction (*HGP,* vol. II, pp. 367–68). Kirk, in KRS, treats Diogenes as an eclectic, influenced by Anaxagoras, Leucippus, and Heraclitus; he does not mention Eleatic strains in Diogenes' thought. An important exception to the general trend is Stokes in *One and Many,* who suggests that "Diogenes had an answer, however, inadequate, to Parmenides" (p. 239), finding the answer in the claims that air is neither created nor destroyed, and that it undergoes alterations (*heteroiōseis*) but not coming-to-be or passing away (p. 240). But Stokes finds Diogenes ignoring many of Parmenides' arguments, as well as those of Melissus. Laks briefly discusses the relation between Diogenes and the Eleatics but does not go as far as Stokes in seeing influence in particular metaphysical doctrines (see *Diogène,* pp. XXIII–XXIV). I follow Laks's texts throughout.

not require that there be but a single thing. It is Melissus, not Parmenides, who argues for numerical monism. So it is worth exploring why Diogenes of Apollonia opts for a single basic entity and whether this innovation in post-Parmenidean thought actually succeeds in meeting Melissus's arguments.[13] Diogenes gives his reason for adopting a single basic entity in B2; but before we examine that passage, it should be noted that Diogenes adopts a number of Eleatic requirements. In B7 he contrasts air with the things that are constituted by it:

> καὶ αὐτὸ μὲν τοῦτο καὶ ἀίδιον καὶ ἀθάνατον σῶμα, τῷ δὲ τὰ μὲν γίνεται, τὰ δὲ ἀπολείπει. (64B7)
>
> And this itself is body both eternal and deathless, by which some things come to be and others pass away.

There is a textual problem in the fragment. Manuscripts D and E of Simplicius's commentary on the *Physics* have τῷ, while F has τό; the Aldine edition printed τῶν. In his edition of Simplicius, Diels followed D and E and opted for τῷ, but in the *Fragmente der Vorsokratiker,* he returned, without comment, to the Aldine version of the line. In his study of Diogenes of Apollonia, Laks argues that τῷ is correct.[14] The context in Simplicius supports τῷ but also shows that while Diogenes is discussing the causative power of air in the coming-to-be and passing-away of other things (as expressed by the τῷ), he is also stressing that air is not susceptible to generation and destruction even as other things come to be and pass away on account of alterations in it.[15] Diogenes is careful to show that his first principle, air, meets the Eleatic requirements of no coming-to-be or passing-away. Diogenes Laertius reports that Diogenes claimed that "nothing comes to be from what-is-not nor passes away into what-is-not" (Diogenes Laertius, *Lives* IX.57 = 64A1). Air certainly meets this requirement, and things other than air, while apparently coming to be or passing away, also satisfy it. Other things may be said to come to be and pass away, but Diogenes clearly means that their generation and destruction is only apparent, as they are really just modified air, and air

[13] In the range of Presocratic thought, including that before Parmenides, Diogenes' theory is not an innovation, for the early Milesians had begun with a single thing that accounted for the multiplicity of the sensible world. I have already suggested (in Chap. IV, Section 1) that Diogenes of Apollonia's return to monism is not a better response than Pluralism to Parmenides, just because it is a monistic theory, but it remains to be seen how well Diogenes' theory is able to answer Melissus.

[14] KRS follow DK, as does Barnes in *PP* (II, p. 274). Laks's discussion appears on p. 32 of *Diogène*.

[15] At *in Ph.* 153.17 Simplicius attributes to Diogenes the view that air is the *archē*; he then goes on to say, just before quoting B7, θαυμαστὸν δὲ ὅτι κατὰ ἑτεροίωσιν τὴν ἀπ' αὐτοῦ λέγων τὰ ἄλλα γίνεσθαι ἀίδιον ὅμως αὐτό φησι (It is amazing that while saying that other things come to be by virtue of alterations in it [air], he nevertheless says that it is eternal).

itself is not subject to generation and destruction.[16] Furthermore, according to B2, air is always the same, no matter what modifications it may undergo. B2 also implies that all air has the same nature (*physis*), for the argument against a plurality of real entities turns on the denial that the apparent plurality of things each have their own nature (*idia physis*). So, Diogenes' air also meets Parmenides' monistic requirement that what-is be single in nature or kind. Because it is all the same, air is not, apparently, divisible into air and non-air, and so it is also continuous, or *xuneches* (see Parmenides B8.25). So, on the face of it, Diogenes of Apollonia has constructed a cosmology that is rational in just the way Parmenides demands, based as it is on a continuous entity that is single in kind and not subject to coming-to-be and passing-away. But, I shall argue, Diogenes' numerical monism ultimately undermines his system, for such a monism will require that air undergo exactly the sort of internal changes that Parmenides rules out. The necessary stability of what-is is signaled by the sign *atremes* (unwavering, unshaking) at 28B8.4, and the capacity of Diogenes' air to become everything by alteration is inconsistent with this sign. But before turning to a fuller examination of this aspect of Diogenes' theory, it is worth considering why Diogenes insists on a single basic entity, thus breaking with the cosmological model of the mixture and separation of a plurality of genuine entities found in Pluralism and Atomism.

An obvious source of influence for Diogenes of Apollonia's return to the Milesian commitment to a single basic entity is Melissus, for it is he who argues that there can be only thing, on the grounds that what-is is unlimited and therefore single. Further, the argument against rearrangement in 30B8 had rendered Pluralistic theories doubtful, for a Pluralistic cosmology in which mixture and separation (as forms of rearrangement) are ruled out cannot succeed in explaining the world reported by the senses.[17] Diogenes was seemingly convinced by Melissus's argument for numerical monism, and he takes care in B2 to emphasize that Pluralistic theories cannot succeed:

> ἐμοὶ δὲ δοκεῖ τὸ μὲν ξύμπαν εἰπεῖν πάντα τὰ ὄντα ἀπὸ τοῦ αὐτοῦ ἑτεροιοῦσθαι καὶ τὸ αὐτὸ εἶναι. καὶ τοῦτο εὔδηλον· εἰ γὰρ τὰ ἐν τῷδε τῷ κόσμῳ ἐόντα νῦν, γῆ καὶ ὕδωρ καὶ ἀὴρ καὶ πῦρ καὶ τὰ ἄλλα ὅσα φαίνεται ἐν τῷδε

[16] There are, however, no extant fragments in which Diogenes of Apollonia claims that generation and destruction are merely appearances, or that they and phenomenal objects are conventional and not real. He asserts (in B2) that sensible items do not differ in their natures and so must really be air. Because air itself neither comes to be nor passes away, he must mean that what we take to be generation and destruction are not real but are only temporary modifications of air, which is a genuine entity. If so, this would account for the report in Aetius (IV.9.8 = A23) that like Leucippus and Democritus, Diogenes says that the perceptibles are by convention (*nomōi*). If this view of Diogenes is right, it would justify the view that A23 actually is a reference to Diogenes of Apollonia and not to Diogenes of Smyrna (see Barnes, *PP*, vol. II, p. 315n.4).

[17] Unless one opts for the radical alternative of denying that rearrangement is real, as Wardy suggests the Atomists did.

τῷ κόσμῳ ἐόντα, εἰ τούτων τι ἦν ἕτερον τοῦ ἑτέρου, ἕτερον ὂν τῇ ἰδίᾳ φύσει, καὶ μὴ τὸ αὐτὸ ἐὸν μετέπιπτε πολλαχῶς καὶ ἠτεροιοῦτο, οὐδαμῇ οὔτε μίσγεσθαι ἀλλήλοις ἠδύνατο, οὔτε ὠφέλησις τῷ ἑτέρῳ ⟨γενέσθαι ἀπὸ τοῦ ἑτέρου⟩ οὔτε βλάβη, οὐδ' ἂν οὔτε φυτὸν ἐκ τῆς γῆς φῦναι οὔτε ζῷον οὔτε ἄλλο γενέσθαι οὐδέν, εἰ μὴ οὕτω συνίστατο ὥστε ταὐτὸ εἶναι. ἀλλὰ πάντα ταῦτα ἐκ τοῦ αὐτοῦ ἑτεροιούμενα ἄλλοτε ἀλλοῖα γίνεται καὶ εἰς τὸ αὐτὸ ἀναχωρεῖ.[18]

It seems to me, to say it in its entirety, that all the things that are are alterations from the same thing and are the same thing. And this is very clear: for if the things that are now in this *kosmos,* earth and water and air and fire and as many others as appear to be in this *kosmos,* if any of these were different from each other, being different in its own proper nature, and were not the same while being changed in many ways and altering, in no way would things be able to mix with each other, nor would advantage or harm come to be from one to another, nor would a plant grow from the earth, nor an animal or anything else come to be, if they were not constituted so as to be the same. But all these, being alterations from the same thing, become different at different times and return into the same thing.

The main argument here is that if there were a plurality of basic entities, each with its own peculiar nature, they would be unable to affect one another.[19] Thus, there could be no combination that would account for the world reported to us by the senses. Diogenes mentions specifically the four roots of Empedocles, earth, water, air, and fire (and the claim that "all these things . . . become different at different times" may be an echo of Empedocles B17.34–35). Insofar as the roots are different, he claims, they cannot truly mix; each must remain separated in isolation from the other. Without such mixture, the obvious features of the *kosmos* would be impossible. But such features are clearly possible, so there must be another mechanism at work. Diogenes explains what it is: all things are really just the same thing, being modifications or alterations of some one thing. He emphasizes that this thing remains the same by claiming that all things, although they "become different at different times," ultimately "return to the same thing," again through alteration. Diogenes does not discuss the mechanism by which alterations in air take place. Clearly, such a mechanism is part of air itself, as there is nothing else that could perform this task. Moreover, by attributing all intelligence to air, and claiming that it has power over all things (B5; with

[18] Text as in Laks. For a discussion of the addition of γενέσθαι ἀπὸ τοῦ ἑτέρου (also adopted by DK), see Laks, *Diogène,* p. 28.

[19] Diogenes does not specifically say that the things he mentions are basic entities. He calls them things in the *kosmos,* or world order, and also refers to "other things that appear in the *kosmos.*" Such locutions are, I think, neutral as to whether they refer to fundamental entities or phenomenal objects. I take him to be enunciating a general principle that would apply at all metaphysical levels.

clear echoes of Anaxagoras's *Nous*), Diogenes seems to imply that air can, as it were, change itself. Because that which accounts for what appears as the generation and destruction of phenomenal things is an aspect of the single thing that genuinely is, this account of a single basic entity avoids Melissus's arguments against rearrangement and would seem, at the same time, to meet his requirement that what-is be unlimited in magnitude.[20]

But Melissus would still seem to have an argument against Diogenes, for Melissus had insisted that what-is cannot alter. In 30B7 he argues, using the same verb as appears in Diogenes' claim, that "if it alters, it is necessary that what-is not be the same, but that what was before be destroyed and what-is-not come to be" (εἰ γὰρ ἑτεροιοῦται, ἀνάγκη τὸ ἐὸν μὴ ὁμοῖον εἶναι, ἀλλὰ ἀπόλλυσθαι τὸ πρόσθεν ἐόν, τὸ δὲ οὐκ ἐὸν γίνεσθαι). Now, Diogenes may simply have ignored, or have been ignorant of, this argument.[21] But, if he is responding to Melissus's arguments in returning to a single basic entity, it would be odd if he failed to see the problem of alteration (particularly as similar arguments are to be found in Parmenides, a point to which I shall return presently). Perhaps Diogenes was aware of the problem of alteration but thought that he had a response to it. Melissus's claim is that if what-is were to alter, there would then be two impossible consequences. First, it would no longer be the same (*homoion*); second, what is would be destroyed and what-is-not would come to be. In B2 Diogenes makes claims that seem to block Melissus's argument. First, he claims that all things that are alterations of or differentiations from the basic entity, air, are differentiations of the same thing (ἀπὸ τοῦ αὐτοῦ) and are the same thing (τὸ αὐτὸ εἶναι). Thus, in altering, he seems to claim, air does not actually become anything different from itself. Various things may be differentiated from the surrounding air but they are, as a matter of fact, not distinct from it. Of anything it may be said that it is (really) air. Thus, despite altering, air has not ceased to be the same. Moreover, Diogenes seems to draw a distinction between alteration and generation. Air may alter but it does not change in its nature, so there is no coming-to-be or passing-away in this case. There are no extant fragments

20 In 30B9 Melissus had argued that what-is cannot be a body: "if it had thickness, it would have parts and would no longer be one" (εἰ δὲ ἔχοι πάχος, ἔχοι ἂν μόρια, καὶ οὐκέτι ἓν εἴη). Diogenes explicitly refers to air as a body in B7. He may well have thought that because air has a single nature, which is the same in every occurrence of air, a plurality of air parts, as it were, would not threaten the essential unity of his basic entity.

21 This seems to be the view adopted by KRS, who assert (p. 437n.1) that "it seems clear, not that Melissus is rebuffing Diogenes, or even vice versa, but that both are reacting in different ways to Pluralist explanations of the world." Diller argued on the basis of similarity of vocabulary that Melissus was reacting to Diogenes of Apollonia rather than the other way around. Kirk, in KRS (cited above), Guthrie (*HGP,* vol. II, p. 368n.1), and Stokes (*One and Many,* p. 337n.14) all reject Diller's arguments, as do Laks, (*Diogène,* p. XXVI, with n. 1), Calogero (*Storia,* pp. 341ff.), and Jouanna ("Rapports," pp. 321 ff.). Laks argues that Diogenes of Apollonia should be placed after Leucippus and Melissus but before Democritus and Socrates (*Diogène,* p. XIX n. 1).

in which Diogenes makes the claims that I am attributing to him, but his assertion that the things that are alterations of air are actually the same thing and that none of them is different in its nature (*physis*) suggests that he could have made this response.

Would such an answer satisfy Melissus (or Parmenides)? Almost certainly not. Parmenides had claimed that what-is is *atremes,* "unshaking," arguing that what-is cannot undergo any change in its basic nature. Diogenes, on the view I have attributed to him, claims that he has met this requirement. But Parmenides could legitimately ask whether Diogenes has proved that what he asserts is indeed the case. Diogenes must show that all things are modifications of air, which does not change in itself, and he does not seem to have done this. He has given reasons why a plurality of fundamental entities may not be able to explain the world as we sense it, but that is not the same as proving that there is a single thing, whose nature remains unchanged throughout the many modifications mentioned by Diogenes (in B5, for instance). He claims that the alterations are many and various (*polutropos,* B5), but he does not actually explain how air can remain just what it is, and the same in its nature, while undergoing all these changes. The claims of B2 are more bravado than proof. Moreover, Diogenes has not satisfactorily met the worry of Melissus B8. There Melissus had argued that a changing world reported by sense experience cannot be grounded in an unchanging entity. Either both must change, or neither. Diogenes insists that air, while altering, does not actually change in itself, yet the sensible world undergoes many changes, and these do not appear to be merely alteration. If everything really is air, how can this be the case? Diogenes does not seem able to account for these changes, so again there is an asymmetry between the metaphysical levels.

Diogenes argued for a monistic theory on the grounds that a plurality of entities, each with its own distinct nature, could not, as a matter of fact, combine in the way necessary to account for the world as it appears to the senses. Different natures would be incommensurable, and thus incapable of the required mixture. But the Pluralist and Atomist theories do not, in fact, suffer from the defect Diogenes attributes to them. Empedocles, who seems to be particularly singled out as the author of a failed theory, provided the mechanism of Love precisely to overcome differences between the roots and to allow for the mixture of the different characteristics necessary to account for the features of bone and blood. Moreover, Empedocles also saw that once things are combined, they must also be subject to dissolution, and that is the job of Strife. Diogenes himself does not actually indicate how the changes are to take place. Theophrastus attributes all these changes to condensation and rarefaction (quoted by Simplicius at *in Ph.* 25.5 = 64A5) and in B5 Diogenes himself attributes the difference between soul and body to temperature, and he also mentions difference in moisture and motion. But there is nothing that accounts for these changes. On this issue Empedocles has the better of

Diogenes. The Atomists, too, avoid the problem of the incommensurability of things mixed, by claiming that all atoms have the same nature. To that extent, their solution is the same as that of Diogenes. But it is better, because there is no alteration in the atoms themselves. Diogenes has no explanation of why things happen as they do, except to say that air is intelligent.[22] But this is not a full explanation (any more than the Atomists' mechanistic account is a full explanation).

Diogenes' theory is a genuine response to Eleatic arguments and should be seen as such, rather than simply as a reversion to older, Milesian, theories. But its monism does not make it a better response than Pluralism or Atomism. All of these theories accept the metaphysical principles argued for by Parmenides, and each, in one way or another, runs afoul of difficulties posed by the later Eleatics, Zeno and Melissus.

2. The Last Presocratic: Plato and the Legacy of Parmenides

With few exceptions, Plato scholars have thought that Plato's interest in Eleaticism is confined to his later period, finding the first evidence of it (and of Eleatic influence) in the *Parmenides* itself.[23] Chief among the exceptions are Solmsen, who in 1971 pointed out the connection between the description of the Beautiful itself in the *Symposium* (at 211a ff.) and Parmenides' description of what-is in 28B8, and Nehamas, whose 1979 article traces the requirement that forms be self-predicating to origins in Parmenides' account of what-is.[24] I shall follow the interpretations of Solmsen and Nehamas, and, in addition, I shall consider further traces of Eleaticism in Plato. The most dramatic evidence of Parmenides' influence on Plato is to be found in Diotima's description of the beautiful itself in the *Symposium,* a passage that is generally accepted as Plato's own account of the nature of the Form of Beauty, and by extension, of the characteristics of all Forms. At the end of the ascent to beauty, the searcher will "suddenly behold something amazingly beautiful in its nature" which is the object of all his searches. Diotima goes

22 To the extent that intelligence plays no real cosmological role in Diogenes' theory, he is subject to the same criticism as that leveled at Anaxagoras by Socrates in the *Phd.* (98b7–c1).

23 Solmsen mentions that Hackforth and Guthrie (who notes links between Parmenides and Plato's claims at *Phd.* 78d) find some Parmenidean influence in the *Phd.* ("Perfect Beauty," p. 202n.3). In his *Plato's Phaedo* (p. 15), Bostock dismisses the possibility of any such influence: "Others have seen ... the influence of Parmenides, who insisted that what genuinely is cannot change. But ... that seems to me to be a rather later influence." Schofield claims that the arguments of *Prm.* are the result of Plato's new-found interest in Eleaticism and do not necessarily express Plato's own opinions (see Schofield, "Neglected" and "Antinomies").

24 See Solmsen, "Perfect Beauty," and Nehamas, "Self-Predication."

on to describe what is said to be "that which is beautiful itself" (211c8–d1: αὐτὸ . . . ὃ ἔστι καλόν):

> πρῶτον μὲν ἀεὶ ὂν καὶ οὔτε γιγνόμενον οὔτε ἀπολλύμενον, οὔτε αὐξανόμενον οὔτε φθίνον, ἔπειτα οὐ τῇ μὲν καλόν, τῇ δ' αἰσχρόν, οὐδὲ τοτὲ μέν, τοτὲ δὲ οὔ, οὐδὲ πρὸς μὲν τὸ καλόν, πρὸς δὲ τὸ αἰσχρόν, οὐδ' ἔνθα μὲν καλόν, ἔνθα δὲ αἰσχρόν, ὡς τισὶ μὲν ὂν καλόν, τισὶ δὲ αἰσχρόν· οὐδ' αὖ φαντασθήσεται αὐτῷ τὸ καλὸν οἷον πρόσωπόν τι οὐδὲ χεῖρες οὐδὲ ἄλλο οὐδὲν ὧν σῶμα μετέχει, οὐδέ τις λόγος οὐδέ τις ἐπιστήμη, οὐδέ που ὂν ἐν ἑτέρῳ τινι, οἷον ἐν ζώῳ ἢ ἐν γῇ ἢ ἐν οὐρανῷ ἢ ἔν τῳ ἄλλῳ, ἀλλ' αὐτὸ καθ' αὐτὸ μεθ' αὑτοῦ μονοειδὲς ἀεὶ ὄν, τὰ δὲ ἄλλα πάντα καλὰ ἐκείνου μετέχοντα τρόπον τινὰ τοιοῦτον, οἷον γιγνομένων τε τῶν ἄλλων καὶ ἀπολλυμένων, μηδὲν ἐκεῖνο μήτε τι πλέον μήτε ἔλαττον γίγνεσθαι μηδὲ πάσχειν μηδέν.
>
> (*Symp.* 210e6–211b5)

> First, it always is and neither comes to be nor passes away, neither grows nor diminishes. Next, it is not beautiful in this way and ugly in that, nor is it beautiful at some time, and not at another, nor is it beautiful in relation to one thing and ugly in relation to another, nor beautiful here and ugly there, as it would be, being beautiful to some and ugly to others. Nor again will the beautiful appear to him as a face or hands or as anything else partaking of body, nor as some *logos* nor as some knowledge, nor will it be in some other thing, such as in a living thing or in earth or in heaven or in anything else; but is itself by itself and with itself, always one in form, all the other beautiful things partaking of it in such a way that, while the others come to be and pass away, it becomes not the least bit more nor less nor undergoes anything.

Solmsen has explored some of the ways that this passage resembles Parmenides' account of what-is, discussing how the characters attributed to the Beautiful itself can be traced to the signs of B8.1–4 and to further arguments in B8. But further Parmenidean influence, and some traceable to Melissus, can also be seen here as well. Taken all together, these reminders of Parmenides and Melissus suggest that Forms are themselves Eleatic basic entities that serve as the foundation of a theory that seeks to explain certain characteristics of objects in the world reported by the senses. Plato, at least in the middle dialogues, deserves to be called the last Presocratic.[25]

[25] Nehamas, in "Self-Predication," calls Plato's "one of the last Presocratic systems"; see p. 98. There is an important difference between Plato and the other post-Parmenidean thinkers discussed here. Plato seeks explanations of a different range of characteristics than had been the objects of explanation by other philosophers. His main interests are in ethical and other evaluative concepts, and in what can be called incomplete predicates, at least prior to the *Ti.* (See Brentlinger, "Incomplete Predicates" and Nehamas, "Self-Predication" on this issue.) There is great controversy surrounding attempts to date or to order Plato's works. In speaking of the "middle" dialogues here, I mean those that come after the earliest Socratic dialogues

The description of the Beautiful begins by asserting that the thing which is "amazingly beautiful in its nature" is something that always is and neither comes to be nor passes away. This matches with Parmenides B8.3, lines that claim that what-is is ungenerable and imperishable (ἀγένητον ἐὸν καὶ ἀνώλεθρόν ἐστιν) and with Melissus's claim that what-is is "always" (especially in fragments B1 and B3).[26] Plato here stresses that *to kalon* (the Beautiful) is something that is, that is a true being, rather than something that comes to be. This distinction between being and becoming is fundamental to the Theory of Forms, and here in the *Symposium,* Plato clearly links that distinction, and the claim that Forms are genuine realities, with Eleatic requirements. Diotima's rejection of growth and diminishment are further rejections of coming-to-be and passing-away and are also grounded in the claim that the Beautiful is a thing that is, just as Parmenides' rejection of growth in B8.6–11 is itself a development of the *krisis* "is or is not." At B8.15 Parmenides makes it clear that all of the preceding arguments, which have repudiated coming-to-be in several forms, are based on the judgment that what-is-not is impossible. Diminishment (*phthinein*) is a type of passing-away and is thus impossible, as is growth. Growth and decay are aspects of growing or living things, mortal things that are subject to coming-to-be and passing-away. The Form, the Beautiful itself, as something that always is (*aei on*) can have no share of such processes, just as Parmenides had argued (B8.6–11).[27]

Further, the Beautiful itself is genuinely beautiful. Indeed, it is what it is to be beautiful; thus it will never be ugly, in any way, at any time, or to any one. It is completely or perfectly beautiful, satisfying Parmenides' claim that what-is is complete (B8.4) and altogether one, cohesive (B8.5–6). At B8.22–25 Parmenides expanded the claim of cohesiveness; what-is is indivisible because it is all alike: "nor is there somewhat more here, which would prevent it from cohering, nor somewhat less there, but all is completely full of what-is" (B8.23–24; also B8.47–48: "nor is there any

---

of search and before the dialogues of the critical period such as the *Th.,* the *Prm.,* the *Sph.* Although there are disagreements about the placement of dialogues within periods, I think that it is both legitimate and helpful to think of Plato's worries as falling roughly into three groups that may be termed "early," "middle," and "late," with transitionary periods between the main groups. The dialogues I have in mind as middle would include the *Ph.,* the *Smp.,* and the *R.,* with the *Meno* as one of the dialogues transitional between the early and middle periods. Recent attempts to group or date Plato's dialogues using stylometrics have proved inconclusive. See Robinson, "Plato and the Computer" and Young, "Computer Dating."

[26] These points are made by Solmsen, "Perfect Beauty," pp. 204–5.

[27] Solmsen thinks that the only claim that is directly traceable to Parmenides is that *to kalon* is not subject to growth; he loosely links the rejection of *phthinein* with Melissus B7.4. But just as growth is a form of coming-to-be, so decay is a type of passing-away, and both are ruled out by Parmenides' claim that what-is is and cannot not be. See Solmsen, "Perfect Beauty," pp. 205–6 with nn. 12 and 13, for his attempts to deal with decay.

way in which what-is could be here more or there less than what-is, since it is all inviolate"). In the same way, being all alike beautiful, *to kalon* can never be ugly in any way, for that would imply that it was somehow less than completely beautiful. Being beautiful is the entire nature of the Beautiful itself (210e4–5); it is all equally full of beauty, as Parmenides might say (compare B8.24), leaving no possibility of what is not beautiful, or ugly. Parmenides likens the perfection of what-is to the bulk of a well-rounded sphere (B8.43–44), and with that simile he stresses the perfection and perspectival neutrality of what-is ("it may be neither somewhat larger nor somewhat smaller here or there" B8.44–45; "equal to itself in every direction, it lies equally in the bounds" B8.48–49).[28] It is the same with the Beautiful. Being completely and perfectly beautiful, it will retain that character no matter who considers it, from whatever point of view.[29] Again, the fundamental notion is the exclusion of what-is-not; any deviation from being *F* is rejected by Parmenides on the grounds that such deviation allows what-is-not, and so what-is completely and perfectly is. In the same way, Plato excludes ugliness, that which is not beautiful, from the Beautiful itself. Here in the *Symposium,* we have Plato filling in the details of the Parmenidean criteria for the nature or reality of something: in this case, the nature of Beauty.

The next step in the description of the Beautiful itself shows that it is not anything bodily, nor anything conceived of as a thought or knowledge. Nor is it dependent on something other than itself, nor is it in anything else. The rejection of anything bodily is surely connected with the various beautiful things that the lover of Diotima's speech has encountered on his ascent to the beautiful, but it can also be connected with Melissus's claim that what-is has no body (B9).[30] Similarly the rejection of Beauty as a kind of *logos* or *epistēmē* is clearly connected with the details of claims made within the *Symposium* itself, but there is an association with Parmenides as well.[31] For Parmenides, what-is is the object of thought and knowledge; the link is made explicitly in B3 and B4, while what-is-not is introduced as impossible in B2 (7–8) on the grounds that it cannot be known or pointed out. But although what-is is what is thought or known or talked about ("to this have all names been given" B8.38), it is not to be identified with a thought or a particular piece of knowledge or a particular speech. It is independent of all these.

28 On the notion of perspectival neutrality, see Mourelatos, *Route,* pp. 129–30.

29 Solmsen discusses this part of the *Smp.* passage on pp. 206–7 of "Perfect Beauty." He points out the parallels with B8.23–24 and B8.44 but does not discuss the passages or their significance, other than to note that they "exclude relativism" and deny imperfections in the Beautiful.

30 The claim can also be linked with Zeno's arguments against physical divisibility.

31 Solmsen claims that "there is nothing in Parmenides that could be compared" with these claims at 211a5–7 ("Perfect Beauty," p. 207).

The independence and perfection of the Beautiful appear at 211b1–2, along with the fundamentally important claim that the Beautiful is "always one in form" (*monoeides aei*). Diotima says that "itself by itself and with itself it is always one in form," stressing that it is separated and different from all the many manifestations of beauty; yet Beauty is the same in every case, for it is *monoeides.* No matter how different each instance of beauty may be, each is a manifestation of the Beautiful, for there is but a single kind for Beauty. That a Form is itself by itself (αὐτὸ καθ' αὑτό) is a favored epithet, appearing several times in the *Phaedo.* It appears at 78d5–6, in the general description of Forms, linked (as in the *Symposium*) with the claim that each Form is *monoeides,* and with the assertion that Forms are unchanging: each Form, Socrates says, always is, "being single in form itself by itself" (μονοειδὲς ὂν αὐτὸ καθ' αὑτό).[32] The locution reappears in the *Parmenides* when Socrates introduces what is clearly the middle period Theory of Forms. He asks Zeno, "Do you not think that there is itself by itself (αὐτὸ καθ' αὑτό) some form of Likeness . . . ?" The notion embodied in the declaration that a form is αὐτὸ καθ' αὑτό can be traced to Parmenides' claim about what-is:

> Remaining the same and in the same, it lies by itself (ταὐτόν τ' ἐν ταὐτῷ τε μένον καθ' ἑαυτό τε κεῖται)
> and remains there steadfast: for mighty Necessity
> holds it in the limits of a bond, which holds it in all around.
> (B8.29–31)

This passage follows the goddess's claim that what-is is changeless (*akinēton*). It lies by itself, far from anything that comes to be and passes away (for coming-to-be and passing-away have been "driven out" by "true trust"). So the contrast here is between something that might seem to change and what-is, which is always the same and steadfast. Likewise, the Beautiful is "itself by itself" and this is contrasted with the many beautifuls that fluctuate in the world of coming-to-be and passing-away. The Beautiful is separated from them, always the same, for it is one in form. This, too is a notion from Parmenides, who claims that what-is is single-in-genus or kind (*mounogenes*).[33] Parmenides argues that to be is to be all, only, and

[32] I take the claim as an assertion. The whole passage is a series of questions about the unchanging character of the Forms, to which Cebes gives an affirmative answer.

[33] Solmsen notes the similarities between 211b1–2 and Parmenides B8.29 ("Perfect Beauty" p. 207). But he is reluctant to link *monoeides* with Parmenides' *mounogenes* (pp. 208–9). He apparently takes Parmenides use to mean "only begotten" rather than "single-in-genus." If this were the case, Plato's *monoeides* would indeed sit uneasily with the Parmenidean claim, for there is surely a plurality of Forms. But the interpretation of Parmenides that I have argued for fits easily with Plato's claim. Parmenides asserts that each thing that is is a unity of a particular kind, a unity that is well summed up in *mounogenes* as Mourelatos, Barnes, and I interpret it (see Chap. II, pp. 71–73).

completely what a thing is. There is but a single way to be that thing, and what is *F* must be so unchangingly, wholly, completely. This means that there can be but a single account of what it is to be *F*, for anything else would allow for differences, shades, and possibilities of being not-*F*. As Parmenides puts it, what-is "is now all together one, cohesive" (B8.5–6 νῦν ἔστιν ὁμοῦ πᾶν ἕν, συνεχές). When Plato asserts that *to kalon* is always one and the same, because it is *monoeides,* he must mean that no matter how many various ways of being beautiful are manifested by sensible things, there is in truth but a single nature of Beauty itself that underlies them all.[34]

The contrast between the perfect unchanging nature of beauty and other things which merely have beauty is underscored at 211b2–5: "all the other beautiful things partaking of it in such a way that, while the others come to be and pass away, it [the Beautiful itself] becomes not the least bit more or less nor undergoes anything." Here we have the Parmenidean claim that what-is is unshaking (B8.4), immobile and unchanging (B8.26–28), not subject to displacement from what it is.[35] But there is an indication of other Eleatic influence here as well. The passage asserts that there is a connection between the Beautiful itself and "all the other beautiful things," those things that will in *Phaedo* be said to be named after the form (see *Phd.* 102b1–2). The *Phaedo* makes clear that the connection is a causal one, that the Form is responsible for the character of the things that participate in it. And in the *Phaedo,* too, it is claimed that the participation of *f*-things in the *F* itself leaves the Form unaffected, no matter how the participants may wax and wane or otherwise change (see 78d1–7). Why does Plato so emphasize that participation, while having a great effect on participants, leaves the Form itself unaffected?

Participation is one of the great mysteries of the Theory of Forms. Its details are unclear in the *Phaedo* (see 100d4–8), and it is one of the central issues that the character Parmenides raises for question in the *Parmenides.* If the Forms are genuine Parmenidean entities, then the analogue for participation in other post-Parmenidean theories would be the Anaxagorean claim that "everything is in everything," Empedoclean mixture, or the mingling and separation of atoms, those mechanisms by which the fundamental and real entities produce or account for the objects of the world reported by the senses. But Melissus had attacked this very feature of those theories, arguing that there is no causal link possible between genuine entities and sensible objects that would explain the latter while leaving the former unscathed by coming-to-be and passing-away. In B8, as we have seen, he insisted that either both the fundamental entities and the sensible objects must change (which is impossible without undermining a theory committed

[34] This point is underscored at 211d8–e4, where the Beautiful itself, "absolute, pure, unmixed," is contrasted with that which is "infected with human flesh and colors." It is said to be "divine single-formed beauty itself" (αὐτὸ τὸ θεῖον καλὸν . . . μονοειδές).

[35] See Chap. II, pp. 83–87.

to the unchanging nature of its real beings) or neither the genuine entities nor the sensible objects change (which is inconsistent with experience); thus no causal connection between the metaphysically basic entity and the world of sense experience is possible. Participation can be read as Plato's answer to Melissus. Having separated the Forms to a realm beyond the sensible, where they neither come to be nor pass away, he then re-connects them to the sensible world through the mechanism of participation. But participation is not the same as mixing and separation, for it leaves the Forms untouched and unchanged, in exactly the way that Melissus's argument in B8 would seem to require.[36] This is exactly what appears in *Symposium* 211b1–5: itself by itself with itself, and single in character, the Beautiful itself accounts for all other beautiful things (because they share in it), but no matter how they may come to be, pass away, or alter, it remains untouched, becoming "not the least bit more or less." This same claim appears in the *Phaedo* at 78d4–7, where it is stressed that a Form, being *monoeides,* and itself by itself, never changes at all: "it admits not a single alteration, not ever, in any way, in any wise" (οὐδέποτε οὐδαμῇ οὐδαμῶς ἀλλοίωσιν οὐδεμίαν ἐνδέχεται).

The Eleatic influence on the description of the Beautiful itself in the *Symposium* and the accounts of Forms in the *Phaedo* seem unmistakable, and given the affinities between this account and the more general discussions of Forms in the *Phaedo,* there seems little doubt that Plato was thinking in Eleatic terms when those dialogues were written. But there is also evidence that the Parmenidean influence was there even earlier, for there are signs of it in some of the earlier dialogues, before the Theory of Forms of the middle period appears.

In the earlier, Socratic dialogues, Plato represents Socrates as engaged in a search for an account of the excellences of character, such as friendship, courage, piety, or beauty. Aristotle says that Socrates was the first to look for the universal definition in such cases, but he is adamant that, in contrast to Plato, Socrates did not separate universals and particulars (*Metaph.* 987a29–b9). One influence on the Socratic search was surely the Sophistic movement, with its emphasis on the particular virtues needed for political success, but there is also Eleatic influence to be found in the conception of that for which Socrates is searching, and the characteristics he claims that the object of his search possesses.[37] Whether or not Socrates actually succeeds in extracting

[36] There are a number of problems here. First, participation remains essentially unexplained in the middle period, as is clear from both the *Prm.* and from Aristotle's comments (*Metaph.* I.987b10–14). Second, the arguments of Part I of the *Prm.* show that Plato is worried that participation actually does affect the Forms, and in a way that is fatal to the theory. Given that participation at the level of the Forms is introduced in Part II of the *Prm.* and used in the Sophist in the blending of Forms, it is clear that Plato thinks that he can solve the difficulties (or dissolve the problem that raises the difficulties).

[37] Here references to "Socrates" are to the character as he appears in the various Platonic dialogues. We simply do not know if the historical Socrates would have characterized the pious,

from his interlocutors the information for which he is looking, and whether or not he himself actually has knowledge of these things, it is evident that Socrates has a clear conception of what the pious, or courage, must be like. That is, he seems certain that he knows the criteria for a successful account of the nature of an excellence of character, for he uses these criteria to evaluate (and reject) suggestions made by his interlocutors.

In the *Euthyphro,* while questioning Euthyphro about the nature of piety or holiness, Socrates claims that whatever the correct account of the nature of holiness is, that single account will cover all cases of holiness:

> ἢ οὐ ταὐτόν ἐστιν ἐν πάσῃ πράξει τὸ ὅσιον αὐτὸ αὑτῷ, καὶ τὸ ἀνόσιον αὖ τοῦ μὲν ὁσίου παντὸς ἐναντίον, αὐτὸ δὲ αὑτῷ ὅμοιον καὶ ἔχον μίαν τινὰ ἰδέαν κατὰ τὴν ἀνοσιότητα πᾶν ὅτιπερ ἂν μέλλῃ ἀνόσιον εἶναι;
>
> (*Euthphr.* 5d1–5)

> Is not the holy the same as itself in every action, and again, is not the unholy in every way opposite to the holy and the same as itself? And everything that is going to be unholy has one single character in accordance with unholiness?

The same point is made at *Laches* 191e10–11: Socrates asks Laches to tell him "what, is courage, being the same in all these cases" (ἀνδρείαν . . . τί ὂν ἐν πᾶσι τούτοις ταὐτόν ἐστιν). The request for a single account to cover all instances also appears in the *Hippias Major.*[38] At 288a8–9 Socrates' rude questioner asks him, "All those things that you say are beautiful, what is the beautiful itself (τί ἐστιν αὐτὸ τὸ καλόν) if these would be beautiful?" The use of the singular article along with *auto* (itself) is an indication that the search is for a single thing, and not a series of things, accounts of which will cover all cases. There is a trivial sense in which whatever account is given (no matter how complex) will be one, for it will be a numerically single account. But Plato's point is not trivial. A unitary account in the proper sense is one in which the one and the same account of the *F* will cover all the cases of *f*-ness that are examined, and it will extend to as yet unexamined cases as well, because the *F*-itself is but a single thing. He here rules out disjunctive definitions, or those that are built up by the addition of new cases. The *F* has a single nature, which is manifested in all the various instances of *f*-ness; the single account of that nature is the object of Socrates' search. In the *Meno* (a dialogue that is transitional between the early and the middle period), Plato

---

the beautiful, friendship, or courage as Socrates does in the dialogues. I take no stand on the contentious (and recently much-discussed) issue of how much of the historical Socrates we can extract from the dialogues. My interest is in examining the traces of Eleatic influences on Plato, the author of all the dialogues considered here.

[38] I accept the *Hp. Ma.* as genuine. Woodruff defends the authenticity of the dialogue and surveys the history of the debate over the question in *Hippias Major,* esp. pp. 93–103. For a recent expression of doubts, see Kahn, "Beautiful."

gives a straightforward statement of the principle.[39] In the discussion of the nature of shape, Socrates says to Meno:

> Ἀεὶ εἰς πολλὰ ἀφικνούμεθα, ἀλλὰ μή μοι οὕτως, ἀλλ' ἐπειδὴ τὰ πολλὰ ταῦτα ἑνί τινι προσαγορεύεις ὀνόματι, καὶ φῂς οὐδὲν αὐτῶν ὅτι οὐ σχῆμα εἶναι, καὶ ταῦτα καὶ ἐναντία ὄντα ἀλλήλοις, ὅτι ἐστὶν τοῦτο ὃ οὐδὲν ἧττον κατέχει τὸ στρογγύλον ἢ τὸ εὐθύ, ὃ δὴ ὀνομάζεις σχῆμα καὶ οὐδὲν μᾶλλον φῂς τὸ στρογγύλον σχῆμα εἶναι ἢ τὸ εὐθύ; (*Meno* 74d4–e2)
>
> We always arrive at a many, but that is not what I want. But since you call these many by some one name, and you say that none of them is not a shape, even though they are opposites to one another, what is this that no less occupies the round than the straight, which you name shape and when you say that the round is shape no more than the straight?

Despite being opposites, straight and round are both shapes, and so there is a single character that they share and a single account of shape that will cover both cases. Although the principle is first explicitly stated in the *Meno,* it is clear that it has been at work in the earlier dialogues as well.

In addition to meeting the criterion of being one and the same in all cases, the object of Socrates' search must function as a pattern or model of the *F* against which to measure *f*-things. The clearest instance of this is in the Euthyphro, at 6e:

> Ταύτην τοίνυν με αὐτὴν δίδαξον τὴν ἰδέαν τίς ποτέ ἐστιν, ἵνα εἰς ἐκείνην ἀποβλέπων καὶ χρώμενος αὐτῇ παραδείγματι, ὃ μὲν ἂν τοιοῦτον ᾖ ὧν ἂν ἢ σὺ ἢ ἄλλος τις πράττῃ φῶ ὅσιον εἶναι, ὃ δ' ἂν μὴ τοιοῦτον, μὴ φῶ.
> (*Euthphr.* 6e3–6)
>
> Show me now what in the world this very character is, in order that, looking to it and using it as a model, I may say that any action done by you or anyone else which is such as it, is holy, and that which is not such as it, is not.

The holy can serve as a pattern or model in all cases, because it is a single thing, and because, it is implied, it is itself holy (I shall return to this presently). An action that is "such as the holy" may be called holy because it resembles the holy that is a model; any action that falls short is unholy. Thus, and this is the third criterion, that for which Socrates searches is explanatory. It is not only a single model or *paradeigma,* to which one may look to judge the *f*-ness of *f*-things. It explains why those things are *f*.[40] The explanatory nature of that for which Socrates searches appears in the *Euthyphro,* along with the claim that it is one:

[39] Nehamas calls this the "one-Name Principle." See "Self-Predication," pp. 99–102.

[40] Woodruff calls this requirement logical causation. See *Hippias Major,* pp. 151–53 and 170–71.

Μέμνησαι οὖν ὅτι οὐ τοῦτό σοι διεκελευόμην, ἕν τι ἢ δύο με διδάξει τῶν πολλῶν ὁσίων, ἀλλ' ἐκεῖνο αὐτὸ τὸ εἶδος ᾧ πάντα τὰ ὅσια ὅσιά ἐστιν· ἔφησθα γάρ που μιᾷ ἰδέᾳ τά τε ἀνόσια ἀνόσια εἶναι καὶ τὰ ὅσια ὅσια.

(*Euthphr.* 6d9–e1)

Don't you remember then that I did not ask you this, to point out to me some one or two of the many pieties, but that character (*eidos*) itself by which all holy things are holy: For I suppose you said that it is by one single character (*idea*) that the unholy things are unholy and the holy things are holy.

Socrates asks for the single thing that is responsible for, causes, and will thus explain, why all holy things are holy and all unholy things unholy. The instrumental dative represents the agency at work here. Not only is there a single account of the *F*, but the *F* itself, of which it is the account, is responsible for the *f*-character of *f*-things. Moreover, because of its single nature in all cases, and its explanatory character, the *F* can be used as a paradigm or model against which to measure *f*-things, as the *Euthyphro* makes clear. For this passage is immediately followed by the one quoted above, in which Socrates asks for a *paradeigma*. The causal and explanatory nature of the *F* is further stressed in the *Hippias Major*. In a series of questions, from 287c1 to d1, it is concluded that it is by justice (*dikaiosunēi*) that the just are just, by wisdom (*sophiāi*) that the wise are wise, by the good (*tōi agathōi*) that good things are good, and by beauty (*tōi kalōi*) that beautiful things are beautiful.

The three criteria that the object of Socrates' search must meet, that it must be one, must function as a paradigm, and must be explanatory, are connected. They are all aspects of what it is to be the true nature of a thing, to be what a thing is, and it is such a nature or the reality of a thing that is the object of Socrates' inquiries. The three requirements are based on a Parmenidean conception of what a genuine thing must be. The demand that the object of Socrates' search must be something that both explains and is responsible for the *f*-characters of *f*-things is a form of the Eleatic claim that what-is cannot come from what-is-not. This is entailed by the *krisis* referred to at Parmenides B8.15 and was the principle at work in all of Parmenides' arguments against coming-to-be, passing-away, and growth. In the Socratic dialogues of search the issue appears as the claim that what is not-*f* cannot be responsible for or cause what is *f*. This is a version of the scholiast's question preserved in Anaxagoras B10 ("for how could hair come from what is not hair and flesh from what is not flesh?"), which also had its origin in the claim that what-is cannot come from what-is-not. The unity requirement similarly is based on a Parmenidean view. Parmenides had argued that to be the nature of a something, a thing must be single in character, and we have seen that requirement echoed in the *Phaedo* and *Symposium* claims that a Form is *monoeides.* The unity criterion is simply an early version of those claims. Insofar as things are called by the same name, they share the same nature, and that nature must be a single thing, for otherwise it would both be and not be *f,* and insofar as it failed to be *f,* it could not account for the nature of *f*-things (thus failing to meet the explanation criterion), and so those things would fail to be *f.* But if something is wholly and completely *f* (thus meeting the unity requirement) and is responsible for the *f*-ness of *f*-things (thus meeting the explanation criterion), it may be used as a standard to judge whether or not anything else is *f.* It also then meets the demand that the object of Socrates' search serve as a *paradeigma.* So the entities that Socrates searches for, the natures of holiness, courage, friendship, beauty, and so on, are themselves Parmenidean basic natures, which Socrates apparently hopes to discover through examining cases with his interlocutors. Socrates is quite certain of the character of the things he searches for; he is less certain of what those entities are. Indeed, in the early dialogues he never succeeds in finding an account of *f*-ness that is adequate, that is, that meets the criteria he has set out.[41] But it is worth noting that Socrates does not treat those criteria as open to question or revision.[42] Rather, they are taken for granted by Socrates; moreover, they are also accepted unquestioningly by his interlocutors.[43] It might seem puzzling that those who converse with Socrates are so ready to accept his account of what the nature of thing must be. But if the basis of Socrates' claims were indeed the Eleatic conception of what it is to be the nature of a thing, Plato could, without being dramatically implausible, present Socrates' criteria as familiar and accepted by all parties to the discussions. So here, too, in Plato's earlier dialogues we also find Parmenidean influence at work.

The metaphysical requirements for being a genuine entity that Plato took over from Parmenides play a fundamental role in a central notion of Plato's mature Theory of Forms: the self-predication of Forms.[44] The Socratic requirements indicated that in order genuinely to be the nature of a thing, an entity must be one in the proper sense, causal and explanatory, and must be capable of serving as a paradigm. Little wonder then that Plato's Forms, his separated version of the entities he depicts Socrates as searching for in the earlier dialogues, are themselves self-predicating. For if Beauty itself is not beautiful, how can anything else be

41 I have discussed some of the reasons for this failure in "Empiricism."

42 See Vlastos, "Elenchus," p. 33 with n. 12. I do not mean to suggest that Socrates conceived of the natures for which he searches as separate entities in the full-blown Platonic sense of the middle period. It is clear, I think, that he does not. On this issue see, for instance, Woodruff, *Hippias Major,* pp.161–80.

43 See Nehamas, "Self-Predication," pp. 93–94 on this issue.

44 This issue has been thoroughly discussed by Nehamas ("Self-Predication"). I accept and use Nehamas's account of self-predication, and I have little to add to his account of the nature of self-predication and its role in Plato's theory.

beautiful?[45] Unless Beauty were beautiful, it would be a thing that is not (insofar as it would be not-beautiful) and as such could not serve as the object of knowledge or as the explanation of the things that participate in it and come to be called after its name. Self-predication is at the core of the Theory of Forms, and it links the theories of Parmenides and Plato. Because Forms are self-predicating, they can be causal explanations and serve as paradigms, while retaining their essential unity. The Beautiful itself is what it is to be beautiful, and Justice itself is what it is to be just (the accounts of Beauty or Justice will fit on the left-hand side of the *is* here) and as such each both meets Parmenidean criteria for what-is and is able to account for the characteristics of objects in the world reported by the senses. Those objects are dependent on the Forms for their characters and fall short of the Forms because they (unlike the Forms) fail to be genuine entities. They are subject to generation and destruction as well as alteration, and while actually being neither *f* nor not-*f*, are called by both names.[46] In the *Phaedo* (at 102bd3), the distinction between being *F* and merely having *f*-ness is made explicitly, and it is clear that only Forms are in the full sense. This is true because, unlike particulars, they are what they are in virtue of themselves, while particulars have their characters in virtue of their participation in Forms. A Form is *F* because of itself, because it itself is the very nature of *f*-ness, and in being such a nature, it meets Parmenidean criteria for what-is. Like other Presocratic theories that work within a Parmenidean framework, Plato sees no difficulty in adopting a theory that is committed to the reality of a plurality of entities, each of which is and is one in the appropriate sense.

But if Plato adopted Parmenidean predicational monism and the Parmenidean account of what-is as early as the so-called Socratic dialogues, making Forms Parmenidean entities, why does he, in the *Parmenides* and other late dialogues, attribute to Parmenides the rather different, numerical monism, that we find there? Later philosophers imputed to Parmenides a commitment to "the One" and to the claim that "the all is one," and it is likely that this interpretation has its origins in Plato's accounts of Parmenides and Eleaticism in the later dialogues. There are, I think, several reasons for Plato's characterization of Parmenides in the later works. It must be kept in mind that Plato probably did not intend his dialogues to be taken as historical documents. The discussion between the characters "Parmenides"

[45] Thus Socrates' otherwise surprising comment at *Phd.* 100c4–6: "If anything is beautiful other than the beautiful itself" (εἴ τί ἐστιν ἄλλο καλὸν πλὴν αὐτὸ τὸ καλόν), it is beautiful because it participates in that Beautiful. What Socrates finds in need of explanation is not why the form is beautiful but how anything else could possibly be beautiful. See Fujisawa and also Nehamas, "Self-Predication."

[46] See *Phd.* 102b1–6, also 74b4–c2. See also Nehamas, "Imperfection" and Vlastos, "Degrees of Reality." In the *R.* the claim is that sensible particulars roll between being and not-being (479d3–5). This claim comes in the midst of a discussion of epistemological states and their objects that is redolent of Eleatic claims. On Eleatic influence in *R.* V, see also Crystal.

and "Socrates" that occurs in the *Parmenides* could not have taken place as it is written.[47] It is clear that other dialogues in which historical figures appear are not meant as accurate records (the *Symposium* and the *Protagoras,* for instance). There is no reason to expect the *Parmenides* to be different. It is important to remember that the purpose of the dialogue is to explore and to criticize certain aspects of Plato's own Theory of Forms, especially the relation of participation, and the conception of Forms at work in the theory. That conception of Forms as Parmenidean entities, each of which is and is one in the Eleatic sense, comes under attack in the negative hypotheses of Part II of the dialogue. There Plato explores not only the nature of the Forms, but also the important question of the relations between Forms. Plato's conclusion is that the conception of what-is at work in that theory is too strong to allow for such standard and necessary claims about the Forms as that they are the same as themselves and different from one other.[48] Plato determines that, in the last analysis, adopting the Parmenidean account of what-is actually commits one to the view that there can indeed be only one thing. At the end of Chapter II (in Section 3), I raised the issue of whether differences between Parmenidean entities can affect the inner unity of what-is, and I suggested that such differences might cause difficulties for the Parmenidean account. I think that Plato's realization of this at the time of the later dialogues (apparently the first sustained exploration of this issue) led him to rethink and to revise the Eleatic account of what it is to be a genuine entity. And because he thought that the Eleatic view entailed a commitment to numerical monism, Plato presents this as Parmenides' view in the *Parmenides* and the *Sophist.*[49] His authority guaranteed that later authors (such as Simplicius) would take his account as historically accurate. As different problems began to worry Aristotle and later philosophers, the influence of Eleaticism faded, and Plato's portrait of Parmenides was mistaken for the original.

Often, Plato's Theory of Forms is characterized as a strikingly creative but essentially unmotivated theory, or as a theory that Plato formulated as a response to the Sophists but without other serious metaphysical and

[47] The mature Platonic Theory of Forms in the mouth of the very young Socrates is a major piece of evidence against the view that the *Prm.* is a historically accurate document.

[48] I argued for this view in a series of papers on the *Prm.* For recent, differing, views of the *Prm.* see Meinwald and Gill.

[49] Barnes suggests that Plato's presentation of Parmenides in the *Prm.* is the result of "a careless conflation" of the views of Parmenides and Melissus: "Melissus soon became the chief representative of the Eleatic school; and Parmenides' obscure verses were read—and misread—in the light of his successor's clear prose" ("Eleatic One," p. 21n.77). While it is true, I think, that the views of Parmenides and Melissus were both important to Plato, there is no reason to think that he carelessly conflated them; he apparently distinguishes between them clearly enough in the middle dialogues. Aristotle, too, recognizes the differences between Parmenides and Melissus.

epistemological precedents.[50] I have argued that Plato's conception of the nature of a thing is inherited from Parmenides, and that the attacks on Pluralism and Atomism by Zeno and Melissus gave Plato reason to think that a nature must be a non-corporeal, predicationally unitary thing. Like the other Presocratic thinkers I have discussed, Plato did not slavishly follow the Parmenidean line. But the arguments of Parmenides and the other Eleatics surely helped to shape Plato's understanding of the philosophical problems to be solved and the structure a successful solution must have, and so his conception of the Forms themselves. Thus Plato, too, belongs in an account of the legacy of Parmenides.

3. Conclusion

This study has argued for an interpretation of Parmenides that makes him a pivotal figure in the development of Presocratic philosophy. On this interpretation, Parmenides' concern is not to reject early Presocratic inquiry into the nature of things, but to reform such inquiry by formulating criteria for a successful account of what there is. The *krisis* at the heart of Parmenides' argument, "is or is not," rules out any candidate for an ultimate entity in an explanation of what there is that is subject to coming-to-be, passing-away, or alteration of any sort. Such an entity must be a whole, complete, unchanging unity: it must be a thing that is of a single kind, *mounogenes.* But it does not follow from this that there can be only one such entity. Parmenides' arguments allow for a plurality of fundamental, predicationally unified entities that can be used to explain the world reported by the senses. Parmenides' own account of that world, the *Doxa,* is, as the goddess says, a deceptive story; but that does not mean that any such account of the world of the senses will, simply by being such an account, be false or deceptive. The error of the *Doxa* is to begin with two entities, Light and Night, that cannot satisfy Parmenides' criteria for an acceptable basic entity. Because Light and Night are opposites that are defined in terms of negations (each is what the other is not), they cannot be whole, complete, unchanging things of a single kind. But the goddess does not rule out the possibility that there could be a successful explanation of the world reported by the senses, one that does not repeat the mortal error of thinking that "to be and not to be are the same and not the same" (28B6.8–9). Such an account would satisfy Parmenides' claims in *Alētheia* while explaining the world of the senses and

[50] Aristotle's references to Heraclitus and Cratylus in Book I of the *Metaph.* (at 987a32–b1) have led to various views about the influence of Heraclitus's account of flux on the theory. While the Heraclitean component is quite important, particularly in Plato's conception of the instability of particulars, it is the views of Parmenides that shape Plato's metaphysical commitments.

would be a rational cosmology. Parmenides himself does not provide this rational cosmology; but his arguments in the *Alētheia* and his likely-seeming story in the *Doxa* provide a model and a standard for such a cosmology.

On this interpretation Parmenides was a positive influence on later Presocratic thought, providing arguments and a model that were accepted and followed rather than stipulating a numerical monism that had to be rejected or avoided. The *chrēmata* of Anaxagoras and the four roots (plus Love and Strife) of Empedocles are themselves unchanging predicational unities of the appropriate sort, which mix and separate to bring about the world reported by the senses. Both Anaxagoras and Empedocles take pains to reject the reality of becoming and to stress the reality of their basic entities, showing how what seems to be change in the sensible world is merely rearrangement of what is genuinely real. The Atomists, too, begin with entities that would be acceptable to Parmenides (and which, unlike the Anaxagorean and Empedoclean basic entities, are not vulnerable to a Zenonian argument from division). For them, both atoms and the void are genuinely real, although they call atoms what-is and void what-is-not. The world of the senses is the result of the temporary mixture of these real entities and is thus subject to rational explanation, through the ability of understanding to grasp the natures of atoms and void.

Thus, the main philosophical theories of post-Parmenidean Presocratic thought are grounded in and indebted to the arguments of Parmenides. This is also true, I have argued, of other late Presocratic thinkers such as Philolaus and Diogenes of Apollonia. In them, and in Plato, Parmenidean presuppositions and arguments (sometimes modified by Parmenides' Eleatic followers Zeno and Melissus) continue to play a fundamental role and extend the legacy of Parmenides into the heart of classical Greek philosophy.

Bibliography

Abraham, W. E. "The Nature of Zeno's Argument against Plurality in DK 29 B 1." *Phronesis* 17 (1972) 40–52.

Algra, K. *Concepts of Space in Greek Thought.* Leiden: E. J. Brill, 1995.

Allen, R. E. *Plato's "Parmenides": Translation and Analysis.* Minneapolis: University of Minnesota Press, 1983.

Asmis, E. *Epicurus' Scientific Methodology.* Ithaca: Cornell University Press, 1984.

Aubenque, P., ed. *Etudes sur Parménide.* 2 vols. Paris: J. Vrin, 1987.

Austin, S. "Genesis and Motion in Parmenides: B8.12–13." *Harvard Studies in Classical Philology* 87 (1983) 151–68.

———. *Parmenides: Being, Bounds, and Logic.* New Haven: Yale University Press, 1986.

Baldes, R. W. " 'Divisibility' and 'Division' in Democritus." *Apeiron* 12 (1978) 1–12.

Barnes, J. "Parmenides and the Eleatic One." *Archiv für Geschichte der Philosophie* 61 (1979) 1–21.

———. *The Presocratic Philosophers.* 2 vols. London: Routledge and Kegan Paul, 1979.

———. *Early Greek Philosophy.* Harmondsworth: Penguin Books Ltd., 1987.

Bennett, J. "The Difference Between Right and Left." In Van Cleve and Frederick, 97–130.

Bicknell, P. J. "Zeno's Arguments on Motion." *Acta Classica* 6 (1963) 81–105.

———. "Parmenides' Refutation of Motion and an Implication." *Phronesis* 12 (1967) 1–5.

———. "A New Arrangement of Some Parmenidean Verses." *Symbolae Osloenses* 42 (1968) 44–50.

———. "Parmenides, Fragment 10." *Hermes* 98 (1968) 629–31.

Blank, D. L. "Faith and Persuasion in Parmenides." *Classical Antiquity* 1 (1982) 167–79.

Bodnar, I. *Being Bound: A Parmenidean Journey* (Budapest: [np] 1990).

Bollack, J. "Deux figures principales de l'atomisme d'après Aristote: L'Entrecroisement des atomes et la sphère de feu." In I. Düring, ed. *Naturforschung bei Aristoteles und Theophrast.* Heidelberg: Stiehm, 1969. 32–50.

———. *Empédocle.* Paris: Les Editions de Minuit, vol. I, 1965; vols. II and II, 1969.

———. "La Cosmologie parménidéenne de Parménide." In R. Brague and J.-F. Courtine, eds. *Herméneutique et Ontologie: Mélanges en hommage à Pierre Aubenque.* Paris: Presses Universitaires de France, 1990. 17–53.

Bormann, K. *Parmenides: Untersuchungen zu den Fragmenten.* Hamburg: Felix Meiner Verlag, 1971.

Bostock, D. *Plato's Phaedo.* Oxford: Clarendon Press, 1986.

Boudouris, K., ed. *Ionian Philosophy.* Athens: International Association for Greek Philosophy, 1989.

Bowra, C. M. "The Proem of Parmenides." *Classical Philology* 32 (1937) 97–112.

Brentlinger, J. "Incomplete Predicates and the Two-World Theory of the *Phaedo*." *Phronesis* 17 (1972) 61–79.

Burkert, W. "Das Proömium des Parmenides und die Katabasis des Pythagoras." *Phronesis* 15 (1969) 1–30.

———. *Lore and Science in Ancient Pythagoreanism.* Trans. E. L. Minar, Jr. Cambridge: Harvard University Press, 1972.

Burnet, J. *Early Greek Philosophy.* 4th ed. London: Adam and Charles Black, 1930.

Calogero, G. *Storia della Logica Antica.* Vol. I, *L'Età arcaica.* Bari: Laterza, 1967.

———. *Studi sull' eleatismo.* 2d ed. Firenze: La Nuova Italia, 1977.

Calvo, T. "Truth and *Doxa* in Parmenides." *Archiv für Geschichte der Philosophie* 59 (1977) 245–60.

Chalmers, W. R. "Parmenides and the Beliefs of Mortals." *Phronesis* 5 (1960) 5–22.

Chantraine, P. *Dictionnaire étymologique de la langue grec.* 4 vols. Paris: Editions Klincksieck, 1968.

Cherniss, H. *Aristotle's Criticism of Presocratic Philosophy.* Baltimore: Johns Hopkins Press, 1935.

Clark, R. J. "Parmenides and Sense-Perception." *Revue des études grècques* 82 (1969) 14–32.

Collobert, C. *L'être de Parménide ou le refus du temps.* Paris: Editions Kimé, 1993.

Cordero, N.-L. "Les Deux Chemins de Parménide dans les fragments 6 et 7." *Phronesis* 24 (1979) 1–32.

———. "L'histoire du Texte de Parménide." In Aubenque, ed., *Etudes,* vol. 2, 3–24.

———. "Zénon d'Elée, Moniste ou Nihiliste?" *La Parola del Passato* 43 (1983) 100–126.

Cornford, F. M. "Anaxagoras' Theory of Matter." 1930; reprinted in Furley and Allen, vol. II, 275–322 (References are to the latter version.)

———. "A New Fragment of Parmenides." *Classical Review* 49 (1935) 122–23.

Couloubaritsis, L. "Considérations sur la notion de *Noûs* chez Démocrite." *Archiv für Geschichte der Philosophie* 62 (1980) 129–45.

Coxon, A. H. "The Manuscript Tradition of Simplicius' Commentary on Aristotle's *Physics* i–iv." *Classical Quarterly,* n.s. 18 (1968) 70–75.

———. "The Text of Parmenides: fr. 1.3." *Classical Quarterly* n.s. 18 (1968) 69.

———. *The Fragments of Parmenides.* Assen: Van Gorcum, 1986.

Croissant, J. "Le Début de la DOXA de Parménide." In *Mélanges offerts à A.-M. Desrousseaux par ses amis et ses élèves.* Paris: Librarie Hachette, 1937. 99–104.

Crystal, I. "Parmenidean Allusions in *Republic* V." *Ancient Philosophy* 16 (1996) 351–63.

Cunliffe, R. J. *A Lexicon of the Homeric Dialect.* 1924; reprint Norman, OK: University of Oklahoma Press, 1963.

Curd, M. V. "Showing and Telling: Can the Difference Between Right and Left Be Explained in Words?" In Van Cleve and Frederick, 195–201.

Curd, P. K. "Some Problems of Unity in the First Hypothesis of the *Parmenides.*" *Southern Journal of Philosophy* 27 (1989) 347–59.

———. "Knowledge and Unity in Heraclitus." *The Monist* 74 (1991) 531–49.

———. "Parmenidean Monism." *Phronesis* 36 (1991) 241–64.

———. "Socratic Empiricism." In K. Boudouris, ed. *The Philosophy of Socrates,* vol. I. Athens: International Association for Greek Philosophy, 1991. 208–16.

———. "Deception and Belief in Parmenides' *Doxa*." *Apeiron* 25 (1992) 109–33.

———. "Eleatic Monism in Zeno and Melissus." *Ancient Philosophy* 13 (1993) 1–22.

———. "Eleatic Arguments." In J. Gentzler, ed. *Method in Ancient Philosophy.* Oxford: Oxford University Press, 1997. 1–28.

DeFillipo, J. G. "Reply to André Laks on Anaxagoras' ΝΟΥΣ." *The Southern Journal of Philosophy* 31 (1993) Supplementary Volume, 39–48.

DeLacey, P. "Colotes' First Criticism of Democritus." In J. Mau and E. G. Schmidt, eds. *Isonomia.* Berlin: Akademie-Verlag, 1971. 67–77.

De Ley, H. "Aristotle, *de Gen. et Corr.* A8, 324b35–325b11: A Leucippan Fragment?" *Mnemosyne* 4th ser. 25 (1972) 56–62.

Denniston, J. D. *The Greek Particles.* 2d ed. Oxford: Clarendon Press, 1954.

Descartes, R. *The Philosophical Writings of Descartes.* Vol. II. Trans. J. Cottingham, R. Stoothoff, and D. Murdoch. Cambridge: Cambridge University Press, 1984.

Detienne, M., and Vernant, J.-P. *Ruses de l'intelligence: La Métis des grecs.* Paris: Flammarion, 1974. Translated by J. Lloyd as *Cunning Intelligence in Greek Culture.* Atlantic Highlands, NJ: Humanities Press, 1978.

Diels, H. *Doxographi Graeci.* 4th ed. 1879; Berlin: Walter de Gruyter, 1965.

———. *Parmenides: Lehrgedicht.* Berlin: Georg Reimer, 1897.

Diels, H., and W. Kranz, eds. *Die Fragmente der Vorsokratiker.* 3 vols. 1951–52; reprint of 6th ed. Berlin: Weidmann, 1974.

Diller, H. "Die philosophiegeschichtliche Stellung des Diogenes von Apollonia." *Hermes* 76 (1941) 359–81.

Dillon, J. "Proclus and the Forty *Logoi* of Zeno." *Illinois Classical Studies* 11 (1986) 35–41.

Dumont, J.-P. "Les Abdéritains et le non-être." *Bulletin de la Société française de Philosophie* 77 (1983) 39–58; discussion reported on 58–76.

English, R. B. "Parmenides' Indebtedness to the Pythagoreans." *Transactions and Proceedings of the American Philological Association* 42 (1912) 81–94.

Finkelberg, A. "The Cosmology of Parmenides." *American Journal of Philology* 107 (1986) 303–17.

———. " 'Like by Like' and Two Reflections of Reality in Parmenides." *Hermes* 114 (1986) 405–12.

———. "Parmenides: Between Material and Logical Monism." *Archiv für Geschichte der Philosophie* 70 (1988) 1–14.

———. "Parmenides' Foundation of the Way of Truth." *Oxford Studies in Ancient Philosophy* 6 (1988) 39–67.

Floyd, E. D. "Why Parmenides Wrote in Verse." *Ancient Philosophy* 12 (1992) 251–65.

Forrester, J. W. "The Argument of the 'Porphyry Text.' " *Journal of the History of Philosophy* 11 (1973) 537–39.

Fränkel, H. "Studies in Parmenides." In Furley and Allen, vol. II, 1–47.

———. "Zeno of Elea's Attacks on Plurality." *American Journal of Philology* 63 (1942) 1–25 and 193–206; rev. reprint in Furley and Allen, vol. II, 102–42.

———. *Early Greek Philosophy and Poetry.* Trans. M. Hadas and J. Willis. Oxford: Basil Blackwell, 1975.

Frederick, R. E., "Introduction to the Argument of 1768." In Van Cleve and Frederick, 1–14.

Freudenthal, G. "The Theory of the Opposites and an Ordered Universe: Physics and Metaphysics in Anaximander." *Phronesis* 31 (1986) 197–228.

Fujisawa, N. "Ἔχειν, Μετέχειν, and Idioms of Paradigmatism in Plato's Theory of Forms." *Phronesis* 20 (1975) 30–49.

Furley, D. J. "Anaxagoras and the Naming of Parts." Unpublished manuscript.

———. "Parmenides of Elea." In *The Encyclopedia of Philosophy.* Vol. 5, 47–51.

———. *Two Studies in the Greek Atomists.* Princeton: Princeton University Press, 1967.

———. *The Greek Cosmologists, Vol. I: The Formation of the Atomic Theory and Its Earliest Critics.* Cambridge: Cambridge University Press, 1987.

———. "Anaxagoras in Response to Parmenides." In Furley, *Cosmic Problems,* 47–65.

———. "Melissus of Samos." In K. Boudouris, ed., *Ionian Philosophy,* 114–22.

———. "Notes on Parmenides." In *Cosmic Problems,* 27–37.

———. "Truth as What Survives the *Elenchos.*" In Furley, *Cosmic Problems,* 38–46.

———. *Cosmic Problems: Essays on Greek and Roman Philosophy of Nature.* Cambridge: Cambridge University Press: 1989.

———. "From Anaxagoras to Socrates." In K. Boudouris, ed. *The Philosophy of Socrates Vol. II: Elenchus, Ethics, and Truth.* Athens: International Center for Greek Philosophy and Culture, 1992. 74–80.

Furley, D. J., and R. E. Allen, *Studies in Presocratic Philosophy,* 2 vols. London: Routledge and Kegan Paul; vol. I, 1970; vol. II, 1975.

Furth, M. "Elements of Eleatic Ontology." In A.P.D. Mourelatos, ed. *The Pre-Socratics.* 241–70.

———. "A 'Philosophical Hero?' Anaxagoras and the Eleatics." *Oxford Studies in Ancient Philosophy* 9 (1991) 95–129.

Gallop, D. " 'Is or Is Not'?" *The Monist* 62 (1979) 61–80.

———. *Parmenides of Elea: Fragments.* Toronto: University of Toronto Press, 1984.

Gill, M. L., and P. Ryan, *Plato: Parmenides.* Indianapolis: Hackett Publishing 1996.

Godfrey, R. "Democritus and the Impossibility of Collision." *Philosophy* 65 (1990) 212–17.

Goldin, O. "Parmenides on Possibility and Thought." *Apeiron* 26 (1993) 19–35.

Gómez-Lobo, A. *Parménides.* Buenos Aires, Editorial Charcas, 1985.

Graham, D. "Heraclitus and Parmenides." Unpublished manuscript.

———. "Symmetry in the Empedoclean Cycle." *Classical Quarterly* 38 (1988) 297–312.

———. "The Postulates of Anaxagoras." *Apeiron* 27 (1994) 77–121.

Groarke, L. "Parmenides' Timeless Universe." *Dialogue* 24 (1985) 535–41.

———. "Parmenides' Timeless Universe, Again." *Dialogue* 26 (1987) 549–52.

Guthrie, W.K.C. *A History of Greek Philosophy,* Vols. I and II. Cambridge: Cambridge University Press; vol. I, 1962, vol. II, 1965.

Havelock, E. A. "Parmenides and Odysseus." *Harvard Studies in Classical Philology* 63 (1958) 133–43.

Heidel, W. A. "Qualitative Change in Pre-Socratic Philosophy." *Archiv für Geschichte der Philosophie* 19, n.s. 12 (1906) 333–79.

———. "Περὶ Φύσεως." *Proceedings of the American Academy of Arts and Sciences* 45 (1910) 79–133.

———. "On Certain Fragments of the Pre-Socratics: Critical Notes and Elucidations." *Proceedings of the American Academy of Arts and Sciences* 48 (1913) 681–734.

Hölscher, U. "Weltzeiten und Lebensyklus: eine Nachpüfung der Empedokles-Doxographie." *Hermes* 93 (1965) 7–33.

———. "Anaximander and the Beginnings of Greek Philosophy." In Furley and Allen, vol. I, 281–322.

Holwerda, D. *Commentatio de vocis quae est ΦΥΣΙΣ vi atque usu praesertim in graecitate Aristotele anteriore.* Groningen: J. B. Wolters, 1955.

Huffman, C. "The Role of Number in Philolaus' Philosophy." *Phronesis* 33 (1988) 1–30.

———. *Philolaus of Croton: Pythagorean and Presocratic.* Cambridge: Cambridge University Press, 1993.

Inwood, B. "The Origin of Epicurus' Concept of Void." *Classical Philology* 76 (1981) 273–85.

———. "Anaxagoras and Infinite Divisibility." *Illinois Classical Studies* 11 (1986) 17–33.

———. *The Poem of Empedocles: A Text and Translation with an Introduction.* Toronto: The University of Toronto Press, 1992.

Jöhrens, O. *Die Fragmente des Anaxagoras.* Bochum-Langendreer: Druck, Heinrich Pöppinghaus o. H.G., 1939.

Jones, B. "Parmenides' 'Way of Truth.'" *Journal of the History of Philosophy* 11 (1973) 287–98.

Jouanna, J. "Rapports entre Mélissus de Samos et Diogène d'Apollonie, à la lumière du traité hippocratique *De natura hominis.*" *Revue des Etudes Anciennes* 67 (1965) 306–23.

Kahn, C. H. "The Greek Verb 'To Be' and the Concept of Being." *Foundations of Language* 2 (1966) 245–65.

———. "More on Parmenides." *Review of Metaphysics* 22 (1968/69) 333–40.

———. "The Thesis of Parmenides." *Review of Metaphysics* 23 (1969/70) 700–724.

———. *The Verb 'Be' in Ancient Greek*; *Foundations of Language,* Supplementary Series, vol. 16. Dordrecht: Reidel, 1973.

———. "Pythagorean Philosophy Before Plato." In A.P.D. Mourelatos, ed., *The Pre-Socratics,* 161–85.

———. "Why Existence Does Not Emerge as a Distinct Concept in Greek Philosophy." *Archiv für Geschichte der Philosophie* 58 (1978) 323–34.

———. *The Art and Thought of Heraclitus.* Cambridge: Cambridge University Press, 1979.

———. *Anaximander and the Origins of Greek Cosmology.* 1960; reprint Philadelphia: Centrum Philadelphia, 1985.

———. "The Beautiful and the Genuine." *Oxford Studies in Ancient Philosophy* 3 (1985) 261–87.

———. "Democritus and the Origins of Moral Psychology." *American Journal of Philology* 106 (1985) 1–31.

———. "Retrospect on the Verb 'To Be' and the Concept of Being." In S. Knuuttila and J. Hintikka, eds. *The Logic of Being.* Dordrecht: D. Reidel, 1986. 1–28.

———. "Being in Parmenides and Plato." *La Parola del Passato* 43 (1988) 237–61.

———. "The Historical Position of Anaxagoras." in K. Boudouris, ed., *Ionian Philosophy,* 203–10.

Kerferd, G. B. "Parmenides Through His Fragments." (Review of K. Bormann, *Parmenides*) *Classical Review* 23 (1973) 129–31.

———. "Anaxagoras and the Concept of Matter before Aristotle." 1969; reprinted in A.P.D. Mourelatos, ed. *The Pre-socratics,* 489–503.

Ketchum, R. J. "Parmenides on What There Is." *Canadian Journal of Philosophy* 20 (1990) 167–90.

Kingsley, P. "Empedocles and His Interpreters: The Four Element Doxography." *Phronesis* 39 (1994) 235–54.

———. *Ancient Philosophy, Mystery, and Magic: Empedocles and Pythagorean Tradition.* Oxford: Clarendon Press, 1995.

———. "Notes on Air: Four Questions of Meaning in Empedocles and Anaxagoras." *Classical Quarterly,* n.s. 45 (1995) 26–29.

Kirk, G. S. *Heraclitus: The Cosmic Fragments.* Cambridge: Cambridge University Press, 1954.

Kirk, G. S., and J. E. Raven. *The Presocratic Philosophers.* Cambridge: Cambridge University Press, 1957.

Kirk, G. S., J. E. Raven, and M. Schofield, *The Presocratic Philosophers.* 2d ed. Cambridge: Cambridge University Press, 1983.

Kirk, G. S., and M. Stokes, "Parmenides' Refutation of Motion." *Phronesis* 5 (1960) 1–4.

Klowski, J. "Antwortete Leukipp Melissos oder Melissos Leukipp?" *Museum Helveticum* 28 (1971) 65–71.

Konstan, D. "Anaxagoras on Bigger and Smaller." In M. Capasso, F. de Martino, and P. Rosati, eds. *Studi di Filosofia Preplatonica.* Napoli: Bibliopolis, 1985. 137–57.

Kripke, S. "Identity and Necessity." In S. P. Schwartz, ed. *Naming, Necessity, and Natural Kinds.* Ithaca, NY: Cornell University Press, 1977. 66–101.

Kühner, R., and Gerth, B. *Ausführliche Grammatik der griechischen Sprache.* 4 vols. 3d ed. 1890–1904; reprint Hannover: Hahnsche Buchhandlung, 1976.

Lacey, A. R. "The Eleatics and Aristotle on Some Problems of Change." *Journal of the History of Ideas* 26 (1965) 451–68.

Laks, A. "How Should We Read Parmenides' Proem? Some Preliminary Remarks on the Legitimacy of Allegory." Unpublished manuscript.

———. *Diogène d'Apollonie: La Dernière Cosmologie présocratique.* Lille: Presses Universitaires de Lille, 1983.

———. " 'The More' and 'The Full': On the Reconstruction of Parmenides' Theory of Sensation in Theophrastus, *De Sensibus,* 3–4." *Oxford Studies in Ancient Philosophy* 8 (1990) 1–18.

———. "Mind's Crisis: On Anaxagoras' ΝΟΥΣ." *The Southern Journal of Philosophy* 31 (1993) Supplementary Volume, 19–38.

Lanza, D. *Anassagora: Testimonianze e Frammenti.* Florence: La Nuova Italia, 1966.

Lesher, J. H. "Perceiving and Knowing in the *Iliad* and the *Odyssey.*" *Phronesis* 26 (1981) 2–24.

———. "Heraclitus' Epistemological Vocabulary." *Hermes* 111 (1983) 155–70.

———. "Parmenides' Critique of Thinking: The *poludēris elenchos* of Fragment 7." *Oxford Studies in Ancient Philosophy* 2 (1984) 1–30.

———. "Xenophanes on Inquiry and Discovery: An Alternative to the 'Hymn to Progress' Reading of Xenophanes' fragment 18." *Ancient Philosophy* 11 (1991) 229–48.

———. *Xenophanes of Colophon: Fragments.* Toronto: University of Toronto Press, 1992.

———. "The Emergence of Philosophical Interest in Cognition." *Oxford Studies in Ancient Philosophy* 12 (1994) 1–34.

———. "The Significance of κατὰ πάντ' ἄ⟨σ⟩τη in Parmenides Fr. 1.3." *Ancient Philosophy* 14 (1994) 1–20.

———. "Mind's Knowledge and Powers of Control in Anaxagoras DK B12." *Phronesis* 40 (1995) 125–42.

Lloyd, G.E.R. *Polarity and Analogy: Two Types of Argumentation in Early Greek Thought.* Cambridge: Cambridge University Press, 1966.

———. "Who Is Attacked in *On Ancient Medicine*?" In Lloyd, *Methods and Problems in Greek Science,* 49–69. First published in *Phronesis* 8 (1963) 108–26.

———. *Methods and Problems in Greek Science.* Cambridge: Cambridge University Press, 1991.

Loenen, J.H.M.M. *Parmenides, Melissus, Gorgias.* Assen: Van Gorcum, 1959.

Long, A. A. "Thinking and Sense-Perception in Empedocles: Mysticism or Materialism?" *Classical Quarterly* 16 (1966) 256–76.

———. "Empedocles' Cosmic Cycle in the 'Sixties." In A.P.D. Mourelatos, ed., *The Pre-socratics,* 397–425.

———. "The Principles of Parmenides' Cosmogony." 1963; reprinted in Furley and Allen, vol. II, 82–101.

Longrigg, J., "Philosophy and Medicine: Some Early Interactions." *Harvard Studies in Classical Philology* 67 (1963) 147–75.

———. "Zeno's Cosmology?" *Classical Review* 22 (1972) 170–71.

———. "The Roots of All Things." *Isis* 67 (1976) 420–38.

———. "Elements and After: A Study in Presocratic Physics of the Second Half of the Fifth Century." *Apeiron* 19 (1985) 93–115.

Lovejoy, A. O. "The Meaning of Φύσις in the Greek Physiologers." *The Philosophical Review* 18 (1909) 369–83.

Luria, S. "Die Infinitesimaltheorie der antiken Atomisten." *Quellen und Studien zur Geschichte der Mathematik* 2 (1932) 106–85.

———. *Democritea.* Leningrad: Nauka, 1970.

Mackenzie, M. M. "Parmenides' Dilemma." *Phronesis* 27 (1982) 1–13.

———. "The Moving Posset Stands Still." *American Journal of Philology* 107 (1986) 542–51.

———. "Heraclitus and the Art of Paradox." *Oxford Studies in Ancient Philosophy* 6 (1988) 1–37.

Makin, S. "Zeno on Plurality." *Phronesis* 27 (1982) 223–38.

———. "The Indivisibility of the Atom." *Archiv für Geschichte der Philosophie* 71 (1989) 125–49.

———. *Indifference Arguments.* Oxford: Blackwell, 1993.

Mann, W. "Anaxagoras and the *Homoiomerē.*" *Phronesis* 25 (1980) 228–49.

Manchester, P. B. "Parmenides and the Need for Eternity." *The Monist* 62 (1979) 81–106.

Mansfeld, J. *Die Offenbarung des Parmenides und die menschliche Welt.* Assen: Van Gorcum, 1964.

———. "The Chronology of Anaxagoras' Athenian Period and the Date of His Trial" Part I: "The Length and Dating of the Athenian Period." 1979; reprinted (with Part II, "The Plot against Pericles and His Associates." *Mnemosyne* 4th ser. 33 [1980] 84–95) in Mansfeld, *Studies in the Historiography of Greek Philosophy.* Assen: Van Gorcum, 1990. 264–306.

———. " 'De Melisso Xenophane Gorgia': Pyrronizing Aristotelianism." In *Studies in the Historiography of Philosophy.* Assen: Van Gorcum, 1990. 200–237.

———. "Critical Note: Empedocles and His Interpreters." *Phronesis* 50 (1995) 109–15.

Marcovich, M. *Heraclitus: Greek Text with a Short Commentary (Editio Maior).* Merida, Venezuela: Los Andes University Press, 1967.

Mason, R. "Parmenides and Language." *Ancient Philosophy* 8 (1988) 149–66.

Matson, W. I. "Democritus Fragment 156." *Classical Quarterly,* n.s. 13 (1963) 26–29.

Matthen, M. "A Note on Parmenides' Denial of Past and Future." *Dialogue* 25 (1986) 553–57.

———. Review of Coxon, *The Fragments of Parmenides. Philosophical Review* 100 (1991) 153–57.

McGibbon, D. "The Atomists and Melissus." *Mnemosyne,* 4th ser. 17 (1964) 248–55.

McKirahan, R. *Philosophy Before Socrates.* Indianapolis: Hackett Publishing, 1994.

Meinwald, C. C. *Plato's "Parmenides."* New York: Oxford University Press, 1991.

Millerd, C. E. *On the Interpretation of Empedocles.* 1908; reprinted New York and London: Garland, 1980.

Minar, E. L., Jr. "Parmenides and the World of Seeming." *American Journal of Philology* 70 (1949) 41–55.

Moorhouse, A. C. "ΔEN in Classical Greek." *Classical Quarterly,* n.s. 12 (1962) 235–38.

———. "The Origin and Use of O, H, TO ΔEINA." *Classical Quarterly,* n.s. 13 (1963) 19–25.

———. "A Use of OΥΔEIΣ and MHΔEIΣ." *Classical Quarterly,* n.s. 15 (1965) 31–40.

Morrison, J. S. "Parmenides and Er." *Journal of Hellenic Studies* 75 (1955) 59–68.

Mourelatos, A.P.D. "*Phradzō* and Its Derivatives in Parmenides." *Classical Philology* 60 (1965) 261–62.

———. *The Route of Parmenides.* New Haven: Yale University Press, 1971.

———. "Heraclitus, Parmenides, and the Naive Metaphysics of Things." In E. N. Lee, A.P.D. Mourelatos, and R. Rorty, eds. *Exegesis and Argument: Studies in Greek Philosophy Presented to Gregory Vlastos.* Assen: Van Gorcum, 1973. 16–48.

———. "Determinacy and Indeterminacy, Being and Non-Being in the Fragments of Parmenides." *Canadian Journal of Philosophy* (1976) Supplementary Volume II, 45–60.

———. "Alternatives in Interpreting Parmenides." *The Monist* 62 (1979) 3–14.

———. "'Nothing' as 'Not-Being:' Some Literary Contexts that Bear on Plato." 1979; reprinted in J. P. Anton and T. Preus. *Essays in Ancient Greek Philosophy, Vol. 2.* Albany, NY: SUNY Press, 1983. 59–69.

———. "Δημόκριτος: Φιλόσοφος τῆς Μορφῆς," *Proceedings of the First International Congress on Democritus, Vol. I.* Xanthi: International Democritus Foundation, 1984. An English abstract, "Democritus, Philosopher of Form," appears on 118–19.

———. "Quality, Structure, and Emergence in Later Presocratic Philosophy." In J. Cleary, ed. *Proceedings of the Boston Area Colloquium in Ancient Philosophy.* Vol. 2. Lanham, MD: University Press of America, 1987. 127–94.

———. "'X is Really Y': Ionian Origins of a Thought Pattern." In K. Boudouris, ed., *Ionian Philosophy,* 280–90.

———. ed. *The Pre-socratics.* 1974; reprinted Princeton: Princeton University Press, 1993.

Nehamas, A. "Predication and Forms of Opposites in the *Phaedo.*" *Review of Metaphysics* 26 (1973) 461–91.

———. "Plato on the Imperfection of the Sensible World." *American Philosophical Quarterly* 12 (1975) 105–17.

———. "Self-Predication and Plato's Theory of Forms." *American Philosophical Quarterly* 16 (1979) 93–103.

———. "On Parmenides' Three Ways of Inquiry." *Deucalion* 33/34 (1981) 97–111.

———. "Meno's Paradox and Socrates as a Teacher." *Oxford Studies in Ancient Philosophy* 3 (1985) 1–30.

Nussbaum, M. "Eleatic Conventionalism and Philolaus on the Conditions of Thought." *Harvard Studies in Classical Philology* 83 (1979) 63–108.

O'Brien, D. "The Relation of Anaxagoras and Empedocles." *Journal of Hellenic Studies,* 88 (1968) 93–113.

———. *Empedocles' Cosmic Cycle: A Reconstruction from the Fragments and Secondary Sources.* Cambridge: Cambridge University Press, 1969.

———. *Theories of Weight in the Ancient World, Vol. I: Democritus: Weight and Size.* Paris: Les Belles Lettres and Leiden: E. J. Brill, 1981.

———. "Le Poème de Parménide: Texte, Traduction et Essai Critique." In Aubenque, ed., *Etudes,* vol. 1, 1–324.

———. "Empedocles Revisited." *Ancient Philosophy* 15 (1995) 403–70.

Osborne, C. "Empedocles Recycled." *Classical Quarterly.* 37 (1987) 24–50.

———. *Rethinking Early Greek Philosophy: Hippolytus of Rome and the Presocratics.* Ithaca, NY: Cornell University Press, 1987.

Owen, G.E.L. "Eleatic Questions." 1960; rev. ed. reprinted in Owen, *Logic, Science, and Dialectic,* 3–26.

———. *Logic, Science, and Dialectic: Collected Papers in Greek Philosophy.* Ithaca: Cornell University Press, 1986.

———. "Notes on Ryle's Plato." 1970; reprinted in Owen, *Logic, Science, and Dialectic,* 85–103.

———. "Plato and Parmenides on the Timeless Present." 1966; reprinted in Owen, *Logic, Science, and Dialectic,* 27–44.

———. "Plato on Not-Being." 1970; reprinted in Owen, *Logic, Science, and Dialectic,* 104–37.

———. "Zeno and the Mathematicians." 1957–58; rev. ed. reprinted in Owen, *Logic, Science, and Dialectic,* 45–61.

Peck, A. L. "Anaxagoras: Predication as a Problem in Physics." *Classical Quarterly* 25 (1931) 27–37, 112–20.

Pellikaan-Engel, M. E. *Hesiod and Parmenides: A New View on Their Cosmologies and on Parmenides' Proem.* Amsterdam: Adolf M. Hakkert, 1974.

Perry, B. M. "On the Cornford-Fragment (28B8.38*)." *Archiv für Geschichte der Philosophie* 71 (1989) 1–9.

Peterson, S. "Zeno's Second Argument against Plurality." *Journal of the History of Philosophy* 16 (1978) 261–70.

Pfeiffer, H. *Die Stellung des Parmenideischen Lehrgedichtes in der epischen Tradition.* Bonn: Habelt, 1975.

Prior, W. J. "Zeno's First Argument Concerning Plurality." *Archiv für Geschichte der Philosophie* 60 (1978) 247–56.

Raven, J. E. "The Basis of Anaxagoras' Cosmology." *Classical Quarterly,* n.s. 4 (1954) 123–37.

Reale, G. *Melisso: Testimonianze e Frammenti.* Florence: La Nuova Italia, 1970.

Reeve, C.D.C. "Anaxagorean Panspermism." *Ancient Philosophy* 1 (1981) 89–108.

Renehan, R. Review of Coxon, *The Fragments of Parmenides. Ancient Philosophy* 12 (1992) 395–409.

de Rijk, L. M. "Did Parmenides Reject the Sensible World?" In L. P. Gerson, ed. *Graceful Reason: Essays in Ancient and Medieval Philosophy Presented to Joseph Owens, CSSR.* Toronto: Pontifical Institute of Medieval Studies, 1983. 29–53.

Robinson, T. M. "Parmenides on the Ascertainment of the Real." *Canadian Journal of Philosophy* 4 (1975) 623–33.

———. "Parmenides on the Real in Its Totality." *The Monist* 62 (1979) 54–60.

———. *Contrasting Arguments: An Edition of the* Dissoi Logoi. New York: Arno Press, 1979.

———. *Heraclitus: Fragments. A Text and Translation with a Commentary.* Toronto: University of Toronto Press, 1987.

———. "Parmenides and Heraclitus on What Can Be Known." *Revue de Philosophie Ancienne* 7 (1989) 157–67.

———. "Heraclitus and Plato on the Language of the Real." *The Monist* 74 (1991) 481–90.

———. "Plato and the Computer." *Ancient Philosophy* 12 (1992) 375–82.

Rösler, W. ΟΜΟΥ ΧΡΗΜΑΤΑ ΠΑΝΤΑ ΗΝ. *Hermes* 99 (1971) 246–48.

Ross, W. D. *Aristotle's Metaphysics.* Oxford: Clarendon Press, 1924.

———. *Aristotle's Physics.* Oxford: Clarendon Press, 1936.

Sanders, K. R. "Much Ado about 'Nothing': ΜΗΔΕΝ and ΜΗ ΕΟΝ in Parmenides." Unpublished manuscript.

Schofield, M. "Did Parmenides Discover Eternity?" *Archiv für Geschichte der Philosophie* 52 (1970) 113–35.

———. "A Neglected Regress Argument in the *Parmenides.*" *Classical Quarterly,* n.s. 23 (1973) 29–44.

———. "Doxographica Anaxagorea." *Hermes* 103 (1975) 1–24.

———. "The Antinomies of Plato's *Parmenides.*" *Classical Quarterly,* n.s. 27 (1977) 139–58.

———. *An Essay on Anaxagoras.* Cambridge: Cambridge University Press, 1980.

———. Review of Sider, *The Fragments of Anaxagoras. Classical Review* 32 (1982) 189–91.

Schrenk, L. P. "World as Structure: The Ontology of Philolaus of Croton." *Apeiron* 27 (1994) 171–90.

Schwabl, H. "Sein und Doxa bei Parmenides." *Wiener Studien* 76 (1953) 50–75.

———. "Hesiod und Parmenides: zur Formung des parmenideischen Prooimions." *Rheinisches Museum für Philologie,* n.s. 106 (1963) 134–42.

Sedley, D. "Two Conceptions of Vacuum." *Phronesis* 27 (1982) 175–93.

Sider, D. "Confirmation of Two 'Conjectures' in the Presocratics: Parmenides B 12 and Anaxagoras B 15." *Phoenix* 33 (1979) 67–69.

———. *The Fragments of Anaxagoras: Edited with an Introduction and Commentary. Beiträge zur Klassischen Philologie* 118. Meisenheim am Glan: Anton Hain, 1981.

———. "Empedocles B96 (462 Bollack) and the Poetry of Adhesion." *Mnemosyne,* 4th ser. 37 (1984) 14–24.

———. "Textual Notes on Parmenides' Poem." *Hermes* 113 (1985) 362–66.

Silvestre, M. L. "Significato e Ruolo del *Nous* nella Filosofia di Anassagora." *Il Contributo* 12 (1988) 29–52.

———. "Simplicius' Testimony concerning Anaxagoras." In Boudouris, ed., *Ionian Philosophy,* 369–74.

Sinnige, T. *Matter and Infinity in the Presocratic Schools and Plato.* Assen: Van Gorcum, 1971.

Smyth, H. W. *Greek Grammar.* 1920; rev. ed. by G. M. Messing, Cambridge, MA: Harvard University Press, 1956.

Solmsen, F. *Aristotle's System of the Physical World.* Ithaca, NY: Cornell University Press, 1960.

———. "Love and Strife in Empedocles' Cosmology." *Phronesis* 10 (1965) 109–48.

———. "Eternal and Temporary Beings in Empedocles' Physical Poem." 1975; reprinted in Solmsen, *Kleine Schriften,* vol. III, 176–98.

———. "The 'Eleatic One' in Melissus." 1969; reprinted in Solmsen, *Kleine Schriften,* vol. III, 137–49.

———. "Parmenides and the Description of Perfect Beauty in Plato's *Symposium.*" 1971; reprinted in Solmsen, *Kleine Schriften,* vol. III, 202–10.

———. *Kleine Schriften.* 3 vols. Hildesheim: Georg Olms Verlag, vols. I and II, 1968; vol. III, 1982.

———. "The Tradition about Zeno of Elea Re-examined." 1971; reprinted in A.P.D. Mourelatos, ed., *The Pre-socratics,* 368–93.

———. "Abdera's Arguments for the Atomic Theory." *Greek, Roman, and Byzantine Studies* 29 (1988) 59–73.

Sorabji, R. *Time, Creation, and the Continuum.* Ithaca: Cornell University Press, 1983.

Stokes, M. C. "On Anaxagoras." *Archiv für Geschichte der Philosophie* 47 (1965), "Part I: Anaxagoras' Theory of Matter." 1–19; "Part II: The Order of Cosmogony," 217–50.

———. *One and Many in Presocratic Philosophy.* Washington, DC: The Center for Hellenic Studies, 1971.

Stough, C. "Parmenides' Way of Truth, B8.12–13." *Phronesis* 13 (1968) 91–107.

Strang, C. "The Physical Theory of Anaxagoras." 1963; reprinted in Furley and Allen, vol. II, 361–80.

Tannery, P. *Pour l'histoire de la science hellène.* 2d ed. Paris: Gauthier-Villars, 1930.

Tarán, L. *Parmenides.* Princeton: Princeton University Press, 1965.

———. "Perpetual Duration and Atemporal Eternity in Parmenides and Plato." *The Monist* 62 no. 1 (1979) 43–53.

Tarrant, H. "The Conclusion of Parmenides' Poem." *Apeiron* 17 (1983) 73–84.

Taylor, C.C.W. "Pleasure, Knowledge and Senation in Democritus." *Phronesis* 12 (1967) 6–27.

Teodorsson, S-T. *Anaxagoras' Theory of Matter.* Göteborg: Acta Universitatis Gothoburgensis, 1982.

Tugwell, S. "The Way of Truth." *Classical Quarterly,* n.s. 14 (1964) 36–41.

Van Cleve, J., and R. E. Frederick, eds. *The Philosophy of Right and Left: Incongruent Counterparts and the Nature of Space.* Dordrecht: Kluwer Academic Publishers, 1991.

Verdenius, W. J. *Parmenides: Some Comments on His Poem.* Groningen/Batavia: J. B. Wolters' Maatschappij N.V., 1942.

———. "Notes on the Presocratics." *Mnemosyne,* 4th ser. 1 (1948) 8–14.

———. "Parmenides' Conception of Light." *Mnemosyne,* 4th ser. 2 (1949) 116–31.

———. Review of Sider, *The Fragments of Anaxagoras. Mnemosyne* 38 (1985) 403–04.

Vlastos, G. "Zeno of Elea." In *Encyclopedia of Philosophy.* Vol. 8, 369–79.

———. "A Zenonian Argument against Plurality." In J. Anton and G. Kustas, eds. *Essays in Ancient Greek Philosophy.* Albany, NY: SUNY Press, 1971. 119–44.

———. "Degrees of Reality in Plato." In G. Vlastos, ed. *Platonic Studies.* Princeton: Princeton University Press, 1973. 58–75.

———. "A Note on Zeno B1." 1959; reprinted in Furley and Allen, vol. II, 177–83.

———. "The Physical Theory of Anaxagoras." 1950; reprinted in Furley and Allen, vol. II, 323–53.

———. "Plato's Testimony Concerning Zeno of Elea." *Journal of Hellenic Studies* 95 (1975) 136–62.

———. "The Socratic Elenchus." *Oxford Studies in Ancient Philosophy* 1 (1983) 27–58.

von Fritz, K. "NOOS and NOEIN in the Homeric Poems." *Classical Philology* 38 (1943) 79–93.

———. "NOOS, NOEIN, and Their Derivatives in Presocratic Philosophy (excluding Anaxagoras) I." *Classical Philology* 40 (1945) 223–42; and II (subtitled "The Post-Parmenidean Period") *Classical Philology* 41 (1946) 12–34.

———. "Zeno of Elea in Plato's Parmenides." In J. L. Heller and J. K. Newman, eds. *Serta Turyniana: Studies in Greek Literature and Paleography in Honor of Alexander Turyn.* Urbana, IL: University of Illinois Press, 1974. 329–41.

Wardy, R.B.B. "Eleatic Pluralism." *Archiv für Geschichte der Philosophie* 70 (1988) 125–46.

Weiss, H. "Democritus' Theory of Cognition." *Classical Quarterly* 32 (1938) 47–56.

West, M. L. *Hesiod: Theogony.* Oxford: Clarendon Press, 1966.

———. *Hesiod: Works and Days.* Oxford: Clarendon Press, 1978.

Wheeler, S. C., III. "Megarian Paradoxes as Eleatic Arguments." *American Philosophical Quarterly* 20 (1983) 287–95.

Woodbury, L. "Parmenides on Names." 1958; reprinted with revised and additional notes in J. Anton and G. Kustas, eds. *Essays in Ancient Greek Philosophy.* Albany, NY: SUNY Press, 1971. 145–62.

———. "Anaxagoras and Athens." *Phoenix* 35 (1981) 295–315.

———. "Parmenides on Naming by Mortal Men: Fr. B8.53–56." Ed. A. Bowen. *Ancient Philosophy* 6 (1986) 1–13.

Woodruff, P. *Plato: "Hippias Major"; Translated with Commentary and Essay.* Indianapolis: Hackett, 1982.

Wright, M. R. *Empedocles: The Extant Fragments.* New Haven: Yale University Press, 1981.

———. *The Presocratics.* Bristol: Bristol Classical Press, 1985.

Young, C. "Plato and Computer Dating." *Oxford Studies in Ancient Philosophy* 12 (1994) 227–50.

Zafiropulo, J. *Anaxagore de Clazomène.* Paris: Les Belles Lettres, 1948.

Zhmud', L. J.-A. " 'All is Number'?" *Phronesis* 34 (1989) 270–92.

Index Locorum

Index Nominum

This index includes modern authors; for ancient authors, refer to the General Index and to the Index Locorum.

General Index

For names of modern scholars, refer to the Index Nominum; for specific passages from ancient authors, refer to the Index Locorum.